# The First War on Terrorism

# The First War on Terrorism

## Counter-Terrorism Policy during the Reagan Administration

David C. Wills

ROWMAN & LITTLEFIELD PUBLISHERS, INC.
*Lanham • Boulder • New York • Oxford*

ROWMAN & LITTLEFIELD PUBLISHERS, INC.

Published in the United States of America
by Rowman & Littlefield Publishers, Inc.
A wholly owned subsidiary of The Rowman & Littlefield Publishing Group, Inc.
4501 Forbes Boulevard, Suite 200, Lanham, Maryland 20706
www.rowmanlittlefield.com

PO Box 317
OX2 9RU
Oxford, UK

British Library Cataloguing in Publication Information Available

**Library of Congress Cataloging-in-Publication Data**

Wills, David C., 1967–
The first war on terrorism : counter-terrorism policy during the Reagan administration /
  David C. Wills.
      p. cm.
Includes bibliographical references and index.
      ISBN 0-7425-3128-7 (hardcover : alk. paper)—ISBN 0-7425-3129-5 (pbk. : alk.
paper)
      1. Terrorism—United States. 2. Terrorism—United States—Prevention. 3. United
States—Politics and government—1981–1989. I. Title.

  HV6432.W55 2003
  363.3'2'097309048—dc21                                          2003005187

Printed in the United States of America

⊗™ The paper used in this publication meets the minimum requirements of American
National Standard for Information Sciences—Permanence of Paper for Printed Library
Materials, ANSI/NISO Z39.48-1992.

For mom and dad

# Contents

# Preface

In 1994, while I was student-teaching at a southern California high school, a friend gave me a copy of Tom Clancy's *Sum of All Fears*. I was immediately fascinated by the tale of terrorists and their use of weapons of mass destruction. I wanted to learn more. A lot of the non-fictional variety took place during the 1970s and 1980s, but I was a kid at the time and paid little attention to the news. Still, what little I did happen to notice seemed totally irrational to me. As an undergraduate student in 1986, I remember sitting around a television with friends watching reports of the U.S. bombing raids over Libya. We were all glad to see the Reagan administration responding to Qaddafi's provocations, but did not really consider the debate that led up to the retaliation, nor the difficulties and ramifications of such a military operation.

This interest eventually evolved into my doctoral dissertation at the University of Virginia. I remember very distinctly that my chairman was wary about the project and advised caution, saying that research on terrorism had a tendency to be "fringe." But that was in early 1998. Today, of course, the entire civilized world recognizes the importance of the topic. If we are to understand the phenomena, and counter it effectively today and in the future, we must not forget the lessons that were hard-learned by past administrations. That is the point of this book—to remember. The media and decision-makers today talk about the war on terrorism as though it is something new. It is not. President Reagan, in particular, confronted an appallingly large number of attacks, and his administration's successes and failures are instructive for today.

No project of this scope can be done by one person. Although the views contained herein are my own, the following helped shape and direct my research during the long process and deserve much thanks. First, to my friends and family—especially my parents and Dr. Scott Waalkes—who read through the manuscript and provided great feedback. Several professors provided assistance along the way, including Dr. Alan Wyner from the University of California at Santa Barbara, Dr. Phil Williams and Dr. Paul Hammond at the University of Pittsburgh. At the University of Virginia, my committee—Dr. William Quandt, Dr. James Ceaser, Dr. John Owen, and Dr. Philip Zelikow, gave invaluable assistance, as did Ambassador Nathaniel Howell. The unsung heroes of this project are the archivists who responded to my countless Freedom of Information Act requests with professionalism and patience. I am especially grateful to those at the Reagan Presidential Library, including Kelly Barton, Greg Cumming, and Lisa Jones. Lastly, this book would not exist without the generous assistance of the many interviewees who gave their time to help a lowly graduate student. In particular, Ambassador Robert Oakley and David Long have my gratitude, for they not only granted several interviews, but also put me in contact with other administration officials and even read early versions of the book to make sure the facts were right.

Lastly, I should note that while this book is at times critical of the Reagan administration's conduct, the individuals in the bureaucracy—at the Departments of Defense and State, the CIA, and the NSC staff—did their jobs very well. The problems that arose should not rest on their shoulders, but on the decision-makers who at the time failed to give a coordinated, centralized direction to their efforts.

# Introduction

Woe to the government, which, relying on half-hearted politics and a shackled military policy, meets a foe who, like the untamed elements, knows no law other than his own power!

—Karl von Clausewitz, *On War*

Terrorism has been with us for several millennia. Whether it was the Sicarii trying to run the Romans out of Jerusalem or Black September murdering Israeli athletes at the 1972 Munich Olympics, the world has long had to confront political violence meted out by small, radical groups. However, Osama bin Laden's organization is not the first group to use political violence against the United States to make Washington change its policies. In the 1980s terrorism was rampant; from Latin America to Europe and the Middle East, a host of groups demanded changes in American foreign policy and were willing to bomb, assassinate, kidnap, and hijack to pressure the government to act. The events of September 11, 2001, were, despite their horrific magnitude, just a continuation in the long pattern of bloody battles waged by groups that see the targeting of non-combatants as a legitimate tool for accomplishing their policy objectives. In the past, such terrorist activities rarely brought about any change in American policy, although in a few instances terrorist groups and their sponsors met with spectacular success. In the case of September 11, Osama bin Laden and his Al-Qaeda network demand that the United States end its support for Israel and the Saudi regime, and remove its forces from the Persian Gulf, especially from Saudi Arabia. If these things do eventually happen, though, it will be the result of other pressures or interests and not because a terrorist group demanded it. The biggest change in policy that has resulted from September 11 is precisely what bin Laden did not anticipate—a sleeping giant awoke and now seeks to snuff out the scourge of international terrorism.

However, while the Bush administration's "war on terrorism" is of the utmost importance to Western security, substantial hurdles to formulating and enacting an effective and coherent response remain and must not be ignored. For its part, the Reagan administration's own "war on terrorism" and the problems it encountered in molding a consistent and effective policy are enlightening. Despite coming to power in part because of President Carter's handling of the Tehran hostage crisis, the Reagan administration was still unable to regularly muster the political will to engage the problem and consistently adhere to its two-pillared policy: (1) when the terrorists involved in an attack against American citizens could be identified, they would pay a very high price for their actions, and (2) the Administration would grant no concessions to terrorists.

There were many reasons for this inconsistency, but three aspects of the Reagan administration's decision-making process bear closer examination. The first is the president's management style. Because Reagan was not a detail man—especially when it came to foreign policy—he tended to hand the keys of each department or agency to an appointee, fully trusting each with a substantial amount of delegated power. At the CIA, William Casey was told to restore the Agency, bring it in line with Reagan's philosophical beliefs, and was given virtual autonomy to do so. Similar mandates were given to Caspar Weinberger at Defense and George Shultz at State. Because Reagan initially trusted his advisors completely, it was a rare occasion indeed when he would override a cabinet secretary's recommendation, especially when such action would impinge on that department's prerogatives.

Such a system, though, required strong personalities to lead each respective bureaucracy, and Casey, Weinberger, and Shultz all fit the bill. Simultaneously, Reagan's deliberative system depended on collegiality. He assumed, as had happened during his days as governor of California, that his primary advisors could come together to discuss policy differences, hash them out, and then implement a compromise. This type of system works when the participants' beliefs converge, but in the case of Reagan's foreign policy team, diametrically opposing views were manifold. The other necessity for a collegial system to function well is the presence of a strong manager who is able to move the group to a decision and ensure that it is implemented true to the president's wishes. Without a president willing to knock heads and bring his disparate group of advisors to a decision point (or a national security advisor with the delegated power to do the same), any one member of the foreign policy team could stake an extreme position, stubbornly hold to it, and as a result bring the decision-making process to a standstill.

Second is the importance of informal power. Since such power was not a constant during the Reagan years, recognizing the ebb and flow of who was in and who was out—who had the president's ear and why at any particular time—is critical to understanding the administration's decisions. When gridlock occurred, Reagan was likely to listen to his most trusted aide—whoever that was at the time—and implement that advisor's preference (or at least allow it to be implemented without repercussions). If it was a toss-up between two or more trusted advisors, Reagan would split the difference, choosing a course of action that pleased nobody, usually resulting in the administration using inappropriate tools or methods in an attempt to protect or advance U.S. interests. As he had done in California, the president rarely imposed his own views, but rather looked to his advisors to tell him how to handle the problem. At other times, when no one was able to enforce decisions and ensure the integrity of the decision-making process, individual participants were left in a position to take unilateral action that circumvented the desires of the other members of the national security team. In so doing, these individuals or small groups could impose their own solution without consulting, or simply by ignoring, the other players. This led to a variety of policies and responses that sometimes conflicted with and at other times were congruent with Reagan's stated counter-terrorism policy.

Third, in a system where participants could unilaterally impose their own policy preference, or where dissidents could hold up the process by refusing to compromise, these individuals' beliefs become very important. For the study that follows, the key participants' most significant beliefs include:

1. The nature of terrorism—is it war or is it crime?
2. The Middle East—are American interests advanced best by closer relations with Israel or the moderate Arabs (or both)?
3. The use of force—under what circumstances, and for what purpose is it appropriate to use the military?

How then does all of this work in practice? The most famous case study from the Reagan administration is, of course, the arms-for-hostages deal that exploded into the Iran-Contra scandal. Unable to win the freedom of the "forgotten seven"—individual American citizens that had been kidnapped in Beirut by the Iranian-supported Hezbollah during 1984 and 1985, Reagan became increasingly frustrated. The kidnappers demanded the release of the Dawa 17, a group of convicted terrorists serving time in Kuwaiti prisons for a bombing spree there in December 1983. The administration queried the Kuwaiti government about freeing these men to resolve the crisis, but when that did not work, and when ransom-paying initiatives fell through, Reagan began to push his national security team to "do something," asking them almost daily if there was any progress.

At the same time, concern about the situation in Iran was increasing in light of rumors that the Ayatollah Khomeini was ill and could die in the near future. If this happened, a power vacuum would have been created, and it was believed by many in the Reagan administration that the Soviet Union was in a much better position to exert its influence in that oil-rich Persian Gulf state than the United States. Iran was a critical piece in the geopolitical chess game that was the Cold War, and these new concerns prompted the administration to undertake its first major review of policy toward Iran since the Ayatollah Khomeini claimed power during the Carter administration. When the Israeli government approached the U.S. about selling arms to Iran as a part of a new strategic opening that would bolster the moderates in Tehran, the administration initially agreed. However, when Shultz and Weinberger both objected, the NSC staff, with CIA director William Casey's help and Reagan's approval, proceeded with the Iranian initiative anyway. In the end, rather than making a breakthrough in relations with Tehran, the administration rewarded the kidnappers' patrons by providing the weapons Iran desperately needed if it were to continue prosecuting its war against Iraq, and failed to end the hostage crisis.

Arms-for-hostages was able to happen because of a number of factors. First, Reagan's management style was "hands off." When he identified the goal—free the hostages—the NSC staff and CIA proceeded without supervision. Second, the beliefs of the individual participants in the decision-making process significantly impacted their actions. Because Robert McFarlane, John Poindexter, Oliver North, William Casey, and Ronald Reagan all believed that Israel was a strategic asset in the region, they were inclined to believe the Israelis when they claimed that selling weapons to Tehran was *the* way to proceed. In addition, informal power in American counterterrorism efforts had shifted from the Pentagon to the NSC staff, whose desire to punish terrorists more closely reflected the president's wishes, and whose successes enhanced their standing. Meanwhile, the Pentagon's continual caution led to, at various times, missed opportunities, frustration, and humiliation. Since Reagan had authorized the arms sales and because the NSC staff and Casey had the tools with which to act, those who opposed the operation were not able to effectively block the initiative, and it was allowed to continue. If the players involved had maintained different beliefs, if Reagan had clearly opposed the plan, or if the NSC staff and the CIA had not had the formal and informal power to control policy, the arms-for-hostages fiasco would never have happened.

Perhaps the most interesting aspect of the arms-for-hostages deal is that it was not an aberration, but rather was indicative of the way the Reagan administration worked, as the other case studies will show. How then is this pertinent to today's world? The Bush administration's new "war on terrorism" is different in magnitude, but surely faces some of the same difficulties encountered by Reagan and his foreign policy team. While it is unclear how Bush manages his advisors this early in his administration, the divergence of beliefs within his foreign policy team concerning terrorism, the Middle East, and the use of force, however minor, will likely become more important as the first phase of the war comes to a close. For the time being, relative unanimity about how to respond has prevailed in the Bush administration primarily because of the nature of the September 11 attacks, with all involved willing to see the United States respond with force. As the Afghanistan campaign continues, though, cracks in the facade will likely develop and the Bush administration will have to manage differing opinions on a number of substantive questions, including: (1) Should the war against terrorism end after the campaign in Afghanistan (or with the confirmed death of Osama bin Laden)? (2) If not, where should the U.S. focus its attention next? Iran? Somalia? Yemen? The Philippines? Colombia? North Korea? Saudi Arabia? (3) What methods should be used? Air power only? Special forces? Conventional forces? Covert operations? (4) How does the United States define victory? How Bush reconciles the different opinions within his administration will help determine how successful he will be in conducting America's second war against terrorism.

Some may question why this particular study is needed, since much has already been done to explore the Reagan administration's counter-terrorism policies. First, it expands on the good journalistic accounts such as David Martin and John Walcott's *Best Laid Plans* and Bob Woodward's *Veil* by employing new archival research and interviews. New details have been uncovered since these books were published, so the case studies are a more complete, synthesized account of American counter-terrorism policy from an era when it was one of the leading issues of the day. Second, it explains *why* the administration acted the way it did. The aforementioned books are good at telling what happened, but they do not explain what caused the variation in American response. This study will.

# Abbreviations

| | |
|---|---|
| ANO | Abu Nidal Organization |
| BIA | Beirut International Airport |
| CIA | Central Intelligence Agency |
| CINC | Commander in Chief |
| CJCS | Chairman of the Joint Chiefs of Staff |
| CNO | Chief of Naval Operations |
| CPPG | Crisis Pre-Planning Group |
| DCI | Director of Central Intelligence |
| DCM | Deputy Chief of Mission |
| DDCI | Deputy Director of Central Intelligence |
| DDI | Deputy Director, Intelligence |
| DDO | Deputy Director, Operations |
| DIA | Defense Intelligence Agency |
| EO | Executive Order |
| EST | Emergency Support Team |
| EuCom | European Command |
| FAA | Federal Aviation Administration |
| FBI | Federal Bureau of Investigation |
| FEMA | Federal Emergency Management Agency |
| GBL | George Bush Presidential Library |
| HIA | Hoover Institution Archives, Stanford University |
| ICRC | International Committee of the Red Cross |
| IDF | Israeli Defense Forces |
| IJO | Islamic Jihad Organization |
| INR | Department of State's Bureau for Intelligence and Research |
| ISA | Intelligence Support Activity |

| JCS | Joint Chiefs of Staff |
| JSOC | Joint Special Operations Command |
| LAF | Lebanese Armed Forces (the Lebanese Army) |
| LPB | Libyan People's Bureau (Libyan Embassy) |
| MNF | Multinational Force |
| NIE | National Intelligence Estimate |
| NRO | National Reconnaissance Office |
| NSA | National Security Advisor |
| NSC | National Security Council |
| NSDD | National Security Decision Directive |
| NSPG | National Security Planning Group |
| OSS | Office of Strategic Services |
| PLF | Palestinian Liberation Front |
| PLO | Palestinian Liberation Organization |
| RRL | Ronald Reagan Presidential Library |
| SAM | Surface-to-air missile |
| SIC | Senate Intelligence Committee |
| SNIE | Special National Intelligence Estimate |
| SSG | Special Situation Group |
| TIWG | Terrorist Incident Working Group |

*Chapter One*

# Explaining the Reagan Administration's Responses to Terrorism

Let terrorists beware that when the rules of international behavior are violated, our policy will be one of swift and effective retribution. We hear it said that we live in an era of limits to our powers. Well, let it also be understood, there are limits to our patience.

—Ronald Reagan
January 27, 1981

Ronald Reagan came to the presidency promising to restore America's strength and pride after a decade of decline. The new administration's promise of revival stood in stark contrast to the recent past—the Vietnam War, Watergate, and America's most immediate humiliation, the 444-day-long Iranian hostage crisis. That crisis began on November 4, 1979, when radical Iranian students stormed the U.S. embassy in Tehran, taking 90 hostages. As a result, in the year between the embassy seizure and the 1980 election, the Carter administration struggled both at home and abroad. In the Persian Gulf, the administration launched an ill-fated rescue attempt that left eight American soldiers dead in the Iranian desert and the hostages still in Tehran. At home, an ABC program called "America Held Hostage" reminded the nation nightly of the embassy staff's captivity and Carter's inability to free them. Weakened by the crisis (and other factors, including the sour economy), he faced a stiff challenge by Senator Edward Kennedy for his party's presidential nomination.

Many political observers, and Carter himself, regard the Iranian hostage crisis as an important factor in Reagan's triumph in the 1980 general election. A series of NBC News/Associated Press polls support this, showing that most Americans disapproved of the way Carter handled the crisis. By October 1980, only 40% of respondents said that they approved of the president's actions;

and even this number is high when contrasted with his overall marks on foreign policy. An NBC News/Associated Press poll conducted in September 1980 indicated that only 23% of those polled rated Carter's handling of foreign affairs as "excellent" or "good," while an overwhelming 77% said he was doing only a "fair" or "poor" job.[1] Meanwhile, the public's perception of Reagan was far different; the former governor of California projected an attitude of firmness, declaring that under his leadership, the United States would stand up to its enemies and put an end to the humiliations it had recently endured. During a televised speech on October 19, 1980, Reagan declared his intention to combat terrorism, saying, "I will direct the resources of my administration against this scourge of civilization and toward expansion of our cooperation with other nations combatting terrorism in its main forms."[2] During the lone presidential debate, Reagan tiptoed around the question "How would you respond to terrorism?" while defusing the public's biggest concern about his own foreign policy—that he would overreact to threats. Further, he did not openly criticize Carter's handling of the Iranian crisis, because such criticism could have undermined ongoing negotiations to free the hostages. The media, however, was not so restrained. Rather than downplaying the crisis, the major television networks emphasized the failure of the Carter administration's Iran policy; each network aired a one-year anniversary retrospective of the embassy takeover during the first weekend in November, which was also the weekend before the general election. According to one observer, "The weekend [was] drenched with . . . humiliation." However, the election was lost well before November. One of Carter's political advisors later reflected, "The President's chances for reelection probably died on the desert of Iran with the eight brave soldiers who gave their lives trying to free the American hostages."[3]

At his inauguration, Reagan was subtle but firm as he addressed the issue of terrorism. He declared:

> Our forbearance should never be misunderstood. Our reluctance for conflict should not be misjudged as a failure of will. . . . Above all we must realize no arsenal or no weapon in the arsenals of the world is so formidable as the will and moral courage of free men and women. It is a weapon our adversaries in today's world do not have. It is a weapon that we as Americans do have. Let that be understood by those who practice terrorism and prey upon their neighbors.

Reagan understood that with the heightened interest in and attention paid to the issue, terrorism was no longer just another foreign policy issue. It had become a factor in domestic politics that carried with it electoral ramifications. This is why he paid so much attention to it in his rhetoric. This is what led him to proclaim a new policy—one of swift and effective retribution—on the occasion of the Iranian hostages' homecoming.

Once in office, Reagan and his team changed the government's approach on a variety of security issues, and were not shy about drawing a very sharp contrast between the Carter and Reagan administrations. For example, Reagan initially wanted to raise defense spending by 5%, but when it was learned that Carter had proposed identical figures in his final budget, the Reagan team *increased* their increase to 7%, justifying the action by saying, "worldwide, what we're doing in defense must be seen as different from Carter. It must be a symbol of a change in the climate as regards to defense."[4] Futher, the Reagan team believed Carter had failed to deal effectively with Soviet adventurism, and had been especially weak trying to resolve the Iran hostage crisis. According to Robert Gates, then the CIA's Deputy Director for Intelligence, "'weakness' was the watchword applied to every aspect of foreign and defense policy, and intelligence, during the preceding four years."[5] Consequently, the Reagan administration was very sensitive about any comparisons to the previous administration, and sought to differentiate itself by appearing to act with strength and dispatch in foreign affairs, with a special emphasis on responding effectively to terrorism. As one commentator observed, "One of the reasons [Reagan] was elected in the first place, and one of the reasons his popularity has continued at a high level, is the belief of the American public that he would stand up to, would face down, the nation's enemies."[6] Secretary of State Alexander Haig spelled out the first tangible departure from Carter's foreign policy priorities, declaring, "International terrorism will take the place of human rights. . . . The greatest problem to me in the human-rights area today is the area of rampant international terrorism."

The Reagan administration's terrorism policy had two pillars. First, when terrorists attacked American targets, the administration would respond forcefully. It would seek to punish those responsible by a variety of means, including the apprehension of suspects and military strikes. Following the return of the hostages from Iran, many complained about the Carter administration's restraint during the ordeal. In contrast, Reagan "vowed to take an unrelentingly tough line against any such future acts of terrorism."[7] An insight into the new president's thinking was his use of the term "prisoners of war" to describe those hostages. Reagan biographer Lou Cannon observed that this could be taken as a clue that the new president would view further terrorist attacks as *acts of war*.[8]

Throughout the 1980s, Reagan, his spokesmen, and his appointees repeatedly spouted fiery rhetoric, perpetuating the image of the administration's strong counter-terrorism credentials. A few examples:

We intend to find the criminals who harbor and direct [the terrorists]. We will not allow this behavior to go unpunished.[9]

Those who directed this atrocity must be dealt justice. They will be.[10]

From a practical standpoint, a purely passive defense does not provide enough of a deterrent to terrorists and the states that sponsor terrorism. Terrorism is a form of warfare, and history has taught us that to deter war, one must be able to strike back or act preemptively.[11]

The community of civilized nations must also ensure that no criminals such as those responsible for the outrages in Beirut are beyond the reach of justice. If such barbarians are safe anywhere, then no one else can be. . . . But we must not rest so long as there is a haven anywhere for those who practice the barbarity of air [piracy] and terrorism.[12]

The President has issued standing guidance that we should maintain our readiness to respond to terrorist incidents across the board—readiness to surveil, to track, to apprehend. . . .[13]

For us to ignore, by inaction, the slaughter of American civilians and American soldiers, whether in night clubs or airline terminals, is simply not in the American tradition. When our citizens are abused or attacked, anywhere in the world, on the direct orders of a hostile regime—we will respond. . . . I warned that there should be no place on Earth where terrorists can rest and train and practice their deadly skills. I meant it. I said that we would act with others if possible, and alone if necessary, to ensure that terrorists have no sanctuary anywhere.[14]

We have put those who would instigate acts of terrorism against U.S. citizens or property on notice that we will vigorously confront this criminal behavior in every way—diplomatically, economically, legally, and, when necessary, militarily. We have demonstrated our resolve.[15]

The State Department's official policy statement on terrorism likewise declared that the United States would "make state sponsors of terrorism pay a price for their actions."[16]

The second pillar of Reagan's terrorism policy concerned terrorists' demands: making concessions to terrorists was not an option. Virtually every member of the administration agreed that acquiescing to such demands only encouraged terrorist groups to try again, sending a message to the international community that the United States could be coerced easily and regularly. Again, Reagan and his team repeatedly declared the administration's position on the issue of concessions:

There will be no negotiation with terrorists of any kind.[17]

Yielding to violence and terrorism today may seem to provide temporary relief, but such a course is sure to lead to a more dangerous and less manageable future crisis.[18]

The United States has a clear policy of combatting terrorism and of refusing to make concessions to terrorists. . . .[19]

We will make no concessions to terrorists. We pay no ransoms, nor do we permit releases of prisoners or agree to other acts which might encourage additional terrorism. We make no changes in U.S. policy because of terrorists' threats or acts. If U.S. personnel are taken hostage or endangered, we are prepared to consider a broad range of actions appropriate to the threat.[20]

On this point there was no flexibility. The new administration went so far as to criticize the Carter administration for its *negotiations* with Iran in an attempt to free the embassy hostages, and was critical of the arrangement that ended the crisis. In that deal, Iran recovered frozen assets worth 2.8 billion dollars, and the United States agreed to lift trade restrictions imposed after the embassy takeover.[21] A review of the agreement by the new administration produced sharp criticism of the provisions limiting the ability of former hostages to sue the government of Iran, but after some delay, the Reagan administration agreed to honor the pact. "The present administration would not have negotiated with Iran for the release of the hostages," said William Dyess, a State Department spokesman. "Future acts of state-sponsored terrorism against the U.S. will meet swift and sure punishment."

## CONTRASTING RHETORIC AND REALITY

The Reagan team firmly believed that its two-pillared policy was the best way to proceed. This being the case, how did the Reagan administration measure up to its own policy? The arms-for-hostages debacle is a well-known departure, but were there others? If the administration consistently enacted its policy whenever it faced such a crisis, there would be no puzzle—aside from Iran-Contra. But the Reagan administration was far from consistent. Arms-for-hostages was not an aberration.

While domestic politics played a role in the initial rhetoric against terrorism, Reagan and his advisors were also genuinely concerned about political violence against Americans. They wanted to bring those who harmed Americans to justice—be it in the crosshairs of a weapon or in the courtroom, and they believed in the no-concessions pledge. However, the Reagan administration found it extremely difficult to respond forcefully when Americans were attacked, even when the evidence showed who was responsible.

Rather than steadfastly adhering to the pledge of "swift and effective retribution," the Reagan administration utilized a wide range of measures in response to terrorist incidents that can be categorized into five broad categories: (1) Military measures (i.e., "swift and effective retribution"); (2) Non-military efforts (such as implementing economic, legal, and/or political sanctions against an offending state); (3) Provide logistical support to a government where an attack took place (such as increased financial aid for that state's military, or technical support); (4) Acquiesce to terrorist demands; and (5) No response against the responsible party and/or only increase defensive measures (e.g., installing shatter-proof windows at an embassy, erecting concrete impediments to make it harder for suicide bombers to get close to their target, etc.).[22]

An analysis of terrorist incidents against American targets during the Reagan years is instructive. Over 600 such attacks occurred between January 20, 1981 and January 20, 1989. These attacks ranged from the small-scale, like the March 13, 1981, attempted bombing of the America House in Frankfurt, West Germany, to the catastrophic, such as the October 23, 1983, bombing of the Marine barracks in Beirut, Lebanon. Of the 636 attacks identified, the administration only used the military option twice.[23] In the overwhelming majority of cases, the administration did not respond at all (see Table 1).

The glaring statistic is the 94.97 percent of cases in which the administration did not respond, and a word of explanation is necessary. In some instances, the administration did not react against the terrorist organization responsible for the attack, but did improve its anti-terrorist, or defensive, capabilities. This primarily consisted of posting more security at potential targets, and in a handful of cases included re-evaluating terrorism policies and improving intelligence-collecting and analysis capabilities. However, improving defensive capabilities did not advance the policy of "swift and effective retribution," nor was it an active measure against terrorists, and therefore falls into the category of "no response" for the purpose of this study.

No clear pattern emerges from an analysis of these cases, save one. In many of the cases where there was no response, the administration was handicapped by a lack of hard intelligence. Uncertainty about who to retaliate against was a problem in many instances. No administration, regardless of how trigger-happy it might be, would send the U.S. military against a target if there was no evidence against that group.[24] In 251 of the 636 cases, no organization claimed credit or could be positively identified as the guilty party. So the uncertainty factor theoretically explains about 40 percent of the no responses. Put simply, when the administration had insufficient information, it did not act.

**Table 1.   Responses to Terrorism**

| Response | Cases | Percent |
|---|---|---|
| Military measures | 2 | 0.32 |
| Non-military efforts | 11 | 1.73 |
| Logistical support | 2 | 0.31 |
| Acquiesce | 17 | 2.67 |
| No response | 604 | 94.97 |
| Total | 636 | 100.00 |

A second explanation for a "'no response" is that government may lack the tools to respond. Organizational capabilities, such as the real-time ability to locate hostages in order to mount a rescue attempt, the appropriate weapons to battle against terrorists and their sponsors, or jurisdictional power to act are all critical if the government is to mount a counter-terrorist operation. For example, the FBI was unable to investigate overseas terrorist incidents until Congress passed legislation making such acts federal offenses. The FBI has been a prominent player in the counter-terrorism efforts of the United States since it acquired this capability in the mid-1980s.

A further explanation for a "no response" is the magnitude of attack. An overwhelming number of the cases were minor, and simply did not rise to the threshold where presidential attentionl was appropriate. Instead, the bureaucracy managed these incidents without presidential and cabinet-level involvement. No president could justify a military strike for the bombing of a McDonalds restaurant in Paris in which no one was injured (November 15, 1981), or the firebombing of a U.S. serviceman's automobile in Greece (November 15, 1983), or other similarly minor incidents. In such cases, the event was treated as a crime, relegating jurisdiction to local law enforcement agencies. Classifying low magnitude terrorism as crime, and making local law enforcement respond, led to a distinct problem; police may have been able to identify the perpetrators, but were unable to apprehend them. Suspects may have fled the country or blended in so well locally that law enforcement's job was virtually impossible. Sometimes the bad guys just got away.

Where then is the justification for a robust response to terrorism? Most significantly, a certain magnitude of attack needed to be attained. In other words, the detainment of, injury of, and/or murder of an American citizen, or a failed attempt that would have accomplished one of these levels of violence seems to cross the magnitude threshold meriting a response. There were 126 such incidents that met this criterion (see Table 2).

**Table 2.  Terrorist Incidents of Magnitude, 1981–1989**

| Date | Event | Americans Involved |
|------|-------|--------------------|
| 03/02/81 | Pakistan Air hijacking | 6 hostages |
| 03/17/81 | Bazooka attack—Marines, Costa Rica | 3 injured |
| 03/25/81 | Embassy assaulted, El Salvador | no casualties |
| 03/27/81 | Honduran Airliner hijacking | 9 hostages |
| 03/28/81 | Garuda Air hijacking, Indonesia | 3 hostages, 1 killed |
| 04/23/81 | Ambassador Boyatt, Colombia | death threat |
| 05/02/81 | US Occidental plant takeover, Bolivia | 1 hostage |
| 05/24/81 | Turkish Air hijacking | 5 hostages |

(*continued*)

**Table 2. Terrorist Incidents of Magnitude, 1981–1989 (*continued*)**

| Date | Event | Americans Involved |
|------|-------|--------------------|
| 07/01/81 | Eastern Airlines bomb thwarted | 100 passengers |
| 08/31/81 | Embassy bombed, Peru | no casualties |
| 08/31/81 | Air Force HQ bombed, Germany | 18 injured |
| 09/15/81 | General Kroesen assassination attempt, Germany | 3 injured |
| 09/23/81 | USAF personnel attacked, Honduras | 2 injured |
| 10/15/81 | Ambassador Rabb, Italy | death threat |
| 11/00/81 | Embassy Club attack, Sudan | bombing failed |
| 11/12/81 | Ambassador Chapman, France | assassination attempt |
| 12/17/81 | General Dozier, Italy | kidnapped |
| 01/18/82 | Lt. Colonel Ray, France | assassinated |
| 04/01/82 | Embassy bombed, Greece | no injuries |
| 04/17/82 | F. Charloff attacked, Lebanon | 1 injured |
| 04/28/82 | Honduran Air hijacking, Honduras | 13 hostages |
| 06/01/82 | Military bases bombed, Germany | no injuries |
| 07/19/82 | D. Dodge, Lebanon | kidnapped |
| 07/23/82 | American tourists, Zimbabwe | 2 kidnapped and killed |
| 08/09/82 | Café attack, France | 2 killed |
| 08/11/82 | Pan Am flight bombed, Japan | 1 killed, 16 injured |
| 10/02/82 | R. Kehagy, Guatemala | kidnapped and killed |
| 12/14/82 | Military personnel bombed, Germany | 1 injured |
| 12/15/82 | Captain Brombay bombed, Germany | 1 injured |
| 03/07/83 | K. Bishop, Colombia | kidnapped |
| 04/07/83 | C. Wood Kirby, Colombia | kidnapped |
| 04/18/83 | Embassy bombed, Lebanon | 17 killed, 88 injured |
| 05/25/83 | Lt. Commander Schaufelberger, El Salvador | assassinated |
| 08/26/83 | Embassy attack, Kuwait | bombing thwarted |
| 08/30/83 | Tourists, Colombia | 2 killed, 1 injured |
| 10/00/83 | Multiple targets, Egypt | attacks thwarted |
| 10/23/83 | Marine barracks bombed, Lebanon | 241 killed, 80 injured |
| 11/15/83 | Various targets, Jordan | attacks thwarted |
| 11/15/83 | Captain Tsantes, Greece | assassinated |
| 12/12/83 | Embassy bombed, Kuwait | 4 killed |
| 01/18/84 | M. Kerr, Lebanon | assassinated |
| 02/07/84 | K. Shafer, Lebanon | kidnapped |
| 02/10/84 | R. Regier, Lebanon | kidnapped |
| 02/15/84 | L. Hunt, Italy | assassinated |
| 03/07/84 | J. Levin, Lebanon | kidnapped |
| 03/16/84 | W. Buckley, Lebanon | kidnapped and killed |
| 03/26/84 | Consul General Homme, France | assassination attempt |
| 04/03/84 | Military personnel attacked, Greece | no injuries |
| 05/07/84 | Ambassador Jordan, Peru | assassination attempt |
| 05/08/84 | B. Weir, Lebanon | kidnapped |
| 05/18/84 | Ambassador Pickering, El Salvador | assassination thwarted |
| 09/20/84 | Embassy Annex bombed, Lebanon | 2 killed, 20 injured |
| 10/01/84 | Ambassador Pickering, El Salvador | assassination thwarted |

**Table 2.    Terrorist Incidents of Magnitude, 1981–1989 (continued)**

| Date | Event | Americans Involved |
|---|---|---|
| 11/18/84 | Embassy attack, Italy | bombing thwarted |
| 12/03/84 | P. Kilburn, Lebanon | kidnapped and killed |
| 12/04/84 | Kuwaiti Air hijacking, Pakistan | 6 hostages, 2 killed, 2 injured |
| 01/08/85 | L. Jenco, Lebanon | kidnapped |
| 02/02/85 | Military personnel attacked, Greece | 37 injured |
| 02/05/85 | Ambassador Rabb, Italy | assassination thwarted |
| 02/07/85 | E. Camarena, México | kidnapped and killed |
| 02/13/85 | Hotel bombing, Philippines | 4 killed |
| 02/15/85 | Military personnel attacked, Honduras | 1 injured |
| 03/16/85 | T. Anderson, Lebanon | kidnapped |
| 04/13/85 | Restaurant bombed, Spain | 15 injured |
| 05/16/85 | Ambassador's residence bombed, Peru | no injuries |
| 05/22/85 | Embassy attack, Egypt | bombing thwarted |
| 05/28/85 | D. Jacobson, Lebanon | kidnapped |
| 06/09/85 | T. Sutherland, Lebanon | kidnapped |
| 06/11/85 | Royal Jordanian Air hijacking, Lebanon | 2 hostages |
| 06/14/85 | TWA 847 hijacking, Lebanon | 136 hostages, 1 killed |
| 06/19/85 | Marines attacked, El Salvador | 6 killed |
| 06/23/85 | Air India 182 bombed, Canada | 7 killed |
| 07/01/85 | TWA offices bombed, Spain | 1 injured |
| 07/13/85 | Airliner hijacking, Berlin | thwarted |
| 07/19/85 | Embassy bombed, Chile | no injuries |
| 07/22/85 | NW Orient offices bombed, Denmark | 3 injured |
| 08/07/85 | Military personnel, Germany | 1 kidnapped and killed |
| 08/08/85 | Military base bombed, Germany | 2 killed, 19 injured |
| 09/16/85 | Café grenade attack, Italy | 8 injured |
| 10/07/85 | *Achille Lauro* hijacked, Egypt | 12 hostages, 1 killed |
| 11/23/85 | EgyptAir 648 hijacked, Malta | 1 killed, 2 injured |
| 11/24/85 | Military exchange bombed, Germany | 30 injured |
| 12/10/85 | J. Geddes and E. Sohl, Colombia | kidnapped, 1 killed |
| 12/27/85 | Airports attacked, Austria and Italy | 5 killed, 14 injured |
| 04/02/86 | TWA 840 bombed, Italy | 4 killed |
| 04/04/86 | La Belle disco bombed, Berlin | 2 killed, 62 injured |
| 04/17/86 | W. Calkins shot, Sudan | 1 injured |
| 04/17/86 | El Al bomb attempt, England | 220 American passengers |
| 04/18/86 | Officers' club assault, Turkey | attack thwarted |
| 04/21/86 | Ambassador Jordan attacked, Peru | no injuries |
| 04/25/86 | A. Pollick shot, North Yemen | 1 injured |
| 04/27/86 | Embassy attack, México | bombing thwarted |
| 04/29/86 | Ambassador's residence bombed, Chile | no injuries |
| 06/25/86 | Tourist train bombed, Peru | 1 killed, 7 injured |
| 06/26/86 | Various targets, Texas | attacks thwarted |
| 07/12/86 | B. Lawrence, Philippines | kidnapped |
| 07/23/86 | Embassy attack, Togo | bombing thwarted |

(continued)

**Table 2.    Terrorist Incidents of Magnitude, 1981–1989 (*continued*)**

| Date | Event | Americans Involved |
|------|-------|-------------------|
| 09/05/86 | Pan Am 73 hijacked, Pakistan | 45 hostages, 4 killed |
| 09/09/86 | F. Reed, Lebanon | kidnapped |
| 09/12/86 | J. Cicippio, Lebanon | kidnapped |
| 10/21/86 | E. Tracy, Lebanon | kidnapped |
| 11/14/86 | Embassy attack, Egypt | bombing thwarted |
| 01/24/87 | Steen, Turner, Polhill, Singh, Lebanon | kidnapped |
| 04/10/87 | Various targets, Turkey | attacks thwarted |
| 04/24/87 | Military bus bombed, Greece | 12 injured |
| 05/26/87 | Embassy personnel attacked, Egypt | 2 injured |
| 06/09/87 | Embassy bombed, Italy | several injured |
| 06/17/87 | C. Glass, Lebanon | kidnapped |
| 07/07/87 | Aid workers, Sudan | 3 kidnapped |
| 08/09/87 | Restaurant bombed, Honduras | 6 injured |
| 08/10/87 | Military bus bombed, Greece | 10 injured |
| 10/28/87 | Military personnel attacked, Philippines | 2 killed |
| 10/26/87 | Missionaries attacked, Zimbabwe | 2 killed |
| 12/26/87 | USO club attacked, Spain | 6 injured |
| 01/21/88 | G. Carros bombed, Greece | attack failed |
| 02/17/88 | Lt. Colonel W. Higgins, Lebanon | kidnapped |
| 03/19/88 | Military personnel bombed, Greece | 5 injured |
| 04/12/88 | Various targets, USA | bombings thwarted |
| 04/14/88 | USO Club bombed, Italy | 1 killed, 4 injured |
| 06/13/88 | C. Gregory, Peru | assassinated |
| 06/28/88 | Captain W. Nordeen, Greece | assassinated |
| 07/11/88 | Tourist ferry attacked, Greece | no injuries |
| 07/17/88 | Military personnel attacked, Honduras | 6 injured |
| 08/08/88 | Secretary of State motorcade, Bolivia | no injuries |
| 12/21/88 | Pan Am 103 bombed, Scotland | 206 killed |
| 01/03/89 | R. Grover and R. Libby, Colombia | kidnapped |

An analysis of these attacks shows a pattern strikingly similar to the larger statistical study. Despite the policy and rhetoric, the United States responded militarily only twice—after the hijacking of the *Achille Lauro* cruise ship and the bombing of the La Belle disco in West Berlin. In the overwhelming majority of cases, the administration did not react—either because it relied on local law enforcement officials to handle the case, or because the U.S. was unable or unwilling to act. This includes cases of a much larger magnitude than the two cases that elicited a military response, such as the bombing of the Marine barracks in Beirut, the hijacking of Kuwait Air flight 221, and multiple bombings of U.S. military facilities in West Germany.[25]

Even after accounting for magnitude of the attack, a majority of the non-responses remain unexplained. Another potential explanation for this policy option is provided by international law, which indicates that nation-states have responsibilities and obligations to the international community. If governments fulfill these obligations, then the United States would have no legal recourse to intervene with force.[26] First among these, states must refrain from using force against other states. Article 2(4) of the United Nations Charter declares that member states are "to refrain in their international relations from the threat or use of force against the territorial integrity or political independence of any state." This prohibition encompasses a state's use of terrorism and the use of proxies, also known as "indirect aggression." The 1951 Draft Code of Offenses Against the Peace and Security of Mankind, as prepared by the International Law Commission, declares that "the organization, or the encouragement . . . by the authorities of a State, of armed bands within its territory or any other territory for incursions into the territory of another State, or the toleration of the organization of such bands in its own territory as a base of operations or as a point of departure for incursions into the territory of another State, as well as direct participation in or support of such incursions," is an international crime.[27]

Second, states are to prevent the use of their territory for use by groups that attack other states. According to Article 4 of the Draft Declaration on Rights and Duties of States, "Every state has the duty to refrain from fomenting civil strife in the territory of another state, and to prevent the organization within its territory of activities calculated to foment such civil strife." Article 7 says, "Every state has the duty to ensure that conditions prevailing in its territory do not menace international peace and order."[28] Thus, states are required to use their domestic law enforcement mechanisms to prevent terrorist attacks, or to investigate and prosecute perpetrators in the aftermath. If they choose not to prosecute, they have the option of extradition under the traditional legal principle *aut dedere aut punire* ("extradite or prosecute"), but they do not have the legal option of doing nothing.[29]

While international law routinely uses the language of states, most terrorist attacks are aimed at individuals, and can be viewed solely as criminal acts rather than acts of war that merit a military response. However, Abraham Sofaer, the State Department's legal advisor during the latter half of the Reagan administration stated that "where an American is attacked because he is an American, in order to punish the U.S. or to coerce the U.S. into accepting a political position," then sufficient reason exists for the administration to respond.[30] This follows the widely accepted premise that the purpose of any government is to protect its citizens.[31] Ethicist Michael Walzer's definition of terrorism—the random murder of innocent people—seems to allow for states to respond legally. He notes that while soldiers are entitled to kill, that right is based on mutuality and consent—meaning that the only legitimate targets are other soldiers in a combat setting. The deliberate attack on noncombatants "is not a legitimate act of war but a crime."[32]

Third is the concept of nonintervention, which cuts two ways. Long-standing tradition holds that states are not permitted to interfere with the internal affairs of other states. This is a part of the Westphalian interpretation of sovereignty, which is based on territorial integrity and the exclusion of "external" actors from interfering with the internal governmental responsibilities of other states.[33] However, if states fail to live up to their obligations, other states may enact corrective measures. This condition exists when a state fails, that is, when the legitimate governmental institutions that bind a society together collapse.[34] Abraham Sofaer addressed this problem in the 1980s noting that "Several States . . . instead of enforcing their domestic law against or extraditing terrorists, protect, train, support, or utilize terrorist groups to advance policies they favor. Some States, such as Lebanon, are simply unable to exercise authority over terrorists, even if they were inclined to do so. The United States must be free to utilize force with sufficient flexibility to defend itself and its allies effectively against threats resulting from such breaches of international responsibility [under Article 51 of the United Nations Charter]."[35] This is a narrow, unilateral approach of the more broadly accepted justification for intervention in another state. When states are unable or unwilling to "uphold certain standards of justice—usually peace, order, basic human rights—[they] are subject to the intervention of outside states . . . the target states are no longer absolute in their sovereignty."[36] Lending credibility to this argument is Lord McNair, a former president of the International Court. He stated that "a government could lawfully use its force to protect its nationals and their property from violence in a foreign country when local authorities were unable or unwilling to protect them."[37]

When the norm of adhering to international law is taken into account, we would not expect to see a military response to terrorism where the government with jurisdiction was willing and able to deal with it (such as West Germany and France); this is exactly what the evidence shows. The United States often viewed local prosecution of terrorists as an effective (and non-unilateral) way to fight terrorism. For example, when members of the Red Army Faction attacked U.S. bases in West Germany, the local German authorities conducted the investigations and prosecuted the perpetrators rather than the U.S. seeking extradition, attempting to seize the terrorists, or retaliating militarily against them. It is absurd to think that the United States would launch a retaliatory strike against a group located within the territory of a stable ally capable of enforcing its laws. So response in these cases was left to the host governments.[38] However, under the guidelines set out by U.S. policy, the Reagan administration's rhetoric, and international law, we would expect to see military responses in places where governments were unwilling (like Greece) or unable (Lebanon) to prevent attacks and/or investigate and prosecute the terrorists, and against states that supported or conducted terrorist activities.[39] But the evidence does not support this logic.

Some other widely accepted practices may be at play here. For example, states do not launch attacks on the soil of friends or allies. This norm *could* encompass responses to incidents in Greece, México, Egypt, Jordan, Pakistan, the Philippines, and many of the Latin American states. Another possible explanation is that the United States asked permission to send in military units and was denied (whereby the U.S. observed the norm of sovereignty, regardless of that government's alignment). There is evidence for this, but only in a handful of cases, such as the TWA 847 hijacking during its Algerian phases. However, even when we examine only the cases in states that are truly collapsed, or where another state clearly sponsored the attack, the Reagan administration's responses still varied widely.

## FRAMEWORK OF THE STUDY

What then explains the Reagan administration's responses to terrorism? Aristotle once noted that human beings are political animals, and the ramifications of this observation resonate throughout the rest of this research; since governments are constituted of men, the process by which governments reach decisions will necessarily be political. In higher-magnitude terrorism cases, where the responsibility to respond rested with the top echelons of government, it was often the case that the president's foreign policy team either could not agree on a course of action, or lacked the political will to act. As shown in chapters three through seven, a battle raged within the administration over counter-terrorism policy, causing the American response to oscillate between different types of action. This bureaucratic battle resulted from a diverging set of beliefs within the administration about (1) the definition of terrorism, and (2) what type of policy best advanced American interests in the region—one that was closely tied to Israel, or one that courted the moderate Arabs.[40] These two sets of beliefs often coincided, forming coalitions: the terrorism-is-crime/pro-Arab camp and the terrorism-is-war/pro-Israel camp, and the two groups seldom agreed on how to respond. Reagan's informal management system exacerbated the situation by not providing discipline for his advisors, meaning that compromise was rare, and the personal political power of individual players in the administration mattered the most when the President finally decided what to do in each case.

Thus, as I approach the Reagan administration's decision making, I do so with the understanding that foreign policy is the external manifestation of forces inside the state, including the state's decision-making structures, the perceptions, attitudes and beliefs of the decision-makers, and the nature of the interactions between them. Policy is made through a political process, occurring within the context of power relationships where all of the participants are not equal, and where actors' power varies from crisis to crisis depending on statutory responsibility (or informal, ad hoc assignment of responsibility) and presidential confidence. Interests, stakes, risks, and information are filtered through the perceptual lenses of the individual participants, producing competing viewpoints. Each crisis encountered by the decision-making group engages the beliefs of the actors within the power equation at that time and for that issue. The policy option an administration chooses then depends on the domestic political drama produced by these competing beliefs and the power attached to them; because of the dynamic nature of this process, state actions will not be consistent over time.

Therefore, the individuals involved in the process would be known. Chapter 2 asks:

1. Which members of the administration had a bearing on decision making during terrorist crises?
2. What were their beliefs about terrorism and other related issues?
3. What accounts for each player's impact on the choice and action?

Once these three factors are explored, the succeeding chapters will show the dynamism and energy in the process that led to varying responses to a group of similar events. Chapter 3 examines the great debate that began with the bombing of the Marine barracks in Beirut,[41] explores the reasons why there was no retaliation, why the Marines were eventually pulled out, and traces the administration's very public tug-of-war over counter-terrorism policy. Chapter 4 explores the hijacking of TWA flight 847 and the administration's efforts to obtain the passengers' release. Chapter 5 looks at a similar hostage situation—the hijacking of the *Achille Lauro* cruise ship, and efforts to free those detained. Chapters 6 and 7 deal with Libyan terrorism—the massacres at the Rome and Vienna airports, and the bombing of the La Belle disco—and the Reagan administration's attempts to respond to the violence.

# Chapter Two

# The Context of Decision

A President is not bound to conform to the advice of his ministers. He is even under no positive injunction to ask or require it. But the Constitution presumes that he will consult them, and the genius of our government and the public good recommend the practice.

—Alexander Hamilton

Before turning to the crises, we will briefly explore the backdrop against which the Reagan administration made its decisions. Since individuals and their interactions shaped the American responses to terrorism, it is vital to understand the key beliefs of the most important participants, their sources of power, and the atmosphere and structure within which they worked. Thus, three ingredients of the context are examined here: the formal structure of the decision-making process, the major players in the process, and the interactions between them.

## INSTITUTIONAL STRUCTURE

The organizational structure of a decision-making system confers formal power on its members. Because this is so, we seek to know which agency or department has statutory authority to manage a given situation, and what organizational responsibilities are engaged by the event.[1] If, for example, the State Department has a responsibility to organize the response to terrorist attacks against Americans overseas, what power over the decision-making process does this confer on the secretary of state? Is he able to act unilaterally, without regard for the other members of the foreign policy team, because of the power of his office? If so, what is this formal power?

Institutions accrue power through legislation, executive decisions, and custom. Individual decision-makers have power based on their position in the system; their roles confer certain statutory powers that come into play in the decision process; in addition they are provided with certain reputational and informational advantages. For example, political scientist Richard Betts identifies four levels of influence that professional soldiers can exert on the policy process. The generals and admirals are most powerful and persuasive when they are directly involved in deliberations during a given situation and recommend using military force; the advice of military men is hard to ignore when dealing with military matters.[2] The same could be said for others in their areas of expertise, such as diplomacy, intelligence gathering, and espionage, etc. Formal power thus flows from the authority inherent in one's position; it comes from a person's rank and from the jurisdictional power that a position confers on a particular player.

However, most governmental decisions are not made by a single agency or department, meaning that individuals and their organizations generally must cooperate in order to act on any given issue. Richard Neustadt sheds light on this condition, noting that the founding fathers did not create a government of separated powers, but a system of "separated institutions sharing powers."[3] This means that no one player or organization has the ability to unilaterally decide upon and implement a preferred policy. Instead, some coordination must take place between institutions that share joint jurisdiction over an issue area, meaning administration offcials must work together. So how do multiple agencies work together when jurisdictions overlap? What mechanisms are in place to facilitate coordination? Who has the responsibility for shepherding an issue through the government, and which players must cooperate for an issue to be resolved?[4] These are important questions since different parts of the bureaucracy have different and often contradictory goals when dealing with the same issue. By identifying which organizational preferences must be accounted for in the final decision we can predict what options a state will choose.

Congress has enacted several significant pieces of legislation that have shaped the present institutional landscape for national security policy making; these laws created bureaucracies, offices, and positions that contain extraordinary powers in the areas of defense, intelligence, and foreign policy. Although power in its fullest sense derives from more than just statutory authority given to the head of each organization, formal power is nonetheless significant since the responsibility within the national security bureaucracy is divided into so many separate but interlocking jurisdictions. Thus, for a coherent national security policy to emerge, these actors must be able to coordinate their powers and actions for common purposes. Over time, however, individual bureaucracies have developed their own missions, creating unique perspectives and goals within each organization. So if an administration is to succeed in carrying out a coordinated and coherent policy, some method must be found to foster cooperation amongst these agencies. The major centripetal force to that end stems from the president's appointment of the highest-ranking bureaucrats; these appointees normally share some common set of beliefs that will allow them and their organizations to cooperate.

To begin with, however, let us look at what Congress did with regard to foreign policy, national security, and counter-terrorism policy. Through legistation, jurisdictions were created and/or formalized, new powers were granted, and new tools created to combat terrorism. Complementing these laws were a number of presidential directives and one executive order that expanded what the government could do to combat terrorism and designated the responsibilities of the various organizations.

## Legislation

When terrorist incidents occur outside the United States, the principal government agencies charged with the responsibility to respond are the Department of State, the Central Intelligence Agency, the National Security Council staff, and the Department of Defense. The first of these organizations to be established by Congress was the State Department in 1789, with the secretary of state responsible for advising the president on foreign policy matters. The department represents the U.S. government abroad, maintaining diplomatic relations with other governments, negotiating treaties and agreements with foreign governments, recommending and implementing foreign policy under the president's direction, and reporting on the desires and actions of other governments. Key to all of these tasks is the maintenance of amicable relations with foreign governments, which has sometimes led the department to overemphasize pleasing the governments with which it must work.[5]

The National Security Act of 1947 created additional components of the national security structure. First, it reorganized the military services, creating a more unified, integrated Department of Defense whose purpose is to raise and maintain a military capable of protecting the United States and its interests. Second, it created the National Security Council (NSC) to improve the coordination of policy and upgrade the quality of advice flowing to the president, "with respect to the integration of domestic, foreign, and military policies relating to the national security." The statutory members include the president, the vice president, the secretary of state, and the secretary of defense. Its support staff includes an advisor for national security affairs (also known as the National Security Advisor, or NSA), whose job it is to coordinate the NSC's activities and see that the president is presented with all pertinent views concerning the issue at hand. Another advisor to the NSC is the chairman of the Joint Chiefs of Staff, who serves as the principal military advisor to the president. Third, the Act created one other major institution—the Central Intelligence Agency—whose director serves as an advisor to the NSC. The CIA was designed to coordinate the intelligence being produced by a number of intelligence organizations, to evaluate intelligence relating to national security, and to disseminate such intelligence within the government.[6]

In 1981, the Reagan administration created the National Security Planning Group (NSPG), an augmented version of the smaller NSC. Its membership included the president, the secretaries of state and defense, the DCI, the chairman of the Joint Chiefs of Staff, the National Security Advisor, Reagan's top political aides, and was chaired by the vice president. This body was a small forum where the principals could discuss and argue, and was usually the last formal chance to influence Reagan before he made a major foreign policy decision.

In 1984, Congress passed the Act to Combat International Terrorism. This legislation allowed the State Department, for the first time, to offer monetary rewards for information leading to the arrest and conviction of terrorists involved in attacks against American targets. Two years later, the Omnibus Diplomatic Security and Anti-terrorism Act of 1986 expanded the jurisdiction of the FBI, making crimes committed against Americans overseas a federal crime. Further, it allowed the federal government to investigate terrorist incidents that occur overseas and, should extradition back to the United States be successful, to prosecute these terrorists in federal court. Since the implementation of this legislation the FBI has become deeply involved in the American response to overseas terrorist attacks, sending agents to investigate and collect evidence from attacks such as the bombings of Pan Am 103 over Lockerbie, Scotland, the U.S. embassies in Kenya and Tanzania, and the USS *Cole* in the port of Aden, Yemen.

## Presidential Directives

Supplementing legislation were a number of presidential national security directives (formal written orders from the president to his advisors). Known during the Reagan administration as National Security Decision Directives, or NSDDs, they allowed the president to enunciate policy, reorganize certain national security structures to meet his needs, and authorize the government to undertake specific actions, including military ones.

In his draft of NSDD-1, which was prepared at the outset of the Reagan administration, Secretary of State Alexander Haig demanded he be given control over crisis management. Although Reagan wanted to rely heavily on his secretary of state, he was unwilling to grant such broad power to Haig, and instead signed NSDD-3 on December 14, 1981, giving control of the administration's crisis management to the vice president. Supporting the vice president was a newly established interagency group, the Special Situation Group (SSG), whose function was to advise the president during crises. Membership consisted of secretaries of state and defense, the DCI, the chairman of the JCS, the White House chief of staff, the vice president's chief of staff, and the president's political advisors. The SSG was also known by other names during the Reagan years, including the Crisis Management Group, the Planning and Coordinating Group, and the Policy Review Group.[7]

Dissatisfaction with the SSG soon arose as a result of its inability to successfully coordinate the efforts of the State and Defense Departments during the kidnapping of American Brigadier General James Dozier in Italy. As the lead agency, the State Department was supposed to manage terrorist incidents overseas. However, when a military response was desired, or required, State was unable to order action since it was outside the national command authority and lacked the authority to order the military into action.[8] As a result, Reagan signed NSDD-30 on April 10, 1982, which sought to eliminate this problem. First and foremost, it reaffirmed the lead agency concept, designating specific organizations as responsible for coordinating American responses to terrorism and demarcating their jurisdictions. The State Department was responsible for "international terrorist incidents that take place outside of US territory," the Department of Justice took the lead for attacks within American territory, and the FAA was charged with coordinating a response for hijackings within the "special jurisdiction of the United States." The Federal Emergency Management Agency (FEMA) was given responsibility for managing public health aspects of and recovery from terrorist incidents in the U.S. In practice, NSDD-30 changed little.

On April 3, 1984 Reagan signed NSDD-138. This directive marked a significant shift in policy, moving the government away from sole reliance on defensive anti-terrorism tactics toward more offensive counter-terrorism options. There were several important themes, but the most significant had to do with self-defense. In practical terms, it was a declaration of war on terrorism. The administration decided that when efforts to stop such attacks through multilateral means failed, the United States would be prepared to take active unilateral measures to preempt terrorist attacks, including the use of covert actions and counter-intelligence operations, and would henceforth be more willing to use conventional military force against terrorists.[9]

Executive Order 12333, signed by Reagan on December 4, 1981, reaffirmed the DCI's role "as the primary intelligence advisor to the President and NSC on national foreign intelligence," and made him responsible for overseeing and implementing covert actions. However, it did check the bureaucracy's power in one respect, continuing the Carter administration's prohibition of political assassinations.[10]

## THE DECISION-MAKERS

### Informal Power and Politics

Sometimes formal power is not enough to sway a decision in favor of a particular organization's policy preference. In these instances, something is needed beyond the power a player derives from his position. According to Admiral Thomas Moorer, chairman of the Joint Chiefs of Staff from 1970 to 1974, "The way decisions are made depends on whose ego is being bruised, what ambitions they have, and so on; generally speaking, the idea that you can draw a wiring diagram and put all those people in a little box is a fallacy."[11] This in-the-trenches view of decision making contrasts starkly with the box diagram approach. Although an organizational chart may show how decisions are supposed to be made, there are many mitigating factors to this formality. Instead of focusing exclusively on the formal mechanisms of government, we need to explore the interactions, both formal and informal, among officials who have the power to move an issue through the government.

A common misconception held by casual observers of government is that since the president's advisors were all hand picked by him, they will each necessarily reflect his policy preferences. While this is true for the big-picture subjects (there are usually some "shared beliefs" that a president insists upon when choosing his advisors), members of an administration's foreign policy team will likely have divergent views in secondary and tertiary policy areas. Often these differences can be rather substantial and can generate great friction in the decision making process conflict when these issues hit the president's agenda.

This leads us back to the concept of power. Power is the key that holds structure and individuals together. Power is influence. It is ability to get things done and to prevent other things from happening; it is the currency that is used in the bargaining process. The major source of informal power (that is, power not conferred on an actor solely by the position he holds) comes from a person's relationship with the commander in chief, based upon how much confidence the president has in that subordinate. When a participant acts in the name of the president and that actor is known to have close ties to the Oval Office, other actors are much more likely to cooperate than if that power relationship did not exist. Similarly, an actor's credibility with the other participants based on his forthright honesty enhances his power, while a lack of trust amongst the other actors can spell doom. Importantly, power is not a constant. It ebbs and flows for individual players as they do things that make the confidence of the president and the other players change. As one study on decision making observed, "the initial distribution [of power] at the start of a game is at least partly the cumulative result of previous games."[12]

Players guard their power (they will not intentionally squander it by supporting a widely unpopular policy position), and use it when they think they can accomplish some important goal.[13] This certainty means that a variety of outcomes are possible when the policy process takes place. Sometimes the power dynamic means that compromise will be the result. At other times, it means one particular player will "win" the argument by having his preferred option implemented. Alternatively, when power is diffuse, and actors are unbending in their preferences, policy stalemate can occur.

## Perceptions and Beliefs

Whichever type of power is used to influence a decision, the beliefs and behavior of those participants who hold power will help explain which policies are ultimately chosen. Human behavior—whether in governmental decision making or elsewhere—is conditioned by the image, or the subjective perception that individuals hold.[14] Within any political system there will be a set of shared beliefs, or "shared images" on certain issues, but in a pluralistic society such as the United States, there will also be great variation on many others.[15] As political psychologists Harold and Margaret Sprout noted, "What matters in the process of policy making is not conditions and events as they actually are but what the policy maker imagines them to be."[16]

The process by which decision-makers receive and intuit information is not objective. It is the interpretation of the information—the filtering of it through one's belief system—that is consequential. "It is not a river itself that matters as a geographic feature," says David Thompson, "It is whether the inhabitants of both banks think of it as a main artery of their common life, or as a 'natural frontier' between them."[17] Political scientist John Kingdon cites a lobbyist commenting on this phenomenon: "If you have only four fingers on one hand, that's not a problem; that's a situation . . . Conditions become defined as problems when we come to believe that we should do something about them."[18]

Since the individual participants in the decision-making process are so integral to the story, the following pertinent beliefs of the major players are explored:

1. What is the individual's worldview?
2. What should the United States's position be concerning the Arab-Israeli conflict? Should the U.S. identify more closely with Israel or the moderate Arab states?
3. What is terrorism? Is it a type of warfare, or merely a crime? Is it caused by local problems, or is it Soviet-inspired?
4. What is the appropriate use of the military?
5. What are the appropriate means of attaining one's goals within the U.S. government?

In addition, each individual's source of power in the decision-making process is identified.

## Player Profiles

*Ronald Reagan, President of the United States, 1981 to 1989*

*Worldview.* Ronald Reagan saw the world in terms of black and white, good and bad.[19] Central to his view of the world was the Soviet–American rivalry and the righteousness of America's role; he saw the United States as the "last best hope of man on earth."[20] Conversely, Reagan viewed the Soviet Union as the antithesis of all America stood for, inspiring him to describe communism as "the Disease" and "a natural menace," and its proponents as animals, primitives, machines, criminals, fanatics, idealogues, satanic, and profane.[21] He believed it to be a "form of insanity—a temporary aberration which will one day disappear from the earth because it is contrary to human nature."[22] He noted, and then edited out of a speech (because, he later explained, "I didn't have the nerve to say this") a 1961 statement by the American Communist Party's 1976 candidate for president, which said, "I dream of the hour when the last congressman is strangled to death on the guts of the last preacher—and since the Christians seem to love to sing about the blood, why not give them a little of it? Slit the throats of their children [and] draw them over the mourners' bench and the pulpit and allow them to drown in their own blood, and then see whether they enjoy singing those hymns."[23]

Reagan not only saw the Soviets as evil, but also as expansionist— spreading their tentacles everywhere they could, including into the United States. In another radio address, Reagan quoted words attributed to Vladimir

Lenin that further reinforced his beliefs about communism: "It would not matter if three-quarters of the human race perished; the important thing is that the remaining one-quarter be communist."[24] In two May 1977 radio addresses Reagan cited warnings about the Soviets in the then-recently declassified NSC-68. Quoting and discussing that document he said, "'The Soviet Union is animated by a new fanatic faith antithetical to our own [and] *seeks to impose its authority* over the rest of the world.' It calls for the complete subversion or forcible destruction of the machinery of [government and] the structure of society of non-communist nations by means, both violent [and] non-violent, by infiltration [and] intimidation."[25]

Because of the visceral nature of the Cold War for Reagan, the abandonment of anti-communist allies was anathema to him. During the 1980 presidential campaign he went out of his way to say that a Reagan administration would be loyal to its friends, defined as any government that was anti-communist, saying, "There will be no more Taiwans, no more Vietnams. Regardless of price or promise—there will be no more betrayal abandonment of friends by the U.S."[26]

*Middle East.* The President thought that Israel held a unique position in the world, that America's duty to stand by the Jewish state was "iron-clad," and that the best way to guarantee Israel's security was through the peaceful resolution of the Arab–Israeli conflict.[27] While Reagan understood that there were local issues contributing to the conflict ("The real issue in the Middle East has to do with the Arab refusal to recognize [that] Israel has a right to exist as a nation."), the Cold War guided his thinking about Israel.[28] To Reagan, the Jewish state stood as a bastion of democracy against Soviet adventurism in the region. Israel also had a proven, potent military that, combined with its Western orientation, led Reagan to automatically consider the Jewish state as a strategic asset and ally.[29] Commenting on the 1973 Arab–Israeli war, Eugene Rostow once said, "[The Soviet Union] violated . . . promises by supplying, planning, encouraging, and even participating in the Arab aggression against Israel of October 1973." Reagan was impressed by Rostow's argument that the Soviet intention was, "not only to crush Israel, but also to outflank NATO, to neutralize Europe, and to drive us out of Europe and the Mediterranean."[30] Additionally, Reagan saw Soviet incursions and increased influence in Somalia, Ethiopia, South Yemen, and Afghanistan as moves toward the strategically important Persian Gulf.[31] Because of the aggressive Soviet actions in the region, Reagan believed that the best bet for America's interests there rested with Israel. In a mock State of the Union speech given during the 1980 campaign, Reagan asserted that "In the Middle East our alliance with Israel must be continued for both our sakes. Israel is a stable democracy sharing our own values [and] maintains with its combat trained and experienced military a deterrent to Soviet expansion in that troubled part of the world."[32] As Secretary of State Alexander Haig observed, "Israel has never had a greater friend in the White House than Ronald Reagan."[33]

As for the Arabs, Reagan was ready to support those that sided with the United States in the Cold War, and promised not to impose an American "solution" on problems in places such as Lebanon.[34] Regarding the Palestinians, Reagan believed that they were not really a nation with a common heritage and history, doubted the viability of a Palestinian state, and was only willing to propose autonomy for the Palestinians. Reagan also harbored serious doubts about the Palestinian leadership, declaring the Palestinian Liberation Organization, and its leader Yasser Arafat, to be little more than a "terrorist guerilla band."[35] Still, because Reagan viewed the world within the East–West context, the pro-Western Arab states were important and worthy of American attention and support. When the Israeli lobby bitterly complained about the administration's plan to sell AWACS to Saudi Arabia, Reagan responded, "While we must always take into account the vital interests of our allies, American security interests must remain our internal responsibility."

*Terrorism.* As the quotes in Chapter 1 show, Reagan believed terrorist incidents to be acts of war that demanded a righteous retaliation. In addition, he viewed terrorist attacks as illegitimate acts by the Soviet Union's proxies who were intent on undermining the West.[36] Reagan was also very concerned for the fate of individual victims of terrorism. When he heard stories about personal suffering, including those of terrorists' victims, his emotions were immediately engaged; he admitted as much when he said, "I'm a pushover for a hardluck story."[37] Those around him recognized this as well. For instance, National Security Advisor Robert McFarlane noted that, "One of President Reagan's weaknesses was a deep revulsion at the loss of human life and a very strong vulnerability to visual images. . . . Television and films portraying suffering children and women bring to the fore his sense of chivalry and humanity, and it has the power to influence his behavior all out of proportion. It leads him to do something even if it is wrong."[38]

*The military.* Contrary to the popular perception of Reagan as a loose cannon or a Rambo figure,[39] the president was not particularly trigger-happy. In his mind, his administration's massive military buildup was not undertaken so that the U.S. could wage a first strike against the Soviets, but in order to deter a nuclear war. His thinking in 1978 went like this: "We want to avoid a war and that is better achieved by being so strong that a potential enemy is not tempted to go adventuring."[40] In a 1968 essay, Reagan wrote about the important signals that the military can send, and how force can work hand-in-hand with diplomacy. He recounted a crisis in which China threatened to invade Taiwan during the Eisenhower administration; the president sent the Navy in, saying, "They'll have to crawl over the 7th Fleet to do it." Reagan was clearly impressed by this action, commenting, "The invasion of Formosa did not take place; no young men died; and World War III did not follow."[41] Reagan also believed that while evident strength was important, merely having the capability to act was not sufficient to stem aggression. He firmly believed that a vital component to military strength was the political willpower to use it, for to lack it "could tempt the Soviet Union as it once *tempted* Hitler and the military rulers of Japan. . . . "[42]

Tempering his will to use the military was a cautious nature and an overriding desire to avoid civilian casualties. Reagan did not like the military term "collateral damage" to describe unintended civilian deaths. Instead he simply called it "killing people." He disliked the idea of "indiscriminate" bombing because such action meant killing innocent people. Consequently he was reluctant to approve any operation where civilians would be put in danger. Some of Reagan's advisors recognized this and used it to advance their preferred policy options, and forestall those they disliked. Late in his second term, Reagan vetoed a proposed invasion of Panama to capture strongman Manuel Noriega precisely because some of his advisors pointed out that the expected civilian death count might be high.[43]

In a series of speeches about President Carter's reassignment of General John Singlaub from duty in Korea, Reagan implied that the wisdom of the military brass should be respected.[44] He criticized Carter for ignoring the opinions of the Joint Chiefs of Staff and for overriding their advice,[45] and in a September 1977 speech remarked that, "Generals and Admirals shouldn't express pol[itical] opinions but politicians shouldn't express military opinions unless the military is given equal time. We've had two wars now in which strategy has been dictated by political decision—Korea and Vietnam. Our men have never fought more bravely in any war nor under such ridiculous politically imposed restraints. That must never happen again."[46] This view that the military could do no wrong most likely developed during Reagan's first experience with the military; during World War II he served in a propaganda filmmaking unit which romanticized the military, putting the views of the country's military leaders squarely on a pedestal.[47]

Reagan also thought the intelligence community had been shackled and was not able to do its job effectively. He thought that the congressional investigations of the 1970s into the CIA were "witch-hunts" that caused "inestimable harm" to the "Nation's entire intelligence gathering ability."[48] Instead of scrutinizing covert operations, Reagan believed that such operations were inviolate, blasting the press in 1975 for being irresponsible for revealing a CIA operation that aimed to recover a sunken Soviet submarine.[49] He also viewed the congressional oversight committees dimly: "With the history of the Congress for leaking information from investigations, the danger is very real to the point of endangering the lives of men who are serving the United States in that capacity."[50]

*Sources of power.* The president inherits a preeminent position in the decision-making process. He has constitutional powers and prerogatives that no other participant in the national security process can hope to attain; he is the commander in chief, and has the responsibility (both legally and because the American public holds him accountable) for setting the country's policy direction and for making the final decision on all matters of import. Additionally, he has the power to appoint his advisors (with Senate approval in most cases), and ordinarily appoints people who share his beliefs and will at least try to instill the bureaucracy with his values.

As for informal power, political scientist Richard Neustadt informs us that the true power of any president is the power to persuade, which comes from a combination of his formal powers, his reputation, and his prestige. According to Neustadt, five factors are involved in how people perceive the president's ability to persuade: (1) how involved the president is on the issue; (2) the clarity of the president's meaning; (3) publicity given to the president's orders; (4) the president's actual ability to carry out the order; and (5) the sense that what the president wants is right. The president can have enormous power to persuade when these factors coincide in a positive way (i.e., when the president is very involved, his meaning is clear, his decision is publicized [so public opinion can pressure other members of the government to go along with it when they otherwise would not, for fear of adverse political ramifications], he has the means to achieve his goals, and the public agrees with the president).[51] Reagan's score on these factors varied greatly, at times according him great power, and at other times leaving him frustrated and unable to get the bureaucracy to execute his desired actions.

### George P. Shultz, Secretary of State, July 1982 to 1989

*Worldview.* Shultz saw communism as a faltering ideology. In a 1979 speech at Stanford, Shultz asserted, "the Soviet system is incompetent and cannot survive. In the struggle with communism freedom is the ideological victor in the world."[52] Shultz believed the Soviets were aggressive, and that they were expanding their influence into areas critical to the West. In his Senate confirmation hearings, however, he argued that this was due, at least in part, to "diminished American strength and resolve."[53] At the same time though, Shultz thought that, should the opportunity arise, the U.S. could work with Moscow to reduce tensions and resolve major issues, including arms control.[54]

*Middle East.* Many observers believed that when Shultz became secretary of state, he would be no friend of Israel. During his confirmation hearings, he talked of the Palestinian problem as the paramount issue of the region, and spoke of the importance of strengthening relations with the oil-rich Persian Gulf states.[55] Coming from the Bechtel Corporation, which had important ties and contacts in the Arab world, especially in Saudi Arabia, Shultz was thought by many to be decidedly pro-Arab in the Israeli–Arab conflict. Initially this seemed to be borne out as he proposed to build on the Camp David Accords by calling for Palestinian autonomy in an arrangement where the West Bank would be affiliated with Jordan.[56] He also advocated "wide and ever-strengthening ties with the Arabs," noting the common interest shared with them in "resisting Soviet imperialism." He did note though, almost as an afterthought, the importance of America's relationship with Israel.[57] But as a priority in the Middle East, Israel did not appear high on Shultz's list when he began his tenure at the State Department.

However, after Lebanon abrogated a peace treaty with Israel in 1983—in part because of Syrian pressure—Shultz began to modify his views. He placed some blame for the plan's failure on the Saudis, since he had been led to believe that they would be able to persuade Jordan's King Hussein to go along with the plan. Shultz also thought that Egypt had broken a promise to return its ambassador to Israel following the Israeli Defense Force's pullout from Beirut.[58] The failure of the Reagan Plan, coupled with the replacement of Ariel Sharon by the more moderate Moshe Arens as Israel's defense minister, opened the door for a shift; Shultz decided that Israel was the only government that could be trusted to consistently support America's interests.[59]

*Terrorism.* While Shultz did not believe that the Soviets were responsible for every terrorist attack against the United States, he did see some Soviet connections to terrorism. He pointed out that "When Libya and the PLO provide arms and training to communists in Central America, they are aiding Soviet efforts to undermine our security in that vital region."[60] In a speech given at the Jonathan Institute Shultz again fingered the Soviets for supporting terrorism: "Let us understand the Soviet connection without exaggeration or distortion: The Soviet Union officially denounces the use of terrorism as an instrument of state policy. Yet, one does not have to believe that the Soviets are puppeteers and the terrorists marionettes to see a mammoth gap between Soviet words and Soviet deeds. Violent or fanatic individuals and groups will exist in every society. But in many countries, terrorism would long since have passed away had it not been for significant support from outside."[61]

Nonetheless, early in his tenure as secretary of state, terrorism was not a high priority. However, the loss of a trusted advisor in the April 1983 Beirut embassy bombing hurt him professionally and personally, and as a former

Marine, he was deeply affected by the October bombing of the Marine barracks. In fact there was speculation that Shultz planned to resign after the 1984 presidential election, but these terrorist attacks "gave him a renewed sense of purpose and a fire in his gut to do something about terrorism."[62] To the secretary of state, terrorism was no longer just a nuisance, but war. Following the attack on the Marines, Shultz became the administration's most ardent and outspoken proponent of using military force to combat terrorism.

*The military.* Shultz favored combining force and diplomacy in a coordinated effort to attain America's goals, adhering to Winston Churchill's statement that "Superior force is a powerful persuader."[63] Further, he was not afraid to push for a military deployment even when the Pentagon opposed it if he thought the troops presence or use would aid his diplomatic efforts.[64]

*Operating style.* According to political scientist Glenn Hastedt, secretaries of state have a choice when they enter office; they can either become advocates of the State Department perspective (a phenomenon known as bureaucratic capture), or they can remain loyal to the president and his agenda.[65] George Shultz chose the latter, sometimes ignoring the advice of experienced foreign service officers (especially those who argued against countering terrorism with force because that would agitate U.S. relations with moderate Arab states). By training, Shultz was a labor mediator, and as secretary of state was known for the skills he acquired from that experience; he was calm and methodical, a mediator, a problem-solver, an incrementalist.[66] In and out of his department, he was known as the "inscrutable Buddha."[67]

*Sources of power.* Shultz began his tenure with a great amount of presidential goodwill and confidence simply because he was not Alexander Haig. Haig had hastened his own demise by attempting to become the sole foreign policy-maker in the Reagan administration, so Shultz smartly came to the job proclaiming, "It is Mr. Reagan's policy" that he would enact, not his own.[68] Shultz was self-effacing and non-abrasive—also in contrast to Haig. These attributes were inherently attractive to the president, and also helped him maintain a good working relationship with Reagan's national security advisors, especially William Clark and McFarlane.[69] Additionally, Shultz had good access to the president, meeting privately with Reagan weekly.[70] This rapport with and access to the president accorded the secretary of state great influence over the decision-making process when he chose to use it.

*Caspar Weinberger, Secretary of Defense, 1981 to 1987*

*Worldview.* Weinberger viewed the Soviet Union as the paramount threat facing the United States, believing that Moscow had "an intention, a desire, a plan to achieve a major imbalance as represented by a tremendous growth [of arms] on their side," which they could use to coerce the United States.[71] He believed that the U.S. was seen as weak, and that this perception could be dangerous for America. In his Senate confirmation hearings, Weinberger stated that "As long as we are perceived by any potential enemy . . . to be ill-equipped or weak or irresolute or guilt ridden, or unwilling or unable to do anything except be patient, then I think we can expect perhaps increasingly hostile actions against our people abroad, and to my mind, actions that would weaken our position in the world."[72] The only path to safety for the nation was to restore the military might of the United States.

*Middle East.* Like Shultz, Weinberger came to the Reagan administration from Bechtel Corporation. He was considered pro-Arab, concluding that U.S. national security (and access to Gulf oil) depended on good relations with the moderate Arab states, especially Saudi Arabia. Any American military action against a Muslim nation, even against a radical regime, could endanger relations with the all-important Gulf States, and thus threaten American security.[73] Consequently, he pledged "our commitment to do whatever is desired of us by the occupants of [the Gulf States] . . . [this] is going to be a very high priority."[74]

Another factor that could endanger these ties was America's close relationship with Israel; he saw Israel—especially under the leadership of Prime Minister Begin and Defense Minister Sharon—as a complication for U.S. policy in the region rather than an asset.[75] Thus, the secretary of defense sought to distance the U.S. from Israel in order to protect relations with the moderate Arab states. During the U.S. deployment to Lebanon, Weinberger was explicit in this effort, "differentiating in every way possible the 'peacemaking role' assumed by the U.S. Marines and the role of 'illegal temporary occupier' by the [Israeli Defense Forces]."[76] He was also one of the first American officials to talk of a Palestinian *state*—at a time when the PLO was still officially at war with Israel.[77] While others in the administration talked of a strategic relationship with Israel, Weinberger was much less exclusive, saying, "My hope is that the whole of our relationships—not just strategic cooperation but the whole relationship with the moderate Arab nations—will be enhanced. . . . We need several friends in the Mideast—not Israel alone . . . [because of the importance of] access to Mideast oil fields."[78]

While there were times, as cited above, when Weinberger was prepared to stake positions well beyond the administration's line, there were other times when it appeared he was actually working against an agreed administration position so as to enhance the chances of his own preferred policy option. Raymond Tanter tells of one such instance at a meeting between Weinberger and Israeli Defense Minister Sharon in May 1982. During that meeting, Weinberger did not follow the approved interagency talking points that had been endorsed by his own defense department officials, but instead pursued his own agenda. He failed to mention that the administration had finally agreed that the November 1981 Memorandum of Strategic Understanding between the U.S. and Israel, which allowed for the institutionalization of security and strategic cooperation between the two governments, was ready to be implemented. Instead, he alluded to possible American sanctions against Israel if it harmed "vital interests" of the United States.[79]

*Terrorism.*[80] At the outset of the Reagan administration, Weinberger saw terrorism as a danger, but not something that should be actively fought against. It was criminal activity—reprehensible criminal activity—but not warfare. Responding to Shultz's call for preemptive strikes against terrorists, Weinberger said that such "retaliation would be analogous to firing a gun in a crowded theater in the slim hope of hitting the guilty party."[81] He believed that the standard of proof for any U.S. response should be courtroom quality, with the ability to prove beyond any reasonable doubt who was responsible for the attack. There had to be a causal chain of events from attack to suspect to proposed retaliation target before he would endorse military action. At one point during the administration, rather than supporting a U.S. response, he suggested that the United States go to the United Nations and ask that organization to deal with the problem of terrorism.[82]

*The military.* The defense secretary's mandate from Reagan was to reinvigorate the American military. Weinberger tackled his job with great vigor, and despite his reputation as "Cap the Knife"—a budget cutter extraordinaire—he chose to follow one simple guideline: build more of everything.[83] At his Senate confirmation hearings he explained, "We need more firepower." This, because he believed the United States had fallen behind in the arms race with the Soviets, and that if the imbalance grew too great, "you have an inducement to war."[84]

Anything that interfered with the defense buildup was adamantly opposed.[85] So despite his confirmation hearing rhetoric, he was extremely cautious about using the military, for the most part because he did not want to risk the public's goodwill toward the Pentagon by engaging in some military disaster or prolonged operation. If the public were to turn against the military, as it had during the latter stages of the Vietnam War, Weinberger's (and Reagan's) holy cow—the defense buildup—would be endangered.[86] So Weinberger jealously guarded against proposals to use the armed forces that he deemed a risk to the buildup.

Weinberger did not favor using the military as a tool of diplomacy. From the time of his Senate confirmation hearings, and throughout his tenure at Defense he argued, "Employing our forces almost indiscriminately and as a regular and customary part of our diplomatic efforts—would surely plunge us headlong into the sort of domestic turmoil we experienced during the Vietnam War without accomplishing the goal for which we committed our forces. Such policies might very well tear at the fabric of our society, endangering the single most critical element of a successful democracy: A strong consensus of support and agreement for our basic purposes."[87] Referred to today as the Powell Doctrine, it was actually Weinberger who identified six requirements that had to be satisfied before force should be used:

1. The commitment to combat should only be engagements that are vital to the national interest of the United States or its allies.
2. Combat troops should be deployed only with the intent of winning.
3. Forces deployed should be given clearly defined political and military objectives.
4. Relationships between objectives and forces—size, composition, and disposition—must be continually re-assessed.
5. Before a decision to commit forces is made, there must be reasonable assurance that the American people and the Congress support such action.
6. Commitment of U.S. forces should be the last resort.[88]

*Operational style.* According to Hastedt, secretaries of defense too face a choice. They can become either generalists or functionalists. Generalists value and defer to military expertise, while functionalists attempt to strengthen management of and control over the Pentagon. A generalist becomes an advocate for the military in the policy process, while a functionalist "rejects the notion that there exists a unique area of military expertise, and sees himself as first among equals in defense policy making," whereby he attempts to manage the Department of Defense according to the president's wishes.[89] Weinberger's agenda did mirror Reagan's, but for the most part, Weinberger can be considered a generalist, as he deferred to the Joint Chiefs of Staff on most matters of import, including strategy, commitment of troops, and military hardware development and acquisition. He met almost daily with the chairman of the Joint Chiefs of Staff, giving the CJCS an important forum in which to express his preferences. Weinberger's operating style was similar to Reagan's in one important respect; the secretary of defense often deferred to and accommodated the wishes of the military services, whose opinions seemed to reinforce his unwillingness to commit the military to fight low-intensity warfare.[90] When Weinberger had to settle conflict between political appointees from the Office of the Secretary of Defense and the JCS, the joint chiefs almost always won.[91]

Weinberger was trained as a lawyer, was an aggressive debater, and was considered stubborn and confrontational by colleagues. His modus operandi was to determine a preferred policy position on an issue, stake out an extreme position and then never yield, forcing others to compromise. One Reagan administration alumni said "arguing with [Weinberger] is like the Chinese water torture."[92] Another commentator described him as a "fox terrier. He darts out here and there. He races into dangerous areas where angels fear to tread. He's a pretty feisty guy who gets himself into trouble because he talks without thinking and then he refuses to budge."[93]

*Sources of power.* Weinberger had a well of personal goodwill to draw upon with Reagan, stemming from their long-standing friendship which dated back to Reagan's earliest political days in California. In 1968, Reagan appointed Weinberger to be the director of the state's department of finance based on Weinberger's experience as a state legislator and state Republican Party chairman. This was an important position for Reagan, since one of the governor's key beliefs was that government was too large and government spending too high. Reagan needed someone he could trust in that position to carry out his wishes, and Weinberger delivered. Because of this relationship and the resultant trust Reagan had in Weinberger, as well as the nature of Reagan's management style (discussed below), Weinberger had carte blanche from Reagan when he took over at the Pentagon.[94]

## *William P. Casey, Director of the Central Intelligence Agency, 1981 to 1987*

*Worldview.* At the end of World War II, Casey accompanied Allied forces to Dachau, and impressions from the concentration camp instilled in him the unshakable belief that there truly was evil in the world.[95] By 1980 it was the Soviets, not the Nazis, who held that position of preeminence as the cause of the world's troubles; in speech after speech, Casey identified the Soviet Union as the new evil. In one speech he said, "The Soviet Union, of course, remains the principal threat to U.S. security and the primary concern of U.S. intelligence."[96] However, the threat from the Soviet Union was not based solely on great power competition, but on its "fundamentally alien and totally unpalatable value system that threatens our own cherished institutions."[97]

Casey was extremely concerned about the Soviet campaign of "creeping imperialism" in which Moscow fomented revolutions on the West's periphery, especially in the Middle East and Central America.[98] In another speech he warned, "The West once again is engaged in a critical struggle with totalitarianism. This time it is in the form of Marxism-Leninism, and the primary battlefield of this struggle is not on the missile test range or at the arms control negotiating table but in the countryside of the Third World."[99] And while Casey did not believe the Soviets would risk a superpower confrontation in this campaign, he did think they would use surrogates, such as Cuba, Vietnam, Libya, and Nicaragua to covertly work toward their objectives.

*Middle East.* Casey viewed the Middle East through a Cold War lens, and sought allies that could help counter the Soviet threat. Because of this, Casey favored close relations with Israel, seeing in them a strong, reliable ally. Reacting to the Israeli invasion of Lebanon in 1982, Casey was unconcerned about appearances that America was supporting the controversial action by selling Israel weapons made in the United States. He opposed punishing Israel for the invasion, instead wanting to see how American interests in the Levant could be advanced as a result of the attack.[100] At the same time though, Casey was equally concerned with American access to Persian Gulf oil, and was an ardent supporter of pro-Western Arab governments, such as the Jordanians and Saudis, and even groups like the Afghan *mujahedin*, so long as their successes advanced American geopolitical interests. Following a trip through the region in April 1982, Casey sent a memo to Reagan explaining that Libya, Ethiopia, South Yemen, Afghanistan, and Syria were "all working together or under Soviet influence," surrounding "our friends Egypt and Israel and the oil fields of the Middle East."[101]

*Terrorism.* Casey viewed terrorism not as mere criminal activity, but as warfare. He was especially impressed with Claire Sterling's book, *The Terror Network*, which claimed the existence of a communist-inspired "international terrorist circuit, or network, or fraternity."[102] Speaking to a closed session of the Senate Intelligence Committee while the TWA 847 hijacking was still ongoing, Casey testified, "The United States is at war" with terrorism,[103] and in a separate speech, he explained, "International terrorism has become a perpetual war without borders."[104] In a speech given to the American Jewish Committee, Casey accused Libya, Syria, and Iran of using "terrorism as an instrument of foreign policy. They hire and support established terrorist organizations. . . . These countries make their officials, their embassies, their diplomatic pouches, their communications channels, and their territory a safe haven for these criminals available to plan, direct and execute bombings, assassinations, and other terrorist operations."[105]

In an interview with *Time* magazine he said the Soviet Union bore much responsibility for terrorism, saying, "I don't think the Soviets are the masterminds of terrorism or that they control it. But they have for a long time provided support that was vital for terror organizations."[106] In another speech he concluded that "The Soviet Union has provided funding and support for terrorist operations via Eastern Europe and its client nations like Libya and Cuba. With at least tacit Soviet approval many groups have trained together in Cuba, Libya, Iraq, South Yemen, and Lebanon."[107] Elsewhere he was more pointed, accusing the Soviets of indoctrinating those who trained in these terrorist camps with the Marxist-Leninist ideology.[108]

Casey did concede though that not all terrorism was Soviet inspired. "Even if the Soviet Union withdrew all patronage, terrorist activity would certainly continue, perhaps unabated. Terror has other independent patrons, currently the most prominent being Libya. Terrorist training camps are the largest industry in Libya, next to oil."[109] However, the example he cited is telling, since Libya was a Soviet client, and Qaddafi's successes were considered victories for Moscow.

*The military.* Casey was in tune with Shultz when it came to the use of force; the DCI favored military usage in conjunction with diplomacy in order to give American positions some teeth.[110] In a speech to the *Washington Times* editorial board, he argued that "A credible threat of force must be one element of a successful terrorism policy."[111] Adding his voice to the debate within the administration about the use of force he declared, "The United States does not use force indiscriminately. But we are ready to consider an armed strike against terrorists and those who support them where other means of defense or deterrence are not sufficient. We face very difficult and sensitive problems in choosing appropriate instruments of response in each case. Yet, we cannot allow this to freeze us into paralysis." He argued that refusing to use force when it was called for meant losing "both the direct benefits of action and the deterrent value of having the capability to retaliate." As for the level of proof needed to retaliate for a terrorist attack, Casey did not believe the evidence needed to be "beyond a reasonable doubt," insisting on the lower standard of circumstantial evidence.[112]

*Operating style.* Casey's experience as an operative in the Office of Strategic Services (OSS) during World War II instilled in him an operating style that would remain throughout his life. During the war he was an assistant to OSS chief Bill Donovan and was involved in many high-risk, freelance operations, including one that infiltrated some 150 agents into Nazi territory to disrupt the German war effort. When he joined the Reagan administration in 1981, not much had changed for Casey; he ran the CIA as though he were still an OSS operator. One Reagan administration official described Casey as "a gambler. He plays the stock market. He likes to take risks."[113]

Casey's time in the OSS was unfettered by bureaucratic gridlock, and as DCI, he relished those unencumbered, freewheeling days. His deputy, Robert Gates, recalled that Casey "was enormously impatient and frustrated with the career analysts' unwillingness to follow his lead in aggressively looking beyond the walls of the CIA for new information and insights. . . . Casey wanted information and analysis that informed or provoked action. . . . He wanted information that would help target clandestine operations better, or be useful for U.S. propaganda, or assist military operations. . . ."[114] If the bureaucracy—even his own—was unable or unwilling to accommodate him, Casey was not averse to finding other avenues by which he could accomplish his goals.

*Sources of power.* Casey stepped into Reagan's 1980 campaign when it was in disarray, and as the new campaign manager, restored order. Reagan was grateful for Casey's contribution and appointed him to head the Central Intelligence Agency. In addition, Reagan deeply respected Casey's personal achievements and experiences. In the field of finance Casey was a successful Wall Street lawyer and had written several "how to" manuals on personal finance. He was also an amateur historian, having written a book about the Revolutionary War. Further, he had served in previous administrations as the president of the Import-Export Bank and as the chairman of the Securities and Exchange Commission. Perhaps most important was his distinguished service in the OSS.[115] But there was something more, something personal that linked Casey to Reagan. One observer described the relationship with Reagan as "Casey's greatest source of power. Reagan likes Casey for many of the same reasons that he is drawn to Don Regan: Both are bluff Irishmen, self-made millionaires, men of Reagan's generation who love risks and never walk away from a fight. . . . He is an ideological soul-mate of Reagan."[116]

Further enhancing his credibility with Reagan, Casey's analyses seemed almost prescient. In a memo to Reagan early in the administration, the DCI correctly predicted the succession of leadership in the Soviet Union: "Chernenko peaked too soon. Kirilenko faded in the stretch. Grishin is a dark horse, but if I had to bet money, I'd say Andropov on the nose, and Gorbachev across the board."[117]

The new DCI's elevated position was acknowledged by the president when he appointed Casey; although the position does not possess statutory designation of cabinet rank, Reagan made Casey a cabinet member, equal in rank to Shultz and Weinberger. The president also allocated the DCI a roomy office in the Old Executive Office Building, right next door to the White House. Cabinet rank did not just confer a nice office on Casey. It accorded him the right to be more than just a provider of intelligence and manager of the intelligence community; because of his rank, he was justified in advising the president and advocating his policy preferences.

Membership in the cabinet though was not enough to guarantee that Casey had access to the president. Although the two were friends, had Casey been less aggressive, it would have been difficult getting through the protective troika of advisers (James Baker, Micheal Deaver, and Edwin Meese) who shielded Reagan. However, there was not a complacent bone in Casey's body. He insisted on being able to meet privately with the president in order to report on and discuss national security matters, and because of his persistence, was successful.[118]

## Robert McFarlane, Assistant to the President for National Security Affairs, October 1983 to November 1985

*Worldview.* In a 1979 article, McFarlane wrote about the state of superpower relations, explaining that because of nuclear parity, the United States and the Soviet Union faced mutually assured destruction if war broke out between them. However, because of the expansionist nature of the communists, they could be expected to continue devising ways to undermine the West despite the danger. McFarlane concluded, "Even in an era of parity, it is very much in the Soviet interest to avoid confrontations with the United States. Rather, the U.S.S.R. seeks to exploit indirect means—insurgent forces, terrorist groups, subversion, third country governments—to foment crises for the United States."[119]

McFarlane also believed that reliability and credibility were critical ingredients of American power, and vitally important tools in the Cold War confrontation with the Soviet Union. One event that left an indelible mark on him occurred during the U.S. pullout from Vietnam. At the time of the evacuation, McFarlane was a member of the NSC staff and was in constant communication with the American embassy in Saigon. Looking back on that day, he believed that the U.S. had unnecessarily abandoned an ally, thereby critically damaging American credibility. If the United States was going to restore its power and prevail against the Soviet Union, that sort of thing could not happen again.[120]

*Middle East.* In 1981, McFarlane joined Haig's State Department as counselor, and during his time there pushed hard for a strategic military relationship with Israel. He viewed Israel as a potent and valuable ally in a region filled with hostility and instability, and as a bulwark against Soviet expansionism.[121] His concern for the Persian Gulf was based on the need for access to oil. He singled out policy toward oil-rich Iran for re-examination in 1981, in light of reports about Ayatollah Khomeini's ill health and the Soviet invasion of neighboring Afghanistan. But above all, McFarlane's priority in the Middle East was maintaining a healthy relationship with Israel.[122]

*Terrorism.* McFarlane viewed terrorism as "calculated political crimes against people" that were used by the Soviets and their surrogates in an attempt to undermine the West. While he recognized that most attacks did not put the United States in immediate physical danger, he did believe that such attacks must be responded to because "the casualties and the human distress caused by such acts are a worry well beyond their numbers."[123] In other words, continued victimization whittled away at the nation's credibility in the eyes of other international actors when the U.S. did not respond, and threatened to psychologically undermine the American body politic as the mounting attacks demoralized, upset, and frightened the American public.

*The military.* One goal McFarlane had as National Security Advisor was to reorient the American government so it would be both stronger and more willing to use its military and diplomatic power in pursuit of its national interests and goals.[124] In a March 1985 speech, McFarlane called for "a proportional military response against bona fide military targets in a state which directs terrorist actions against us." He did not believe courtroom-quality evidence was needed to strike, saying, "Nor should we need to prove beyond all reasonable doubt that a particular element or individual in that state is responsible for such terrorist acts."[125] If the evidence was convincing, and if intelligence provided a good probability that a military mission against terrorists would succeed, McFarlane was likely to support it.

This willingness to use force was heavily influenced by his graduate school experience at the Institut des Hautes Études in Geneva, Switzerland, where he studied under Louis J. Halle. Halle's lesson was simple: deterrence is the combination of military power and the willingness to use it. McFarlane absorbed Halle's teaching thoroughly, believing that if the United States lacked the will to use its military power, no amount of missiles, planes, tanks, and ships would be enough to influence an opponent.[126] When he was given a position where his opinions influenced policy, he consistently favored showing and using force to compel others to bend to America's will.

*Operating style.* McFarlane's upbringing instilled in him a strong belief in self-reliance; to depend on others, or even to ask for help, was seen by him as a sign of weakness. In an interview with Robert Timberg he explained, "Every person who aspires to be a leader must be self-contained, that to show uncertainty or vulnerability is a weakness. And even to seek advice is evidence that you don't know something, and you should never do that."[127]

McFarlane was typical of Reagan subordinates in that when he thought he knew the president's mind he acted, regardless of what the relevant departments or agencies wanted. If the interagency process could not produce a consensus position that aligned with Reagan's desires, McFarlane was not averse to acting unilaterally. One such example occurred in early 1985 when the State Department wanted to authorize $75 million in commodity credits to Guatemala immediately, but the Treasury Department wanted to see the Guatemalan government's finances reformed first. McFarlane issued a memo on his own authority authorizing $50 million in credits to Guatemala. One White House official noted that McFarlane often signed such decision memorandums "Robert C. McFarlane for the President" without ever showing them to Reagan.[128]

*Sources of power.* McFarlane was Reagan's kind of staffer: nonconfrontational, humble, and collegial. According to McFarlane's staff, his credo was: "There is no limit to what a man can do or where he can go if he doesn't mind who gets the credit."[129] However, this was not enough to guarantee success for McFarlane, since he began his tenure as National Security Advisor by default, as the compromise candidate after two factions in the administration failed to get their own choices approved. That, combined with his lack of a reputation as a foreign policy "heavyweight" meant he started his job with little clout in the administration.

McFarlane also lacked the long-standing relationship with the president that his predecessor possessed. Consequently, other participants could not be certain if he was really speaking for the president. However, McFarlane was able to consolidate his position within the administration by quietly mediating conflicts between Shultz and Weinberger. This, combined with his knowledge about foreign policy, his eagerness to work long and hard hours, his loyalty to the president, and his discretion in dealing with other bureaucratic players, slowly earned him Reagan's trust.[130]

McFarlane's power was enhanced by two other factors. First was the size of his organization. Commentator Leslie Gelb observed that, "staff size . . . is a real measure of power in D.C."[131] Under McFarlane, the NSC staff grew to a size that rivalled Kissinger's when the NSC staff's power was at its apex. The second factor that helped McFarlane achieve power and influence within the administration was his proximity to the president. No one else on the foreign policy team had the sort of access to Reagan that McFarlane did, especially after early 1985 when, in what was seen as a signal of his increased status in the administration, McFarlane's office was moved out of the White House basement.[132] With a new office just down the hall from the president's, McFarlane was able to meet with Reagan three or four times a day—often alone.[133] In this private setting he could discuss issues with the president and thereby influence Reagan's decisions. Adding to this was the NSA's role as gatekeeper, controlling the paper flow of virtually all national security information going to the president. Because of this function, it was McFarlane who presented the president's morning national security brief, and it was McFarlane who put together briefing papers that the president would use to make his decisions.[134] If information is power, then McFarlane held the levers in the White House.

*John Poindexter, Assistant to the President for National Security Affairs, December 1985 to November 1986*

*Worldview.* While Poindexter saw the Soviet Union as an expansionist power, he believed that a number of factors within the United States, including the

Vietnam syndrome and the failure of the Carter administration to stand up to the Soviets, were encouraging Moscow's bad behavior.[135] He thought the Soviets could not be trusted, and consequently viewed such things as arms control as worthless, and tried to persuade Reagan to disavow the SALT II Treaty.[136]

*The military.* During the Vietnam War, Poindexter worked in the Pentagon and had a close-up view of how President Lyndon Johnson and Secretary of Defense Robert McNamara prosecuted the war. Poindexter was disappointed when he saw how domestic politics influenced what the military was allowed to do, where it could act, and what it was prohibited from doing. Poindexter believed that political micromanagement of the war had led to disaster, and this perception would serve as a guide when he later reached the NSC staff.[137] He also believed that military force was a legitimate and useful diplomatic tool, and was willing to advocate rattling—and using—the sabre in order to accomplish policy goals.[138]

*Operating style.* Poindexter was a man with a problem-solver's mentality, and he hated disorder. Professionally, he preferred the classroom to the wardroom, pursuing the more solitary calling of graduate school where he earned a doctorate in nuclear physics. The consequence of this atypical naval career path was that Poindexter spent less time with fellow naval officers, and less time being suffused with the Navy's parochial perspective, leaving him as more of a "free thinker" than the typical naval officer.

There are several significant aspects of Poindexter's operating style. First, his preference for solitude over socializing meant he received less input from and interaction with staff specialists who could help him refine policy, and spent less time developing political relationships that could be used later when he needed help building support for policy options. One former NSC staffer explained, "[Poindexter] told us time and time again that he was more comfortable alone in his office with the door closed, reprogramming his computer, or at home tinkering with his car or making furniture."[139] Perhaps this was a result of his quest for "order and organization," as he described his preferred setting in a paper written during his Naval Academy days.[140]

Second was his implicit trust of both people and the system; his days in the Navy instilled him with the sense that a man could not rise to a position of responsibility unless he was qualified.[141] In the late 1970s, Poindexter served as the executive assistant for chief of naval operations, Admiral James Holloway. During that time, Holloway trusted his aide's judgment and ability to the point that Poindexter rarely bothered the CNO with much paperwork. Said Holloway about his assistant, "He didn't load me up with details. He took care of the details . . . but always reserved for me the decision that should be made by me."[142] It was a style Poindexter would take with him to the White House.

*Sources of power.* Poindexter lacked the reputation and independent stature needed to mediate in the name of the president when disputes arose between the principals. This resulted because his rise to power occurred without his gaining the political experience necessary to be a strong manager.[143] In June 1981, Richard Allen asked him to join the NSC staff as a military aide. During the job interview, Poindexter said he did not have any experience in national security and foreign policy. Allen replied, "Admiral Poindexter, you see this map? There are red countries on this map and green countries; the red countries are the bad ones, the green ones are the good ones, and the rest is my problem. The function for which I'm asking you to volunteer your services don't necessarily involve you in policy."[144] Poindexter took the job and was retained in the same position when William Clark took over the NSC when Robert McFarlane was named NSA. The admiral was then promoted to deputy. Poindexter became NSA when McFarlane resigned two years later.

Despite Poindexter's lack of institutional standing, to Reagan the admiral was a star; he admired Poindexter for his role as crisis manager in the successful mid-air interception of the *Achille Lauro* hijackers.[145] The president trusted Poindexter, due in large part to a comfort level that grew out of the admiral's presence in daily national security briefings, his proven reliability during his stint as McFarlane's deputy, and his unassuming and subordinate attitude toward his superiors.[146]

The appointment of a new chief of naval operations in 1986 is a good example of Poindexter's influence with the president. Traditionally, the secretary of the Navy chooses the new CNO, and the president automatically accepts the nomination; for the commander in chief to do otherwise was unheard of. Secretary John Lehman had selected Admiral Frank Kelso, the commander of the Sixth Fleet for the post, but Poindexter, for a variety of reasons, believed Kelso to be the wrong choice at that time. Instead, he supported the nomination of Admiral Carl Trost. Despite Lehman's intense lobbying for Kelso, including a threat to resign if his candidate was not chosen, Reagan sided with Poindexter and selected Trost.[147]

Poindexter also appears to have used the morning national security brief and his control over the paper flow to the president to good effect. In his congressional Iran-Contra testimony, Chief of Staff Donald Regan recounted how Poindexter and his staff would place extra materials intended only for Reagan in the president's briefing book without showing them to anyone else. When an NSC aide would point out the additional papers to the president, Regan would object: "And I would say, 'Hey, I didn't get that in my book. What happened?' And they said, 'Well, we just gave that to the president.'"[148]

Poindexter was thus able to influence Reagan because of his role as gate-keeper, and his proximity to the Oval Office, as well as the fact that the president genuinely liked and trusted the admiral.

## The Joint Chiefs of Staff

General John Vessey, Chairman of the Joint Chiefs of Staff, 1982 to 1985
Admiral William Crowe, Chairman of the Joint Chiefs of Staff, 1985 to 1989
General Charles Gabriel, Chief of Staff, Air Force
General P. X. Kelley, Commandant of the Marine Corps
Admiral James Watkins, Chief of Naval Operations
General John Wickham, Chief of Staff, Army

Political scientist Richard Betts once observed, "An office orients its occupant in certain directions," especially when that individual has spent a lifetime serving in the same organization. Specifically, most military men plan for the worst-case scenario when preparing for military action, and they assume that the intentions and capabilities of a potential enemy cannot be known with absolute certainty.[149] Another is that the security of the state depends on the maintenance of a strong military. Things that threaten the military's ability to ensure security against America's enemies are to be avoided.[150] Thus, the differences that did arise between the chiefs over counter-terrorism policy were generally due to individual beliefs, not interservice rivalries.[151] For the most part though (except where indicated below), beliefs among the chiefs were fairly consistent.

*Worldview*. General John Vessey's views about the world were typical of all the chiefs. He held the orthodox Cold War view that the Soviet Union's ideology was "the very antithesis of our own values," describing it "as being militant and aggressive, devoid of all moral authority." Vessey believed Moscow's goal was to expand its influence by exporting its Marxist-Leninist ideology—especially to the Third World—by assisting surrogates such as client states and revolutionary movements. One example Vessey cited was Nicaragua, about which he claimed, "Libyan support and PLO extremists are active in training and supplying the Soviet-supported Sandinistas." By exploiting American reluctance to fight in Latin America and elsewhere, Vessey felt that the Soviets sought "to capitalize on every dispute or . . . turn instability to its own purposes."[152]

*Middle East*. The Pentagon's traditional view of the Middle East focused on the importance of the Persian Gulf and the maintenance of good relations with the moderate Arabs, since access to oil was a vital American interest. Admiral Crowe's perception of the Middle East—seeing the region in terms of the East–West conflict—was typical. In a 1978 article he explained, "The starting point in any discussion of U.S. interests in the Persian Gulf comes with clear recognition that 'energy policy is integral to security policy and cannot be considered in isolation.'"[153] As for Israel, closer bilateral relations were seen as problematic. This, because such relations would make it more difficult for Washington to obtain basing rights in the Arab world should the United States need to station forces there to counter a Soviet invasion of Iran, which was seen as a plausible scenario.[154]

*Terrorism.* Terrorism was generally considered a form of low-intensity warfare, although the terrorists themselves were not seen as warriors, since warriors follow a code of honor in which hostilities against civilians are forbidden. Instead, terrorists were viewed as mere criminals. Targets for retaliation were difficult to identify, and therefore, missions to attack such targets were undesirable because of their low probability of success. The exceptions to this line of thinking were the CNO, Admiral Watkins, who was at many times advocating the use of force, and Admiral Crowe, for reasons that will be explained shortly.

*The military.* The uniformed services were reluctant to endorse the use of force as a component of diplomacy, fearing a repeat of Vietnam-era mistakes when Washington engaged in ill-defined missions that lacked public and political support. The Pentagon also did not want responsibility for low-intensity warfare projects such as counter-terrorism operations. Since the military's primary mission was to deter and fight major wars, low-intensity conflict was considered a distraction and a peripheral mission that would draw scarce resources away from more important matters. Therefore, low-intensity conflict generally, and warfare against terrorism specifically, was something the U.S. military should not engage in because of its low priority and high risk. Instead, most at the Pentagon believed that force should be reserved for use against the most significant threat—the Soviet Union.[155] An example of this occurred in 1983, when DCI Casey attempted to turn the Contra support operation in Nicaragua over to the Pentagon, but was unsuccessful because the JCS did not want the military to become involved in a guerrilla war.[156]

Another thing that frightened Pentagon planners about engaging in military action generally, and low-intensity conflict specifically, was the likelihood that American servicemen would die and that innocent civilians would be injured and/or killed. Such casualties were likely to undermine public support for the military and again threaten the Pentagon's ability to carry out its primary mission, leading the military leadership (especially General Vessey) to oppose the employment of force when extensive casualties were likely.[157]

Admiral Crowe brought a slightly different approach to the JCS. For him, the quality of evidence was not the criterion by which to determine whether or not respond to terrorism with force. Nor should casualties or intransigence over the peripheral nature of such missions deter U.S. action. He explained what would make him willing to use force in response to terrorism in an exchange during his Senate confirmation hearings:

> SENATOR WARNER: Weinberger has adopted a philosophy that if there is a clear causal chain between the event and the perpetrators of that event, then in that instance there may rest a case for the use of force. . . .
> ADMIRAL CROWE: My general principle would be to try . . . to determine whether the situation would be better off or worse off after we took action. . . . In using force in a terrorist situation, my view would be to project ahead to determine whether force would produce the results desired. If so, I think the use of force would be justified.[158]

*Operating style.* The chiefs' perspective on the use of force was clear: if the military is utilized, deploy it quickly, massively, and decisively. The armed forces were not a tool to be used in diplomacy, but rather, were meant only to deter war, or to win any war forced upon the United States. Admiral Crowe had a slightly different perspective, primarily because he did not follow the typical naval career path (he earned two graduate degrees, spent time at the State Department, and at a variety of other diplomatic posts). As a result, he did not experience the same amount of institutional immersion as the other chiefs, and was therefore more likely than someone like General Vessey to look beyond the Pentagon's standard parochial perspective for policy options.[159]

*Sources of power.* According to Richard Betts, the military has several levels of influence on the policy process. The military has the most power when it is directly involved in the decision process and recommends *against* the use of force. The chiefs know when it is unwise to act militarily, when the probability of failure is high, and are loath to proceed when the odds are stacked against them. Betts observes that when America's most senior military officers offer this sort of advice, it is difficult for the president to ignore. The next lower level of influence occurs when the military is indirectly involved in the policy process and opposes the use of force, but does not "explicitly recommend against the use but presents alternatives or gives only conditional endorsement to the plan." While military action is their bailiwick, if the chiefs do not explicitly and categorically oppose some action, other policy-makers may view the Pentagon's reluctance as political, and not as a result of some imminent threat of disaster. Beneath that level is when the military supports the use of force. When the military leadership is involved in the policy process and supports using force, its influence is fairly low because the advice is seen as "superfluous," since a consensus to act among the civilian leadership probably already exists.[160]

## REAGAN'S DECISION-MAKING STYLE

President Theodore Roosevelt once remarked that the best executive chooses good men, delegates responsibilities to them, and has "the self-restraint to keep from meddling with them while they do it."[161] Reagan extolled this approach in an interview about his managerial philosophy, advising others to "Surround yourself with the best people you can find, delegate authority, and don't interfere as long as the policy you've decided upon is being carried out."[162] Reagan was able to do this successfully, especially in his first term, because his agenda was clear and limited. He campaigned on and tried to govern by a small set of priorities; every other policy matter was considered peripheral, and attempts were made to keep them off the presidential agenda.[163]

One factor that made it possible for Reagan to avoid the details, and for him to be what many have described as incurious and passive,[164] was that he had a clear set of core convictions on many of the big-picture policy questions that made decision making easy, even programmatic. Without an in-depth analysis, he could, for example, easily decide in favor of countering the Soviets, or lowering taxes, or reducing regulation.[165] He also was extraordinarily trusting of the people who worked for him, leading him to uncritically accept information that was provided by his advisors.[166]

Reagan had no real political experience prior to running for the governorship of California. However, his years in Sacramento allowed him to grow familiar with many of the domestic policy issues he would face in Washington. But the same cannot be said about foreign policy. While Reagan did have very strong feelings about the Soviet Union, beyond that, he had very few specific ideas with which to direct American foreign policy. So when he arrived at the White House, he replicated the successful decision-making process he had previously employed in Sacramento, relying extensively on his advisors, especially for advice on foreign policy.

Additionally, the president was not particularly interested in the minutiae of policy, and consequently did not like to receive a lot of detailed paperwork.[167] He preferred verbal briefings to memos, but when he did receive memos, he liked them short. During his stint as the governor of California, his staff developed the mini-memo, a single-page brief that summarized the issue under consideration, listed the possible options and their ramifications, and made a recommendation.[168] Use of the mini-memo continued during his presidency, with Cabinet Secretary Alfred Kingdon preparing two- to three-page memos that summarized the positions of each pertinent advisor for the issue at hand and outlined the pros and cons for each proposed alternative.[169] Toward the end of his first year, Reagan apparently thought he was still being sent too much paperwork and had his advisor Ed Meese resolve the problem. In a memo to Ray Tanter of the NSC staff, National Security Advisor Richard Allen wrote, "Ed Meese has asked that we not send so much paper to the President."[170]

Another aspect of Reagan's management style came directly from his experience as governor of California. When he entered that office, he recognized his lack of managerial experience and consequently structured his administration so that day-to-day management by him was unnecessary. By delegating power, Reagan believed "that the powers of the President [would] radiate out into the Cabinet offices."[171] Chief of Staff Donald Regan described how the system worked: Reagan "laid down no rules and articulated no missions . . . [thus conferring enormous] latitude on his subordinates."[172] This system worked because Reagan controlled the appointment process more extensively than any of his predecessors, even over low-level appointments, ensuring that only ideologically pure loyalists were appointed.[173] So despite this latitude given to his appointees, it was assumed that each would act in accordance with a common set of shared beliefs, thus ensuring Reagan's will would be done. As a study on Reagan's governorship noted, "Because cabinet officials were indeed decision-makers and were widely known as such within government, they were powerful managers of the departments below them. . . . In this way, Reagan's delegation of power became *centralized* in the cabinet where he could oversee it."[174]

Political scientist Roger Hilsman has compared Reagan's system of delegation to that of Henry II; the murder of Thomas à Becket was not explicitly ordered, but when the King lamented, "Is there not one who will rid me of this low-born [turbulent] priest?" his subordinates took the royal desire as a command, and put the archbishop to death.[175] The people who worked for Reagan readily adapted to this managerial style; as one Sacramento aide recalled, "Every day I would imagine myself in the place of the governor and think 'What would Reagan do?'"[176] Because Reagan had such a consistent philosophy, and because Reagan truly trusted his appointees and overtly delegated enormous power to them, they believed that they could make decisions unilaterally, knowing that Reagan would likely approve. However, this left room for abuse. A staff aide from Sacramento recounted one instance when the governor's trust was taken advantage of: "We instituted, for the first time in the history of California, regulation of insurance agents' fee commissions under Ronald Reagan and he never knew anything about it. They guy who had been responsible for it said, 'I know his philosophy; that's against Ronald Reagan's philosophy, but there are times where you have to overcome philosophy."[177]

Another important aspect of the president's managerial style was his aversion to conflict and his dislike for disciplining or firing subordinates. As his wife Nancy observed, "He doesn't function well if there are tensions. He likes everybody to like one another and get along."[178] A former California aide put it this way: "Ronald Reagan has never even disciplined a maid."[179] Many examples abound, including his reluctance to fire Casey over "Debate-gate" even after a congressional investigation concluded that "the better evidence indicates that Carter debate briefing material . . . entered the Reagan-Bush campaign through its director, Casey."[180] Reagan was also reluctant to fire Alexander Haig in 1982 when it became clear the secretary of state was out of step with the administration, and the president was unwilling to settle the many vehement differences between Shultz and Weinberger. A week after the 1984 election, McFarlane raised the issue of the Shultz–Weinberger conflict, saying, "I must tell you, Mr. President, we do not have a team in national security affairs." Reagan acknowledged the fact, and allowed McFarlane to outline the conflict, where he noted that the two secretaries rarely agreed on anything. The National Security Advisor explained that there were two ways to manage the problem. First, the president could become more active, more disciplined, and more involved in the decision process so as to ensure that the policy decisions he made would be enacted faithfully. The other option was to fire either Shultz or Weinberger—McFarlane preferred firing Weinberger—and rebuild the national security team around the "survivor." Reagan said he would not choose between them. He trusted Shultz, and while he did not always like the advice Weinberger provided, he was not going to fire a friend. Instead, Reagan instructed McFarlane, "So what I want you to do is just make it work."[181]

Because Reagan lacked the knowledge (and perhaps the confidence) to drive most foreign policy decisions in a particular direction, and because he assiduously avoided conflict, the president preferred that his national security team work on the basis of collegiality. As he had done in Sacramento, he set up a system where his main advisors would come together and "round-table" a problem in search of a consensus position. While this approach worked when the issue was one where there was broad agreement, when opinions diverged, the system devolved into a competitive, even conflictual one that caused the structured, well-designed interagency process to degenerate into a bureaucratic state of nature.[182] One former NSC staffer described the situation when collegiality broke down: "The players invariably are strong people with definite views. This leads to bitter infighting. . . . The organization dealing with the crisis is far less important than the personalities of key actors."[183] This infighting, in the absence of strong management (either from the president or his NSA), invariably led to stalemate in the policy process. Former National Security Advisor Zbigniew Brzezinski aptly described Reagan's system in this state, comparing it to the Polish feudal practice known as *liberum veto*, in which a lone dissenting nobleman could stall or kill a proposal that everyone else wanted.[184]

When such an impasse was reached, the NSA would summarize the divergent views and alternatives in an "options paper" for Reagan, from which he could choose. Usually Reagan would select some middle ground, giving none of his advisors what they really wanted, while not completely shutting any of them out either. When Reagan's subordinates clashed, as they did when the topics at hand were how to respond to terrorism, U.S. policy in the Middle East, and how and when to use the military, decisions that were consistent with stated policy were unlikely to occur. Instead, the wide range of responses the Reagan Administration utilized depended on the specifics of the individual terrorist incident, and on which advisor had Reagan's ear at the time. It was a rare occasion indeed when the beliefs and interests of all of the national security team's players converged at the point where "swift and effective retribution" could become reality, as many of the following chapters will demonstrate.

One caveat to this, though, concerns Reagan's emotional involvement with terrorism. The president once admitted that he was a "sucker" for a hard-luck story. When his emotions were engaged, such as during a hostage crisis, his will to take a particular action (along with his position in the governmental hierarchy) was sufficient to drive American action in a particular direction. In the chapters that follow, the president's concern and anger at the outset of each crisis would move the administration to prepare for action. However, as time passed, his anger inevitably cooled and he would revert to his prior modus operandi, allowing his advisors to determine how the U.S. would respond.

Such was the case in the next chapter—the bombing of the Marine barracks in Beirut, Lebanon.

*Chapter Three*

# The Marine Barracks Bombing in Beirut

The violence done to Lebanon will overwhelm you.

—Habakkuk 2:17

## BACKGROUND

By June 1982, the drums of war had been beating along the Israeli–Lebanese border for some time. Israeli Defense Minister Ariel Sharon was looking for a reason to invade Lebanon and "clean out" the Palestinian Liberation Organization (PLO); he got it on June 3, 1982, when Palestinian gunmen attempted to assassinate Israeli ambassador to Great Britain, Shlomo Argov. When informed by his intelligence community that the evidence clearly identified the Abu Nidal Organization (ANO) and not the rival PLO as the responsible party, Israeli Prime Minister Menachem Begin replied, "They're all PLO . . . Abu Nidal, Abu Shmidal. We have to strike the PLO!"[1]

On June 6, Israeli forces invaded Lebanon. On their drive toward Beirut, the Israeli Defense Forces (IDF) had to traverse territory populated primarily by Shia Muslims. Although the Shia had agreed to stay out of the fight, the Israeli occupation of southern Lebanon served to ignite a radical activism within certain elements of that community. On their drive north, the Israelis also engaged the Syrian military. Within the first few days of action the IDF decimated the Syrians, destroying a large quantity of Soviet-supplied armaments, including 89 aircraft, 19 anti-aircraft batteries, and more than 350 tanks.

Within a matter of days, the IDF was at the outskirts of Beirut, pounding away at suspected PLO strongholds with artillery and airstrikes. Philip Habib, Reagan's special envoy to the Middle East, described the situation: "They

were bombing the shit out of [Beirut] day after day."[2] The carnage was catastrophic, and the media quickly broadcast pictures of the siege, including reports of numerous civilian casualties, to the rest of the world. In Washington,
President Reagan saw the pictures and was appalled.

As early as July 6, there was a move to send American troops to Lebanon
to help stabilize the situation. From his vantage point in the region, Habib
sent a cable back to Washington arguing for the deployment of troops as part
of a multinational force to help facilitate the departure of the PLO from
Lebanon. However, Reagan and his top advisors wanted no part of the conflict and rejected Habib's recommendations.[3]

In August 1982, after a particularly brutal shelling of Beirut by the IDF,
Michael Deaver, one of Reagan's closest political advisors, decided he had to
talk to the president about the situation because he was distraught over television pictures showing the seemingly indiscriminate deaths of civilians. He
walked into the Oval Office and told the president, "I can't be a part of this
anymore. The bombing, the killing of children. It's wrong. And you're the one
person on the face of the earth right now who can stop it. All you have to do
is tell Begin you want it stopped." After a quick conferral with Secretary of
State George Shultz, Reagan phoned the Israeli prime minister and demanded
the shelling be stopped. A few minutes later Begin called back to say the appropriate orders had been given.[4]

By August of 1982 it had become clear that if the Lebanese government
was going to reestablish sovereignty over its territory, the PLO had to leave.
If that happened, it would clear the way for the IDF, and even the Syrians and
Iranians, to withdraw as well. A breakthrough occurred when PLO leader
Yasser Arafat agreed to evacuate his forces from Beirut, putting Habib in a
position to broker a deal that allowed for their withdrawal as well as an end
to the Israeli siege of Beirut. If the PLO fighters agreed to give up their heavy
weapons, the Israelis would let the men go—some by boat, and others overland to Syria.

### The First Deployment of the Marines

Habib's goal for the Marine deployment in Beirut was to advance U.S. policy toward Lebanon. That policy included: (1) the withdrawal of all foreign
forces from Lebanon, (2) a sovereign, independent Lebanon, and (3) security for Israel's northern border. However, not everyone in the administration agreed with Habib's answer to the problem, which led to a heated debate. Shultz and National Security Advisor William "Judge" Clark favored
sending the Marines as a contingent of an international peacekeeping force.

The NSC staff wanted the Marines sent in as well, but for a much more limited reason—credibility. NSC staffer Geoffrey Kemp explained, "The idea was that the effort would be a real assertion of superpower strength . . . that if you're a superpower, you've got all these goddamned forces that you've built up for one reason or another, and you can't use them in a situation like this, then you've got a prostrate country."[5]

From the start, Secretary of Defense Weinberger and the Joint Chiefs of Staff (JCS) were at best unenthusiastic about sending the Marines into Beirut.[6] General John Vessey, the chairman of the Joint Chiefs, explained that the JCS viewed the Marine deployment as "a mistake: for the United States to put its forces between the warring factions in Lebanon . . . we respectfully asked the Secretary [of Defense] to convey those views to the President urgently—that we not get American forces involved in Lebanon."[7] Chief of Naval Operations Admiral James Watkins commented that the mission of peacekeeping, or "presence," was of great concern to the chiefs, because the assignment was so vague. The military much prefers being told "who to shoot at."[8] According to Francis J. "Bing" West, the assistant secretary of defense for international security affairs,

> The Pentagon fought as hard as it could for as limited a role as possible. . . . The Department of Defense didn't want our troops going in at all in that kind of situation. There wasn't a military mission. It's difficult to talk with a military man when you want to talk about political symbolism. We could understand why people might want us there as a symbol and a guarantee, but a symbol and guarantee of what? It wasn't peacekeeping; there wasn't really a peace to keep. It wasn't taking out some hostiles. It didn't strike us as being an appropriate mission to use American military force, and it struck many in the Pentagon as having a high degree of danger, without explicit orders as to what the Marines would do in that kind of situation.[9]

At one point senior State Department officials were so frustrated with what they saw as the Pentagon's intransigence that they "jokingly offered to call for several hundred volunteers from the Foreign Service" to serve as peacekeepers.[10]

When it was apparent that the president was going to send in the Marines over the military's opposition, the Pentagon shifted its efforts from blocking the deployment to controlling its details. Weinberger and the JCS succeeded in limiting the Marines' mission in Beirut to the absolute minimum. Habib had wanted the troops there for sixty days; the Pentagon cut it to thirty, and also succeeded in limiting where the Marines could go. Habib wanted some of the Marines to help patrol the so-called Green Line separating East and West Beirut, but the Pentagon succeeded in restricting the Marine presence to just the airport and harbor areas.[11]

Italy and France joined the United States to form a Multinational Force (MNF), which entered the Lebanese capital to facilitate the PLO's evacuation. One reason that Arafat had agreed to leave was Habib's guarantee that the MNF—and the U.S. specifically—would protect the civilian Palestinian population left behind in Beirut.[12] When the United States deployed the Marines to Lebanon though, they were not allied with any specific force, but were to be purely neutral.

The first elements of the U.S. MNF presence went ashore on August 24, and the PLO evacuation went off without any major hitches; between August 28 and September 1, thousands of PLO fighters departed. Although the Marines were to stay for 30 days—until September 24, Weinberger unilaterally ordered them out early, and the Marines were withdrawn by September 10. One State Department official characterized the withdrawal as "precipitous . . . [the Marines] were out two weeks before anybody expected them to be." Another official said, "What I remember is that Weinberger actually [made] a public statement that we're getting out, and everybody's pretty much taken by surprise. Whether he told the President or not I don't know, but I don't know of anybody else who knew about it." It should have come as no surprise though; when Weinberger visited the troops in early September, he indicated that the Marines would be withdrawn as soon as possible.[13]

Despite the Pentagon's resistance to a large role in Lebanon, the NSC staff pushed for a very broad military mission. Dr. Geoffrey Kemp recalled the NSC staff arguing that "the President should use this opportunity to take a major gamble and put in, or consider putting in, more forces rather than less, with an ultimatum to both Syria and Israel that we are determined to let Lebanon be Lebanon, and if necessary France, Italy, and the United States, and hopefully some others at some point, will ensure that this is done."[14] Under NSC direction, the Pentagon even developed a plan that would have deployed some 63,000 American servicemen in Lebanon; their mission would have been to disarm the various Lebanese militias, "secure ports and borders, and take over ground held by Syria and Israel."[15] Shultz, who feared Congress would not support such a large operation, joined the Pentagon in its opposition to the larger plan.[16]

Instead, the Reagan administration opted for the diplomatic option, and on September 1, Reagan announced a new peace initiative for the Middle East. The plan, which came to be known as the "Reagan Plan," called for Jordan's King Hussein to open negotiations with Israel on behalf of the Palestinians in search of a resolution on their status and that of the West Bank. The plan envisioned some sort of Jordanian-administered Palestinian entity there.

On September 14, the prospects for peace in Lebanon took a significant blow when President-elect Bashir Gemeyel was assassinated. The Reagan administration and the Israeli government had counted on Gemeyel to impose order in Lebanon and to make peace with its Jewish neighbor, but with him gone, it did not appear that there was anyone else strong enough to do the job. Middle East envoy Morris Draper described the situation: "The Americans were very badly hit by the loss of Bashir Gemeyel because he was a strong person and a very close friend of the United States. . . . He was indebted to the United States for many things including his election in which we had given him strong support. . . . His loss was very discouraging."[17] As a result of the new power vacuum, and contrary to their own stated objectives, the Israelis moved the IDF into Beirut.

## The Second Deployment of the Marines

When the IDF moved into Beirut, they conducted some "mop-up" operations to purge the city of any remaining PLO fighters. One trouble spot the IDF focused on was the Palestinian refugee camps, where the Israelis believed terrorists were hiding. The Israelis could not, however, enter refugee camps on a search-and-destroy operation without sustaining considerable international condemnation. Instead, they allowed Phalange militiamen—from the Lebanese faction controlled by the Gemeyel family—to enter the Sabra and Shatilla camps on September 16; the Phalange slaughtered over 700 civilians, including women and children. The official Israeli government inquiry into the massacre—the Kahan Commission—placed indirect responsibility for the killings on Defense Minister Sharon. Sharon was sacked and replaced by Moshe Arens, who happened to have very good relations with Secretary of State Shultz.

When Bashir Gemeyel's brother, Amin, was elected president on September 21, he immediately called for a redeployment of the MNF into Beirut. The death of hundreds of civilians so horrified Reagan that it was almost a foregone conclusion that the Marines would be sent back in. Geoffrey Kemp observed, "We had promised to protect the Palestinian civilians, it was our allies, the Israelis, who permitted the massacre to happen, and it was our boy Bashir Gemeyel's troops that did the killing."[18] Assistant Secretary of Defense Richard Armitage recalled that the massacres "shocked us. It just shocked everyone. It was so horrible and none of us could believe that the Israelis just stood by while the Phalangists committed these atrocities in the worst possible way . . . if you look at the film footage . . . it is pretty amazing if you put it in the context of the time. We were not showing bodies all the time, and these bloated Palestinian bodies, they were just unbelievable. Women, kids, dogs. Pretty brutal. I guess, although the Defense Department again resisted going back in [we felt so much] morose guilt that we ended up going back."[19] The French government claimed that the massacre would have been avoided if the MNF had stayed for the entire 30 day mandate, bolstering the moral argument to go back in.[20] According to one State Department official, "Reagan virtually said: 'I don't want to hear any objections,' and he didn't." Although Weinberger and Vessey opposed returning to Beirut, the Pentagon did not actively work against the redeployment.[21]

Perhaps because of the guilt-laden circumstances, the second deployment of the Marines was much more hurried and much less considered. Instead of identifiable goals with which to measure the success of the mission, the Marines were sent in as an "interpositional" force, to separate the warring parties and help stabilize the environment so that the Lebanese government could reestablish control over its territory. Consequently, their rules of engagement were extremely mild; because the Marines were on a peacetime deployment, their guns were not readied for combat. The guidelines issued to each Marine read: "When on post, mobile or foot patrol, keep loaded magazine in weapon, bolt closed, weapon on safe, no round in the chamber. . . . Do not chamber a round unless told to do so by a commissioned officer." If their lines were crossed by another force, they were to warn the offenders that they were in an unauthorized area. If the intruders did not withdraw, the Marine's commanding officer was to be notified, and he would decide what to do next. The troops could only return fire if fired upon, and only to ensure their safety.[22]

When the Marines returned on September 29, they carried orders to "establish a presence" and to "establish [an] environment that will permit the Lebanese Armed Forces [LAF] to carry out its responsibilities in the Beirut area, and be prepared to protect U.S. forces and conduct retrograde and withdrawal operations from the area."[23] The Marine presence, though, was limited; when the Marines went back in, they took up position at the Beirut International Airport, ostensibly because it was an easy site to resupply and, if necessary, to evacuate from. Weinberger insisted on that location because he thought it was the safest possible place for the troops.[24] To fulfill the other part of their mandate, the Marines began joint training missions with the LAF.[25]

One of the most significant ramifications to come from the Israeli invasion—one that would critically affect the American experience in the Middle East throughout the rest of the decade—was the introduction of Iranian Revolutionary Guards into Lebanon's Bekaa Valley. Although Tehran claimed the guards were sent to Lebanon to fight the Israeli invasion, they were in fact, according to the State Department's David Long, "there to organize, train and indoctrinate a militant Lebanese Shia political and terrorist organization from their headquarters, the old Shaykh Abdallah barracks near Baalbek."[26] They were directed by Iran's ambassador to Damascus, Ali Akbar Muhtashamipur, in an attempt to realize Iranian leader Ayatollah Khomeini's assertion that,

"We consider [Lebanon] to be part of Iran."[27] The new organization was called Hezbollah (meaning Party of God), and was led by Lebanon's most influential Shia cleric, Sayyid Muhammad Husayn Fadlallah.

Adding confusion to the situation was the near-simultaneous emergence of the Islamic Jihad Organization, which was, in fact, a part of Hezbollah.[28] Since Shia Islam holds that terrorism is against Islamic law, Hezbollah used the *nom de guerre* Islamic Jihad to hide its involvement in a plethora of terrorist attacks that would plague Westerners and Israelis throughout the 1980s.[29] A CIA assessment dated September 25, 1984 noted, "We do not believe that Islamic Jihad is a distinct organization with identifiable leaders. The term Islamic Jihad (Islamic Holy War) more likely is an umbrella name used by a number of Iranian-dominated Shia extremist groups in Lebanon. . . . [The name] has been identified with" a number of groups, including the Hezbollah, Islamic Amal, the Husayni Suicide Commandos, the Council of Lebanon, the Hizb al-Dawa of Lebanon, the Muslim Students' Union, and the Jundallah.[30]

## The Embassy Bombing in Beirut

Habib's attempts to broker a peace deal continued into the spring of 1983. However, the Reagan Plan suffered a mortal blow on April 10 when Jordan's King Hussein announced that he would not enter negotiations with Israel on behalf of the Palestinians, primarily because his relations with Arafat had soured. So for the moment, the Reagan administration's diplomatic efforts ground to a halt.

A week later, on April 18, a suicide bomber drove a pickup truck loaded with an estimated 2,000 pounds of explosives into the front of the U.S. embassy in Beirut. Upon detonation, the center of the building collapsed, killing 63 people, including 17 Americans. Among the dead were most of the CIA's Beirut station, one member of Delta Force, and Robert Ames—the CIA's leading expert on the Middle East—who was meeting with the station at the time.[31]

A heretofore-unknown group calling itself Islamic Jihad claimed credit for the attack, and that meant Hezbollah, and thus, Iranian involvement.[32] Intelligence indicated that the Iranian Foreign Ministry had been planning something, but the details were unclear. Journalist Bob Woodward reported that the National Security Agency had broken Iran's diplomatic codes and was reading the cable traffic between Tehran and the Iranian embassies in Beirut and Damascus. A review of those intercepts revealed that some sort of attack against an American target was in the works, and that a payment of $25,000 had been authorized for the "unspecified operation."[33] The base of operations for the Iranian outpost in Lebanon was the Sheik Abdullah barracks in

Baalbek, and the National Reconnaissance Office [NRO] had satellite photographs showing a mock-up of the embassy there.[34] Still, the evidence was circumstantial and did not definitively provide a clear picture of who was ultimately responsible. Geoffrey Kemp concluded that Iran was involved with the bombing, but was uncertain about the level of Syrian involvement.[35] However, as Noel Koch observed, it would have been "unlikely that they would have been able to move out of Baalbek through East Beirut and into West Beirut without the Syrians knowing what the target was . . . this couldn't happen without Rifaat al Assad [Syrian President Hafez al Assad's brother and head of Syrian intelligence] concurring."[36]

Woodward claims that after the bombing, William Casey sent a CIA team to Beirut to determine who had destroyed the embassy. According to his account, the investigation revealed that a Syrian intelligence officer had come to Beirut to install the explosives in the truck. However, this information was viewed with suspicion because of the intelligence-gathering method used; one of the CIA officers dispatched to Beirut apparently interrogated suspects using an electric-shock device in order to extract confessions, and one suspect died.[37]

Official Washington was stunned by the bombing. Despite the rhetorical attention given to terrorism over the previous two years, nothing—not even the kidnapping of Brigadier General James Dozier in Italy—grabbed the administration's attention like this did. A diplomatic mission had been attacked and all but destroyed. The anger was widespread, but nobody really knew what to do about it. General Vessey explained later, "Although it was a great tragedy, it seemed like an inexplicable aberration."[38] Reagan wrote in his diary, "Lord, forgive me for the hatred I feel for the humans who can do such a cruel and cowardly deed."[39] But such anger was not enough to move the administration to action. Consequently, the administration did not seriously explore retaliation, but instead, according to General Willie Y. Smith of the U.S. European Command, focused on "how to protect ourselves."[40]

However, when Weinberger saw Shultz on television talking about how "his" facility had been attacked, the secretary of defense grew worried that the State Department hierarchy would push the president into supporting a rash military action. So in early May, Weinberger ordered an Intelligence Support Activity (ISA) team to Beirut to investigate the "intelligence failure" that led to the embassy bombing.

ISA teams are small units of special operations forces that are officially attached to the Army, but receive their tasking directly from the JCS or the secretary of defense. They are described as straddling "the intelligence and special operations world[s],"[41] collecting intelligence, conducting reconnaissance, and locating targets for later conventional and special operations.[42]

When the five-member group arrived in Beirut, they contacted the many individuals and organizations in the intelligence business, including the various American contingents, the Israelis, the French, and the numerous Lebanese sources. They discovered that there was an abundance of raw intelligence in Beirut, but that it was not being centralized. They wrote a report for Weinberger proposing the creation of an intelligence fusion center, where all available sources of intelligence would be brought together, collated, and disseminated to the pertinent organizations (whether it be the American diplomatic mission or the Marines). Second, they encouraged better intelligence cooperation and coordination with the Israelis, who had been on the ground in Beirut for some time. Third, they recommended that the imagery and signals data analyzed by the intelligence community in Washington be forwarded to people in the field at a much faster rate.[43]

The report was finished in the first week of June, and upset almost everyone who read it. The European Command, the Navy, and the Marine Corps were all angry over recommendations about how to do their jobs better. Nonetheless, the ISA team forwarded the report to Deputy Assistant Secretary of Defense for International Security Affairs Noel Koch, who in turn sent it to Weinberger. For the time being, the report was buried, and its recommendations shelved.[44]

Ultimately, Reagan responded to the embassy bombing with a stiffened resolve and a renewed urgency to see the peace process move forward. Following the attack he declared, "Because of this latest crime, we're more resolved than ever to help achieve the urgent and total withdrawal of all . . . foreign forces. . . . With this in mind, I've asked the Secretary of State to visit the Middle East next week. His primary purpose will be to bring to a successful conclusion the negotiations in Lebanon."

## The May 17 Agreement

Following the embassy bombing, the Reagan administration renewed its efforts to broker a peace deal in Lebanon. The day the embassy was bombed, Reagan reaffirmed to President Gemeyel that he would press on with the peace process.[45] Later he told the American ambassador to Lebanon, Robert Dillon, "This tragedy, however awful, must not distract us from our search for peace in Lebanon and elsewhere."[46] Ten days after the bombing, Shultz personally began a new round of intense diplomacy. These talks produced an agreement that in principal meant peace between Israel and Lebanon, only the second such agreement between Israel and an Arab state. One aim of the agreement was the removal of all foreign forces from Lebanon, although a key codicil to the agreement said that Israel did not have to withdraw its troops if Syria did not.[47] In what turned out to be a major mistake, however, Syria was intentionally kept out of the peace talks. During a meeting between Israeli Foreign Minister Yitzhak Shamir and Reagan in Washington, the president proposed "leav[ing] the Syrians on the outside looking in."[48] Instead of having direct Syrian involvment, Shultz hoped that the Saudis and Egyptians would use their influence on Assad to compel compliance with the troop pullout. Most of the region's American ambassadors, Habib, and Assistant Secretary of State for Near East Affairs Nick Veliotes warned that the plan would never succeed without Syrian involvement. Shultz ignored them and pressed ahead.[49]

Shultz's hope for an agreement was short-lived. Almost immediately after the May 17 Agreement was announced, one Syrian official said Damascus "would do all it could to foil the agreement," and on May 19, Syrian Foreign Minister Abdul Halim Khaddam said Syria would take action against the Lebanese government for making peace with Israel.[50] The Gemeyel government was quickly ostracized by Damascus for signing the accord, and it became common knowledge that Syria was aiding Lebanon's Druze militia in an effort to undermine Gemeyel and the May 17 Agreement. When Habib traveled to Damascus to discuss a troop withdrawal, Assad refused to see him and declared the American envoy persona non grata because of his role in keeping Syria out of the negotiations. Some had an inkling that this sort of reaction was coming though; a CIA report prepared after the Reagan Plan was unveiled indicated that if an agreement was reached for the withdrawal of the IDF, it was unlikely that Syria would go along. The State Department's Bureau of Near East Affairs had similar concerns.[51]

After Assad banned Habib in Damascus, Reagan had little choice but to replace his envoy to the Middle East. Turning to someone already within the administration, the president named Robert McFarlane as his new representative, and sent him to the region with a single mission: get Syrian and Israeli troops out of Lebanon so the Lebanese government can reestablish control over its territory.[52]

McFarlane discovered quickly that his new job would be nearly impossible. Assad made it clear that he would not pull his troops out, and took great exception when McFarlane referred to Lebanon as a sovereign nation. McFarlane came to believe that Syria would only withdraw its troops from Lebanon if it were compelled to do so by a considerable show of American force. He directed two of his aides, Howard Teicher and Philip Dur, to develop a list of options. Dur came up with the idea to station the battleship *New Jersey* off the coast of Lebanon "as a symbol that the United States meant business." Its 16-inch guns could hurl an artillery shell the size of a Volkswagon bug into the Shouf Mountains some miles away.[53]

## The Mission Changes

Throughout the summer, the Marines succeeded in maintaining the appearance of neutrality in the midst of considerable chaos. However, their association with the LAF was bound to irritate some faction in Lebanon, and by early August the Marines were being intentionally fired upon. On August 28, the Marines returned fire for the first time, marking them not just as targets, but as combatants. On September 1, Walid Jumblatt, the leader of the Druze militia, announced that the Marines would be considered enemy forces and therefore legitimate targets in the ongoing civil war.

On July 20, the Israeli Knesset voted unanimously to withdraw the IDF from the Shouf and move them south to the Awali River. Since it was now clear that Syria was not going to go along with the troop withdrawal, the United States now faced the prospect of Syrian forces filling the void left by the departing IDF. Following intense American lobbying to forestall the Israeli withdrawal from the strategic high ground which overlooked the Beirut Airport and the Marine positions, the IDF began to redeploy southward on September 4. McFarlane then proposed deploying the Marines in joint patrols with the LAF into the Shouf, but his proposal was shot down by the NSPG. Instead, the Phalange militia quickly moved into the Shouf, but was defeated by the Druze, who were supported by Syrian and PLO forces.

Between September 9 and 11, Reagan met secretly with his foreign policy team—Bush, Shultz, Weinberger, Clark, Casey, Meese, Baker, and Vessey. After an NSC meeting on September 10, Reagan signed NSDD-103, which laid out the administration's objectives in Lebanon. They were: "(a) to restore the sovereignty of the Government of Lebanon throughout its territory, (b) obtaining the complete withdrawal of all foreign forces, and (c) ensuring the security of Lebanon's borders, especially the northern border of Israel." It reiterated the mission of the MNF as supporting "the Government of Lebanon in deterring hostilities by maintaining an active presence in the Greater Beirut area."[54]

On September 10, Reagan wrote in his diary that, "We may be facing a choice of getting out or enlarging our mission."[55] At a subsequent meeting, McFarlane, just back from the Middle East, proposed that the United States launch air strikes against Syrian positions in Lebanon "to stun the Syrians and get them to stop causing trouble." Weinberger opposed any such escalation, fearing the United States would be pulled into a much broader conflict.[56]

The LAF, which had tentatively moved into the Shouf on its own, was quickly faced with a large and belligerent force of Druze, Syrians, Palestinians, and perhaps some Iranians, as it stood to defend the market town of Suq al-Gharb. When the LAF was attacked on September 11, and appeared to be faltering, McFarlane cabled Washington requesting American military intervention to save the Lebanese Army and its positions in the Shouf. In what came to be known as "the sky is falling cable," he argued that "this is not a civil conflict . . . forces were comprised of a PLA brigade and Iranian elements. . . . We may well be at a turning point which will lead within a matter of days to a Syrian take over of the country north of the Awali [River]."[57] Reagan was alarmed by the Cold War overtones and agreed, authorizing American naval gunfire to support the LAF. In an addendum to NSDD-103 on September 11, Reagan determined that the town of Suq-al-Gharb was "vital to the safety of U.S. personnel in Beirut, and the U.S. diplomatic presence," and authorized the American commander in Beirut, Colonel Timothy J. Geraghty, to call in naval and air strikes to defend that area from hostile takeover.[58] He also issued broader rules of engagement for the Marines; the new rules were known as "aggressive self-defense," and were authorized on September 13, but were still relatively soft, and still mandated "unchambered" rounds in weapons.[59]

When the LAF attacked Druze and Palestinian positions in the Shouf on September 19, and began to run low on ammunition, the Lebanese Ministry of Defense decided it needed U.S. naval gunfire support. A request was put to Army Brigadier General Carl Stiner, the JCS liaison with the LAF, who passed it on to McFarlane. The request was approved and four American warships, the *Virginia, John Rogers, Bowen,* and *Radford* fired for five hours. The Lebanese government reported that the enemy forces "broke and ran" as a result.[60]

While the events of September 19 seemed to improve the situation around Beirut, as the United States increased its support for the Lebanese Army, it was seen as siding with the Gemeyel government by even more Lebanese factions and as just another participant in the war. As a result, over a period of months the hostilities directed against the Marines grew, so much so that just two days before the attack on the Marine barracks, the JCS met to discuss concerns about the troops' safety.[61]

Meanwhile, congressional anxiety over the role of the Marines, and the increasing casualties, was on the rise. Officially, the administration wanted Congress to extend the deployment for at least another eighteen months, while some individuals wanted no limit at all, including General P. X. Kelley, the Commandant of the Marine Corps. He argued, "If you make it too short they'll wait you out; if you make it too long, they'll blow you out."[62] At a meeting with a large number of members from the House of Representatives, assistant secretary of state Nick Veliotes addressed congressional concerns.

He argued that the administration needed the full eighteen months to depoliticize the deployment—to put off the next decision on what to do with the Marines until after the 1984 presidential election. Congress ultimately approved the request, although a number of members—on both sides of the aisle—were uncomfortable with the decision. Veliotes recalled that after the meeting, Congressman Trent Lott "called me over and he said, 'Now you go back . . . we're going to vote, we're going to give you eighteen months but you go back and tell the Secretary of State and the President that we really mean three or four months. We expect this to be wrapped up.'"[63]

On September 23, McFarlane met with the Syrian president in Damascus. After the meeting had dragged on for four hours, McFarlane told Assad, "President Reagan feels quite strongly about the importance of reconciliation in Lebanon, of the restoration of Lebanese sovereignty over its entire territory, and the withdrawal of all foreign forces. As a sign of that commitment, the battleship *New Jersey* will be sent to augment the Sixth Fleet in the next week." The news had its anticipated effect. When McFarlane proceeded to Beirut, he was able to secure a cease-fire, which was announced on September 25. For a time, it appeared that the situation in Beirut was under control.[64]

On October 17, Reagan shuffled his foreign policy team, appointing McFarlane as his new National Security Advisor and promoting Admiral John Poindexter to deputy NSA. The next day, the NSPG met to discuss the administration's strategy for Lebanon. After opening the meeting, McFarlane asked Shultz to "lead a discussion on the recommended course of action and the next steps for decision."[65] However, the meeting eventually turned to a Weinberger proposal to immediately withdraw the Marines to ships waiting offshore. Although Weinberger and the JCS opposed the mission, intelligence indicated a heightened probability of a terrorist attack against the Marines, prompting them to push for this new initiative. The proposal was shelved after other principals persuaded the defense secretary to drop the issue.[66]

## Grenada

Meanwhile, the growing crisis in Grenada had forced the administration to consider what it might do if the situation got out of control in that tiny Caribbean nation. Earlier in the year, Reagan had lamented about the "Soviet-Cuban militarization" of Grenada, and the JCS feared that the island would be used as a forward base for Soviet surveillance craft.[67] The murder of leftist Prime Minister Maurice Bishop by even more radical elements in Grenada and concern for the safety of roughly 1,000 American citizens on the island prompted the administration to act. At an NSPG meeting on October 22, a consensus emerged that the situation in Grenada had deteriorated so much that the administration should proceed with Operation Urgent Fury—the invasion of Grenada.[68]

## THE CRISIS

### The Bombing

At 6:22 am (Beirut time) on Sunday, October 23, a yellow Mercedes truck laden with the equivalent of 12,000 pounds of explosives entered the airport parking lot in front of the Marine barracks, circled to gain speed, and then crashed through a barbed wire fence. It sped past a sentry post guarding the facility, slammed into the barracks, and detonated. The building collapsed, killing or mortally wounding 241 military personnel—220 Marines and 21 Navy medical personnel.[69] Minutes later, another suicide bomber attacked the headquarters of the French MNF contingent, killing 58.

First word of the bombing came to Washington in a cable to the National Military Command Center at midnight EST (7:00 am in Beirut). It read:

> A large explosion at BLT 1/8 Hq Bldg collapsed the roof and leveled the build-ing. Large numbers of dead and injured. Are using MSSG 24 and Italian MNF medical and will medevac out of LLS Brown . . . French report a Bldg in their sector also bombed . . . unknown injured; BLT Hq destroyed. Amplifying info to follow.[70]

### The American Response Unfolds

Trying to maintain a business-as-usual appearance prior to the Grenada oper-ation, the president and his entourage had traveled to the Augusta National Golf Course in Georgia for a long weekend. McFarlane got first word of the attack in a phone call at around 2:00 am EST from the White House Situation Room. McFarlane immediately had the president and the secretary of state awakened, whereupon the NSA quickly briefed them on the few details he did know, telling them, "It's not confirmed yet, but it looks like two hundred or more fatalities."[71] Reagan was devastated. According to an account McFar-lane gave to journalist Robert Timberg,

> Reagan looked stricken. God, he said, just think of those poor guys, their fami-lies. His voice trailed off. He looked away and shook his head. When he turned back, the grief had melted away, replaced by what McFarlane called "an expres-sion of hatred and wish for revenge that I never saw in him before or since." . . . Those sons of bitches, said Reagan, let's find a way to go after them.[72]

The three men discussed the situation and possible U.S. responses for two hours. One option they considered was pulling the Marines out, but McFarlane argued against the move, and the three reached a consensus that the troops should stay.[73]

Reagan and his entourage returned to Washington that morning. On his way into the White House the president told reporters, "I think we should all recognize that these deeds make so evident the bestial nature of those who would assume power if they could have their way and drive us out of that area, that we must be more determined than ever that they cannot take over that vital and strategic area of the Earth." When he got to the Situation Room, he was, according to NSC staffer Oliver North, in a "white rage" declaring, "We'll make them pay."[74]

Upon hearing the initial evidence, NSC staffer Howard Teicher wrote a memo to McFarlane recommending that the United States immediately begin planning for a retaliatory strike. Despite suspected Iranian complicity, "it was clear in my mind the U.S. had to answer this immediately. . . . I argued we should hit targets associated with Syrian-sponsored terrorism in Lebanon." Under Secretary of State Lawrence Eagleburger also counselled in favor of a retaliatory strike. "It made very little difference whom you clobbered, so long as you clobbered somebody who had it coming. They all talk to each other."[75]

That morning, the NSPG met at 9:00 am to discuss both Lebanon and Grenada. Present were Reagan, Bush, Shultz, Deputy Secretary of State Kenneth Dam, Under Secretary of State Lawrence Eagleburger, Assistant Secretary of State Langhorne Motley, Weinberger, Vessey, General P. X. Kelley, Deputy Director of the CIA John McMahon, political advisors Meese, Baker, Deaver, and a small group of NSC staffers, including McFarlane, Robert Kimmitt, Geoffrey Kemp, and Oliver North.[76]

McFarlane opened the meeting with a quick recap of the situation, and was followed by McMahon with an intelligence update. McMahon noted that no group had claimed responsibility for the attack, but suspicion was already centering on the Syrians, the Iranians, and their surrogates.[77] Weinberger and Vessey explained the military situation in Beirut, and Shultz gave a quick briefing on the diplomatic front. When the updates were through, a short discussion ensued. At the end of the morning meeting, Reagan observed, "This is an obvious attempt to run us out of Lebanon. . . . The first thing I want to do is to find out who did it and go after them with everything we've got." At 10:40, the meeting recessed.[78]

The group reconvened at 4:00 pm, and a retaliatory strike against Hezbollah sites in Lebanon's Bekaa Valley was discussed. Civilian installations that could be at risk in an attack were identified, including a school and a hospital,[79] and a specific Navy proposal to launch Tomahawk missiles from the battleship *New Jersey*, which was just off the coast of Beirut, was debated.[80] Weinberger opposed any retaliation, later defending his opposition to the plan saying, "I'm not an eye-for-an-eye man. . . . I have no objection to bombing Baalbek if you're going to accomplish something with it, if you're going to stop future terrorism with it. . . . But we didn't have the conclusive kind of target information that I think is essential."[81] Armitage explained Weinberger's rationale, saying, "Many of us felt that that kind of retaliation was a sort of 'feel good' exercise rather than a sharp, tight, military response."[82]

Unlike the Pentagon's civilian leadership, the joint chiefs were not unanimously opposed to a retaliatory strike. CNO Watkins favored an attack, saying, "I wanted to go because I felt the confluence of information was almost overwhelming."[83] On the other hand, Marine Commandant General P. X. Kelley opposed retaliation for two reasons. First, he did not think the administration had a good target to hit because of the collateral damage that would have resulted. Second, he feared that such an attack would result in more violence against the Marines.[84] Vessey opposed an attack on moral grounds, saying, "It [is] beneath our dignity to retaliate against the terrorists who blew up the Marine barracks."[85] He also opposed an attack on more practical grounds, believing the United States was not in a good position to retaliate, since the Marines in Beirut were still vulnerable and retaliation might invite further terrorist attacks.[86]

While the Tomahawk option was ruled out, a strike plan using planes from carriers in the Mediterranean began to develop. Shultz and McFarlane supported this approach, as did Vice President Bush. The JCS, although hesitant to use more force in Lebanon, agreed on a target for the proposed strike—the Sheikh Abdullah barracks in Baalbek. Following the discussion, Reagan said, "Well, let's go after it. Let's plan the mission, get ready and quick, and if possible do it with the French. But do it."[87]

At the end of the meeting, McFarlane summed up what had been decided. "As I understand it, Mr. President, you want the Pentagon to commence planning a retaliatory mission." Reagan agreed. The president also affirmed that McFarlane had been given the authority to discuss a joint action with the French. With this, McFarlane proceeded to write a directive/memo and delivered it to Weinberger that read, "Please undertake military-to-military contacts for an early attack in the Baalbek area."[88] McFarlane also instructed two of his aides, Poindexter and Dur, to contact the French about a cooperative effort. Poindexter discussed the possibility of a joint attack with President Mitterrand's military advisor, Jacques Salnier, and the two agreed to work on a plan to hit the Sheikh Abdullah barracks in Baalbek.[89]

During the afternoon, McFarlane and Kemp authored NSDD-109, which Reagan signed the following day. It held Iran and its Lebanese surrogates responsible for the bombing, and ordered comprehensive efforts to identify and punish those responsible for the attack. It also directed, on General Vessey's recommendation, the dispatch of General Kelley to Beirut to study the Marines' situation and to make recommendations for improving their security. Kelley subsequently requested that the FBI send agents to Beirut to investigate the bombing.[90]

That evening, Principal Deputy Press Secretary Larry Speakes spoke to reporters and outlined the administration's view of the day's events. "These attacks were clearly designed to weaken our determination and to disrupt the efforts of the Government of Lebanon to regain control and sovereignty over the country. . . . We will not yield to international terrorism, because we know that if we do the civilized world will suffer and our values will be fair game for those who seek to destroy all we stand for. . . ." He then proclaimed, "We also intend to respond to this criminal act when the perpetrators are identified."

On October 24, Reagan tried to justify the Marine presence in Lebanon in anticipation of growing negative public opinion, and hinted broadly at retaliation during a luncheon with regional broadcasters:

> Are we to abandon the thousands of Lebanese who yearn for the simple freedoms and privileges we take for granted. . . . The struggle for peace is indivisible. We cannot pick and choose where we will support freedom. If it's lost in one place, all of us lose. If the Soviets and their surrogates can feel confident that they can intimidate us and our allies in Lebanon, they will become more bold elsewhere. . . . The United States will not be intimidated by terrorists. . . . We will not allow this behavior to go unpunished.[91]

The international community was quick to press restraint upon Reagan. In a letter to Reagan, Egyptian President Hosni Mubarak urged the U.S. to "apply maximum self-restraint in the face of such acts of cowardice," and to "defeat the purpose of their perpetrators by not playing into their hands."[92] German Chancellor Helmut Kohl told the president that "only a political solution can lead to a reconciliation." British Prime Minister Margaret Thatcher asked Reagan to "think carefully about retaliating for the bomb attack." In a response to Thatcher drafted by the State Department, Reagan "set the record straight on U.S. intentions to engage in measures of self-defense against the perpetrators of the bomb attack."[93]

In Amman, Jordan, American Ambassador Richard Noyes Viets met with King Hussein late on October 23. Viets reported that the king was "in a mood of profound despair. He seemed physically in shock over the carnage . . . and he was deeply concerned over the ultimate impact this tragedy could have on our political will to stand fast in the region." Hussein was less concerned about an immediate American reaction. Rather, his main concern was about the bombing's long-term implications for a diplomatic settlement in Lebanon. He wanted the U.S. to get tough with both Israel and Syria, "without distinguishing between friend or enemy." He felt that neither had any business in Lebanon and that neither should be allowed to negotiate a preferential role for itself prior to withdrawal.[94] In a subsequent meeting between Hussein and Viets, the king urged Reagan to stay the course in Lebanon. "If the arrival of [the MNF] was a bluff, then the bluff has been called. It leaves the United States and its European partners and, indeed, the free world, the choice of either withdrawing urgently from Lebanon, and by implication, leaving the Middle East to whatever is its destiny or taking the alternative course—if you have the resolve and the means—of calling for an urgent, total and unconditional withdrawal of all foreign forces from all sovereign Lebanese soil."[95]

In the afternoon, a series of telephone conversations took place between American and French officials about the situation, including one from Reagan to Mitterrand. When the two spoke, Reagan told the French president, "For our part, we plan to retaliate . . . once we have determined who perpetrated this heinous crime."[96] The American ambassador to Paris, Evan Galbraith, reported that Shultz and his counterpart, Foreign Minister Claude Cheysson, had also spoken.[97]

The administration also faced some initial pressure from Congress, especially from the Democrats, to pull the Marines out of Lebanon. Democratic Senator Ernest Hollings and former Senator George McGovern called for the immediate withdrawal of the Marines, and Senator Gary Hart said, "The continued slaughter of U.S. personnel cannot be tolerated. . . . It is clear that a U.S. military presence in the area is not the right answer." Representative Sam Gibbons said much the same, but in terms everyone understood: "I have only three words to say—Lebanon: Reagan's Vietnam." On October 24, House Speaker Tip O'Neill and Senate Majority Leader Howard Baker spoke with Reagan about the situation, and the congressional leaders agreed to not push for a quick withdrawal.[98] It helped that O'Neill believed that partisanship should end at the water's edge. He squelched the Democrats' dissent during a party caucus shortly after the bombing, arguing that it was not the time to "undermine Reagan's efforts to resolve the crisis." The Speaker appears to have been persuasive. Congressman Les Aspin, a Democrat from Wisconsin, explained that he had planned to vote for a withdrawal of the Marines "basically to send the President a message," but changed his mind after hearing O'Neill's pleas.[99] The resolution to pull out the Marines failed on a vote of 153 to 274.

Despite these domestic and international pressures, most in the Reagan administration believed that U.S. retaliation was fully justified. In a memo from Shultz's executive secretary, Charles Hill (and Brennan McKinley), to Mc-Farlane, Hill and McKinley suggested that Reagan's upcoming televised address to the nation about Grenada and Lebanon include an announcement of "the U.S. intention to retaliate against hostile forces which attack U.S. forces."[100]

Within hours of the blast, an order went out to implement the buried ISA report that had recommended the establishment of an intelligence fusion center in Beirut. Over the next few days, Assistant Secretary of Defense Noel Koch put together a notebook pertaining to the ISA report that included police reports, messages, and cables back and forth between Koch and the ISA team. The notebook set out everything that had been discovered about the intelligence shortcomings in Beirut, and included the objections to the report's recommendations from the European Command (EuCom). Koch called the notebook "the most inflammatory document that had ever been constructed because it just said . . . you have gotten 241 people killed for the convenience of some people's careers." He sent a copy of the notebook to Weinberger, but according to Koch, "Colin Powell [Weinberger's assistant] intercepted it and called me or came up, I think he called me and he was really irate, because he knew the significance of this. 'Why did I put this together?'" Powell asked. "Because I think we need a record on how we got these people killed," Koch replied.[101] Koch does not believe the secretary ever saw it.

On October 25, Reagan held a question-and-answer session with reporters. Meese prepared one set of talking points that included reiterating America's interest in Lebanon, proclaiming again, "We will not be driven [out] by terrorism."[102] Another set of talking points for the meeting was prepared by the NSC staff, and it outlined the reasons for not pulling out the Marines:

1. We would encourage terrorists.
2. We would give up the chance for a negotiated settlement producing a unified, democratic Lebanon.
3. We would leave the Lebanese to suffer bloody internal strife and chaos.
4. We might allow anti-Western, Syrian forces to fill the vacuum.
5. By so doing, we might threaten both Israel and the West—thus risking a major escalation of the conflict.

Additional margin notes made by Poindexter reflect his concerns should the Marines be pulled out. He asked, "Can we allow [the] demise of Israel?" and "Can we allow [a] threat to NATO['s] *southern border?*"[103]

During an early afternoon meeting with the press, Reagan used these points
to discuss the situation in Beirut:

Many Americans are wondering why we must keep our forces in Lebanon. Well,
the reason they must stay there until the situation is under control is quite clear:
We have vital interests in Lebanon, and our actions in Lebanon are in the cause
of world peace . . . seeking a withdrawal of all foreign forces from Lebanon and
from the Beirut area while the new Lebanese government undertakes to restore
sovereignty throughout that country. By promoting peace in Lebanon, we
strengthen the forces for peace throughout the Middle East.

Peace in Lebanon is key to the region's stability now and in the future. To the
extent that the prospect for future stability is heavily influenced by the presence of
our forces, it is central to our credibility on a global scale. We must not allow international criminals and thugs such as these to undermine the peace in Lebanon.

He issued a veiled threat to the bombers, saying there was "evidence linking the
perpetrators of this latest atrocity to others that have occurred against us in the
recent past, including the bombing of our Embassy in Beirut last April." Finally,
he reiterated his resolve to stay the course and not withdraw the Marines.

On October 27, after attending an extremely emotional memorial service
for the victims of the Beirut bombing at Camp Lejune, North Carolina, Reagan made a nationally televised address about events in Lebanon and
Grenada. In it he again defended the rationale for having the Marines in
Lebanon, and outlined the administration's next steps:

Every President who has occupied this office in recent years has recognized that
peace in the Middle East is of vital concern to our Nation. . . . Four times in the
last thirty years, the Arabs and Israelis have gone to war. And each time, the
world has teetered near the edge of catastrophe. . . . Those who directed this
atrocity must be dealt justice, and they will be. . . . If we were to leave Lebanon
now, what message would that send to those who foment instability and terrorism? If America were to walk away from Lebanon, what chance would there be
for a negotiated settlement producing a unified democratic Lebanon? . . . Can
the United States . . . stand by and see the Middle East incorporated into the Soviet bloc? . . . The events in Lebanon and Grenada, though oceans apart, are
closely related. Not only has Moscow assisted and encouraged the violence in
both countries, but it provides direct support through a network of surrogates
and terrorists.

The same day, the carrier *Eisenhower* was ordered to the eastern Mediterranean from Naples, Italy.

Meanwhile, Shultz was meeting with the other MNF foreign ministers in
Paris. In a memo to Reagan discussing the meeting, Shultz was upbeat about the

continued MNF mission, saying, "The meeting, in my view, was successful, with my three counterparts firm on the need to demonstrate to our publics and the world-at-large that we will not be intimidated by terrorism." While the French, British, and Italians were ready to keep their MNF contingents in Beirut, they were concerned that the U.S. "not act precipitously." Shultz told the group that the Administration was "still evaluating the intelligence, but that in light of reports that those in Lebanon responsible might strike again, any U.S. response was less reprisal than self-defense." Despite this difference, they unanimously agreed that the ultimate path to security depended on the success of the political process in Lebanon, the reconciliation of the various Lebanese factions, and the removal of all foreign (i.e., Israeli, Iranian, and Syrian) forces from Lebanon.[104]

On October 28, the president approved a draft directive, which he signed the following day as NSDD-111. This document authorized renewed strategic cooperation with Israel and increased the amount of American military and financial aid going to that country. It also modified the Rules of Engagement for the Marines, expanding their ability to support the LAF outside the Suq-al Gharb, including "LAF positions controlling strategic arteries to Beirut . . . in danger of being overrun by hostile forces."[105]

Two days later, Deputy Secretary of State Kenneth Dam appeared on the news program *Face the Nation* and disclosed the existence of "circumstantial evidence" of "rather deep Iranian involvement" in the bombing. He continued, "We certainly believe the Syrians must have been cognizant of what was going on," and issued a veiled threat to the terrorists, saying, "Retaliation comes in many shapes and sizes, and we're looking at all of the options."[106]

In response, Syrian Foreign Minister Faruq Ash-Shar' said that the accusations against Syria were "not based on tangible evidence" and warned of the "consequences" of any retaliation. He claimed that the Reagan administration was trying to exploit the bombing "to carry out a prepared plan of aggression against Syria." He concluded by saying, "Supposing that—and this is very likely—that those who have carried out the bombing attacks had no connection whatsoever with any state and that their connection was only with God. In this case the American Administration should retaliate against God."[107]

Likewise, in a meeting between the American Ambassador to Damascus Robert Paganelli and Syrian Chief of Staff General Hikmat Shihabi, the Syrian claimed his government had no prior knowledge of the attack and did not condone or approve of such actions. Paganelli responded by saying the U.S. did not believe that "an operation of this magnitude and sophistication could not, repeat, could not have happened without the Syrians knowing about it in some way, given the ubiquitous Syrian presence in Lebanon." He noted the probable Iranian connection, but said that the "Iranian presence in Lebanon was possible only because the Syrian government permitted it and sustained it logistically." He said that Syria had the power to get the Iranians out, and that the U.S. had repeatedly asked them to do so; their continued presence and troublemaking in Lebanon indicated that the Syrian government acquiesced in their activities.[108]

Meanwhile, the intelligence community's effort to determine who attacked the Marines was paying off. Ultimately, the CIA was able to conclude, "The bombings on October 23 of the United States and French MNF headquarters were carried out by Shia radicals armed, trained and directed by Syria and Iran."[109] This conclusion was reached by compiling an overwhelming amount of intelligence:

1. A National Security Agency intercept showed that the Iranian Foreign Ministry had ordered the Iranian Ambassador to Damascus Ali Akbar Muhtashamipur to conduct a major attack against an American target in Lebanon.

2. Another intercept on October 22 showed that Muhtashamipur in turn had ordered Abu Haydar Musawi, the leader of the previously unknown group called the Husayni Suicide Forces, to obtain weapons from Yasser Arafat's Fatah organization and "undertake an extraordinary attack against the U.S. Marines."

3. DCI Casey contacted the Israeli intelligence agency Mossad and asked them to investigate the bombing. The Israelis came back with information showing that the Iranian Embassy in Damascus had paid fifty-thousand dollars to a Lebanese man named Hassan Hamiz. The money that financed the attack came from Iran, and was funneled to Hezbollah by Ali Akbar Muhtashamipur.

4. The Mossad also identified two planners of the attack: a Syrian intelligence lieutenant colonel and a "grandfatherly man with a black turban and brown robes," who was later identified as Sheikh Mohammad Husayn Fadlallah, Hezbollah's spiritual leader.

5. Intelligence also showed that the Syrian officer in charge of operations in Lebanon, Colonel Ghazi Caanan, had approved and coordinated the bombing.

6. The CIA discovered that the Husayni Suicide Forces had conducted the attack. This group was under the command of the Iranian Revolutionary Guard in Baalbek. In an interview with *The Times of London* on October 28, Musawi denied responsibility for the bombings, but he went on to praise the bombers, saying, "I personally consider this deed is a good deed which God loves and which his prophet—may God praise his name—loves. I bow before the souls of the martyrs who carried out this operation." He concluded by saying that he hoped to participate in future "operations."

7. Still another intercept showed that the Iranian Revolutionary Guards in Baalbek had requested permission from the Iranian embassy in Damascus to conduct the attack.

8. Another individual connected to the bombing was Immad al-Haj Mugniyeh, the security chief for Hezbollah. It was believed that he also masterminded the Embassy bombing in April.

9. A week before the bombing, Hosein Sheikholislam, a member of the Iranian Foreign Ministry and a leader of the 1980 takeover of the American embassy in Tehran, visited Damascus, and departed on October 22.

10. The Lebanese intelligence service reported that the Iranian embassy in Beirut was evacuated just *before* the bombing, indicating that they knew something was about to happen. This report was confirmed by the French Commander in Beirut, whose headquarters was directly across the street from the Iranian embassy. He told General Kelley that "of the twelve persons who departed rapidly from the Iranian Embassy within 15 minutes of the attacks (fully clothed and in a hurry), ten have been identified as Syrian military officers."

11. The FBI's investigation showed that a powerful plastic explosive, PETN, had been used to blow up the Marine barracks, while another plastic explosive, hexogen, had been used to destroy the French MNH headquarters. Both compounds were extremely difficult to obtain outside of military channels, which implied the involvement of a government.

12. According to the French newspaper *Canard Enchaine*, Iranian military officers not sympathetic to the Ayatollah's regime warned French intelligence services several weeks before the bombings that six terrorists had left Iran to carry out attacks against French targets in Beirut. The French apparently thought the attacks would be aimed at the embassy and not the MNF. French Defense Ministry officials indicated that the attacks had been organized by the Syrians and carried out by Iranians.[110]

Because of this and other evidence, the State Department placed Iran on its official list of terrorist states on January 18, 1984.

During late 1983, the NSC staff was working on options to curtail Syria's influence in Lebanon. One proposal examined by Donald Fortier and Philip Dur was an unofficial position paper suggesting that the United States encourage Turkey to destabilize Syria. It reads in part: "When Assad challenges Israel and the Marines in Lebanon, he knows that if Israel attacks him it cannot occupy all of Syria. Assad feels he can always retreat to the North and set up a smaller state and with stronger Alawite control. However, if Turkey is brought into the calculations of Rifaat [Assad] (the real power in Syria) and Hafez (the President of Syria) their calculations will be totally different and would be impossible to add up without losing their power. If Syria is attacked by Turkey from the north the Alawite stronghold will be gone at the start and Assad and his supporters will have to fall back on an ocean of hateful Sunni moslems in the south where they will be eaten like lost sheep. Therefore the pressure on Syria should come from Turkey and not from the Marines and or Israel."[111] Another proposal was floated to bomb the Iranian embassy in Damascus.[112] However, neither proposal ever got past the initial discussion stage.

As planning for a retaliatory strike in Lebanon's Bekaa Valley continued, Reagan resumed his normal schedule. From November 9 to 14, the president was out of the country, paying state visits to Japan and South Korea. McFarlane accompanied the president on the trip, and upon returning, asked Poindexter how the planning was progressing. Poindexter told him that "everything's pretty much ready to go," although Weinberger could be a problem.[113]

On November 10, Syrian forces had fired SAM-5 surface-to-air missiles at an American F-14 over Lebanon. Although the Syrians missed, this was still a new and unprecedented escalation—and one that was directly attributable to Damascus. However, Weinberger was loath to see American involvement deepen in Lebanon, and did all he could to keep public opinion from demanding a military response. When asked about the incident, the secretary of defense said he did not think the latest attack was "unusual or surprising," and did not think it was any sort of an escalation. While he was claiming that the U.S. did not know if the Syrians had done the firing, Damascus announced that it had indeed fired on American warplanes that day.[114]

Two days later, the French government announced that they had reached a common conclusion with the U.S. government about who was responsible for the bombings on October 23. After extensive intelligence sharing, the French said it was definitely Musawi and Hezbollah.[115]

## The Retaliation Plan

The plan to launch retaliatory strikes was developed by Deputy CNO Vice Admiral James "Ace" Lyons and Rear Admiral Jerry Tuttle, the commander of Sixth Fleet, then in the eastern Mediterranean.[116] In preparation for the attack, two additional carriers were ordered to the Mediterranean on November 5—the *Independence* and the *John F. Kennedy*. The European Command's General Lawson explained that "the Navy staff came up with the idea that the only thing that was needed was to go bomb Baalbek into oblivion," using planes launched from French and American carriers.[117] The specific target was the Sheik Abdullah barracks, home of Iran's Revolutionary Guards and Hezbollah.[118]

On November 14, Shultz announced that the administration would no longer discuss retaliation against the terrorists, which was a standard ploy that the government used, in effect a press blackout, before commencing a major operation. When Reagan returned from his trip to Asia later that day, the NSPG met to discuss the retaliatory option. Present were Reagan, Bush, Daniel Murphy (from the vice president's office), Shultz, Eagleburger, Weinberger, Casey, Vessey, Admiral Art Moreau, Meese, Baker, McFarlane, and Poindexter.[119] In addition to the Sheikh Abdullah barracks, the intelligence community had identified a specific target—a hotel in Baalbek used by Musawi's group. By using video footage shot by CBS News, they were even able to identify the floor of the hotel where the terrorists lived. General Vessey told Reagan that the Navy plan was ready to go, and that smart bombs would be used to pinpoint-target the specific hotel floor, thus keeping collateral damage to a minimum. However, he cautioned that there was a chance that some American planes could be shot down by the recently upgraded Syrian anti-aircraft sites, and that the attack would increase the probability that the Marines still in Beirut would be targets of more terrorism. Despite these warnings, Reagan gave the go-ahead for the strike, ordering it to proceed on November 16.[120]

Weinberger said the operation would proceed, but raised one reservation, saying he "would monitor the situation for developments that might require a change in plans." Reagan could not imagine anything like that happening. Still, Weinberger indicated he would "keep an eye on it."[121]

Following the meeting, McFarlane and Poindexter were worried that Weinberger might find a reason to delay the attack. So Poindexter sent a cable to the military advisor to French President François Mitterrand indicating that Reagan had given the go-ahead.[122]

At this point in the story, there are two versions of what happened next.

## Version Number One

In the first version, Poindexter recalls, "There's no doubt in my mind that the President, in Cap and Jack Vessey's presence, approved the cooperation with the French and carrying out a raid when the forces were ready."[123] This version holds that Vessey did in fact send the strike plan to the Sixth Fleet by secret courier, with a copy to EuCom's General Bernard Rogers.[124]

On November 15, the commander of the Sixth Fleet, Admiral Tuttle, sent a message through EuCom that his forces were ready to conduct the attack and requested authority to proceed. The next morning, McFarlane was waiting for news that the attack had begun. When he spoke by phone with someone from the White House Situation Room, he was told that the attack was still on, the carriers *Eisenhower* and *Kennedy* were poised to strike, but the Pentagon had not yet issued the execute order. Howard Teicher recalled that Reagan had in fact directed that an execute order be issued, but it never was.[125]

When McFarlane reached the White House, he was told that the execute order still had not been sent. Poindexter lamented, "I don't think they're going to do it." A short time later, Vice Admiral Art Moreau, the assistant to General Vessey, phoned Poindexter and informed him that Weinberger had ordered the fleet to "stand down."[126]

At around 6:30 am EST, Weinberger called McFarlane and said, "Well, I have decided that we really ought not to go ahead with this. There are complications."

"Cap, what has gone wrong?" asked McFarlane.

"No, Bud, there are just too many factors here that are uncertain and I do not believe it is prudent to go," replied Weinberger.[127] "We just weren't ready. We needed more time."[128]

"The President isn't going to be able to understand this, Cap. You were there. You saw how strongly he felt about this," replied McFarlane.

Weinberger countered, "I'll be glad to talk to him. But I thought it was the wrong thing to do."

After ending the conversation with Weinberger, McFarlane went to see the president and told him what had happened. "I don't understand. Why didn't they do it?" asked Reagan.

"There's no excuse for it, Mr. President," replied McFarlane. "You approved this operation, and Cap decided not to carry it out. The credibility of the United States in Damascus just went to zero. There's no justification. The Secretary of Defense was wrong, and you ought to make clear to him how you feel about it."

At this point, the president wavered. "Gosh, that's really disappointing. That's terrible. We should have blown the daylights out of them. I just don't understand." He never called Weinberger to demand an explanation.[129]

Those who had supported the retaliatory strike were upset, including the president. However, one top aide later said, "But he didn't pick up the phone and say, 'What has gone wrong and why?' He was visibly sighing and head shaking, but he's not the kind of person who would ever strongly discipline anybody."[130]

Despite the American stand-down, the French did attack, using planes from the carrier *Clemenceau* to attack the Sheikh Abdullah barracks and the hotel used by Musawi as his headquarters in the Bekaa Valley. The Israelis, who suffered a suicide bombing attack on the IDF in Tyre on November 4, also retaliated.[131]

## Version Number Two

The second version claims that at the last minute, the president canceled the mission. In his memoirs, Reagan explains,

Our intelligence experts found it difficult to establish conclusively who were responsible for the attack on the barracks. Although several air strikes were planned against possible culprits, I canceled them because our experts said they were not absolutely sure they were the right targets. I didn't want to kill innocent people.[132]

In an interview with *U.S. News and World Report* on December 15, 1983, Reagan lamented, "One of the hardest things . . . is to prove that the terrorist attacks are sponsored by a government. For example, these groups that are taking credit for the recent suicide attacks are believed to have an Iranian connection."[133]

General Vessey did his utmost to slow momentum toward a retaliatory strike. Even after State Department officials had gone on record saying they believed Iran and Syria were responsible, Vessey appeared on *Meet the Press* and declared, "I really don't know who did it. . . . I wish I did."[134] The general also claims that he was notified at the last minute about the proposed attack—so late in fact, "that there wasn't time even to write alerting messages and get them out" to the Sixth Fleet. Vessey denies that Reagan ever gave an execute order.[135]

While Reagan says he called off the attack, Weinberger claims to have "no memory" of the president even coming close to ordering an attack. He says that there were "some discussions in a very inconclusive way of possibly taking an air raid, some sort of a single shot raid, just to do some damage in Baalbek."[136] On the morning of November 16, Weinberger recounts a phone call from the French defense minister, Charles Hernu, who told the secretary of defense that French planes were about to launch airstrikes against Syrian positions in the Bekaa Valley. Weinberger says he wished the French good luck and added, "Unfortunately, it is a bit too late for us to join you in this one."[137]

## Another Military Option

Within five days of the attack on the Marines, General Vessey ordered another ISA team to Beirut to prepare recommendations for ways in which the United States could retaliate against the terrorists responsible for the barracks bombing. However, due to bureaucratic red tape, the group did not depart for Lebanon until early December.[138]

Once in Beirut, the ISA team worked closely with CIA station chief William Buckley to put together a "comprehensive list of military retaliatory options that our Beirut experience indicated were possible." These options included intelligence operations that would compromise the operational security of Musawi's organization, as well as specific proposals for the "precise use of military force against select targets," such as Syrian anti-aircraft sites and the residence of Sheik Fadlallah. Each proposal took into account, and largely ruled out, the possibility of significant collateral damage.[139] The team also laid the groundwork for the introduction of special operations forces in Beirut for missions against Fadlallah and Musawi.[140]

Before departing Beirut in mid-January 1984, the team briefed Buckley on their recommendations. The station chief supported the proposals, as did the deputy CINC of EuCom, General Lawson. Not everyone was happy with the report though; it was met with antagonism in the Pentagon, where a two-star admiral was reportedly "beside himself" over the plan. After the leader of the ISA team briefed director of the White House Military Office Edward Hickey on the report, the White House staffer observed, "You know, if the President knew about your recommendations, he would order them to be done. The President is not afraid to take action. Unfortunately, they'll never make it to his office. They," indicating the senior staff at the Pentagon, "will never let it get through the bureaucracy." The report was quickly buried as the debate in Washington shifted from a retaliatory strike to the Marine pullout.[141]

Continued Syrian attempts to shoot down American warplanes led to another NSPG meeting on December 1, attended by Reagan, Bush, Shultz, Donald Rumsfeld (the new Middle East envoy), Weinberger, Vessey, Casey, UN Ambassador Jeane Kirkpatrick, Meese, Baker, Deaver, and McFarlane.[142] During the meeting, Reagan authorized new rules of engagement for the Marines, termed "vigorous self-defense," in which "Responsive attacks will be used to destroy targets originating fire if this can be done with minimum collateral damage." In a draft NSDD agreed to by Kirkpatrick, Shultz, and Casey, the new rules stated, "In the event the above action can not be carried out due to risk of collateral damage or lack of precise information on the source of fire, destructive fire will be directed against discrete military targets associated with known hostile forces, including PSP and Syrian military targets in unpopulated areas of Lebanon."[143] The NSPG met again the next day to continue deliberations on NSDD-117, which was subsequently approved. On December 3, the Syrians fired again on American warplanes conducting reconnaissance over Lebanon and this time the U.S. responded. Later that day General Vessey met with Reagan at Camp David and recommended a strike against Syrian anti-aircraft sites. The president, still perhaps smarting over his administration's non-response to the Marine bombing, approved the retaliatory strike. According to one of his advisors, Reagan thought, "the Pentagon would kick the shit out of the Syrians" this time.[144] American naval forces launched a retaliatory raid on December 4, but it was not the overwhelming attack Reagan had envisioned. Instead, it was a small, haphazard attack, resulting in the loss of two American planes, the death of one pilot, and the capture of another by Syrian forces. Jesse Jackson eventually secured the pilot's freedom during a mission to Damascus.[145]

### Retreat

In reality, the president had three options in the aftermath of the Marine barracks bombing. First, the United States could "soldier on" with its efforts to find a diplomatic solution that would allow the Marines to withdraw from a "stabilized" Lebanon. Second, it could enlarge the peacekeeping mission of the Marines and its role supporting the Gemeyel regime. Third, the Marines could be withdrawn.[146]

Throughout November and December, Reagan and Shultz defended the mission, declaring that the United States was not going to abandon the Lebanese government. Shultz claimed that "If we are driven out of Lebanon, the message will be sent that relying on the Soviet Union pays off and that relying on the United States is fatal."[147] However, extensive rhetoric to the contrary, the groundwork was already being laid for the Marines' withdrawal.

Inside the White House there were fears—as early as the first week of November—that the American presence in Lebanon could be Reagan's political undoing. Comparing the situation to Carter's Iran disaster, the president's political advisors, especially Chief of Staff James Baker, his deputy Michael Deaver, and Senate Majority Leader Howard Baker, believed that public support for the president's Lebanon policy would be temporary, a manifestation of rallying around the flag.[148] They believed that as time passed, this support would dissipate, and the Democrats would then use the issue to defeat Reagan and Republican congressional candidates in the 1984 election.[149] Because of this, they counseled Reagan to get the Marines out of Lebanon right away.[150] As McFarlane put it later, a presidential election "does concentrate your mind."[151]

Reagan was clearly conflicted over the Marine presence. Time after time he had stated the importance of the mission and his intent to stay the course. However, on December 14, he created some wiggle room for himself in the event that he ordered a withdrawal. At a news conference the president conceded, "If there was such a collapse of order that it was absolutely certain that there was no solution to the problem in Lebanon," he would pull the Marines out. On January 3, he was still defending his policy, responding to concerns raised by House Speaker Tip O'Neill, saying, "He may be ready to surrender, but I'm not." In his February 4 weekly radio address, he again argued that there was "no reason to turn our backs and to cut and to run."

The situation at the Pentagon was quite different. Weinberger and the chiefs had never wanted the Marines sent to Beirut in the first place, and for months had been advocating a pullout. In December, Weinberger tasked Assistant Secretary of Defense Richard Armitage to prepare a study reassessing U.S. policy objectives in Lebanon and to propose how those objectives might be attained. Armitage produced a paper entitled, "Strategy for Disengagement in Lebanon."[152] There was no question about the Pentagon's position.

Also in mid-December, a number of subcabinet officials—Dr. Fred Iklé, Richard Armitage, and Vice Admiral Art Moreau (all from Defense), Ambassador Richard Murphy and Rear Admiral Jonathan Howe (from State), and Admiral Poindexter (from the NSC staff)—met informally to discuss the Lebanon situation, to review options, and to make recommendations. The consensus position was to withdraw the Marines.[153] After conferring with their principals, the group wrote an unofficial "nonpaper" in which they concluded that the May 17 Agreement between Israel and Lebanon was not working and "the solution to the Lebanese crisis was not to be found through a continued or increased employment of American military force."[154] The paper did not reflect consensus at the top levels of government, but did indicate that the lower, subcabinet levels were reconciling themselves with the inevitable.

At the same time, McFarlane was still searching for ways to salvage the mission. At a subcabinet meeting on December 24, McFarlane presented a proposal written by Dennis Ross, the Pentagon's deputy director of the Office of Net Assessment, which argued that the best the U.S. could hope for in Lebanon was to negotiate some concessions from Syria, in return for which the U.S. would offer to withdraw the Marines. For this to work though, President Assad had to be convinced that without these concessions, the Marines were going to stay for the long haul. Consequently, McFarlane argued in favor of moving the Marines to a more defensible location, but still on the ground in Beirut.

Weinberger's opposition killed that idea. He and the Joint Chiefs wanted the Marines out of Lebanon altogether. By January, Richard Armitage explained, "We were desperate to get out. If we could get [the Marines] on the ships, we could see no reason why we would ever have to return."[155]

Congress was becoming a factor as well. Although they had authorized an additional eighteen-month deployment shortly before the bombing, both sides of the aisle were now saying that the mission should end. In mid-December, congressional Democrats began pushing Speaker O'Neill to put the Marine mission in Beirut "at the top of the agenda of issues to be discussed during the second session,"[156] and Dante Fascell, the acting chairman of the committee on Foreign Affairs, talked about "assert[ing] Congressional authority" over the mission.[157] On December 19, the House Armed Services Committee released the findings of its investigation into the bombing. It concluded that the administration should thoroughly review its policy in Lebanon "from the standpoint of how the Marine mission fits into the policy to determine if continued deployment of the Marine unit, as part of the Multinational Force (MNF) of French, British, and American units is justified."[158] The committee also issued a veiled warning to Reagan, saying, "The failure of the administration to adequately reexamine its policy and relate it to present conditions will only mean that such reexamination will have to be done by the Congress."[159] This pressure on the administration was compounded by public opinion polls showing that 57 percent of Americans wanted the Marines out.[160]

Also adding pressure was an inquiry into the attack conducted by the Pentagon. Following the bombing, Secretary of the Navy John Lehman wanted the Navy to investigate the bombing. He discussed the idea with General Kelley, who said that since placing responsibility for preventing the bombing meant investigating overlapping jurisdictions (and multiple services), Weinberger was the one who should decide who would conduct the investigation. Lehman finally agreed, and the proposal was forwarded to the secretary of defense.[161] On November 7, Weinberger impaneled the Department of Defense Commission on the Beirut International Airport (BIA) Terrorist Act of 23 October 1983, also known as the Long Commission. The commission, chaired by retired Admiral Robert Long, issued its report on December 20, and was critical of the way the Marines were deployed in Lebanon, as well as of the administration's overall counter-terrorism policy. It concluded that the Marines in Beirut were "not trained, organized, staffed, or supported to deal effectively with the terrorist threat in Lebanon."[162] Another problem cited was the lack of sufficient and timely intelligence tailored to the specific needs of the commanding officer of the Marine contingent in Beirut. The commission recommended, just as the ISA report had after the Embassy bombing in April, the creation of an all-source fusion center that would provide "all-source intelligence support to U.S. military commanders involved in military operations in areas of high threat, conflict, or crisis." It also argued that the United States needed "an active policy" to combat terrorism since "a reactive policy only forfeits the initiative to the terrorists."[163] Lastly, it called on the Reagan administration to reexamine the means of achieving its objectives in Lebanon.

McFarlane later explained how the deteriorating situation in Lebanon changed his position on the Marine mission. "Gently but persistently, Jim [Baker] began to say, 'Bud, what is the light at the end of the tunnel here?' And I had to tell him, 'There really isn't any.'"[164] With a military escalation ruled out and pressure building from all quarters to pull the Marines out, Reagan's National Security Advisor reexamined the options open to the administration. McFarlane "recommended to the President that, since we could not go to war with Syria, that we ought to get out of there. I did feel that there was a way we could have gotten out that would have preserved our interests, and

I still think that, had it not been for the total collapse of Lebanon's Army, that we could have. But it did collapse and I think I should have recognized the inevitability of that collapse perhaps earlier on."[165]

On January 3, 1984, the NSPG met to discuss the administration's "next steps in Lebanon." Present were Reagan, Donald Gregg (from Bush's office), Shultz, Rumsfeld, Dam, Weinberger, Iklé, Casey, Vessey, Moreau, Kirkpatrick, Alton Keel (from OMB), Baker, Deaver, James Jenkins (White House staff), McFarlane, Fortier (NSC staff), and Kemp.[166] Among the topics discussed were: a reassessment of short-term and long-term goals in Lebanon, the security of the Marines in Beirut, the proposed JCS plan to redeploy the Marines, and an assessment of the effectiveness of the LAF.[167] McFarlane also expressed his concern about leaks to the press, telling the group, "I am pretty mad about the way we have been backed into a situation so that we are reduced to considering redeployment of our forces in Lebanon in *response* to a public debate stimulated by leaks from within our government. Let me give you two recent examples: There were detailed stories in the press about the contents of the Long Commission Report *before I'd ever seen it* and today the press has details of the JCS proposals on the redeployment of the Marines *which we are meant to be considering at this meeting*."[168]

After a visit to the region, Rumsfeld came down in favor of withdrawal. His rationale, though, differed significantly from that of the Pentagon and the White House. Rumsfeld and his aide Howard Teicher believed that the U.S. still had a role to play in Lebanon, but that the Marines were no longer a part of the administration's strategy—they were just sitting ducks. And since the Pentagon would not allow the troops to move beyond the airport, they were no longer a part of the power equation in Lebanon. As Peter Rodman later explained it, "The power that was relevant was offshore. So the sensible strategy was to pull the Marines out and simultaneously expand the [Navy's rules of engagement to] shape the outcome of this battle" between the Lebanese Army and its enemies.[169]

By mid-January, even though Shultz was virtually the last member of the administration still pushing to keep the Marines in Beirut, he seems to have believed that his position would soon prevail. During a meeting with French Foreign Minister Cheysson in Stockholm, Shultz told his counterpart that "the U.S. support for maintaining participation in the Multinational Force was strengthening again after some weakening in the aftermath of the Long Commission Report," and that Reagan's resolution on this matter was still strong. He continued, "Those in the U.S. who advocated the withdrawal . . . would find that they had made a mistake." Cheysson said that public opinion in France would not affect their involvement, but he had no illusions about the other MNF partners, observing "there were already strong pressures within both Italy and Britain to pull out and such pressures could come again in the United States."[170]

On January 21, Reagan's senior advisors met to discuss the proposed withdrawal. Weinberger argued that the Marines should be pulled out immediately since there were no constructive military options left. Baker, Deaver, and Meese agreed with the secretary of defense. Shultz must have finally seen the writing on the wall, advocating an intense naval bombardment against Syrian positions *after* the withdrawal.[171]

On January 26, the NSC met to debate a JCS plan for moving the troops offshore, and the NSPG met on February 1 for a follow-up discussion. By now, redeployment was truly gaining momentum. Weinberger continued his attack, using the Long Commission Report to support his argument for the immediate withdrawal of the Marines. Shultz was out of the country in early February, so Eagleburger represented the State Department at the NSPG meeting. He insisted that to pull out would send the wrong message, but Reagan remained noncommittal.[172] Later that day though, the pullout was accepted in principle and codified when Reagan signed NSDD-123. In it he ordered "The Secretary of Defense and the Chairman, JCS, in coordination with the Secretary of State [to] develop, for the President's review, a proposed timetable for the phase down of the USMNF military personnel ashore and a plan for the continuing U.S. military presence offshore."[173]

Also on February 1, the House of Representatives ratcheted up the pressure on Reagan, passing a non-binding resolution calling for the "prompt and orderly" withdrawal of the Marines. Polls show that in early February, 74 percent of Americans wanted the Marines withdrawn.[174] Although the congressional action increased political pressure on the administration to withdraw, the final blow to American participation in the MNF was the deterioration of events in Lebanon during the first week of February. The LAF and the Gemeyel government collapsed, leaving the Marines without a government or army to support. These events, combined with the constant fighting between Weinberger and Shultz, led McFarlane to finally agree that the Marines should come home. Subsequently, on February 7, Weinberger and McFarlane convened a meeting of the NSPG to discuss the withdrawal option once again. A still undecided Reagan was on his way to Santa Barbara for vacation, and did not attend the meeting. In addition, the lone stalwart in favor of staying was not at the table that day; Shultz was on a trip to Grenada. In his stead, Under Secretary of State Eagleburger attended and argued again for keeping the troops in Beirut, claiming that a pullout would damage American credibility throughout the world. However, the rest of the group, including Vice President Bush, concluded that it was now time to withdraw the Marines. Weinberger recommended calling it a "redeployment" instead of a withdrawal or a retreat—a semantic wordplay intended to mask the reality of the action. That way, he suggested, American forces would be at the ready to go back in if they were needed. Regardless of what it was called, the plan called for the Marines to withdraw from their positions at the airport to ships offshore. Everyone also recognized that once the Marines had departed, there was no way they would be allowed to go back in. When the meeting ended, Bush called Reagan aboard Air Force One and told him that everyone except State thought the Marines should go.[175]

Completing his about-face on Lebanon, the president accepted the recommendation and ordered the withdrawal.[176] Within days, the administration notified the British, French, and Italian governments that the U.S. was pulling out of Beirut. This came as no surprise, as these governments had already reached similar decisions. The British pulled out on February 7, the Italians were gone by February 21, and the Marines were out by February 26. As the Americans withdrew, the battleship *New Jersey* pummeled the Shouf in a final spasm of violence.

Sometime between February 7 and the day the Marines finally withdrew, Reagan sat down and penned an explanation for the mission and his rationale for pulling them out. In the opening he pondered whether or not the efforts and the cost in American blood had served a useful purpose. He thought so, justifying the mission in terms of Israel's security and the peace process. But it is also clear that personal stories of tragedy helped push the president to support a "presence" mission whose purpose was to establish security and stability:

> It is almost impossible for us to imagine the savagery to which the people of Beirut had been subjected and what a change was made by our presence. A young woman sent me a letter her sweetheart had smuggled out with someone leaving Beirut. He told her of the terror and hardship when the fighting had been going on— 17 days straight living in the cellar. Then he told of the difference our Marines had made. He added, without them there would have been a massacre of all the Christians in Beirut. . . .
>
> A woman wrote a letter to me that her daughter had only been able to go to school 2 out of the previous 8 years. She then wrote that because of our Marines her daughter could at least live a normal life.

He believed that the Syrians were responsible for the failure of the peace plan, and said that the Marines were now coming home "because they did all that could be done."[177]

## The Aftermath

The bombing of the embassy, followed by the Marine barracks disaster, deeply affected Reagan and his entire staff. The failure to respond to these attacks was unacceptable to many in the administration, and a small group of officials set out to change the American approach. Although these attacks, and the great loss of American life, set the stage for a change in policy, it was actually an attack with no American casualties that convinced Reagan that his administration's counter-terrorism policy needed a reevaluation.

In the summer of 1983, Armenian terrorists attacked the Turkish embassy in Lisbon, killing seven. No Americans were killed or injured in the attack, but when Reagan saw the carnage, he reacted emotionally. As Noel Koch recalled, "A mother and a child were involved and the President just didn't like it. So [Reagan] said, 'That's it. We're going to work with other governments and put a stop to this once and for all.' So I called Ollie and said, 'Let's do something with this—let's start to push it.' And [North] said, 'I'm already on it.'"[178]

North drew up a draft NSDD that included a provision authorizing covert operations that would "neutralize" terrorists. Considering the prohibition on assassination contained in Executive Order 12333, this provision appeared to some, including deputy director of the CIA John McMahon, to be illegal.[179] But the March 16, 1984 kidnapping of William Buckley, the CIA station chief in Beirut, seems to have pushed CIA Director William Casey firmly to Shultz's position that force should be used in response to terrorism. Based on advice from CIA chief counsel Stanley Sporkin, Casey overrode McMahon's objections. The DCI allowed the language to stay because, according to Sporkin's opinion, neutralizing terrorists was not the same as assassination; assassination only meant the killing of foreign political leaders.[180]

While the NSDD was being drafted and debated, Shultz sponsored a terrorism discussion on March 24, inviting all of the senior administration officials and five outside experts to participate. Those in attendance included Shultz, Weinberger, FBI Director William Webster, DDI Robert Gates, Meese, General Witt Rice (from Joint Special Operations Agency), Koch, Kenneth Dam (from State), and Poindexter. The group recognized that there had been significant problems coordinating a response in the past, and sought common ground to base future responses upon. Koch characterized the effort as "a watershed meeting, after which the whole tenor and tone of the Administration's anti-terrorism policy shifted substantially."[181]

Reagan signed the new NSDD, numbered 138, on April 3. However, this version did not have the "neutralize" terminology that had been proposed by North and endorsed by Casey. Nonetheless, NSDD-138 was a seminal shift in the administration's officially sanctioned approach to terrorism, with a preamble declaring that "the U.S. government considers the practice of terrorism by any person or group in any cause a threat to our national security." It went on to declare, "States that use or support terrorism cannot be allowed to do so without consequences . . . the United States has the right to defend itself." To accomplish this, it authorized the FBI and the CIA to establish top-secret paramilitary units to join the Pentagon's special operations forces in undertaking guerrilla warfare against terrorists. It authorized the use of sabotage, killing (though not "neutralization" or assassination), preemptive and retaliatory strikes, deception, and expanded the intelligence community's responsibility and power to collect information on terrorists. These new efforts were to focus especially against state sponsors of terrorism, including Iran, Libya, Cuba, Nicaragua, North Korea, and the Soviet Union. Koch described the new policy as "a quantum leap in countering terrorism."[182]

In an effort to alter the public's opinions about terrorism and the appropriate methods of governmental response, Shultz embarked on an offensive that included a series of important speeches. On the day NSDD-138 was signed, the secretary of state gave a speech entitled "Power and Diplomacy in the 1980s" to the Trilateral Commission. In it, he subtly criticized the approach of Weinberger and the JCS, saying, "It is increasingly doubtful that a purely passive strategy can even begin to cope with the problem of terrorism." Instead, he advocated a proactive approach, arguing, "It is more and more appropriate that the nations of the West face up to the need for an active defense against terrorism."[183]

With this, the split within the administration had gone public, and both Weinberger and Bush publicly questioned Shultz's approach. In response, Shultz gave a speech at the Jonathan Institute on June 14 in which he asked, "Can we as a country—can the community of free nations—stand in a solely defensive posture and absorb the blows dealt by the terrorists?" Expanding on the concept of proactive counter-terrorism he continued, "I think not. From a practical standpoint, a purely passive defense does not provide enough of a deterrent to terrorism and the states that sponsor it. It is time to think long, hard, and seriously about more active means of defense—about defense through appropriate preventative or preemptive actions against terrorist groups before they strike."[184]

Shultz's efforts did not go unanswered. The first to respond were the terrorists in Lebanon. As if to drive home the impotence of American counter-terrorism policy, on September 20, a vehicle loaded with explosives weaved its way through an elaborate set of concrete "dragon's teeth" intended to slow down would-be attackers, and destroyed the U.S. embassy annex at Aukar in East Beirut. The explosion killed 24, including two Americans.[185]

Overhead satellite photographs of the Bekaa Valley showed that Hezbollah had created a mock-up of the annex and had been practicing for the attack.[186] Intelligence also discovered that Iran had shipped explosives to Baalbek through its embassy in Syria just before the attack.[187] In addition, Islamic Jihad phoned Agence France-Presse and announced, "The operation goes to prove that we will carry out our previous promise not to allow a single American to remain on Lebanese soil." McFarlane believed the evidence was conclusive saying, "We had them dead to rights."[188]

Even with the new policy spelled out in NSDD-138, a debate ensued over how to respond. Despite the certainty of responsibility, the Pentagon opposed retaliation, claiming it would be difficult to hit the correct target. Military officials apparently advised against an attack because intelligence indicated that the Hezbollah leadership rarely met together, making airstrikes either inefficient if the U.S. went after the entire leadership (meaning a campaign of ongoing strikes), or ineffective since it was unlikely that one strike would hit all of the intended targets. The military also repeated its standard argument that such strikes would inevitably lead to high numbers of civilian casualties. They also opposed infiltrating special operations forces into Beirut to conduct more "surgical" strikes because it would be too difficult to pull off successfully. Meanwhile, Weinberger said that airstrikes "would damage America's real interests" (i.e., relations with the Arabs), and claimed that the evidence was not really as solid as McFarlane and Shultz claimed. He also argued that it was impossible to know if those who had perpetrated the attack were actually still at the Sheik Abdullah barracks; therefore, any such attack would likely miss the guilty party.[189] Additionally, Reagan's political advisors were not prepared to support a retaliatory strike less than two months before the 1984 election, especially after the disastrous operation against Syrian antiaircraft sites back in December. Opposition to a strike appears to have been so widespread that there were rumors Shultz was "chided" for "getting carried away in bringing" up the idea of retaliation.[190]

However, Shultz was not prepared to give up. On October 25, he gave perhaps his most eloquent speech on the topic before an audience at the Park Avenue Synagogue in New York City. Citing terrorism as a threat to democracy and modern civilization, he said, "The magnitude of the threat posed by terrorism is so great that we cannot afford to confront it with half-hearted and poorly organized measures." He cited a number of obstacles that had inhibited a robust response in the past, singling out confusion and "an Orwellian corruption of language" that obscures the public's understanding of terrorism. "How tragic it would be if democratic societies so lost confidence in their own moral legitimacy that they lost sight of the obvious: that violence directed against democracy or the hopes for democracy lacks fundamental justification." He continued by proposing that "It is time for this country to make a broad national commitment to treat the challenge of terrorism with the sense of urgency and priority it deserves . . . violence and aggression must be met by firm resistance." He praised Israel's strong, confident resort to force in the face of terrorism and said, "the rest of us would do well to follow Israel's example." In that vein he argued, "To combat [terror-ism], we must be willing to use military force" to retaliate for or to preempt terrorist attacks at a moment's notice. He concluded by saying,

> There will not be time for a renewed public debate after every terrorist attack.
> We may never have the kind of evidence that can stand up in an American court
> of law. But we cannot allow ourselves to become the Hamlet of nations, worry-
> ing endlessly over whether and how to respond. A great nation with global re-
> sponsibilities cannot afford to be hamstrung by confusion and indecisiveness.
> Fighting terrorism will not be a clean or pleasant contest, but we have no choice
> but to play it.[191]

Despite the obvious failure of the administration's response to terrorism in Lebanon, a number of administration officials continued to dissent from Shultz's press for a new, more proactive counter-terrorism policy. The day after Shultz's October speech, Vice President Bush took issue with some of Shultz's propos-als, saying, "We are not going to go out and bomb innocent civilians or some-thing of that nature. I don't think we ever get to the point where you kill 100 in-nocent women and children just to kill one terrorist. I don't think we have reached that point." Bush cited the need to avoid collateral damage as the main difficulty when contemplating retaliation.[192] While Shultz had not advocated killing scores of civilians in pursuit of a single terrorist, Bush's words effectively defined Shultz's approach as immoral and therefore, unacceptable.

Also dissenting was the hierarchy at the Pentagon. Back in May, Wein-berger had intended to respond to Shultz's Trilateral Commission speech with one of his own, but encountered considerable opposition. When General Kel-ley reviewed a draft of the speech, he objected to it because Weinberger's cri-teria for using force would give the enemy too much insight into how and when the U.S. would respond militarily. General Kelley explained, "What you're doing is telling the enemy okay, here's my road map. Let them won-der, let them wonder what the hell. Truthfully, let them wonder, don't give them all of the things which have to be done." Reagan also objected to the speech, and made Weinberger put off its delivery until after the election.[193] When the secretary of defense finally got his chance, he gave a speech that outlined what became the Weinberger doctrine (later the Powell doctrine— a set of six stringent tests or preconditions that had to be met before he would approve the use of force ([for the list, see Chapter 2])).[194] It was clear that the spirit of NSDD-138 had not yet taken root; Shultz and Weinberger were still diametrically opposed to one another on counter-terrorism policy.

Despite the split between his advisors, Reagan seems to have genuinely wanted to punish terrorists who killed Americans. On November 13, he took another step toward Shultz's position and signed an unnumbered and still classified NSDD. This new directive gave legal protection to covert teams that undertook "pre-emptive self defens[ive]" operations against terrorists in the event that some U.S. law or executive order was broken, such as the one barring assassination. Following the December hijacking of a Kuwaiti airliner in which two Americans were killed, Oliver North proposed to Poindexter that the U.S. "move quickly to place our experts on-scene in Beirut. . . . We could reap considerable benefit from a U.S.-assisted LAF strike against Hizb 'Allah [sic] as a response to the murders and atrocities perpetrated in the hijacking."[195] What came of this proposal is not known. However, on March 8, 1985, an attempt was made to assassinate Hezbollah's spiritual leader Sheik Fadlallah in Beirut. A car bomb exploded near the Bir al Abed mosque, killing 92 and injuring over 250, but missing Fadlallah. The bombing was traced to an American-trained squad of Lebanese; while the administration claimed that the operation was "unauthorized," the plan to go after terrorists using surrogates was subsequently "rescinded."[196]

Noel Koch lamented that NSDD-138 "was simply ignored. No part of it was ever implemented."[197] The fundamental reason that it failed was that the bureaucracy never wholly embraced the proactive approach. Indicative of this disagreement was a statement by Robert Sayre, the head of the Office of Counter-terrorism in Shultz's State Department. In August 1984 he argued that terrorism "is essentially a policy matter and not a military matter." Instead of responding forcefully, Sayre said that the best way to deal with terrorism was to deal with its "root causes," concluding that, "It is possible to deal with terrorism on a legal basis. There is no need to resort to extra-legal measures."[198]

This approach would be put to the test within a matter of months with the hijacking of TWA flight 847.

*Chapter Four*

# The Hijacking of TWA Flight 847

Salus populi suprema lex esto.[1]

—Cicero

## BACKGROUND

Lebanon has a long history of internecine violence, much of which stemmed from the problematic National Covenant of 1943. This agreement allocated government posts and seats in the National Assembly to various religious groups based on their percentage of the population from the 1932 census; in 1932 the ratio stood at six Christians to five Muslims. Over the next several decades, the Muslim growth rate outpaced that of the Christian population, but the allocation of governmental positions remained static. Muslims increasingly saw this situation as unfair and began agitating for change. Strains between the Muslim and Christian communities erupted into civil war in 1975. In 1976, the Syrians intervened, ostensibly to save the Christian militias from defeat, and have effectively controlled the Bekaa Valley ever since.

Shia Muslims, who make up some 40 percent of the Lebanese population, began trying to gain a larger share of representation in the government in 1974 when Sayyid Musa al-Sadr, the religious leader of the Shia, established the "Movement of the Disinherited."[2] The following year the movement formed a militia known as Amal (Arabic for "hope"), and in 1980, Nabih Barri, the Lebanese government's minister of justice, took the reigns of the new militia. Barri's ties with the West were extensive; his legal education took place in Paris, his ex-wife and children lived near Detroit, and he owned a second home in Michigan. Within a few years of Barri's takeover, Amal splintered, with Islamic Amal, Hezbollah, and Islamic Jihad—all Shia organizations supported by Iran—going their separate ways. The primary difference of opinion was over the future shape of Lebanon, with Barri and Amal committed to a secular Lebanon, while the other groups wanted to create an Islamic republic based on the Iranian model. Amal's primary goal was to gain more power for the Shiites in Lebanon, and Barri sought to do this by dominating and politically unifying West Beirut. When the U.S. Marines pulled out of Lebanon in 1984, Amal seized the Beirut airport and systematically eliminated Muslim opposition in the city. At the same time, Barri worked to consolidate his control over the other Shia factions in Beirut by attempting to bridge the gap between the moderates and the Iranian-backed radicals.

During Israel's 1982 invasion of southern Lebanon, the Israeli military detained thousands of Lebanese and Palestinians, initially holding them at Ansar, Lebanon. When the Israeli Defense Forces withdrew from Beirut and portions of southern Lebanon in September 1983, they moved some 700 to 800 detainees from Lebanon to a prison at Atlit, Israel, and in November began the first of several prisoner exchanges, swapping 4,500 Lebanese and Palestinians for six Israelis. In June 1984, through the good offices of the International Committee of the Red Cross, Israel swapped 291 Syrian prisoners of war, 21 other prisoners, and the remains of 70 Syrian soldiers for 6 Israeli soldiers and the bodies of 5 more. Then on May 20, 1985, the Israeli government agreed to an exchange with the Popular Front for the Liberation of Palestine, trading 1,150 Palestinian prisoners— many of whom had been charged with violent crimes—for three Israelis held by the group. The agreement was enormously unpopular with the Israeli public, and subsequent releases were put on hold. Among those remaining in Israeli custody were the 700 militiamen that had been moved from Ansar to Atlit prison.

According to Article 49 of the Fourth Geneva Convention, "Individual or mass forcible transfers, as well as deportations of protected persons from occupied territory to the territory of the Occupying Power . . . are prohibited, regardless of their motive." Article 4 defines protected persons as "those who, at a given moment and in any manner whatsoever, find themselves, in case of a conflict or occupation, in the hands of a Party to the conflict or Occupying Power of which they are not nationals." The governments of Lebanon and the United States believed the Atlit prisoners fell under these provisions and urged Israel to release the detainees and cease violating international law. The Israelis, while not agreeing with this interpretation, said that some of the detainees would be released in the future according to pre-established judicial procedures.

## THE CRISIS

### Day One: Friday, June 14

At 10:10 am local time,[3] two Shia Lebanese gunmen hijacked TWA Flight 847 while en route from Athens to Rome and diverted it to Beirut. Among the 145 passengers and eight crew members were 129 Americans. The first thing the hijackers did after taking control of the plane was to collect the passengers' passports and search for Israeli citizens. Finding none, they expanded their search to include Americans with Jewish-sounding names and those with U.S. military identification cards, singling them out for potential violence.[4]

Meanwhile in Athens, Greek police arrested Ali Atweh, who had unsuccessfully attempted to board TWA 847 with the two hijackers. Atweh was the apparent leader of the trio and told authorities that the two hijackers were Shiites from Lebanon.

Just before noon the plane was allowed to land at Beirut International Airport, but only after pilot John Testrake reported that one hijacker had pulled the pin on a grenade and threatened to blow up the plane unless it was permitted to land. Once on the ground, the hijackers demanded that the plane be refueled, threatening to kill an American passenger in ten minutes if the demand was not met. Calling themselves "Oppressed of the Earth," the hijackers read a statement to the control tower demanding the release of Arab prisoners held in Israeli jails. They also condemned U.S. operations in the Arab world, Washington's military and financial aid to Israel, and the March 8, 1985, car bombing in South Beirut that targeted Hezbollah's spiritual leader Sheik Fadlallah.[5]

After refueling the plane, Testrake convinced the hijackers to release some of the passengers, arguing that after taking on so much fuel, the plane was 15,000 pounds overweight, and would have difficulty taking off.[6] As a result, 17 women and 2 children were released. At 1:30 pm, the plane took off and headed west.

First word of the hijacking arrived in Washington at the Federal Aviation Administration's (FAA) communications center at 3:35 am EST.[7] This was followed by cables to the State Department from the American embassies in London and Paris that told what little they knew about the incident. London reported that the hijackers had arrived in Rome the previous day from Beirut, and also indicated that the Beirut airport had blocked the runway to prevent the hijacked

*Chapter Four*

plane from landing.[8] Almost immediately, crisis management teams gathered at the FAA, the Pentagon, and in the White House Situation Room.[9] At the State Department a task force headed by Assistant Secretary of State Richard Murphy and Ambassador Robert Oakley, director of the State Department's Office of Counter-Terrorism, was organized to monitor and coordinate the department's response to the hijacking, and to gather and relay information to the policymakers who would need it.[10]

At 10:00 am, the first interagency meeting took place at the White House. With Poindexter chairing, the Terrorist Incident Working Group (TIWG) tried to determine who was behind the hijacking; early evidence pointed toward Syria and Iran, as the event exhibited similarities to the hijacking of a Kuwaiti airliner in December 1984 when American citizens were specifically targeted. Iran and Syria were suspected in that hijacking. With that information, the group began discussing pressure points that could be exploited against the hijackers and their sponsors. One option was to use military action, and Principal Deputy Assistant Secretary of Defense for International Security Affairs Noel Koch advised that Delta Force—the Army's special operations unit—be deployed to the region; the group concurred and made the recommendation.[11] To facilitate the introduction of Special Forces into the region, an Emergency Support Team (EST) was formed, with David Long, a Middle East specialist in the State Department's Office for Combating Terrorism, as its leader. The EST's role was to serve as the vanguard for any mission, to advise the U.S. ambassador in the country where an operation was contemplated, and to provide expertise to the local host government. To facilitate these tasks, the team included regional and functional specialists from State, CIA, Delta, as well as some communications experts.[12]

TIWG also discussed the hijackers' new demand to be allowed to land at Algiers. Initially the Algerians had refused to grant the plane landing rights, but the group agreed to ask the Algerian government to reconsider, believing that the Algerians were experienced negotiators and might be able to resolve the crisis. They also thought Algiers to be a far more manageable location than the alternatives—somewhere in Libya, or back in Beirut.[13] So as the plane headed west over the Mediterranean, the watch officer at the State Department contacted Ambassador Michael Newlin in Algiers and informed him of the hijacking. The ambassador was instructed to request that Algerian President Chadli Bendjedid allow the plane to land despite Algeria's policy against granting landing rights for hijacked planes. Newlin was also instructed to request that once the plane landed, it not be allowed to depart. Within 45 minutes of the request, Bendjedid's chief of staff told Newlin that the plane would be allowed to land based "on humanitarian grounds." The flight arrived at Houari Boubedienne International Airport at 3:30 pm, and was immediately surrounded by the Algerian *mukhabarat* (intelligence agency) and military.[14]

During the five hours the plane spent in Algiers, the Algerian government's first priority was to get the hostages off the plane, and it succeeded in winning the freedom of most of the women and children.[15] During the negotiations, the hijackers demanded the release of all Shiite Muslims held prisoner in Israel, and warned against any rescue attempt, claiming the plane was booby-trapped with explosives.[16] The hijackers also demanded to meet with the U.S. ambassador, but Ambassador Newlin was not available; he was delayed at the embassy writing down a message from President Reagan to Bendjedid. Deputy Chief of Mission Nathaniel Howell was on scene monitoring the situation and was joined by Ambassador Newlin just before the plane departed.[17] However, neither diplomat met with the hijackers.

When the Algerians would not allow the plane to take off, the hijackers threatened to begin killing passengers unless they were allowed to depart. The threat was taken seriously, and the plane was permitted to depart Algiers at 8:25 pm; it headed back toward Beirut. At about the same time in the United States, a transport plane carrying the twenty-man EST departed from Andrews Air Force Base headed for the British base at Akrotiri, Cyprus. Long planned to proceed from there to Beirut to lay the groundwork for a possible rescue mission.[18]

## Day Two: Saturday, June 15

After Flight 847 left Algeria, the U.S. government asked the Lebanese government to prevent the plane from landing at Beirut International Airport, and urged the Syrian and Cypriot governments to accept the plane if it was successfully diverted from Beirut. When the airliner approached Beirut, the air traffic controllers initially denied landing permission, but eventually acquiesced to the hijackers' demands, allowing the plane to land at 2:20 am. The hijackers requested that a negotiator from the Amal militia meet the plane, and when one did not arrive quickly enough, they shot Navy Petty Officer Robert Stetham in the head and threw his body from the plane. As they did so, the hijackers shouted, "We have not forgotten the massacre of Bir al-Abed," in reference to the car bomb that had targetted Sheikh Fadlallah in Beirut. Within minutes, the U.S. government knew that an American had been killed.[19]

Following the murder of Stetham, Amal militiamen surrounded the plane, and up to twelve heavily armed Amal and Hezbollah members boarded the plane to take charge of the hijacking. One of those who boarded was Immad al-Haj Mugniyeh, a terrorist involved with the bombing of the Marine barracks and responsible for the kidnapping of several Americans in Beirut. Passengers with Jewish-sounding names and those with U.S. military identification—twelve persons in all—were removed from the plane and taken to a secret location in Beirut.

After daybreak, the plane took off again for Algiers, and the United States government once again instructed Newlin to ask the Algerians to allow the plane to land. The State Department also wanted him to request permission for the EST and Delta Force to enter the country. Newlin considered the Delta request a bad idea; he thought the Algerians would see their arrival as a fait accompli rescue mission, and this was something the Algerians would not permit. He called Washington, and in a conversation with Robert Oakley said, "This is very, very bad . . . tell the Secretary . . . to cut off and stop this talk about Delta Force because that is going to . . . it [will] never work. Any sort of attempt without Algerian consent . . . I don't think the Algerians [will] ever consent to have a foreign military force operate on their territory and . . . if you try to do this you would immediately be faced with armed opposition from the Algerians, and the terrorists would probably blow up the plane with everybody in it."[20] Both Long and General Richard Lawson, the deputy commander of U.S. forces in Europe (EuCom), concurred, and no such request was made.[21] At the same time, the Algerians were not about to launch a rescue operation either because, as Nathaniel Howell said, "It wasn't their style."[22] However, the Algerians did grant permission for the EST to enter the country on the condition that it not mount an of armed rescue mission of its own.

That morning in the United States the Delta commando team, led by General Carl Stiner, took off and headed for Cyprus. The special operations entourage included six planeloads of equipment and over 200 people—a self-sufficient team with everything needed to conduct a rescue operation.[23] Contrary to the wishes of the TIWG, Stiner's departure was delayed because the Pentagon wanted to keep the force in the United States until Flight 847 had come to its final resting place.[24] According to the NSC staff's Howard Teicher, "The military felt extremely strongly that until they knew exactly where they were going, they would be better off at Ft. Bragg. That would preserve the 'integrity of command' and they would not have to move all the hardware from place to place."[25]

The EST and Delta teams were on the way to the region when Flight 847 departed Beirut again for Algeria. Consequently, the American teams were immediately redirected from Cyprus to the NATO base at Sigonella, Sicily, so they could be closer to the hijacked plane. Once on Italian soil, with the possibility of sending special operations forces into Algeria fading, Long took one-third of his original team and discreetly headed to Algiers via Marseilles on a commercial flight.[26] General Stiner also continued planning for a rescue operation and had TWA fly a duplicate of the hijacked Boeing 727 to Sigonella so his team could practice for an assault, and possibly to use to "fly [Delta] into Algiers under pretext of bringing in a fresh crew for 847."[27] This option was a faint possibility though, especially with the additional armed terrorists that had boarded the plane in Beirut, reports that a number of hostages had been taken off the plane in Lebanon, and the lack of Algerian permission.

In Washington, information was still sketchy. In a morning meeting at the CIA, Casey told Chief of Staff Regan he feared that if the plane returned to Beirut, the hijackers would kill ten more hostages. Despite Algeria's unwillingness to allow American special forces to attempt a rescue, the planning for just such an operation had to move forward. Casey noted that the forces in Sicily would be ready to go in two and a half hours. Following the meeting, Regan briefed the president.[28]

Shultz also sent a status report to the president indicating that more terrorists had boarded the plane in Beirut, and that one "still unidentified American" had been murdered. The organization responsible for the hijacking remained unknown, although the administration did know that the hijackers were supported by Hezbollah. Additionally, despite Amal's presence aboard the plane, there was some indication that Amal was not responsible for the initial hijacking; the hijackers were demanding the release of a prisoner in Cyprus, but Amal operatives would have known that the man in question had been released into Amal custody back on May 30.[29] Consequently, the State Department passed assurances to the Algerian government that this particular demand was moot. In a second status report that day, the secretary of state informed Reagan that a number of passengers had been removed from the plane during its short stop in Beirut.[30] Meanwhile, Casey met with his deputy, John McMahon, and NSC staffer Oliver North to discuss leverage the United States might have against Iran.[31]

At this stage, the administration had several operations in motion. First, Delta Force was positioned in Sicily for a possible rescue attempt.[32] Second, quiet diplomatic talks were underway. National Security Advisor Robert McFarlane sent messages to Syrian president Assad, Algerian president Bendjedid, and Lebanese president Amin Gemeyel, asking each to use their influence to help bring the hijacking to an end.[33] Additionally, Assad was asked to contact Iranian and Shia leaders and urge them to influence the hijackers to release the passengers to Algerian authorities.[34] At the behest of the administration, the International Committee of the Red Cross (ICRC) quietly intervened to see if it could arrange a "staggered swap of passengers for Shiite prisoners held in Israel."[35] During the day, a five-man ICRC team went to Algeria, and when Flight 847 landed, they and a few Algerian officials were allowed to board the plane to check on the remaining hostages. On another diplomatic front, the U.S. charge d'affaires in Tel Aviv, Robert Flaten, called the home of Israeli defense minister Yitzhak Rabin, but was told that the minister was out. Flaten left a message that read, "If [the hijackers] approach Israel, please negotiate with them."[36]

When the plane arrived in Algiers at 7:50 am, the hijackers issued a communiqué demanding that the fate of several "hero[es]" be disclosed, and demanded that "brother Afi Miytahi," who was held by Cypriot authorities, be released. They also threatened to blow up the plane if any move was made against them, adding, "We have come out in order to be martyred. To return without implementation of our demands is a dishonor to us."[37]

Later, the hijackers issued another communiqué, demanding that Greece release their "brother fighter Ali" [Atweh] and Cyprus release "brother fighter Paris Al-Riyat." They also indicated that they would not release any of the remaining passengers so "long as the Israeli authorities do not release the brothers detained in their prisons." A threat was added to this demand: If the Atlit prisoners were not released by the next morning, "the price for not releasing the detained brothers by the Israeli authorities will be paid."[38]

In Madrid, the Spanish government said it would not comply with another hijackers' demand to release two members of Amal sentenced to 23 years in prison for acts of terrorism in Spain.[39] However, the Greek government was seriously considering the demand made on them. When Ambassador Newlin learned of this, he phoned Robert Oakley and argued, "This gives us a chance; if the Greeks are willing to release this individual and he can be brought here, then the Algerians can trade him for more hostages." Oakley and Shultz opposed any such trade, but Newlin continued, "You should not interfere or try to stop the Greeks from doing something that they want to do if it will help the Algerians." Ultimately, the Greek government flew Atweh to Algiers, where he was exchanged for several Greek passengers and another batch of Americans.[40] In all, the Algerians were responsible for the release of 61 passengers and the five flight attendants.

Meanwhile, Newlin delivered another request to the Algerian government asking that the plane not be allowed to take off again, "even if that meant shooting out the tires."[41] Thinking that this might be a precursor to an American rescue, the Algerians indicated that they opposed any military operation on their soil. Bendjedid did not want the Americans entering the country and did not want the embarrassment of having to publicly decline a U.S. request to admit Delta. Nonetheless, the Algerian government kept the plane on the ground, which was as much as the administration could hope for. Shultz believed that this would give the Algerians an opportunity to bring the crisis to an end peacefully, but if the standoff dragged on, Shultz thought the Algerians might eventually be persuaded to permit a rescue attempt. Even if the Algerians never agreed to such an operation, everyone in the administration agreed on one point: "anything but Beirut."[42]

Late that evening, someone from the Algerian foreign ministry approached Newlin and told him that they could probably persuade the hijackers to release the passengers if the United States could guarantee that Israel would release the Atlit prisoners—something the Israelis had already talked about doing. Newlin, however, declined to give such assurances, explaining, "I cannot on the basis of my instructions tell you that the Israelis will do this." The Algerian replied, "I may have to take action on my own responsibility," which Newlin took to mean that the Algerians were willing to offer this guarantee to the hijackers anyway.[43]

Within the administration there was considerable debate about whether the U.S. could or even should launch a mission without Algerian permission. Despite the Algerian position, the NSC's North and some officials at the Pentagon continued to advocate this option. In an evening meeting between McFarlane and Regan, the Delta option was discussed again, with the two agreeing, "The President must protect Americans." Another government, presumably the Israelis, volunteered to join in a rescue attempt "if needed."[44] However, both Shultz and Bush opposed the idea, and it was eventually dropped.[45]

## Day Three: Sunday, June 16

At 8:00 am, before the deadline for Israel to release the Atlit detainees had passed, and over the objections of Ambassador Newlin, TWA 847 departed Algiers and again headed for Beirut. Apparently, the hijackers had become worried about press reports that U.S. military forces were en route to the scene.[46] While Delta was not on its way to Algiers, Long and his small team were. They arrived on an Air Algérie plane shortly after Flight 847 departed.[47]

While the plane crossed the Mediterranean again, officials at the Pentagon brainstormed about how they could get Flight 847 to a location where Delta could mount a rescue operation. Because Beirut was a permissive environment for terrorists, and the difficulties for American forces to operate there were many, American ambassador to Lebanon Reginald Bartholomew urged Nabih Barri to prevent the plane from landing there. According to Noel Koch, "We wanted to divert the plane to Larnaca, where Delta could get at it." The idea was to have Captain Testrake fake an emergency so he would have to land on Cyprus. Once there, Delta could storm the plane.[48]

As the plane approached Beirut International Airport again, the hijackers found the runway blocked with fire trucks to prevent a landing. However, as Flight 847 approached, pilot Testrake urgently radioed the Beirut tower:

We have no choice, we have no choice. The hijackers have insisted that we have to land regardless, even if we have to crash the aircraft.

The trucks were removed and Flight 847 landed again in Beirut. Once this happened, the Delta option became much more difficult; General Stiner believed there was nothing he could do there, and General Lawson concurred.[49]

At 7:00 am EST, Shultz, Weinberger, McFarlane, Casey, Poindexter, Regan, and General John Vessey held a conference call with the president, who was at Camp David. Reagan was told that the plane was back in Beirut after the pilot of TWA 847 tried unsuccessfully to land in Cyprus where "measures [were] set to take [the] plane if it landed there."

After a brief break, the conference call reconvened at 8:30 am, and Shultz indicated that the hijackers were demanding food and fuel. In addition, he reported that the State Department had asked the Lebanese government to keep the plane on the ground, and noted that contingents from the Amal militia were arriving at the airport.

On the military front, the president was told that Delta Force was en route to the region and would arrive on Cyprus in three hours. Seal Team Six was en route to the scene as well.

The group then discussed the possibility of launching a rescue mission in Beirut. Shultz explained that Ambassador Bartholomew did not think the Lebanese government would be very helpful because it was so "unsure of itself." The group agreed that the "worst case scenario [was] going into Beirut without [the] support of locals . . . [we] would have a lot of casualties." One of the participants, probably General Vessey, recommended, "[The] best plan [is] to go in after dark to lessen casualties." He indicated that additional forces would probably be required to secure the area, but that "to get on [the] plane [would] need only a few. Lots of casualties in any event." Planning to put forces into Algiers continued as well, should the plane return there.

Reagan was told that Barri was not worried about the American hostages that had been taken off the plane. The Amal leader had indicated that he knew where the passengers were and that his men guarded them.

The group agreed to meet again at 9:30 am for another update.[50]

In Tel Aviv, thousands of right-wing Jewish settlers rallied against the recent release of 1,100 Lebanese in exchange for three Israeli soldiers, and opposed the release of the Atlit detainees. The Israeli cabinet was in agreement with the protesters, with one spokesman saying, "Israel itself will not enter into any negotiations for an exchange of Lebanese Shiite detainees for the American hostages held by the terrorists." Defense Minister Rabin told a group of Israeli reporters that "the Americans will have to crawl on all fours before we even discuss" releasing the detainees. However, another spokesman indicated that Israel "would consider a formal U.S. request to swap the prisoners for the passengers." Rabin did concede that the government of Israel would meet with Red Cross representatives, but would make no "substantive commitments" until the Reagan administration clarified its position on the hijackers' demand for the release of the Shia prisoners.[51]

On the military front, the Israeli Defense Force went on alert amid concerns that a refueled TWA 847 might head for Israel and further embroil the Israelis in the crisis. At least four Israeli gunboats were moved to the Lebanese coast near Beirut Airport, and Israeli planes overflew the area.

Back in Beirut, the hijackers refused to negotiate with anyone but Amal. Nabih Barri, as the leader of Amal, agreed to mediate for the terrorists, and met with the ambassadors of the United States, France, and Spain in an effort to end the crisis.[52] Over the course of the day, Barri clearly established that he was in control of the situation in Beirut, exemplified by his order that an ill passenger be moved to the American University Hospital for treatment. Barri's involvement was fortuitous for the United States. No longer were those holding the passengers faceless and nameless. By co-opting the hijackers and taking control of the standoff, Barri made himself the focal point of American pressure.

When the NSPG conference call reconvened at 9:30 am—this time without the president, Casey told the group that Beirut was "the worst place" for the plane to be, saying that even Tehran was preferable.

According to Shultz, the Jordanians had indicated that they would allow the plane to land in Amman and would then use their forces mount a rescue operation; he had already approved the plan in case the plane headed for Jordan. The secretary of state also said that Syria's President Assad had sent a message saying he wanted to help, and that his country welcomed McFarlane's attempt to work with the Barri. Shultz also said that according to the Red Cross, the hijackers claimed that they would kill the remaining passengers or blow up the plane if their demands were not met.

Weinberger provided a military update, explaining that elements of the 82nd Airborne were on alert, but he said that he was not sure how they should be used. McFarlane reported that it was likely the plane would continue to shuttle back and forth across the Mediterranean, and suggested that the U.S. have forces at both ends should they be needed quickly. General Vessey informed the group that the assault team on Cyprus was prepared to go back into Algiers "in any fashion" if the plane returned there.

The group agreed to have a formal NSPG meeting upon the president's return to Washington.

At 9:45 am, Regan called the president and advised him to return to the White House for a formal NSPG meeting. The chief of staff then coordinated with McFarlane and set up the session for 1:00 pm that afternoon in the Situation Room.

During a 10:30 am conference call (again without Reagan), Shultz reported that the hijackers had asked for Barri to intervene. Vessey said that he had spoken with Senator Barry Goldwater, and McFarlane noted that the rest of the congressional leadership was also being briefed on the crisis. Casey said that he had located the hostages that had been removed from the plane; five were in the custody of Hezbollah, while Amal controlled the others. At the end of the meeting, Regan confirmed that no one would speak about the hostage situation on the morning news programs (Weinberger was scheduled to appear on David Brinkley's show that day).[53]

When Reagan arrived at the White House, he took some questions from the press corps and issued a threat to the terrorists. He warned the hijackers to release the hostages "for their own safety," adding that "there have been instances in which hijackers have found that action is taken that resulted in their death or capture." When asked if he was still opposed to negotiating with terrorists, he replied, "This has always been a position of ours, yes." On asking Israel to release the Atlit detainees he said, "This is a decision for them to make, and the decision isn't so simple as just trading—the decision is, at what point can you pay off the terrorists without endangering people from here on out, once they find out that their tactics succeed."

Despite Reagan's conciliatory tone toward Israel, the administration was extremely angry. The Israeli government had asked that the top level of the Reagan administration issue a "formal" request for the release the detainees, and had said it would only "consider" the request, implying that it might say "no."[54] In addition, such a request would mean that it was America, not Israel, that was caving in to the terrorists' demands. Some observers believed that criticism of Israel's position remained private because the Reagan administration did not want to undermine the politically moderate Shimon Peres and risk bringing the conservative Likud Party back to power. If that happened, the Middle East peace process would be severely hampered, since the Labor Party seemed much more willing to negotiate with Israel's neighbors than the hard-line Likud.

Following his impromptu question-and-answer session with the press, Reagan attended a 1:00 pm NSPG meeting in the White House Situation Room with Bush, Shultz, Weinberger, Casey, McFarlane, Regan, General Vessey, FAA Administrator Donald Engen, James Baker, Craig Fuller (from the vice president's office), Don Gregg, Deputy Press Secretary Robert Sims, and NSC staffers Oliver North, Howard Teicher, and John Poindexter.[55] Reagan began the meeting wanting to end the hijacking quickly, even if that meant conducting a rescue operation. According to notes taken at the meeting, the president based this on a belief that the public would demand satisfaction for the hijacking and the murder of the as-yet-unidentified American soldier.[56] One senior advisor later said, "From the beginning, [Reagan] approved of the concept of using everything on the menu."[57]

Casey opened the meeting with an intelligence update, explaining that the ten passengers previously removed from the plane "were being interrogated" and that Barri knew where they were. He added an ominous note, reporting that the five hostages being held by Hezbollah "may be in Tehran." He also reported that the hijackers were asking that the Spanish, British, and French ambassadors, as well as representatives from the International Red Cross, meet at Barri's house in Beirut to try and resolve the crisis.

The discussion then turned to diplomatic options. The group immediately and unanimously opposed giving in to the terrorists' demands and reaffirmed the policy of no negotiations with, or giving concessions to, terrorists. Instead, Reagan instructed the State Department to encourage Arab governments and the Red Cross to talk to the hijackers; perhaps the terrorists could be persuaded to release the passengers.

Another option explored was an approach through Syria and its Lebanese allies. The NSC staff believed that in order to free the hostages, Assad's help was necessary, and to get that help, the United States needed to convince the Syrian leader that resolving the crisis was in his interest. McFarlane briefed the group on the various Lebanese factions, explaining that since Amal had taken charge of the hostages in Beirut, it was now in a position to help, or be pressured to help, and therefore should be approached. McFarlane knew Nabih Barri from a 1983 trip to Beirut, and believed the Amal leader co-opted the hijacking because [Barri] "saw an opportunity here to elevate his own standing within the Shiite community by winning the release of the prisoners in Israel." Reagan liked the Amal option and directed McFarlane to contact Barri.[58]

Reagan had already sent a letter to Syrian president Assad asking him to use his influence with Barri to end the crisis,[59] and Shultz now reported that "[Barri] has been stimulated by Assad who has replied to the President's letter." Shultz also said that the Spanish ambassador might have gone to the airport in response to the terrorists' demands. The secretary's biggest problem, though, was what to say to Israel. Reagan suggested sending a message to the hijackers, saying, "free the hostages and the U.S. would have the Israelis release the detainees." According to NSC staffer Howard Teicher, Bush, Weinberger, Vessey, and Casey had no problem with this approach; they wanted to "beat up on the Israelis" for detaining the prisoners at Atlit and to push the Israeli government for their quick release.[60] Shultz adamantly opposed the idea saying that such a move "would amount to a direct swap of hostages for prisoners."[61] Shultz won this argument, and the State Department was only asked to produce a survey of public and private statements made by the government of Israel about the Lebanese detainees.[62]

In addition, Shultz noted that Red Cross officials had informed him that they would not take part in any negotiations and would not be attending the meeting with the ambassadors and Barri. The secretary also reported that the Algerians claimed to have developed a relationship with the hijackers, that they thought it possible to resolve the hijacking peacefully, and were requesting that Delta Force not enter their country should Flight 847 return to Algiers.

Weinberger cautioned about a rescue operation in Beirut, commenting that there was "a lot of firing in Beirut," but then conceded that the gunfire was not connected with the hijacking. Next, he said that some American special forces were on Cyprus, only forty minutes from Beirut, and suggested that a night operation would minimize the number of casualties. He also reported that an advance team was already in Beirut, scouting the airport, and that the Sixth Fleet was in position to strike should the president order it. He argued that this small number of special forces would have to suffice, because mobilization of other troops would immediately leak.

General Vessey proceeded to explain what would be necessary to carry out the rescue option, including moving the rest of Delta from Sigonella to Cyprus in preparation for deployment to Beirut. However, since Amal controlled the Beirut airport, and because it could be assumed that they would resist any American attempt to free the hostages, a large force—including Army Rangers—would be necessary to secure the surrounding area while Delta Force conducted the rescue. Like Weinberger, Vessey believed that it would be very difficult to preposition the troops and still retain the necessary element of surprise. This "hostile atmosphere of Beirut" frustrated Reagan immensely.[63] In any event, Vessey thought that there would be many casualties if American forces went into Beirut, believing that due to the large number of hijackers aboard the plane, at least fifteen casualties were "almost assured." The general indicated that a night strike had the best chance of success since Delta Force was trained for such a contingency and had practiced rescue missions on a similar plane. However, he recommended that the "only safe way [to end the crisis] is to talk them out."

When the group debated the rescue option, predictably, Shultz was in favor of a forceful move to end the hijacking. Weinberger and Vessey cautioned that such an operation could provoke radical Shiites to conduct even more violent attacks *inside* the United States. They added that any operation should be carefully planned and have a high probability of success, but insisted that Vessey's plan lacked the latter. When it was clear that an agreement on a rescue mission could not be reached, other military contingencies were discussed, including the possibility of bombing the runway at the Beirut Airport if the plane prepared to leave again. The carrier *Nimitz* was ordered to proceed to the Lebanese coast in case this option became necessary.[64]

FAA Administrator Engen then added information about the plane's crew, saying that the captain was "able and stable," as was the first officer. He noted that the engineer "is very religious and has been beaten." Overall, he reported that the entire flight crew was under strain, but doing reasonably well. Officials from TWA had told Engen that with enough rest, the crew could continue flying the plane if the hijackers demanded it. However, he indicated that TWA was worried that if the plane went to Tehran, communication difficulties with the crew would result. He also said that there was also a risk of mechanical failure if the long flights continued, especially since the hijackers were keeping one of the plane's engines running constantly to keep the air conditioner going. Lastly, he said that the plane's captain had indicated that he and the crew could not escape out the cockpit window, which would have deprived the hijackers of a pilot.

Shultz was discouraged about the situation, lamenting, "If it stays in Beirut, this is bad." However, he thought that the group needed to consider what to do if the plane moved again, and wanted to know why the plane was still at the end of the runway, wondering if the hijackers suspected that a rescue attempt was coming. He also said that he had sent a message to Iran through the Swiss requesting permission for the plane to land should it head for Tehran. Next, he read a letter from the hostages aboard the plane:

June 16, 1985

Dear President Reagan,

We the undersigned 32 American hostages aboard flight 847 are writing you freely, not under duress. We implore you not to take any direct military action on our behalf. Please negotiate quickly our immediate release by convincing the Israelis to release the 800 [Lebanese] prisoners as requested. *Now*.[65]

The president asked about the Israeli position on releasing the prisoners, and Shultz replied that Israel was willing to talk to the Red Cross, noting that "this is an invitation for us to ask for [the prisoners'] release." However, Shultz again argued that if "we do release" the Israeli detainees, the hijackers would win. He also wanted the U.S. military to "take out the airport in Beirut as a place to land."

This launched the group into a further discussion about whether or not to ask the Israelis to release the Lebanese detainees. Shultz recommended letting time pass in hopes that the Barri meeting or the Red Cross visit to Israel would bear fruit. He advised, "Sit still, don't change policy," especially in light of the Algerian success in freeing many of the passengers. "Don't negotiate and appear to be blinking," he said. "Don't force the pace of Israeli negotiations." He noted that Barri was in a position to help. McFarlane agreed, counseling the president to "buy time."[66]

Regan wanted to know if there was "any disabling gas" that could be used to immobilize the highjackers. The answer was no. The chief of staff thought that something like that should be developed for similar crises in the future.

Baker shifted the discussion to security aboard airliners in general, asking if there could be more armed guards aboard American planes. Engen replied, "We have stepped up security at major domestic airports and on overseas flights."

McFarlane brought the discussion back to the immediate crisis, asking what the U.S. should do if the hijackers wanted to take off again. The group discussed a number of options, with one point of agreement: "Obviously Algiers is best," although Damascus and Tehran were also considered good alternatives. Shultz said his department was doing all it could to influence those governments.

The president asked, "How much longer can the plane go on? [It would be a] real tragedy if [there was] a crash." He then explained that he thought the key to resolving the crisis was Israel's position on the detainees.

Weinberger, responding to Reagan's latter comment noted, "If we give in then [the hijackers] may up their ante." He counseled, "Say nothing now, let the talks go on. We [should] not negotiate. Let others do as they will and we [will] respect their decision."

Recapping a rescue mission, General Vessey said that the military could get troops into Beirut aboard helicopters and would move to do so in Algiers as well, but again warned that alerting more troops for such an operation would produce unwanted publicity.

Reagan ordered that nothing be said about Israel's readiness to release the detainees in the future and that there should be no comment about American armed forces being deployed, though he observed, "Rumors will persist." He did ask about keeping the plane on the ground in Beirut, wondering, "Should we crater the airfield?" The group's consensus was to wait until the hostages were released before taking that sort of action.

The chief of staff noted, "[We] must think about what to do when this is over. The public will want retaliation. So [we need to determine] who is responsible and what do we do."

The meeting ended with a decision to let the diplomatic efforts proceed while continuing to prepare for military action.[67]

After the meeting, spokesman Larry Speakes reiterated the administration's official position: "We do not make concessions. We do not give in to demands. And we discourage other governments from doing this." Privately, however, some administration officials admitted that the U.S. would not criticize Israel if it did release the Lebanese detainees.

The first hint that the White House was paying attention to the domestic political audience came in a memo from Elizabeth Penniman to David Chew. In it, she cataloged Reagan's previous statements on terrorism so that the president's remarks during this crisis would remain consistent.[68]

## Day Four: Monday, June 17

After Lebanese radar picked up unidentified aircraft approaching from Israel and Cyprus, Amal reinforced the Beirut airport, putting its militia on alert and surrounding the airport with rocket launchers, bazookas and anti-aircraft guns. Because Amal believed an American or Israeli rescue attempt was coming, Barri had the remaining passengers removed from the plane and taken to undisclosed locations in the Beirut suburbs. However, he did leave the three-man flight crew aboard the plane with several guards. During a press conference Barri explained, "I'm trying to bring all the passengers from the plane to outside the airport because I'm afraid something [might] happen to them and I'm responsible now." However, he threatened that if Israel did not release the Lebanese detainees, the hostages would be returned to the custody of the original hijackers, "to do with them as they pleased."

American television networks became participants in the drama when Amal allowed them to start interviewing the hostages; the networks supplemented their coverage by interviewing the hostages' families—all of whom urged President Reagan to do what the terrorists asked. CBS Evening News interviewed five of the hostages, who talked about being angry and frustrated with the administration's response. One of them, Steve Traugott, said, "I want to make a very strong demand that some positive action is taken towards releasing some of the Shiite prisoners held by Israel and to stop the political posturing for face-saving purposes." These interviews served the hijackers' purposes, increasing domestic political pressure on the administration to ask Israel to release the detainees.

Barri met with the Italian and British ambassadors who told him "not to underestimate the anger of the Americans."[69] They hinted at what the United States might do if the standoff continued, pointing to the annual U.S.-Jordanian joint military exercise—Operation Shadow Hawk—that was just getting underway.[70] Rumors that Delta was in or around Beirut also helped convince Barri and Assad that an American military response was imminent.

Despite mounting pressure in Washington, Reagan and Chief of Staff Donald Regan decided to keep a "business as usual" posture "as much as possible," which meant the president would maintain his regular schedule.[71] Reagan believed that he should not fall into the same trap that Jimmy Carter had during the Iran hostage crisis, becoming, in essence, hostage to the crisis. Pat Buchanan recalled that "there was a conscious determination not to cancel a single meeting."[72]

In response to the NSPG's request for Israeli statements about the detainees, the State Department provided a summary review that showed the Israelis intended to release the men, and that those still incarcerated would be returned to Lebanon when "their villages were 'quiet' and 'when the security situation warrants.'" This helped a consensus emerge within the administration that the best way for the crisis to end would be for Israel to release the prisoners—but only after the TWA hostages were released. This would enable both sides to get what they wanted without any party having to "cave in."

McFarlane informed the president that he would "talk . . . with Barri, Israel, and the Red Cross to make each give way." He thought the administration should not change its policy on concessions and that "there can be a deal without our direct involvement."[73] Later that morning, McFarlane and Barri talked for about thirty minutes. Speaking from a prepared script, McFarlane told Barri, "You hold the key," and that it was Barri's game to "win or lose."[74] In so doing, McFarlane placed the responsibility for resolving the crisis on Amal. Presidential spokesman Larry Speakes publicly reinforced this, saying, "We have made it plain what we want Barri to do, and that is to use his influence to resolve this situation. We believe he's capable of doing that. We believe he is the key to the solution there and if he wishes to step forward and take that leadership role and use his influence, then we think it could go a long way toward resolving the problems involved—the complex problems involved in this situation, *perhaps including the release of the Israeli detainees.*" He continued, "If the hijacking situation were relieved, then that would certainly put us back at status quo and seemingly put the Israelis back in position to proceed with their announced plan," implying that the hijackers could attain their objectives, in time, by releasing the passengers.

In Jerusalem, the Israeli government formally ended the Red Cross option when it announced that an ICRC request for the release of the Lebanese detainees "would not suffice" as a substitute for an official U.S. request. Additionally, an Israeli spokesman explained, "Israel itself will not enter into any negotiations for an exchange of Lebanese Shiite detainees for the American hostages held by the terrorists. However, if the United States government, on a senior level, will turn to the Israeli government and request that it release the Lebanese detainees, the government of Israel will consider such a request." In an attempt to further distance his government from the crisis, Israel's police minister Chiam Bar-Lev told Israeli State Radio that the hijacking was an American problem and that Israel would not act unilaterally to end the crisis. Responding to a request from Barri, the secretary general of the United Nations, Javier Pérez De Cuéllar, proposed a role for his organization in resolving the crisis—provided all parties approved. Pérez De Cuéllar noted,

> It is to be recalled that the U.N. has available in Lebanon the observer group in Beirut and UNIFIL in the south. As regards to Beirut, I am ready to instruct the observer group to receive for safe conduct out of Lebanon all of the passengers and crew of TWA 847.
>
> As regards south Lebanon, it will be recalled that earlier this year when the Government of Israel transferred the former inmates of the Ansar camp to Israel the Government stated its intention to return those inmates in due corse. . . . I am prepared to instruct UNIFIL to observe the repatriation of these from Atlit to insure that their repatriation is carried out in a speedily and orderly manner.[75]

Privately the Reagan administration was outraged with Israel for undercutting the administration and for continuing to put the responsibility of conceding to the hijackers on Reagan. It was also clear that the administration had to talk privately with Israel about the situation very soon.

On the military front, the aircraft carrier *Nimitz*, the cruiser *South Carolina*, and the guided-missile destroyer *Kidd* moved into position off the coast of Lebanon, and a Marine amphibious task force aboard the *Spartanburg County* left Gibraltar headed to the eastern Mediterranean.[76] The *Kidd* carried an eaves-dropping system code-named "Classic Outboard" that could prove useful since the entire CIA station in Beirut had been wiped out by the 1983 embassy bombing, and the subsequent kidnapping of the new CIA station chief William Buckley.[77] Intelligence experts at the Pentagon proposed infiltrating an ISA team into Beirut to locate the hostages, suppling them with false identities—as German businessmen or tourists on a snorkeling trip. Oakley opposed the plan, arguing that if Amal did not recognize the men as people who should be at the airport, they would likely be chased off, kidnapped, or killed.[78] Thus, Barri's removing the passengers from the plane made any rescue attempt exponentially more difficult. Oliver North and Howard Teicher wrote about this situation in an NSC staff update, saying, "This will significantly confound any possible rescue effort by our forces."[79]

## Day Five: Tuesday, June 18

Responding to the Greek release of Ali Atweh, Barri released the remaining Greek hostages, leaving 37 passengers and three crewmen captive. Barri acknowledged that the passengers, except for those removed from the plane on

June 14, were being held together in south Beirut, and that the crew remained aboard the plane. He also confirmed that some of his men were with each group of hostages to ensure their safety. Barri continued to urge the United States to pressure Israel to release the Atlit prisoners, saying, "If Israel does not release them, then, I, as a mediator, will wash my hands of the case." The ramification of this statement was clear—if the United States and Israel did not give in, Barri would hand the passengers back to the original, more violent and less predictable hijackers. Reinforcing the seriousness of this prospect, at the Beirut airport, the original hijackers (who were still aboard TWA 847) threatened to blow up the plane over Tel Aviv if Israel did not release the Atlit detainees. Shortly thereafter, however, a message was sent from the headquarters of Amal to the hijackers, ordering the gunmen to "stop this nonsense and childish games. You are not to make any such threats."

Meanwhile, Assad sent a reply to Reagan's request for help, asking, "Can we understand that the U.S. will exert efforts for the release of the Lebanese prisoners, especially since the U.S. considered the holding of them in Lebanon and their transfer outside of Lebanon as a violation of the Geneva Convention and make the U.S. government's position public?" In response, and without conferring with the State Department, Larry Speakes announced that the United States "would like Israel" to "go ahead and make the release" of the prisoners. Caught completely by surprise at the announcement, Shultz angrily went to Reagan to complain. Reagan sided with Shultz and publicly contradicted his own spokesman; the president declared, "the United States would make no deals and would not ask other governments to deal with terrorists either."[80]

In a further effort to reestablish his administration's earlier hard-line position, Reagan instructed Ambassador Bartholomew to tell Barri to "let our people go or Israel will never give in and we'll never ask them to." At the State Department, spokesman Bernard Kalb raised the stakes for Amal, saying, "[Barri] has accepted responsibility for the safety and well being of the hostages and we have made clear we consider the prompt resolution of this matter to be his responsibility."

As part of the ongoing diplomatic effort, the administration tried to get Israel to recommit to freeing the detainees at some unspecified time in the future. At the daily operations meeting, Reagan agreed to privately tell the Israelis that they were "allowed to give [the] Lebanese prisoners in exchange for all [American] prisoners."[81] He did not seem to view this as giving in to the hijackers' demands since the Israelis had already planned to release the men, and because the U.S. had already protested the detainees' transfer to Israel before the hijacking. The first step in this process was to get the Israelis to agree to a Red Cross visit to ascertain the status of the Lebanese detainees.

By accomplishing this, the administration believed it could cobble together an unspoken agreement in which each party's objectives were met, and the U.S. and Israel could not be accused of conceding to the terrorists' demands. There was also some discussion of rattling Barri's cage by conducting military fly-overs of the Beirut airport, Baalbek, and West Beirut, causing sonic booms that would serve as a warning to the Amal leader. Other proposed moves included blockading the Lebanese coast until the hostages were released, cutting off gas and oil deliveries to Beirut, threatening to cut off aid and supplies to the city, and other retaliatory measures.[82]

In the evening, Reagan held a regularly scheduled televised press conference. During the opening statement he announced a number of measures aimed at airport security and terrorism, including an order to explore an expansion of the armed sky marshals program. He also made another public call for the unconditional release of the hostages and restated the American position: "Let me further make it plain to the assassins in Beirut and their accomplices, wherever they may be, that America will never make concessions to terrorists. To do so would only invite more terrorism. Nor will we ask nor pressure any other government to do so. Once we head down that path there would be no end to it, no end to the suffering of innocent people, no end to the bloody ransom all civilized nations must pay." He also declared, "the linkage that has been created" between the hostages and the Atlit detainees "makes it impossible for [the Israelis] and for us" to proceed with the Israeli government's previously announced intention to release the prisoners. Following his opening statement, questions about the hijacking dominated the news conference. The president admitted to experiencing frustration over the situation, saying, "I have pounded a few walls myself," but vowed to wait out the terrorists, although he admitted that he had been tempted by thoughts of retaliation. However, in an attempt to lower the public's expectations for a rescue while calming the jittery hijackers, he seemed to rule out such an attack because it would victimize the innocent, and because he could not guarantee that those responsible would be hit. He lamented the lack of reliable intelligence, saying, "You have to be able to pinpoint the enemy. You can't just start shooting without having someone in your gunsight." He saw another downside to any military operation, acknowledging that retaliation "would probably be sentencing a number of Americans to death."

All of this was intended to address the American public's growing concerns. A *Washington Post*–ABC News poll showed that public opinion was mixed on how the administration should proceed, with 58 percent of Americans favoring negotiations with the terrorists, and 41 percent believing that the U.S. should ask the Israelis to release the Atlit detainees. When asked if Israel should release the prisoners without an American request, 60 percent said yes. Meanwhile, 53 percent said they approved of "retaliation against countries that give aid and comfort to the terrorists."[83] Although the preferred methods varied, the public was unanimous on one point—it wanted the administration to resolve the crisis.

## Day Six: Wednesday, June 19

In the morning, the U.S. government asked that the Red Cross meet with the hostages to verify their well-being. The Red Cross was also asked to query Israeli prime minister Peres about his government's plans to release the Atlit detainees. The Israeli response was to be forwarded to the Americans, and then passed on to Barri in hopes that the answer would satisfy him, whereupon he would free the hostages. On a parallel track, the Algerian government worked to broker a similar arrangement in which they would convince Barri to release the hostages in return for a "silent but firm American guarantee" that the Israelis would release their prisoners by a definite date.[84] At the same time, Shultz finally sent a reply to the United Nations, welcoming the offer for help.

Meanwhile, new intelligence confirmed that Hezbollah, not Amal, controlled six of the passengers that had Jewish-sounding names. This meant that pressure solely against Barri could not guarantee the release of all the hostages. Hezbollah's cooperation was needed as well. Still, Barri was seen as the most important player in the game. When Syrian president Assad made an unannounced visit to Moscow to meet with Soviet president Mikhail Gorbachev, the Soviet leader insisted that Assad "use his influence [on Amal] to keep the hostages from being harmed."[85] Assad now had a reason for getting involved: his group in Lebanon—Amal—was not solving the problem, and if Barri failed, the balance of power in Lebanon would likely shift to the anti-Soviet Iranians. Upon his return to Damascus, Assad immediately scheduled a meeting with Barri.

On Capitol Hill, McFarlane briefed senators about the hijacking. Most were generally supportive of the administration's efforts. Senator Daniel Patrick Moynihan wanted to know if TWA had done "all it could to protect [passengers with] Jewish names." Senator Patrick Leahy wanted to know how the U.S. planned to proceed, asking, "Is it likely that we can work a deal to get only some back?" When asked how the U.S. would prevent terrorism from becoming a long-term problem, McFarlane indicated that the key was improving the country's intelligence capabilities.[86]

In Washington, Shultz worked to increase the pressure on Barri. Speaking before the Senate Foreign Relations Committee, the secretary of state said that Barri risked international ostracism if he failed to release the hostages.

Shultz also reiterated what Reagan was saying—that the administration would not negotiate with, and would give no concessions to, the hijackers. He also implied how Amal could successfully attain its goals in the crisis, saying, "The hijacking and the demands and so on have stopped at this point the flow of release of [the Atlit] prisoners."

In Beirut, an ABC News crew was allowed to interview Flight 847's crew of John Testrake, Philip Marseca, and Benjamin Zimmermann. As journalists Charles Glass and Julie Flint stood on the tarmac, Testrake leaned out the cockpit window to answer questions while one of the hijackers held a pistol to his head. Glass asked, "Captain, many people in America are calling for some kind of rescue operation or some kind of retaliation. Do you have any thoughts on that?"

Testrake responded, "I think that we'd all be dead men if they did because we're continually surrounded by many, many guards."

When Glass asked for a comment about whether the U.S. should ask Israel to release the Atlit detainees, Testrake replied, "No, I have no comment." During interviews with some of the passengers, however, several captives asked Reagan to press the Israelis to release the detainees. Testrake's "no comment" suggests that this session was unscripted and uncoerced, making his first comment about retaliation all the more potent.

These interviews greatly disturbed the Reagan administration. Beyond giving the hijackers a forum to publicize their demands, the nationwide coverage added pressure on Reagan to resolve the crisis by giving in to the terrorists' demands. One positive side effect of the interviews, though, was new intelligence; it was now confirmed that, except for the crew, all of the other Americans had indeed been removed from the plane and were somewhere else in Beirut just as Barri had claimed. The launch of a rescue mission was now impossible since the intelligence community did not know the location of most of the hostages.

In addition, the military option faced a number of other difficulties. First, law enforcement officials feared that a retaliatory strike against terrorists in Lebanon could lead to attacks in the United States; one FBI official said that a nationwide Islamic terrorist "infrastructure" was ready to "spring into action."[87] Second, worries over the public's reaction were mounting. A memo from NSC staffer Rodney McDaniel to McFarlane noted that "[s]erious support for military retaliation occurs only when hostages are harmed or killed or when time passes with no resolution of the situation and the pressures build to 'do something.'" For now, the public wanted the crisis resolved peacefully, with McDaniel noting, "The public opinion pattern developing now is similar to that found during the Iranian hostage incident."[88] The implications were clear; like the Carter administration, the public would initially support the president, but as the crisis dragged on, public support could evaporate.

So the search for options continued as the various diplomatic efforts played out. McFarlane explained to reporters, "I think it's safe to say that the President has directed us to do everything with institutions that are in a position to influence change." North even suggested having Jesse Jackson try to negotiate with the hijackers for the passengers' freedom.[89]

During a previously scheduled trip in Indiana, Reagan again expressed his concern for the hostages. At a meeting with the Moorseville Chamber of Commerce, the president said, "To the families of those here from your own state, I think we are all praying—that's all—I've been praying ceaselessly for them and for their safety." That evening Reagan spoke at the Annual Convention of the Jaycees in Indianapolis and declared, "We're continuing to do everything that we can to bring all credible influence to bear, to get our people freed and returned home safe and sound. . . . But let me say, we must not yield to the terrorist demands that invite more terrorism. We cannot reward their grisly deeds. We will not cave in." After the speech, the president and Chief of Staff Regan met with the family of hostage James Hoskins. Reagan told the family that the government was doing all it could to free their son; Hoskins's mother replied by asking the president not to do anything that would endanger the life of her son.[90]

The administration's troubles with terrorism were exacerbated by a number of unrelated terrorist attacks that day: (1) guerrillas in El Salvador killed 15 people at an outdoor café, including four off-duty U.S. Marines and two U.S. businessmen; (2) a communist group detonated a bomb at the airport in Frankfurt, Germany, killing three and wounding forty—none of which were Americans; and (3) four days later, Sikh extremists blew up an Air India flight over the Atlantic killing all 329 persons aboard, including seven Americans.[91]

### Day Seven: Thursday, June 20

In the morning, Amal staged a news conference with five of the hostages at the Beirut Airport. Allyn Conwell, the elected spokesman for the forty captives, said he had "personally verif[ied]" that all of them were in good shape. Reading from a prepared statement he continued, "We as a group, most importantly, beseech President Reagan and our fellow Americans to refrain from any form of military or violent means as an attempt, no matter how noble or heroic, to secure our freedom." He went on to discuss the Lebanese detainees saying, "It is also our hope, now that we are pawns in this tense game of nerves, that the governments and peoples involved in this negotiation, will allow justice and compassion to guide their way. We understand that Israel is holding as hostage a number of Lebanese people who undoubtedly have as equal a right and as strong a desire to go home as we do." He concluded by warning that if negotiations failed, he and the other hostages would be given back to the original hijackers. The conference ended abruptly when the more than 200 reporters in attendance attempted to push closer to the passengers and Amal militiamen began punching the journalists to keep them back.

In Washington, members of the administration viewed the news conference and a set of interviews taped for ABC News as propaganda that Amal had coerced out of the hostages. The State Department issued a statement calling the news conference a "cruel exploitation" of the hostages and deplored the alleged singling out of those passengers with "Jewish-sounding names" and U.S. military affiliations.

Back in Lebanon, Hezbollah's Sheik Fadlallah said that if Israel released the Lebanese detainees, he would use his influence to gain the release of the small group of Americans controlled by his group. However, despite this aura of Shiite unanimity, there were signs of growing strain. Aboard the plane there was a confrontation between the Amal reinforcements and the original Hezbollah hijackers over media access; when Amal held a news conference at the airport, the Hezbollah members fired warning shots at reporters to keep them away from the runway.

The Israelis continued to insist that the only way the detainees could be released would be if the United States formally requested such an action. Speaking on ABC's *Nightline* on Wednesday night, Defense Minister Rabin said, "The United States government has to make up its mind. What do they want to do? It's first and foremost their decision."[92] However, Rabin's statements only increased the administration's consternation toward the Israeli government; Reagan dryly noted in his diary that "the Israelis are not being helpful."[93] The Israeli position was not playing well with the American public either. An ABC News–*Washington Post* poll showed that by a two-to-one majority, Americans thought Israel was not doing enough to free the TWA hostages, while only 41 percent thought that Reagan should formally ask the Israelis to free the detainees. At the same time, Reagan's job-approval rating edged upward to 62 percent, with most Americans saying the president was handling the crisis well.[94]

At 10:00 am EST, Reagan attended an hour-long meeting of the NSPG. Present were Bush, Weinberger, Shultz, Casey, General Vessey, Regan, McFarlane, Poindexter, Meese, and Craig Fuller.[95] The Algerian government relayed through Ambassador Newlin that Barri would free the hostages if he had "a date certain" when Israel would release the Lebanese detainees. The group decided to take the Algerians up on the offer, while pursuing a similar plan with the Syrian government. McFarlane explained that Assad was willing to help because "They see Barri being built up and as their pawn."[96]

Chief of Staff Regan objected to the path diplomacy was taking, arguing, "We are negotiating. Why not admit it and get the hostages [out]. Work on Israel, get their prisoners, swap through an intermediary, and then blast—either verbally and/or lethally and economically the hijackers, Shiites and Israelis [for making us to suffer public humiliation]." He also pointed out that the "Carter syndrome" was being "put on the President," thus raising the specter of tarnishing Reagan's perception as a strong and effective leader.

The president asked, "What if I call Barri and ask [him to] give [the hostages] back, and work on the Israelis, but not as a quid pro quo."

Following some discussion of the president's suggestions, Shultz recommended sending a cable through Ambassador Bartholomew to "get on record so Barri can't run with an unstructured call that the President made a deal with him." The cable could be followed by a call from Reagan later if necessary. Shultz indicated that the alternative to Barri was to deal directly with Syria, whereupon the president asked if he should call Assad. He was told that the Syrian president was in Moscow.

As for the approach to Israel, McFarlane cautioned, "Nothing [should] be in writing so that we are never seen to have been brokering a deal." The group concurred and decided Shultz or his emissary should approach the Israeli ambassador to the United Nations to ask what Israel would do with the Lebanese detainees if the hijackers no longer held the TWA hostages.[97]

The group also discussed the formation of a task force to evaluate U.S. counter-terrorism policy. Casey had initiated the idea during the previous week and had already spoken with Weinberger about it, enlisting the secretary of defense's support. After McFarlane and the DCI conferred, the National Security Advisor tasked North to draft a new NSDD authorizing the new task force.[98]

Following the meeting, spokesman Larry Speakes read a presidential statement announcing the appointment of Vice President Bush to head the task force reviewing American and allied counter-terrorism and anti-terrorism policies. Its goal was to determine "what actions, military and otherwise, we and our similarly threatened friends can take to end this increasingly violent and indiscriminate but purposeful affront to humanity." The statement showed Reagan's frustration at the recent spate of terrorism. Reagan also issued a warning saying, "No nation on earth has been more generous to others in need. But we also have our limits—and our limits have been reached. We cannot allow our people to be placed at risk simply because they are blessed in being citizens of this great Republic." The United States would, in the future, consider responding—with the "military or otherwise"—to stop the attacks. But this vow had a provision; any U.S. response would be "appropriate and proportionate" to the terrorist attack, not indiscriminate retaliatory strikes, which were "pointless anger."

Later that day, Attorney General Meese met with Transportation Secretary Elizabeth Dole and FBI director William Webster to discuss steps that could be taken to enhance airport and airline security. Dole favored expanding the sky marshall program, but Webster was skeptical, arguing, "Past experience shows marshals can easily become captive[s] of the hijackers." He also said that sky marshals were too expensive to train, and that the program was simply not cost effective. Instead, Webster believed that a program of enhanced inspection and screening at airports was "the most promising approach."[99] Reagan chose to expand the marshall program though, signing a directive authorizing the action (NSDD-180) on July 19.[100]

Enacting the plan approved by the NSPG, Shultz directed his executive assistant, Charles Hill, to open a back channel with Israel's ambassador to the United Nations, Benjamin Netanyahu. Displeasure with Israel's statements was conveyed, and the American position on concessions was reiterated. Netanyahu was asked to clarify Israel's intentions regarding the Lebanese detainees once the American hostages were released. Netanyahu replied that the only obstacle to freeing the detainees was the hijackers' demand. Hill requested that Prime Minister Peres specifically be asked the following: "What can we expect Israel to do about all the Ansar prisoners on the assumption that there are no TWA 847 hostages being held?" Hill emphasized that the administration was only seeking a clarification; this was not to be construed as a request or suggestion to free the Lebanese detainees.[101]

Netanyahu agreed to ask Peres, but wanted to know if the Hill–Netanyahu discussion was the only back channel. As far as Hill knew, it was. But, he was wrong. Simultaneously, at McFarlane's direction and with Shultz's knowledge, NSC staffer Howard Teicher had opened similar discussions with the Israeli prime minister's chief advisor for domestic issues. Teicher and the Israeli aide worked on an arrangement for the simultaneous release of the passengers and the detainees, but rather than calling it a quid pro quo exchange, Teicher characterized the arrangement saying, "It was a subtle [thing]—we communicated about what might happen if certain steps were taken."[102]

In addition, the CIA had submitted the same questions to Mossad. Casey phoned Shultz with the reply: "[The government of Israel] intended to release gradually the Shiite detainees in accordance with security developments. However, we do not intend to release them under blackmail from the hijackers." Shultz was upset about the additional back-channel and thought McFarlane was responsible, angrily confronting him about it. McFarlane denied that he was responsible.[103]

On the diplomatic front, three other things were happening. First, Alexandre Hay, the president of the International Red Cross, met with Reagan, and later with McFarlane.[104] Reagan asked the organization to ascertain the condition of the American hostages, but the president made it clear that he was not asking the ICRC to help resolve the crisis. Publicly, Hay claimed, "We are not involved." Second, a number of countries, including Austria and Switzerland, became involved when they told Barri they would be willing to help facilitate an exchange of prisoners between Amal and Israel. Third, the administration discreetly briefed its allies on the American position; the *New York Times* reported that the administration told several friendly governments that if the Americans were released "unconditionally," Israel would then release the 766 Shia prisoners—but only if there was no formal linkage. Shultz denied the story.[105]

Despite the focus on the diplomatic track, the NSC staff continued to look for other options should diplomacy fail. In a memo from NSC staffers Donald Fortier, Jock Covey and North to McFarlane, a recommendation was made to explore an "application of force" against the hijackers and their sponsors.[106]

## Day Eight: Friday, June 21

At the Beirut Airport, hundreds of Hezbollah sympathizers demonstrated, shouting "Death to America" and "Death to Reagan." Following the rally, Barri repeated his warning that if the United States and Israel did not release the Lebanese detainees, he could not guarantee the safety of the hostages.

At the same time, it was looking more and more like Hezbollah, Iran, and Syria were responsible for the original hijacking; British intelligence sources claimed that the hijacking was masterminded by Iran and supported by Syria. These sources claim that Iran set the hijacking in motion back in April when Khomeini recalled his ambassador to Damascus to plan potential terrorist operations against Western targets. Tehran wanted to overshadow Nabih Barri by conducting "spectacular terrorist operations against the United States and Israel," so as to shift the balance of power in the Shia population away from Amal and to the Iranian-supported groups. A secondary objective was to obtain the release of followers held by Israel, Cyprus, and Spain. Once he returned to Damascus, the Iranian ambassador conferred with the leader of Hezbollah and Muhammad al Abad, the Syrian official in charge of Iranian affairs to coordinate a new terrorist offensive. The Syrians approved of the operation and the group later met at least three times in May to coordinate the hijacking.[107]

Meanwhile, the Algerian option began to gain momentum; Algiers planned to ask that the passengers be turned over to the Algerian government. At the same time, the Algerians would tell Barri that Israel would continue releasing the Lebanese detainees.[108] To that end, Peres's reply to the Hill–Netanyahu exchange arrived in Washington. It said:

1. If the hijacking had not taken place, we would have continued with a gradual release of the detainees, depending upon developments in southern Lebanon.
2. We have not set a timetable for their release.
3. In view of the hijacking, we are not inclined to do this in a way that would appear to give in to the terrorists.
4. Israeli law says that detainees may appeal to a board headed by a district judge.
5. As the result of such an appeal board decision, we have to release some 31 detainees next week.

It should be noted that one-third of the detainees are not Shiites, but Palestinian members of terrorist organizations apprehended in Lebanon.

That afternoon, the secretary of state and Peres spoke. The prime minister said he supported the tough position the United States had taken, and Shultz gave his assurance that the United States would make no concessions to the hijackers—and would not ask others to do so either. In turn, Peres again indicated that Israel would restart the release of the Lebanese detainees once security conditions in southern Lebanon permitted it. Further, the Israelis indicated that they would release 31 of the prisoners the following week, but emphasized that the release should not be linked to the hijacking.[109]

Despite this cordial exchange, disagreement over whether or not to publicly ask Israel to release the detainees continued. According to Shultz, the chorus of voices that advocated asking the Israelis publicly continued to grow. Philip Habib favored cutting a deal, arguing, "Get Israel's commitment to release the 766, then go make a deal for the TWA release." Abraham Sofaer, the State Department's legal counsel agreed. To him, getting the Israelis to do something they had already publicly said they were going to do was not a real concession.[110] But overt, public pressure was not forthcoming largely because of Shultz's opposition. Instead, the United States applied more subtle pressure on Israel. With the blessing of the Reagan administration, Thomas Ashwood, the chairman of the International Federation of Airline Pilots Association met with Peres's counter-terrorism advisor, Amiram Nir, and suggested that his organization might support an international boycott of Tel Aviv's Ben Gurion Airport. While the Israeli government rejected the "proposal," it got the message, and started to work more constructively toward an American–Israeli agreement.[111]

Meanwhile, the White House continued its business-as-usual approach, with the president traveling to Dallas to promote his tax plan. However, after a speech at the Lions Club International convention, he did meet with a few hostage families. Then it was on to Camp David for the weekend.

### Day Nine: Saturday, June 22

As the crisis stretched into its ninth day, Reagan's political advisors' attention to public opinion continued to grow. Pat Buchanan sent a memo to Chief of Staff Donald Regan discussing President Carter's poll numbers during the Iran hostage crisis. A Gallup poll taken early in that crisis showed that 76 percent of Americans approved of the way Jimmy Carter had handled the crisis. The memo noted, however, that, as Carter's standoff dragged on over the next few months, his approval rating dropped to 40 percent. Buchanan then sounded the alarm: "If we are at 61 percent approval—then, 10 days into this one, we have the same approval as Carter had two months into his. What this suggests is that the American people, having gone through this same trauma, no longer have the patience they once did."[112] This was a serious problem for an administration that had campaigned on Carter's inability deal effectively in foreign affairs.

In an effort to garner Syria's help, the State Department sent talking points to the American embassy in Damascus for talks with the Syrians:

> We understand the domestic constraints under which Barri must operate, and that his influence over Hezbollah is limited. Nevertheless, he should not delay in moving to release the passengers and crew, and must be made to understand this.
>
> At the same time, we know that Barri will need the firm support of Syria to take this action. We hope that you will act promptly to give him that support, in accordance with the President's message to President Assad. . . . The continued detention of the passengers, crew, and aircraft constitutes a specific impediment to Israel's publicly-expressed policy to release the Atlit prisoners.
>
> We also understand that senior representatives of the Iranian Government may soon visit Damascus. We believe that it would be useful for senior Syrian officials to take this opportunity to directly and strongly urge your Iranian visitors to use their influence with those groups in Lebanon with which Iran is in contact to urge not only the release of the passengers and crew of TWA 847, but also the release of the American, British, and French kidnap victims—some of whom have now been in captivity for more than a year.[113]

The intelligence community now added a new piece to the hijacking puzzle. According to a State Department cable, the "ABC news tape shows an Iranian in the cockpit of TWA 847. He was guard for hostage aircrew during plane-side interview and spoke Farsi. One of the other guards was identified as one who took part in [Royal Jordanian Air Lines] hijack."[114]

## Day Ten: Sunday, June 23

Following a secret meeting of the Israeli cabinet, Defense Minister Rabin and Prime Minister Peres went on American television to announce the release of 31 Lebanese detainees the next day. Rabin said that the release was "a result of the legal procedure in accordance to the Israeli law," not pressure from the American government. Peres asserted, "We did release the 31 in accordance first of all with the laws of our country. Every detainee has the right to appeal to a special committee and if the committee decides to release them, so we do." However, despite claims that the release was not linked to the crisis, Peres telephoned Shultz at two in the morning to inform him personally of this "unrelated action."[115]

Publicly, Shultz said he would be happy if the move led to the release of the U.S. hostages, but also denied any linkage. Concerning the remaining detainees, Shultz publicly threw the ball back into Israel's court, saying, "Do we want to get ourselves in a position where we invite people who have a grievance somewhere to grab some Americans and then assert a connection and cause us to try to put pressure on somebody to do something about it? We certainly don't want to invite that pattern of behavior. Israel will have to decide for itself what it wishes to do about those prisoners . . . that's not connected with the problem in Beirut."[116] It did not go unnoticed, though, that the number of Lebanese released—31—matched the number of hostages being held by Amal and Hezbollah.

On the diplomatic front, the U.S. contacted a number of governments, including Switzerland, Sweden, and Austria, to see if they would ask Barri to release the hostages on humanitarian grounds. However, it was now clear that Syria and Iran were the ones who had to be convinced to act. Several times during the week, Reagan contacted Syrian president Assad, and on the news show *This Week with David Brinkley*, Shultz stated, "Syria is in a position to exert influence, and we have said that, and President Assad has said that he will try to do that." In addition, some officials privately started talking about threatening to attack Syria in order to force Assad to resolve the crisis.

On his way home from a trip to Libya, Iranian parliamentary speaker Hashemi Rafsanjani stopped in Damascus at the behest of the Syrian president. Following a meeting with Assad, Syrian vice president Abdul Halim Khaddam, Iran's ambassador to Syria, Muhtashamipur, and the Iranian minister in charge of the Revolutionary Guards, Moshen Rafiq-Doust, Rafsanjani publicly criticized the hijacking, saying, "Had [Iran] known in advance about this kind of action, it would have acted to prevent it." While in Damascus, Rafsanjani also met with Hezbollah's spiritual leader, Sheik Fadlallah, during which the Iranian leader pushed Hezbollah to release its group of passengers.[117]

## Day Eleven: Monday, June 24

As promised the day before, Israel released 31 of the Lebanese detainees from Atlit prison. In Beirut, Nabih Barri declared the release insufficient, saying, "I want the 700 plus." He also added a new demand—before the hostages could be released, all American warships off of Beirut's coast had to leave Lebanese waters. Despite the progress made over the previous days, Barri feared that, in light of his response to the Israeli release, the U.S. would attempt a rescue operation, or would launch a retaliatory strike after the crisis ended.

The administration responded to Barri's latest statement by reaffirming Amal's responsibility for the well-being and release of all of the hostages. However, a spokesman did reiterate the U.S. position on the Lebanese detainees, saying, "We believe the transfer is inconsistent with the Fourth Geneva Convention."

At the White House, the business-as-usual façade finally broke down; overriding the rare consensus of Shultz, Weinberger, and McFarlane, Reagan cancelled his Fourth of July vacation so he could remain at the White House, at the center of the crisis. In the afternoon, the NSPG met again, with Reagan, Shultz, Weinberger, Casey, Vessey, Regan, McFarlane, Poindexter, and Treasury Secretary James Baker in attendance.[118]

McFarlane opened the meeting by stating that the Algerian diplomatic initiative was progressing, but that Assad was being "cryptic." Shultz added that the Algerians claimed to need "three days to get back into Beirut." This was unsatisfactory to Shultz, who complained, "[They] need to speed up the time frame." He also reported that Barri was probably in Damascus meeting with Assad at that very moment.

Casey said there were "signs that Iran is directing [the hijackers, but that] Barri is sharing control [of the hostages]." The DCI deduced, "This will result in the negotiations being dragged out." He then advocated a two-step administration strategy. First, get the hostages out without conceding anything to the hijackers, perhaps with the help of Algeria. Contrary to the administration's stated position, Casey had no problem with Barri releasing the Americans "after the Israeli release without reference to security in Southern Lebanon." Once the hostages were free, Casey proposed that the administration "declare West Beirut an international quarantine zone [in which the U.S. would] stop air traffic, [close] ports, and send an envoy to Assad to secure Lebanon's borders with Syria." He suggested that the U.S. take "further steps if the hostages are harmed," such as disrupting the delivery of electricity to Beirut. Casey also wanted to tell American citizens to "get out" of Lebanon right away.

Shultz said that closing the Beirut Airport could be effective since a number of international airlines used the facility, and suggested that the U.S. rescind American landing rights to any airline that continued flying into Beirut.

McFarlane suggested continuing the diplomatic track a little longer before resorting to Casey and Shultz's proposals. Regan agreed, saying that he thought the U.S. should continue to work with Algeria, Syria, and Israel for another 48 hours, "72 hours max," before adopting a more aggressive option.

Casey proposed that if "Israel gives assurances to Barri [about the detainees and if] Barri gives assurances to Israel over security in Southern Lebanon—once this is agreed to, Israel could release [the Lebanese prisoners] and Barri could release [the hostages]."

Regan suggested that either the president or Shultz talk to Barri and tell him, "Our patience is being exhausted," whereupon the president outlined a potential call in which he would demand that Barri "either . . . give up the hostages or we do other things that will cause problems."

Weinberger tried to put a damper on the idea, arguing, "a blockade needs more ships and more time." Shultz wanted to know, "Is the Eastern Mediterranean [still] a Soviet lake as it was in 1970 and 71?"

Weinberger admitted, "We'd have to meet Soviet ships [while] resupplying."

Reagan asked, "What if we talked to Gorbachev? [Tell him] we want our people back," and appeal to him about international terrorism.

Vessey indicated that some sort of quarantine operation was possible in Lebanon because the ports were in the hands of the pro-Western Christian militias, but warned that this would "put control [of access in and out of Lebanon] into the hands of Assad."

Reagan thought he should talk to the Syrian president about the situation, suggesting that he ask Assad to "tell [Barri] he can be a hero by releasing our people or he can be stubborn and we will begin some actions" against Beirut if the hostages were not released.[119] Shultz said he would work on a call to Assad for the following day.[120] He also said he would continue working on the Israeli approach, noting that he had a "discreet list of things [he could] do."

The discussion then turned to what the U.S. should do if the terrorists harmed more of the hostages. McFarlane outlined a number of options. First was a naval blockade against Lebanon. Second, the administration could "go through the other diplomatic steps . . . to prepare the public [for more forceful action]. Third, "Let the U.N. go ahead [and try to resolve the crisis] to show we tried," and perhaps let the Red Cross try again as well. Fourth, "In a legal sense in 48 hours, [we will have] exhausted all [other] possibilities. Then we can justify [military] actions."

This turned the group back to the final diplomatic push. Baker supported a presidential phone call to the Syrian president but not to Barri. This way any deal would be brokered through a third party and would not be a direct quid pro quo. Shultz said he could talk to the Soviet ambassador to Washington, Anatoly Dobrynin that day to inform him of pending action. He also said he could call a meeting of the International Transportation Association to put a boycott of Beirut Airport into motion.

"How long is this process [going to take]?" asked Regan. "We don't have the luxury of waiting. Public opinion will desert the President [and we'll face the] Carter syndrome." Baker and Casey agreed that time was of the essence. The president concurred, saying, "We cannot wait. [We] must move ahead."

Shultz said he did not know how long it would take, but reiterated that diplomacy "does take time." He then gave Reagan a paper by NSC staffer Peter Rodman about negotiations during Carter's Iranian hostage crisis, entitled, "The Hostage Crisis: How Not to Negotiate," and encouraged the president to read it. Shultz then pushed ahead, arguing, "Power goes with diplomacy. [We] must think through what to do and then do it." He proposed the U.S. immediately call for the quarantine of Beirut Airport.

Casey thought that Shultz's proposal was insufficient, explaining, "Closing the airport is just the first step. [It] may not be successful, so we must have another thing to do [just in case]."

McFarlane suggested, "A time line is needed to show when we have to be ready for what."

General Vessey then observed that the Israelis were seen as "losing ground. [They] are getting very nervous."

The secretary of defense agreed, saying, "The legal basis for holding [the Lebanese detainees] by Israel is very weak."

"[We] need an American who can talk to Israel and to Amal about security in Southern Lebanon," suggested McFarlane.

The president agreed, saying that the U.S. needed to find a "bargaining position to let Barri out with a whole skin."

After some final discussion, the group agreed that a timeline for future options to end the standoff should be developed and would be discussed at another NSPG meeting the following day.[121]

## Day Twelve: Tuesday, June 25

During the day, the ICRC visited all of the American hostages and arranged for the release of one who was ill. This proved to the Reagan administration that even if Barri did not *control* all of the hostages, he still maintained enough power to *produce* all of the hostages.

In Washington, McFarlane met with members of Congress at a bipartisan congressional leadership luncheon. In a talking-points memo written by Oliver North and Christopher Lehman, McFarlane was urged to "use this opportunity to push our position on the House/Senate Conference [regarding] aid to the Nicaraguan freedom fighters." North and Lehman believed the primary concern of the congressmen and senators would be the hijacking, but they nonetheless urged the National Security Advisor to "take advantage of the current terrorist situation and make our case for CIA distribution of aid [to the Contras]."[122] North later said that this was done because certain members of Congress were "establishing a moral equivalency between the Nicaraguan resistance and the Hezbollah. It was just a ludicrous argument but nevertheless that's what prompted it."[123]

That afternoon, Reagan—whose patience was wearing thin—attended an NSPG meeting in the Situation Room with Shultz, Weinberger, Casey, Vessey, Regan, McFarlane, Poindexter, and Baker.[124] The group reviewed plans to extricate the hostages, as well as plans to "press forward with a campaign against terrorism," including a "top-to-bottom" review of current diplomatic efforts, and an assessment of whether they would bear fruit. The group also reviewed an NSC staff-prepared "timeline" or "escalation ladder" that the U.S. could follow to resolve the hostage situation should it continue much longer. These options were intended to ratchet up the pressure on Barri and his allies, while setting a deadline for concluding the crisis. McFarlane described it as an attempt to "alter the climate in which Barri makes decisions."[125]

One military option was to close the Beirut Airport by bombing the runways and enforcing an aerial blockade with warplanes based on nearby aircraft carriers. Shultz supported this option, as did the State Department's legal advisor Abraham Sofaer.[126] Casey argued for airstrikes against Hezbollah bases in the Bekaa Valley, but Weinberger and Vessey still cautioned against that approach, raising the specter of killing innocent civilians and damaging U.S. relations with the Arabs. At the extreme end of the timeline was "declaring war on terrorism" and going after any state that sponsored terrorists.[127] To that end, day number ten's action was to launch Tomahawk missiles against targets in Damascus.[128]

After the group reviewed the proposed timeline, McFarlane summarized, "If we agree on a calendar we can ask the Deputies on the [CPPG] to work up the [appropriate] cables" to Syria and the other involved governments.

The president then remarked that the Rodman paper given to him by Shultz the previous day had impressed him. The article's first lesson was that "to announce that force is ruled out is to consolidate the adversary's victory to relinquish control over events."[129] "We cannot be just sitting here," complained Reagan. "It's [been] eleven days. [We] must have action. I want our people back!"

Shultz agreed, saying, "I like the plan, though [there has been] no chance for deep evaluation. [We] must have better intelligence that we can make public to make our case" before launching military action.

"I'll get it," responded Casey.

Shultz wanted to know, "What weapons are we ready to use?"

"When we know the mission, we will select the [weapons]," replied Weinberger. "[However] if we use weapons, hostages will probably be killed."

Shultz then asked, "What brings this to an end—if the hostages are killed, what is our end?"

"I'm not willing to give up on the hostages being brought out alive," exclaimed the president.

McFarlane outlined proposed military actions in Lebanon. Weinberger confirmed the plans, saying that "by day eight, we attack. [But with] four Soviet allies [we] must figure [on] retalition. We may not be able to stop [it, and] other [groups] may want to prolong [the crisis]."

Shultz asked, "Is eight days too quick? [We] should ask Americans to leave Beirut and Lebanon. . . . [There's] not much time here to negotiate, nor to see the results of action. Have we discarded the Israeli option?"

"What about U.S. citizens [leaving other countries in the region] before we move, as for example, in Libya?" asked Baker.

The president responded, "Let's concentrate on Barri. What pressure [do we] put on him? [Could we] mine harbors?"[130] He directed McFarlane to "Make it clear that we're considering [a blockade] so that it gets the attention of those people and Nabih Barri,"[131] and then added, "Tell him we can and will do more."

Regan asked, "Is there no way to bring in Israel?" He was told that using the Israelis to help rescue the hostages or retaliate against Amal and Syria would disturb American relations with the Arab nations, so Israel could not be a player.

After discussing how to handle Barri, Casey recommended that the administration approach Assad first and warn him of impending military action if the crisis was not resolved quickly.

"Why not, first," suggested Regan, "put economic pressure onto Barri— close off the airport, [make sure] no revenues [go] to Amal and any other economic help. Second, put the Palestinians to work. [The two] are enemies. If Barri has trouble he can't focus only on the hostages. Third, play Assad to put peer pressure on Barri."

Baker thought that the administration could "do several things together— close the airport by [not allowing any] flights, [talk to Assad] and work on Israel to release their hostages simultaneously."

Casey added, "Also warn Americans we cannot protect them."

Regan did not like the DCI's comment, saying, "If we send that signal, the press will interpret it as a sign we will do more. It won't be all bad to get TV reporters out of Lebanon." The meeting finally wound down with a discussion of the continued press coverage coming out of Beirut.[132]

Following the NSPG meeting, Reagan briefed congressional leaders on the crisis. Senator Alan Cranston's response was typical of both Republicans and Democrats: "I would support any of the steps that I heard about today. I believe the President is handling this in a very responsible way."

Following these meetings, Larry Speakes told reporters that Reagan's patience was running out. "The President will let diplomacy run its full course before taking further steps, but he is prepared to take whatever action is necessary." He announced that Reagan had set a deadline of "a day or two" longer for the passengers' release. If there was no movement by then, he said the U.S. would consider isolating Lebanon to put pressure on the Shiite hijackers. Speakes went on to say that in order to end the crisis, the United States would also consider taking action against Syria, Libya, and Iran—all state sponsors of terrorism. Pentagon sources also informed the media that the Navy could easily impose a blockade on Beirut with the ships it already had stationed off the Lebanese coast.

Meanwhile, public and private pressure brought to bear on Israel convinced that government that it had to act. Israeli prime minister Shimon Peres sent president Reagan a letter announcing a shift in the Israeli position. No longer was the hostage situation an "American problem" as previously defined. Instead, he suggested U.S.–Israeli cooperation, and said that Israel would do whatever the U.S. wanted. He also conceded that if the U.S. wanted Israel to grant the hijackers' demand to release the Atlit detainees, a public request was no longer necessary. This allowed the back-channel discussions to move forward, culminating in an exchange of letters between Reagan and Peres formalizing an arrangement in which the passengers would be released, followed shortly thereafter by the repatriation of the Atlit prisoners.[133]

## Day Thirteen: Wednesday, June 26

The administration's tough approach began to bear fruit. After being pressured by Assad to find a solution, Barri offered to transfer all of the hostages to the French or Swiss embassy, or to Syria, where they would be held in "escrow" until the release of the Atlit detainees. As an incentive for France to get involved, Barri added that if the transfer were conducted as proposed, he would see to it that two Frenchmen who had been kidnapped in May would be released as well. However, he again demanded the departure of all American ships from the coast of Lebanon, and added a new requirement, saying,

"I want a promise from the United States that no attack—no retaliation against Lebanese territory—from them or from the Israelis" would occur once the situation was resolved.

On the Syrian front, Assad sent a message to Reagan saying that progress was being made. The Syrian president then asked, "what if the hijackers were informed that Syria would guarantee the release of the Lebanese prisoners after the TWA passengers were freed?" Shultz sent a reply through the American deputy chief of mission in Damascus, April Glaspie:

> It has been the position of the United States throughout this event that the hijacking and hostage-taking is preventing the planned release by Israel of Atlit prisoners. Therefore you may inform the Syrians that the President believes that Syria may be confident in expecting the release of the Lebanese prisoners after the freeing of the passengers of TWA 847, without any linkage between the two subjects. This is the President's view only if this refers to all passengers and crew and if "Lebanese prisoners" refers to the Lebanese Shiites now held in Atlit.
>
> You should in addition urge that Syria do all it can to bring about the release of all hostages in Lebanon in addition to the hostages from TWA 847.
>
> The United States reaffirms its publicly stated position regarding the illegality of the transfer of prisoners from Ansar to Atlit. The United States will be active on this issue.[134]

In Washington, Reagan attended another NSPG meeting in the Situation Room with all of the previous participants except for Jim Baker. At the start, the group was briefed on the latest developments. First, Assad was now asking for a guarantee that if the American passengers were released, Israel would free their detainees as well. Those attending the meeting were adamant that there be no linkage between the release of the TWA passengers and the Atlit detainees, although Shultz informed the group that Israeli prime minister Peres was "confident" the Lebanese detainees would be released. This message had already been forward to Assad, with a positive response. Second, the group was told about Barri's escrow proposal, which came about as a result of being "leaned on by Assad while in Damascus." Third, the group was informed that Barri was releasing one of the hostages for health reasons. However, the Amal leader maintained his demand that the Sixth Fleet leave the eastern Mediterranean and that Israel release the Lebanese detainees.

Weinberger balked at the demand on the Navy, arguing, "[There should be] no agreement restricting fleet movement."

Reagan said he wanted the hostages "in safe hands, but [we] cannot leave them in someone else's custody." Further, the president said, "[I want] 47 hostages—all [of them], not just the TWA passengers," in reference to the other Americans kidnapped off the streets of Beirut over the previous year.

The NSPG then discussed how to get the hostages safely out of a Western embassy in Beirut, after which Shultz crowed, "This is a response to our pressure." Still, Chief of Staff Regan wondered, "Are we making a deal with terrorists?" Shultz rationalized the unfolding deal, saying, "[We] focus on Assad to prevent this." Then changing the subject he reported, "The Syrians have asked about press reports of possible sanctions against them, Iran and Libya." The group discussed this for a moment and decided that rather than talking publicly about sanctions against Syria, it would be better to talk in terms of how Syria could be helpful.

General Vessey then noted that the Red Cross had recently seen all 37 passengers in one place, but that Hezbollah still controlled four of them. Further, Vessey said that Amal was now offering a guarantee that it would not launch raids against Israel from southern Lebanon.

Regan asked if the Soviets could use their influence with Assad to end the crisis, but was told that it was not desirable to have Moscow pressure Assad nor to be seen [as helpful] in the eyes of the world.

McFarlane then outlined the steps decided on the previous day. First, there would be no presidential call to Assad. Rather, he would send a cable. Next, concerning attempts to close Beirut Airport, the group maintained that nothing should be done at present, but that a diplomatic effort should be prepared to commence as soon as the crisis ended. Third, planning for possible military strikes would continue.

Next, the discussion turned to the future, with the group agreeing that all Americans should be ordered out of Lebanon, and that economic sanctions against Lebanon should be prepared.

Casey recounted the taking of the plane—as told by an informant. Apparently, Hezbollah planned and executed the attack, but Amal took over once the plane was on the ground in Beirut. Vessey corroborated Casey's version, saying it was a Hezbollah member that had killed Stetham, but it was Barri's decision to remove the passengers from the plane and split them up.

The discussion turned to the Barri proposal, which Chief of Staff Regan described as a "breakthrough."[135] Weinberger also voiced support for the escrow offer, saying he believed "Assad should hold the hostages."

There were concerns that prevented Barri's proposal from being unconditionally endorsed. Most importantly, the escrow embassies could become new targets of terrorism. After all, car bombs blowing up embassies in Beirut was nothing new. That left the transfer of the hostages to Damascus as the most popular of an unpopular set of ideas.[136] At least in Syria the hostages would be protected by Assad, who had his own interests in resolving the crisis. Since Syrian troops occupied much of Lebanon, the main threats to this domination came from Israel, the PLO, and perhaps Shia factions loyal to other regional powers. By resolving the crisis, Assad would remove any justification for the Israelis to move north again, and would bolster the Syrian-supported Amal at the expense of Iranian-backed Hezbollah.

Shultz agreed that the focus should be on Syria, saying, "Assad can handle the situation and if he has the hostages, he feels Israel will release the Lebanese prisoners."

The group concurred that the proper solution was for all of the hostages and detainees to be released right away, and unanimously agreed that the administration should impose a 24-hour news blackout to build pressure on Barri and Assad.[137]

Following the meeting, Shultz contacted French foreign minister Roland Dumas and requested help.[138] Dumas then contacted Israeli prime minister Peres and asked what the Israeli position would be concerning the Lebanese detainees if the American hostages were transferred to the French embassy in Beirut, adding that the French did not want to accept the hostages for more than a day or two. Much to the chagrin of Dumas, the Israelis were unwilling to give a specific timetable for the detainees' release.

However, a "no-deal deal" was slowly taking shape. Oakley later described the Israeli approach as a clever formula. He explained the Israeli position: "Once the TWA hostages are released, we will resume the release of prisoners which has been temporarily interrupted—we're not producing a quid pro quo, we're just doing something that we intended to do anyway, but we're not going to do it until the hostages are released."[139] Officially there was no linkage between the hostages and the Lebanese detainees, but if Assad persuaded the hijackers to release the passengers, the release of the detainees would occur shortly thereafter.

As decided upon during the day's NSPG meeting, the Reagan administration declared a news blackout on the hostage situation. After saying that Barri's demand that the U.S. Navy stay outside of Lebanese waters would be no problem—since the ships were already twelve miles off the coast, officials in Washington refused all other comment on the crisis. This was done because, as White House spokesman Larry Speakes later acknowledged, "We began to pick up intelligence . . . that every word we spoke was being picked up over there by the hijackers and others and instantly reacted to."[140] The news blackout was intended to intensify pressure on the hijackers and make them think that if the U.S. had stopped releasing information, military action was imminent if the hostages were not released immediately.[141]

## Day Fourteen: Thursday, June 27

In the morning, there was widespread media speculation that the transfer of the hostages to a friendly embassy was at hand. Barri stated, "We're in the end . . . of this thing." However, the Europeans now rejected Barri's escrow proposal; both Switzerland and France had initially agreed to accept the TWA hostages, but only if there were no strings attached; French Foreign Minister Dumas declared that France would not become "substitute jailers" and that the hostages should be released "unconditionally."[142] The Italians told the U.S. embassy in Rome that they too would only accept the hostages if there were no conditions attached to the transfer.[143] Austria announced that it was prepared to accept the passengers, but only for a short time.

Syria's government-controlled newspaper reported that Syria would do all it could to resolve the crisis, thus publicly committing Assad to the task. However, there was no mention of Barri's escrow offer, leading to speculation that Assad "favor[ed] moving the hostages [to Damascus], but not placing them under Syrian control."[144] Deputy Chief of Mission Glaspie sent a cable from Damascus to the State Department confirming this. She reported that she had conveyed Shultz's latest message to Assad's advisors, that the Syrians had pronounced the U.S. position "good," and that "the end should be in sight." Another cable to Damascus seemed to solidify the tentative arrangement. In it, Shultz authorized Glaspie to tell the Syrian government that "the United States has no plan of action against Syria," thus allaying any fears that after the crisis ended, the United States would retaliate against Syria. Damascus then informed Barri that they had received the assurances necessary to complete the deal.[145]

Now however, with the end of the crisis finally in sight, the administration changed *its* demands. The new official line not only called for the release of the TWA hostages, but for the other seven Americans previously kidnapped in Beirut as well. While giving a speech in San Francisco the night before, Shultz called for the release of "our hostages—all 46 of them—immediately— unharmed and unconditionally." This change resulted from a newfound confidence and belief that the U.S. now held the advantage. However, while the administration chose to push for the release of the "forgotten seven," Reagan was not prepared to risk losing all of the hostages for their sake. The other hostages were part of a wholly separate political dynamic and were held by an Iranian-controlled group with no connection to Amal. So the "all or nothing" talk was essentially a bluff.[146]

## Day Fifteen: Friday, June 28

In Valletta, Malta, a senior Maltese official approached the U.S. ambassador there with an "unsolicited offer of assistance" to help resolve the crisis. The official proposed a five-step scenario. First, he would contact Barri, "relying

on the Maltese language which is quite similar to the Arabic of the Eastern
Med . . . ('After all, we are both Phoenicians')." Second, having worked out
an "understanding" with Barri, the Maltese official would travel to Beirut.
Third, Barri would release the Americans, sending them to Israel, while the
Maltese official remained as a "token hostage." Fourth, the freed Americans
would "appeal to the Israeli government in their capacity as private citizens
to release the Shi'ites now in detention." Fifth, Israel, "responsive to the plea
of private American citizens who had just endured such hardship, would lib-
erate the Shi'ites now in detention." The U.S. response was cautious, with the
ambassador saying he thought it was "a well-meaning but greatly muddled
proposal which comes from a warm human being the decency of whose motives I have no cause to question."[147]

As part of the effort to add the forgotten seven to the deal, the administration continued its dialogs with Israel and Syria while planning to send an emissary (possibly Vernon Walters) to Iran, and "us[ing] an emissary already "inside" Beirut." However, these prospects were dimmed when those holding the
other seven rejected the demand that their captives be included in a larger deal.

While on a trip to Chicago, the president met with more TWA hostage families and the family of Beirut hostage Father Lawrence Jenco. Later at a
luncheon with community leaders from Chicago Heights, Reagan derided the
criticism from one of the hostages about the administration's new demands,
saying, "I don't think anything that attempts to get people back who have
been kidnapped by thugs and murderers and barbarians is wrong to do. And
we are going to do everything that we can to get all of the Americans back
that are held in that way." At his next meeting with citizens of Chicago
Heights, the president's position hardened. He told the group:

> When terrorism strikes, civilization itself is under attack. No nation is immune.
> There's no safety in silence or neutrality. If we permit terrorism to succeed any-
> where, it will spread like a cancer, eating away at civilized societies and sowing
> fear and chaos everywhere. This barbarism is abhorrent. And all of those who
> support it, encourage it and profit from it are abhorrent. They are barbarians. . . .
> We cannot accept these repeated and vicious attacks against our nation and its cit-
> izens. Terrorists, and those who support them, must, and will, be held to account.

In the evening, press reports said that the hostages' release was imminent.
Ending its news blackout, the White House released a statement: "We have
heard the reports. We are in touch with appropriate authorities in both
[Lebanon and Syria]." Around the same time, the president phoned Assad to
offer American assurances that Israel would release the Lebanese detainees
once the hostages were released. This was the final step of the intricate diplomatic dance that ended the crisis. It did, however, include one important pro-

vision to maintain some leverage over Barri: Israel would not release any of the detainees until all of the Americans were freed.

At the White House, Reagan's staff began preparing a statement and press guidance "questions and answers" announcing the release of the hostages. However, the State Department and the NSC staff disagreed over how much praise to give to Barri and Syria. Evidently, the NSC staff won the argument because Poindexter and McFarlane changed the "tone" of the statement so it gave less credit to Assad and Barri.[148] At the same time, Reagan wrote a letter to be delivered to Assad once the hostages were released. While thankful for Assad's help, the letter made clear that Reagan expected Assad's help freeing the "forgotten seven" and other foreign hostages, saying, "Efforts to secure their release must be intensified." The president also complained about the situation in Lebanon, saying, "Nor does our moment of satisfaction in any way diminish the fact that parts of Lebanon, and Beirut International Airport in particular, have become operating bases and safe-havens for terrorists. Civilized nations must act to deal with this horrible reality and to ensure that the Beirut Airport does not remain a base of hijacking operations. Here, too, I would expect your support."[149]

## Day Sixteen: Saturday, June 29

By morning, the release appeared to be a done deal. When Assad called Barri and passed along the American guarantee, the passengers were on the verge of freedom. An American C-141 flew to Damascus to pick up the hostages, while another carried a reception team to the Rhein-Main Air Force base near Frankfurt. In Beirut, most of the hostages gathered for departure, and the TWA crew filed a flight plan to Damascus. At around 4:00 am EST, reports from Beirut indicated that the hostages had been released and were en route to Damascus, while a statement from the Syrian government seemed to confirm this: "The hostages were freed today and will be transferred to Damascus where they are expected later today." In a morning press briefing, Larry Speakes announced that the hostages would travel overland to Damascus and then on to Frankfurt by air.

However, three hours later, the hostages were still in Beirut, and four of the hostages held by Hezbollah had not been delivered to the rendezvous point. Apparently, Reagan's fiery rhetoric the day before had frightened the Hezbollah leadership, which now feared that once all of the hostages were freed, the United States would retaliate against targets in Lebanon.

While talking to reporters, Barri explained that the Hezbollah group holding the four missing hostages had a new demand: "We are still awaiting guarantees that no retaliatory strike will be undertaken [against Lebanon] after the hostages are released. Guarantees must be given to Syria. If these guarantees are provided tonight, they will be released tonight. If not, we are not in a hurry. Tomorrow, the day after, who knows?"

Assad too was seeking another public statement about American intentions toward Lebanon, so the U.S. embassy in Syria cabled Washington explaining what was necessary; a restatement of the administration's formal policy concerning the sovereignty of Lebanon would be accepted by Hezbollah as a nonretaliation pledge. However, this was not enough for Assad, who added that he now wanted the Atlit detainees transferred to Syria instead of being released directly back into Lebanon. Instead, Shultz called Assad's bluff and passed word to Damascus reiterating that the detainees were a separate matter and that the issue should be discussed "after the present situation is clarified."[150]

While some in the administration, including McFarlane, thought that Hezbollah's move was more about making Barri and Amal look bad than a real fear of retaliation, another nonbelligerency statement on Lebanon was something that could be accommodated. That night, Reagan approved of the release, and McFarlane had Teicher direct the State Department to re-issue its standard policy statement on Lebanon: "The United States reaffirms its longstanding support for the preservation of Lebanon, its government, its stability and security, and for the mitigation of the suffering of its people." The State Department complied at 10:00 pm.[151]

In the event that Barri and Assad were not able to deliver the group held by Hezbollah, the administration decided to make an urgent appeal to the Iranian government for help. After receiving instructions from McFarlane, North contacted Iranian Speaker Rafsanjani through a "pre-arranged channel" and asked him to intervene and help secure the release of the four passengers held by Hezbollah.[152]

After the morning release attempt failed, a remarkable meeting took place in Damascus between officials from Syria, Iran, and Hezbollah. Assad was furious at Hezbollah's move and made his displeasure known. According to Glaspie, the Syrian president was "frustrated, humiliated, and pulling out all the stops to get the hostage holders to release everyone."[153] His vice president contacted the Iranian Revolutionary Guards headquarters in Baalbek and issued an ultimatum: release the hostages or get out of Lebanon.[154] Assad also dispatched to Beirut his intelligence officer in charge of Syrian affairs in Lebanon, Brigadier General Ghazi Caanan, to monitor the release. As additional incentive to facilitate the release, Assad promised to sell Scud missiles to Iran.[155]

## Day Seventeen: Sunday, June 30

At 3:30 am EST, Glaspie cabled McFarlane to report that Syrian officials claimed to have "solved the problem" that prevented the previous day's release; Hezbollah was now willing to go along with the arrangement. At around 1:30 pm in the Middle East, all of the hostages from Flight 847 crossed the border into Syria from Lebanon aboard a convoy of Red Cross vehicles and headed for Damascus. When McFarlane briefed Reagan on the situation, the president responded, "That's very welcome news. Let me know when they are wheels up." In Beirut, Barri said that the release occurred because of assurances made by the Reagan administration that the U.S. would not retaliate. Still, the White House continued to insist that "There were no concessions. We made no deals." However, off-the-record administration and Arab sources said that the United States did indeed provide assurances to Syria that Israel would resume the release of the Lebanese detainees quickly.[156]

President Reagan spoke to the American people that night in a nationally televised address and declared, "The 39 Americans held hostage . . . are free, safe, and at this moment, on their way to Frankfurt, Germany. . . . They will be home again soon." Then he warned,

> We will not rest until justice is done. We will not rest until the world community meets its responsibility. We call upon those who helped secure the release of these TWA passengers to show even greater energy and commitment to secure the release of all others held captive in Lebanon. And, we call upon the world community to strengthen its cooperation to stamp out this ugly, vicious evil of terrorism. . . . Terrorists be on notice: We will fight back against you in Lebanon and elsewhere.

Despite the assurances given to Assad, in a subsequent interview with Independent Network News, Robert McFarlane indicated that the U.S. might still be preparing for retaliation against "The root sources of terrorism, where people are trained, where they are housed, fed, sustained over time—and there are two or three strategic locations, in the Middle East in particular where that is the case."

## Monday, July 1

In the morning, Israeli State Radio announced that 300 of the 735 Lebanese prisoners held at Atlit prison would be released within 48 hours, claiming that the decision to repatriate the men had been made prior to the hijacking. As for the other 435 prisoners, the Israeli cabinet maintained that the decision to release them would be based upon the security situation in southern Lebanon.[157]

At the behest of Casey, the president sent a cordial note of thanks to Iranian leader Rafsanjani, but when Reagan phoned Assad to thank him for his help, the president turned angry and demanded that Syria bring the hijackers to justice so he would not have to act further. "This is murder. Tell him it was murder," Reagan said to a translator. The hijackers had disappeared in Beirut, but with so many Syrian troops in Lebanon, Reagan was certain that Assad could capture them, saying, "We know you have ways of finding out who they are." For his part, Shultz said that the United States already knew the identities of the original hijackers and would take legal and "other" steps to bring them to justice.[158]

## The Aftermath

In a form of mild retaliation, the Reagan administration called for "legal action and diplomatic steps" to close Beirut International Airport. On July 1, Reagan signed an order that suspended landing rights in the United States for two Lebanese airlines—Middle East Airlines Airliban and Trans-Mediterranean Airways—ordered two American carriers—Pan Am and TWA—to discontinue cargo flights to Beirut, and encouraged other countries to follow suit.[159]

Despite assurances to the contrary, some in the administration still wanted to see some sort of military retaliation. When it was learned that the leadership of the Iranian Revolutionary Guards planned to meet with Hezbollah at the Sheik Abdullah barracks in the Bekaa Valley, specialists from the Defense Intelligence Agency and aides to the JCS came up with a plan to bomb them. It was also suggested in some quarters that the Pentagon work up attack plans for other targets, including Hezbollah's Camp of the Holy Martyrs at Janta, Lebanon, and the Hotel Khawam in Baalbek, which was used by Hezbollah as a military training school. The plan called for the use of cruise missiles armed with conventional warheads fired from a submarine in the Mediterranean. The Joint Chiefs rejected the plan, calling it "too barbaric and too technologically risky."[160]

While the State Department and the NSC staff favored retaliation, arguing that not acting would undermine America's credibility, the military option fell out of favor for several reasons. First, the seven Americans previously kidnapped in Beirut remained captive, and would probably be murdered in response to any American military action. Reagan admitted in his diary that while the NSPG did discuss retaliation, the seven remaining hostages "limited" what the U.S. could do.[161] Second, a number of governments, including those of Algeria, Saudi Arabia, and Jordan—all friendly Arab states—indicated that they opposed retaliation. Thus, any retaliatory attack would likely damage relations with these American friends. Third, within the administration itself there was no consensus on the matter. Weinberger and the Joint Chiefs were against an attack, claiming a reprisal would both incite anti-American sentiment and undercut American allies in the region. "Military efforts" that were to be discussed at a Cabinet meeting on July 1 were even deleted from the agenda on June 27—well before the crisis ended.[162] Fourth, the public did not support retaliation. An ABC–*Washington Post* poll found that by a two-to-one margin, Americans opposed a military response.[163]

On July 6, David Ignatius of the *Wall Street Journal*—a paper normally supportive of the administration—wrote, "Ronald Reagan, for all his tough talk, has failed to develop a coherent antiterrorism policy. The impotence of U.S. policy has been dramatically demonstrated by the hijacking of TWA Flight 847."[164] Two days later, Reagan discussed the problem in a speech before the American Bar Association. Harkening back to history, he quoted President Teddy Roosevelt: "The American people are slow to wrath, but when the wrath is once kindled it burns like a consuming flame." He also cited Japanese Admiral Yamamoto, who said of the United States after his forces attacked Pearl Harbor, "[I fear] we have only awakened a sleeping giant and his reaction will be terrible." Reagan then declared, "The American people are not—I repeat, not—going to tolerate intimidation, terror and outright acts of war against this nation and its people. And we're especially not going to tolerate these attacks from outlaw states run by the strangest collection of misfits, looney toons and squalid criminals since the advent of the Third Reich."[165]

*The Vice Presidential Task Force on Combatting Terrorism.* After Reagan signed NSDD-179 in June, Retired Admiral James Holloway was chosen as the Executive Director of the new panel, whose membership included representatives from a number of cabinet departments (State, Treasury, Defense, Justice, Transportation), the CIA, the Joint Chiefs of Staff, the FBI, the NSC staff, the White House, and the Office of Management and Budget. The panel was directed to "Evaluate national policy and priorities, current programs, interagency coordination, international cooperation, legislation, public attitudes and awareness on terrorism."[166]

After several months of study, there was consensus on most issues, but the group had one significant disagreement. In a memo from Holloway to Bush, the admiral described the problem. "Because of the lack of central direction" in counter-terrorism policy, it was proposed "to add a National Coordinator for terrorism located in the National Security Council at the senior level." While the CIA and the Pentagon favored the move, the Department of State and the National Security Advisor opposed it. They preferred the "present arrangement with the [State Department's] Ambassador-at-Large serving as coordinator." Any change would have been seen as a judgment against Shultz—reducing the State Department's authority and influence over counter-terrorism policy—and would have constituted a victory for Weinberger. However, to avoid a politically discordant report, the group decided to keep the coordinating role at State.[167]

The Task Force delivered its report to Reagan on December 20, 1985, and following an NSPG meeting to discuss it on January 7, 1986, Reagan signed a new NSDD implementing the findings. In a key passage of the public version, the Task Force recommended that, "the Interdepartmental Group on Terrorism should prepare, and submit to the NSC for approval, policy criteria for deciding when, if and how to use force to preempt, react and retaliate."[168] It also (1) recommended establishing a permanent, full-time position within the NSC staff for coordinating the U.S. counter-terrorism program; (2) recommended making the murder of American citizens outside the country a federal crime (which was subsequently done); and (3) reaffirmed the policy that the U.S. would not give concessions to terrorists.

*The suspects.* On January 13, 1987, one of the suspected hijackers, Mohammed Ali Hamadei, was arrested carrying a suitcase filled with liquid explosives in Frankfurt, Germany. Upon learning of the arrest, the United States formally requested the extradition of Hamadei to the United States to stand trial for the hijacking. Within a few days though, two German nationals were abducted in Beirut, and the kidnappers demanded that Hamadei be released instead of being sent to the United States for trial. Otherwise, they would kill the hostages. After a lengthy deliberative process, the Germans decided against extradition and opted to try Hamadei in Germany using the "universal law principle," by which German courts could claim jurisdiction over serious crimes such as hijacking, regardless of where the offense occurred or the nationality of the victims.

The Reagan administration was split concerning how much pressure to bring on the Germans. The Justice Department wanted to press hard, the institutional view being that if Hamadei was not tried and convicted in an American courtroom, it would be a failure for U.S. counter-terrorism policy and a concession to terrorists. On the other hand, the State Department and the NSC staff were not willing to hold Germany's feet to the fire, and were prepared to declare victory so long as Hamadei was convicted and his sentence was substantial (i.e., life in prison). One NSC staffer objected to Justice's position, saying, "We deliberately did not wish to create the symbolic choice of either extradition or a failure of counter-terrorism policy." When the Iran-Contra revelations came to light, the Justice Department shifted to the State Department's position. Associate Attorney General Steve Trott explained, "We cannot impeach ourselves. We can't let ourselves get in a position where we say, 'Don't negotiate with terrorists,' and then we send arms to Iran, and deal [Nicholas] Daniloff for [Gennadi] Zakharov." Joseph diGenova, the U.S. attorney responsible for the indictment against Hamadei conceded, "We'd lost the bully pulpit on this issue." Ultimately, Reagan put the issue to rest when he met with German chancellor Helmut Kohl in Venice on

June 3, 1987. He told Kohl that he sympathized with the German position and would understand if they tried Hamadei themselves. Shortly thereafter, Germany announced it would do exactly that.[169]

One of the German hostages was released in September 1987, and the other in September 1988. In May 1989, a German court found Mohammed Hamadei guilty of hijacking TWA flight 847 and murdering Robert Stetham. He was sentenced to life in prison.

In mid-1987, the opportunity arose to apprehend another suspect—Fawaz Yunis—who had boarded the flight in Beirut as one of the reinforcements, and was referred to in the June 22 State Department cable. A source used by the Drug Enforcement Agency was familiar with Yunis and provided information on his whereabouts. After a series of meetings that included officials from the CIA, FBI, NSC, and the Departments of Defense, Justice, and State, a plan was hatched to bring Yunis to justice. The plan, Operation Goldenrod, was to set a trap for the terrorist in international waters near Cyprus, luring him there with the promise of a job running drugs. On September 13, 1987, the plan was set in motion. When Yunis arrived on the yacht where he thought he was meeting a drug lord, the FBI arrested him and moved him to the USS *Butte*. The *Butte* then steamed four days to the western Mediterranean where it met up with the aircraft carrier *Saratoga*. The prisoner was transferred to the *Saratoga*, and then flown back to Andrews Air Force Base in Maryland. He was tried in a U.S. court, convicted, and sentenced to thirty years at Leavenworth.[170]

Caspar Weinberger described the hijacking of TWA Flight 847 as the "beginning of a war." The subsequent top-to-bottom review of U.S. counterterrorism policy makes it seem as though the entire government was finally prepared to address the problem in a coordinated and serious way. This newfound resolve would be put to the test a few short months later with the hijacking of the cruise ship *Achille Lauro*.

*Chapter Five*

# The Hijacking of the *Achille Lauro*

We bag the bums!

—*New York Daily News* headline,
October 11, 1985

## BACKGROUND

In 1977, Mohammad Zaidan Abbas (Abul Abbas) founded the Palestinian Liberation Front (PLF), a radical Palestinian terrorist group that had splintered from the Popular Front for the Liberation of Palestine—General Command (PFLP-GC) over the PFLP-GC's support for Syria's invasion of Lebanon. In the early 1980s, the group conducted a number of spectacular terrorist attacks against Israel, including one in 1982 using hang gliders to attack an oil refinery near Haifa, and a 1983 attack on northern Israel using hot-air balloons launched from Lebanon. In 1982 when the PLF itself splintered into three factions, Abbas vowed loyalty to Arafat and was rewarded in November 1984 with a seat on the PLO's executive committee and one on the even more exclusive ten-member inner cabinet.

As part of the PLF's ongoing campaign against Israel and its supporters, Abul Abbas directed a group of his operatives to board the cruise ship *Achille Lauro* at Genoa, Italy, and seize control of the vessel sometime during its voyage.[1] Five days before departure, the hijackers' operational leader (and a relative of Abul Abbas) Issa Mohammed Abbas was arrested by Italian authorities who, upon searching his car, found four Kalashnikov rifles, eight grenades, and some detonators.[2] So, when the ship set sail on October 1, the

PLF cell—composed of Majed al Molqi, Hallah al Hassan, Ali Abdullah, and Abdel Ibrahim—was one man short.

## THE CRISIS

### Day One: Monday, October 7

On Monday, October 7, the *Achille Lauro* set sail from Alexandria, Egypt, after dropping off most of its passengers for a day excursion to the Pyramids. The passengers were to re-embark the cruise ship that night in Port Said before continuing on to a port call at Ashdod, Israel. Most of the 750 passengers opted for the bus tour, leaving only 97 passengers, including twelve Americans, aboard. Counting staff and crew though, there were more than 400 people still on board. Over the previous week, one of the ship's stewards had become suspicious of the would-be hijackers based on their passports. These documents were from three separate, non-Arab countries (Argentina, Portugal, and Norway), despite the fact that the group travelled together and all four men were clearly of Arab descent. When the steward entered the terrorists' room thinking they were at lunch, he walked in on the four cleaning their weapons. With this, the terrorists' hand was forced, and they took control of the ship.[3]

The first thing the hijackers did was sort through the passengers and single out the American and British citizens, who were then placed on deck and surrounded by open cans of gasoline. Next, they used the ship's radio to announce that they had taken control of the ship. They did not specify which ship though, saying only that they had taken an Italian cruise ship. Israeli intelligence quickly began monitoring the radio transmissions from the vessel, many of which showed that from the moment the hijackers took control of the ship, they were in constant radio contact with Abul Abbas in Beirut.[4]

At CIA headquarters, analyst Jerry Agee went to inform Charles Allen, the CIA's national intelligence officer for counter-terrorism, about the hijacking. Agee was able to indentify the ship as the *Achille Lauro*, describing it as "bigger than the 'Love Boat,'" and noting that there were some Americans aboard.[5] Allen immediately notified the NSC staff of the situation, whereupon Deputy National Security Advisor John Poindexter instructed NSC staffer Oliver North, "Why don't you get your group together and come up with some recommendations?" North quickly sent out an e-mail to the Terrorist Incident Working Group (TIWG) calling for a meeting later that day.[6]

By the time the group met, the ship had already sailed away from the Egyptian coast. The TIWG reviewed the situation, formulated some options for the president, and forwarded them to National Security Advisor Robert McFarlane. Present were Poindexter, Robert Oakley (from State), Noel Koch (from Defense), Lieutenant General John Moellering (from the Joint Chiefs of Staff), Oliver "Buck" Revell (the FBI's executive assistant director for investigations), Lowell Jensen (from the Justice Department), Fred Fielding (from the White House counsel's office), Charles Allen, and Oliver North.[7]

At the outset, Poindexter said that he wanted a passenger list so they could figure out how many Americans were on board. Koch countered that a headcount could wait, and that the first order of business should be the dispatch of the special operations unit SEAL (Sea-Air-Land) Team Six to the region. He argued that this hijacking was the best opportunity yet to use American counter-terrorism forces, explaining that so long as the ship remained at sea it was isolated and vulnerable. "We can take that sucker down," said Koch.[8] Oakley initially advocated a "wait-and-see" posture, but the group eventually agreed with Koch and agreed to recommend dispatching an Emergency Support Team (EST) to Rome and Joint Special Operations Command (JSOC) forces to the Mediterranean.[9] They believed that, even without an operational plan, it was better to get the forces on their way since it took half a day to get them into the region—better to have them sit and wait until the president decided what to do. At the very least, dispatching SEAL Team Six would allow the option of a rescue mission.[10]

The TIWG also recommended that the State Department contact the other governments with hostages aboard and urge them to maintain a firm stance against the hijackers. The group also advised that the State Department contact the governments of Syria, Lebanon, and Cyprus, and ask that they refuse to let the ship enter their ports.[11] The group believed that isolating the *Achille Lauro* increased the probability that the crisis could be brought to an end peacefully; so long as the ship remained at sea, the hijackers would not be able to play to the media as the hijackers of TWA Flight 847 had done in Beirut. Also, conducting a military operation at sea did not require the permission of any other government and would help ensure operational secrecy. Lastly, it would be logistically easier to carry out such an operation on the open sea.[12]

As planning for a rescue option moved forward, the administration faced two significant problems. First, the ship was registered in Italy, and thus subject—at least nominally—to Italian sovereignty, so when David Long arrived in Rome with the EST, he met with key members of the Italian government to discuss the situation. While Defense Minister Giovanni Spadolini favored a rescue operation, Foreign Minister Giulio Andreotti preferred a negotiated end to the hijacking. After a short debate, Spadolini prevailed, and the Italians gave their blessing to an American operation. JSOC would conduct the rescue, with the Italians standing close by for public relations. Accordingly, while the main force of JSOC, headed by General Carl Stiner, landed at the NATO airfield at Sigonella, Sicily, a small group was sent on to the British base at Akrotiri, Cyprus to prepare for the operation.[13]

Since the *Achille Lauro* was now observing radio silence, the second problem the U.S. faced was locating the ship. Speculating that it had not gone far, NSC staffer Jock Covey wrote, "[The] Egyptians are presently behaving as if ship were in international waters, but that may be wishful thinking. [It is n]ot clear if they have or will make [an] effort to prevent ship leaving Egyptian waters if it [is] still within 12 [nautical miles]."[14] To verify its location, North called Major General Uri Simhoni, the military attaché at the Israeli Embassy in Washington to see if he could help. Within minutes, Simhoni called back with the ship's exact location, which North passed on the National Security Agency.[15]

## Day Two: Tuesday, October 8

On Monday night, Italian prime minister Bettino Craxi had directed a question to the administration asking if the U.S. "was amenable to simple contacts with the hijackers." It was not. Tuesday morning, American ambassador Max Rabb met with Craxi and told him that the administration wanted the hijackers punished. Rabb then expressed the United States government's "great concern" about reports that American hostages might be killed, and offered America's "readiness to furnish any assistance requested by Italy."[16]

In the hours after North conferred with Simhoni about the location of the *Achille Lauro*, the ship eluded its watchers. This upset many in the Reagan administration who thought that the military should have been conducting a more aggressive search. At the NSC staff, Navy captain James Stark vented his frustration in an e-mail to Poindexter:

> I understand our reluctance to tell the JCS how to run their show, and am not suggesting that we do so. But I am concerned that 24 hours after the start of the hijacking, we still do not have a good fix on the ship, and the two naval surface units in the area do not appear to be attempting to close on it, [redacted], while we may not want to make any suggestions, would it be in order for you to call JCS and simply discuss the location problem and how they intend to solve it? My understanding is that *Sara[toga]* has not been ordered to proceed at best speed to the Eastern Med[iterranean].[17]

While the NSC staff debated the propriety of making suggestions to the Pentagon, Shultz felt no dilemma. Early in the morning, he phoned Weinberger to pointedly ask whether the Sixth Fleet had been ordered to search for the hijacked ship. According to Shultz, Weinberger said it had not. Shultz then encouraged Weinberger to begin looking, to which Weinberger replied, "The cruise ship is faster than our ships. It can outrun us." Shultz did not buy this argument, believing that the Navy's resources—ships, planes, and radar—

should be sufficient to locate the *Achille Lauro*. Shultz called Weinberger again and impressed upon the secretary of defense his desire to keep the cruise ship "in Egypt's orbit," as opposed to some less controllable environment (like Beirut), or someplace where the U.S. would have to deal with a difficult leader (such as Syria's Assad). Weinberger replied that the cruise ship was 25 to 30 nautical miles off of Port Said, and that Egyptian helicopters were watching it. If it tried to leave, the American destroyer *Scott* could move to intercept. With this, Shultz briefed McFarlane. The two agreed that keeping the ship in or near Egyptian waters was the best approach.[18]

Shultz next phoned the American ambassador to Egypt, Nick Veliotes, and told him that the administration wanted to handle the hijacking using a cooperative U.S.–Egyptian approach and instructed him to ask the Egyptians to keep the ship in their territorial waters. Veliotes replied that the *Achille Lauro* had left hours ago.

At 8:15 am EST, Egyptian Defense Minister Abu Ghazala notified the administration that the ship's location was "confirmed"— 15 nautical miles off Tartus, Syria.[19] When the ship arrived in Syrian waters, the hijackers issued two demands. First, they wanted the release of Samir al Qantari (a PLF member imprisoned since a failed April 1979 raid on Nahariya, Isreal), and a group of fifty Palestinian prisoners held in Israeli jails, many of whom were identified as members of Force 17, a commando unit of the PLO.[20]

Second, they wanted permission to dock. The Syrian foreign ministry immediately summoned American ambassador William Eagleton and the Italian chargé d'affaires to inquire about their governments' positions on the matter. Assad wanted nothing to do with the hijackers since he knew which PLF faction they represented (one not supported by Syria), and was unwilling to allow the ship dock "unless the United States and Italy decide to negotiate." Damascus also passed on the hijackers' request that the American, Italian, British, and West German ambassadors to Syria proceed to Tartus to commence negotiations. While the Syrians awaited a response, the Syrian Navy kept the *Achille Lauro* at bay outside the Tartus harbor.[21]

After some deliberation, the administration determined that it wanted to keep the ship out of Tartus, and set out, through diplomatic channels, to express its view. TIWG drafted cables for State to send to Syria, and Shultz directed Dick Murphy, the assistant secretary of state for Near East Affairs, to contact the Syrians and ask them to prevent the ship from docking. Shultz wanted the ship kept away from port because of what had transpired during the TWA hijacking; with both terrorists and hostages accessible to television cameras, the situation had quickly become a media circus where the terrorists drove the pace and direction of the crisis—at least for a time. However,

Murphy was in favor of letting the ship dock. Since the hijackers were from the Abul Abbas faction of the PLF, and Assad and Arafat were not seeing eye-to-eye, Murphy argued that Assad would probably order his forces to storm the ship and bring the episode to a conclusion not favorable to the terrorists. Murphy lost the argument.[22]

Shultz also cabled a message to Ambassador Eagleton for delivery to Assad:

—we understand the ship is now approx 15 miles off Tartus;
—it is the firm policy of the USG that terrorists should not be given sanctuary;
—we know that President [Assad] has spoken out firmly against [terrorism] and against giving in to demands;
—we therefore strongly urge that the government of Syria not give sanctuary to the ship;
—we also note that any country which gives sanctuary for such ship becomes fully responsible for the ship and for the safety of all the people on board.[23]

At the president's morning national security briefing, the President was given a CIA spot commentary that concluded the hijackers did "not belong to PLO Chairman Arafat's Fatah Organization." Instead, the CIA believed that the Palestinian Liberation Front was responsible. In addition, it confirmed that an as yet unknown Palestinian official was en route to Cairo to help defuse the crisis. Reagan was also told that Italian prime minister Craxi would probably try to employ "a mix of military posturing and quiet diplomacy" to end the hijacking.[24] Shultz suggested that Reagan order American forces to "take action to intercept" the *Achille Lauro*, but Reagan was not willing to order the assault at this stage. Instead, he decided to discuss the situation at an NSPG meeting later that day.[25]

By 2:42 pm in Tartus, the Syrians still had not allowed the ship to dock. Because of the long wait, one of the hijackers—Majed Molqi—radioed the port authorities to ask where the negotiators were, and declared, "We will start killing at 1500" if they did not arrive before then. A few minutes later he called again and warned, "We cannot wait any longer. We will start killing." Frustrated by inactivity, Molqi shot wheelchair-bound American passenger Leon Klinghoffer in the head and chest, and ordered the body thrown overboard. At 3:23 pm Molqi returned to the radio and transmitted, "What are the developments, Tartus? We will kill a second. We are losing patience."[26]

The administration was aware of the murder almost immediately. The Syrian Foreign Ministry notified Ambassador Eagleton that a "Leon Glen Ghosser" (rendered from the Arabic spelling of the name) had been killed, followed shortly by news that the hijackers had killed "Mildred Hoss."[27]

Meanwhile, JSOC troops had arrived in the region and began preparing to mount an assault. The rescue plan entailed Navy SEALs boarding the ship at night and retaking it from the hijackers. Reports that there were up to "200 kilos of dynamite on board" did not dissuade planners, who had tentatively agreed to execute the plan on Wednesday night.[28] When Shultz spoke with chairman of the JCS, Admiral William Crowe, about the preparations, Crowe siad that he would present the plan for the president's approval at the afternoon NSPG meeting. Shultz reiterated the need to keep the cruise ship away from Beirut.[29]

Later that afternoon in Rome, Rabb met again with Craxi and notified the Italian prime minister of America's intent to storm the ship. He explained that the United States government believed the reports about American citizens being killed were authentic and said that the situation was "intolerable." On Reagan's orders, Rabb told Craxi that the U.S. opposed negotiating with the hijackers, and that the rescue mission would go on Wednesday evening without Italian help "should any divergence emerge as to the necessity for it." Craxi disagreed with the American position, arguing that the ship was Italian, and that reports of passenger executions had not yet been confirmed. Instead of a military assault, the prime minister called for negotiations.[30]

At Tartus, the hijackers were contacted via Radio Monte Carlo by someone calling himself "Abu Khaled," who instructed them to sail the ship back to Port Said. Immediately, U.S. intelligence analysts scrambled to identify this Abu Khaled.

Back at the White House, the NSPG met following a White House reception for Singapore's prime minister Lee Kuan Yew. In attendance were Reagan, George Bush, Craig Fuller (from the vice president's office), Michael Armacost (sitting in for Shultz, who could not attend due to a scheduled meeting with Lee) and Oakley from State, Weinberger and Armitage from Defense, Attorney General Meese, Casey, Clair George and Charles Allen from the CIA, Dr. Alton Keel from the Office of Management and Budget, Admirals Crowe and Art Moreau from the JCS, and Don Regan, McFarlane, Poindexter, and North from the White House.[31]

After Poindexter recapped the situation, Casey gave an intelligence briefing, explaining that the hijackers claimed to belong to the Palestinian Liberation Front, but since there were three factions, the question remained, "which one?" This was an important question because identifying the correct faction could have a bearing on the outcome of the crisis. The faction headed by Abul Abbas was pro-Arafat and was the most likely to end the crisis peacefully. A second faction, led by Taalat Yaacoub, was opposed to Arafat and had aligned with Syria. This faction might kill passengers and thus necessitate the use of JSOC. A third faction had recently splintered from the second, and was headed by Abdul Fitah Ghanem. It opposed Arafat as well, and was also likely to kill passengers, thus requiring a rescue mission.

The CIA thought it unlikely that Abbas's faction was responsible because of Arafat's close ties to Italy and Egypt; such an attack would damage the PLO's relations with both nations. Instead, the CIA thought Yaacoub's faction was responsible because it had the "best resources for carrying out the hijacking." This group also had a motive—to discredit Arafat and derail the peace process.[32]

Meanwhile, the State Department's analyses came to different conclusions. Officials at the State Department's Bureau for Intelligence and Research (INR) discovered that the only PLF leader who ever used the name Abu Khaled was Abul Abbas, which confirmed intelligence passed to the United States by the Syrians and Jordanians.[33] One INR official thought that the hijackers "were probably going to Ashdod [the cruise ship's next stop in Israel] and something had happened aboard the ship. Their hand was forced and they probably panicked and decided to take it."[34] Now armed with reliable intelligence, Morton Abramowitz, the head of INR, informed Armacost and Oakley. Abramowitz told the two that a military operation would be risky and pointless since Abbas, a loyal Arafat ally, was likely to end the crisis without any more bloodshed.[35]

However, State's Bureau of Near Eastern Affairs argued that pinning the attack on Abbas was tantamount to blaming Arafat himself, and that such an accusation would put a damper on the Middle East peace process. One State Department official explained the problem, saying, "There is a resistance because it is very difficult to place blame on Arafat. Because if you do this, you brand him as a terrorist, and what do you have left? How do you negotiate, and how do you get out of this mess? As long as you have Arafat and the PLO at least you have something in the Middle East, not Abu Nidal and some of these hard liners. So I think there's a conscious effort to give the benefit of the doubt." Because of this, the State Department was unable to provide a consensus position paper for Shultz.[36]

The contradictory analyses about the identity of the hijackers seemed to have forced the group to focus on a rescue operation. Crowe outlined the assault plan but noted that the helicopters necessary for the operation were presently involved in NATO exercises nearly a day's steaming time away from the *Achille Lauro*. Consequently, the earliest an assault could take place would be Wednesday evening.[37]

Reagan noted in his biography that "It was time . . . to strike back at the terrorists, even though we all agreed that attacking the ship would be a high risk operation."[38] Still, based on the INR analysis, Armacost and Oakley recommended delaying the mission until the identity and intentions of the hijackers were clarified. Weinberger, too, was not enthusiastic about the rescue attempt, but as Reagan looked over the passenger list, he commented, "These are not spring chickens, Cap." The president then directed the operational planning to proceed and had Weinberger issue the following orders: (1) deploy JSOC to the Mediterranean (including both Seal Team Six and Delta Force so Stiner could mount an assault at sea or in a harbor, depending on the situation once he arrived on scene); (2) alert the Sixth Fleet (and the *Saratoga* battle group, then in the northern Ionian Sea) that a rescue mission might be in the offing; (3) call short a port call for the destroyer *Scott* and have it put to sea immediately to track the hijacked ship; and (4) deploy the Sixth Fleet's flagship *Coronado* from its home port in Gaeta, Italy. The president closed the meeting by telling Admiral Crowe to "take no prisoners."[39]

Back at Tartus, the *Achille Lauro* finally moved out to sea. When this happened, however, naval surveillance lost the ship again. In addition, the satellite that could have located the cruise ship was not tasked to search in the right area.[40] This left the intelligence community guessing about where the cruise liner was headed next, with some thinking it was sailing for Port Said as Abul Abbas had instructed, while others believed it was headed to Larnaca, Cyprus.[41] The Pentagon's intelligence agencies were further hampered by Weinberger; according to NSC consultant Michael Ledeen, the secretary of defense ordered that no one in the Pentagon (including the Defense Intelligence Agency and Naval Intelligence) ask the Israelis about the ship's location.[42]

Unsure of the ship's location once again, Oakley and North contacted Amiram Nir, Israeli prime minister Shimon Peres's special advisor on counterterrorism, and asked for help.[43] When Nir reported back, he said that the ship was near the Israeli–Lebanese border, headed south. Simultaneously, the CIA's Charles Allen confirmed that the anonymous Palestinian official headed to Egypt was none other than Abul Abbas, which meant that the *Achille Lauro* was headed back to Egypt.[44] With this new intelligence, the administration was not going to let the ship slip away again; American warships carrying SEAL Team Six moved into position, shadowing the cruise ship from just over the horizon.

## Day Three: Wednesday, October 9

In addresses to the Italian parliament, Foreign Minister Andreotti spoke of the "special importance" of his country's relationship with the PLO, while Defense Minister Spadolini declared that Rome wanted to avoid an American military response. Adding to the pressure to refrain from acting militarily, the CIA said it now believed that there were seven to twelve hijackers aboard the ship instead of just four, which would make any rescue operation much more difficult.[45] Still, Reagan approved Crowe's plan and ordered JSOC to storm the ship that night.[46] When it was finally confirmed that the cruise ship was heading back to Port Said, Egyptian foreign minister Esmat Abdel Meguid contacted the ambassadors of countries with citizens still aboard and asked whether they thought the ship should be allowed to dock or whether Egypt should deny permission as the Syrians had done.[47] Events were outpacing diplomacy though, and before responses could be formulated, the *Achille Lauro* arrived in Egyptian waters. When the ship appeared, Egyptian authorities blocked its attempt to enter Port Said harbor and surrounded it with four naval vessels.[48]

At around 5:00 am, Israeli intelligence notified Washington that the ship was "in the Egyptians' orbit," anchored off of Port Said. Once it was there, Abbas instructed the hijackers via ship-to-shore radio to apologize to the passengers and to treat them well. Also, the ship's captain radioed Egyptian authorities and said that everyone was alive and well, and that the hijackers wanted to come ashore.[49]

With the ship now in their waters, the Egyptian government found itself in a quandary. The Americans were angry, suspecting that at least one passenger had indeed been killed. If the terrorists surrendered to Egyptian authorities, the Americans would demand that the hijackers be extradited to the U.S. for trial. It would be politically impossible, however, for the Egyptian government to give up fellow Arabs to the Americans. Besides, Egyptian president Hosni Mubarak believed that the United States would be content so long as the hijackers faced trial somewhere, and a deal proposed by Arafat seemed to offer some hope. The PLO chairman phoned Italian prime minister Craxi around noon and said that the ship could be released "with all its passengers safe and sound" if the governments of Egypt and Italy agreed to turn the hijackers over to the PLO for trial.[50] The Italians and Egyptians both liked the idea. Next, Meguid notified the ambassadors of the United States, Great Britain, and West Germany that the hijackers now demanded that they join the negotiations.

At 2:00 pm in Cairo, Italian ambassador to Cairo Giovanni Migliuolo hosted a meeting at the Italian embassy where he tried to convince the other three ambassadors to accompany him to Port Said to negotiate with the hijackers. Veliotes and the others opposed the idea, arguing that such a visit would raise the stakes of the crisis by increasing publicity for the hijackers and would only embarrass the governments involved. As the ambassadors were debating, Meguid summoned the four to his office, where the Egyptian foreign minister presented an arrangement. The hijackers would surrender to Egyptian authorities, but all present had to guarantee that their governments would not press for extradition. In order to get the answer he wanted, Meguid told the group that the Egyptian government would cease all contacts with the hijackers in twenty minutes unless all four ambassadors agreed to the terms. Although the Egyptians were basing the deal on the premise that all of the passengers were unharmed, Veliotes would not agree, arguing that even if the crisis ended without bloodshed, the hijackers were responsible for seizing the ship and should be punished. The American ambassador added that the twenty-minute deadline—with the implication of bloodshed if they did not all agree to Cairo's terms—was out of order. Nonetheless, he and the other ambassadors agreed to contact their governments and relay the request. Rather than heading back to their respective embassies, though, the four stayed at the foreign ministry so as to avoid the large group of reporters that had gathered outside.[51]

When Veliotes called Washington, Shultz opposed the Egyptian proposal as did the State Department's legal advisor, Abraham Sofaer, who wanted the hijackers put on trial in the United States. Reagan, though, was resigned to the deal, saying, "It is Egypt's call," and was not willing to order an assault on the ship while it was under Egypt's control—especially when there was continued uncertainty concerning casualties. However, if any American had been harmed, the president expected the Egyptians to arrest and prosecute the hijackers. Consequently, with JSOC no longer able to act, Reagan ordered the team to stand down and return to the United States.[52] Still, Shultz disagreed with Reagan's position and had Armacost instruct Ambassador Veliotes not to agree to any arrangement with the hijackers.[53]

At around 3:30 pm, as the meetings in Cairo continued, word arrived that the hijackers had surrendered. Meguid announced, "It's all over. They've left the ship without guarantees." Veliotes, assuming that no passengers had been killed, congratulated the foreign minister on ending the hijacking peacefully. However, Meguid failed to mention that the Egyptians would turn the hijackers over to the PLO, and contrary to his assertion that the hijackers had surrendered without condition, the Egyptians had in fact given assurances to the hijackers that they would not be extradited, and that they would be granted safe passage out of Egypt.[54]

In Washington, the administration was livid. After enduring the two-week TWA ordeal only to have the hijackers disappear into the slums of Beirut, they did not want to see history repeat itself here. Consequently, White House spokesman Larry Speakes announced, "We believe those responsible should be prosecuted to the maximum extent possible." At State, Armacost called the CIA's Clair George and asked him to "Follow those guys."[55] The administration was not ready to concede defeat just yet.

While the Americans fumed, Meguid announced that because no passengers had died during the crisis, "the four hijackers have left the ship and are heading out of Egypt." At this, Veliotes headed to Port Said to inspect the situation firsthand. Meanwhile, his deputy was instructed to see Mubarak and tell the Egyptian president that it was "imperative" that the hijackers not be set free.[56]

At the State Department, Shultz met with the Tunisian ambassador to urge Tunisia—home of the PLO's headquarters—to help keep the hijackers in Egypt. He also sent a similar message to the Jordanians. In addition, Reagan sent a cable to Mubarak expressing displeasure that the hijackers had been allowed to go free. However, close cooperation with the United States was a hard sell in the Arab world, particularly after Israel's October 1 airstrikes on the PLO's headquarters in Tunis.

Despite earlier reports from Syria that two Americans had been killed by the hijackers, these deaths had yet to be confirmed. Exemplifying this uncertainty, the State Department put together draft press guidance for two contingencies, depending on whether or not an American had been killed, with both documents reiterating U.S. displeasure that "those responsible have been allowed to go free by the Government of Egypt."[57] A CIA assessment explained, "It remains unclear whether the two killings of Americans claimed yesterday actually occurred."[58] But when Veliotes boarded the ship around midnight, he learned the truth, and immediately radioed the news to an aide, saying, "Leon Klinghoffer was murdered by the terrorists off of Tartus when they were trying to get the attention of the Syrians. In my name, I want you to call the foreign minister. Tell him what we've learned, tell him the circumstances, tell him that in view of this and the fact that we, and presumably they, didn't have those facts, we insist that they prosecute those sons of bitches."[59]

When this reached Washington, North and Stark drafted a "strongly worded" message from Reagan to Mubarak asking that the hijackers be turned over to the United States, or at least to the Italian government, for trial. After McFarlane approved it, the message was forwarded to the State Department for clearance, and then to Reagan, who authorized sending it to Mubarak.[60] Shultz also instructed the embassy in Cairo to insist that the Egyptians arrest and prosecute the hijackers. He then attempted to phone Mubarak, but was unable to get through. Shultz was able to reach Meguid around 1:20 pm EST, and armed with the information about Klinghoffer's death, demanded that the hijackers be detained. The secretary of state indicated that Attorney General Meese was already preparing an indictment against the hijackers, and that the U.S. would make a formal extradition request in the very near future. Meguid replied that it was too late. The hijackers were gone.

### Day Four: Thursday, October 10

At noon on Thursday, President Mubarak told reporters, "[The hijackers] left Egypt already. I don't know where they went, but they possibly went to Tunis. When we accepted the hijackers' surrender, we did not have this information [about Klinghoffer's death]. This information emerged five hours after the surrender. In the meantime, the hijackers had left the country." A message from Mubarak repeating the claim arrived during an early morning NSC meeting but was immediately dismissed. McFarlane directed North to verify Mubarak's claim, and then asked where the JSOC forces were. North told him they were at Gibraltar, en route back to the United States.[61]

As to verifying Mubarak's claim, North first checked with American intelligence, but came up empty. So North and fellow NSC staffer Howard Teicher phoned Simhoni to see if Israel knew the hijackers' whereabouts. After some quick checking, the Israeli called back and said that the terrorists had not left Egypt yet; Mubarak was lying. Charles Allen was able to confirm the Israeli-supplied information when the CIA directed more of its intelligence-gathering assets against Egypt, including contacting a CIA agent planted inside Mubarak's office. The National Security Agency also stepped up its efforts against Egypt, intercepting a phone call in which the Egyptian leader ordered his aides to get the hijackers out of the country. Another monitored conversation had Mubarak telling Meguid that the hijackers were still in the country and that Shultz was "crazy" to think Egypt would give up its PLO brothers. All of this intelligence was forwarded directly to the White House Situation Room and provided conclusive proof of Mubarak's deception.[62]

As this information was coming in, the State Department was preparing instructions for Veliotes' meeting with Mubarak. The ambassador was to tell the Egyptian president two things: (1) we have information contrary to his public statements concerning the whereabouts of the hijackers; and (2) "letting the pirates go will surely rock the U.S.–Egyptian relationship." Simultaneously, Armacost was meeting with the Egyptian ambassador to Washington to make the same points. The message was also passed to the Egyptian government through intelligence-community connections.[63]

At the NSC staff, Stark had an idea. He thought that if the U.S. could get sufficient intelligence, it might be possible to intercept the plane the terrorists were using to leave Egypt, likening the proposed operation to the one during World War II that killed Japanese admiral Yamamoto. After all, he figured, if the plane was going to be over international waters on its way to Tunis, it would be within range of the American warplanes aboard the carrier *Saratoga*. They could force the plane to land somewhere sympathetic to the American position, and once on the ground, the hijackers could be taken into custody and flown straight back to the United States.[64] Stark discussed the idea briefly with Howard Teicher, and then brought the proposal to North. North liked the concept, so the three discussed possible locations where the plane could land, settling on the NATO base at Sigonella, Sicily. The three of them also contemplated a more fundamental question—how to find the plane if the Egyptians did fly the hijackers to another country. Teicher suggested contacting "our Israeli friends," and subsequently called Simhoni.[65]

North then took the idea to McFarlane and Poindexter. McFarlane was just about to leave with the president on a trip to Chicago, so North quickly explained, "We can intercept them and force them down at a friendly base, transfer them to one of our planes, and fly them back here for trial." McFarlane liked the idea and said, "It's a possibility. Work out the details. Call me in Chicago."[66]

Poindexter liked the idea as well and called an old friend, Admiral Moreau, who also happened to be Admiral Crowe's assistant, and explained, "It looks like they are going to be leaving today. What do you think about discussing in the Pentagon the possibility of intercepting the airplane?" Moreau conferred with Crowe, and they both endorsed the plan. Moreau called Poindexter back and told him, "If the President authorizes it, I think we can do it." He also indicated that Crowe would need "a go-ahead from the Secretary of Defense" before launching the operation.[67]

Crowe then set the plan in motion, calling General Richard Lawson, the Deputy Commander of U.S. Forces, Europe, to tell him that something was in the offing. Lawson, in turn, called his operations officer, Admiral James Dorsey, and had him set up an air picket for the intercept. Dorsey then called Admiral Jerry Houston at a naval command center in London to make the arrangements. Houston wanted to know what kind of aircraft he was arranging to intercept, but Dorsey did not know yet. Next, Admiral Frank Kelso, the commander of the Sixth Fleet, phoned Rear Admiral David Jeremiah—the battle group commander aboard the *Saratoga*—and instructed him to put together an operational plan. Within 45 minutes, Jeremiah launched his intercept "package," consisting of six F-14s, two A-6 tankers, and two E-2C radar aircraft.[68] The JSOC forces headed home were redirected from Gibraltar to the NATO base at Sigonella, where, if all went smoothly, they would take the hijackers into custody and return them to the United States for prosecution.

Crowe next went to see Deputy Secretary of Defense William Taft and informed him, "I've checked the forces, and we can intercept. I've told the Navy to assume they are going to do it and to make arrangements to put interceptors in the air corridor."

Taft replied, "That's fine. I think it's a good idea, but I have to let Weinberger know." Weinberger was in Ottawa at a session of the Canadian parliament, and as the intercept plan gained momentum, Taft scrambled to reach him. When he did, he got back to Crowe and said, "Weinberger's on the phone and he's against it. In fact, he's irate."

Weinberger couched his opposition to the plan in terms of policy, but was also upset that he had not been in the loop when the operation was planned.

When Crowe and Weinberger were connected, the secretary of defense said, "What the hell's going on? That's a terrible idea. I'm dead set against it, interfering with civilian aircraft. We'll be castigated all over the world."

"Well," Crowe responded, "the original request came from the White House. We've responded, and if those terrorists are aboard I'm for getting them and taking the heat."

Weinberger was not moved. "Just stop everything. I'll call the President."

"All right," said Crowe reluctantly. "I can call it off, but my information is that the aircraft may be taking off momentarily. It may even be in the air already. If we're going to intercept, we've got to do it with dispatch. We're going to have to get at it."[69]

The planning was moving along quickly now, with the NSC staff assuming the lead agency role; it conceived, planned, and facilitated the intercept because Poindexter believed he had too little time to shepherd the proposal through the normal interagency deliberative process.[70] He was also confident that the plan would work because, according to Noel Koch, "We had intelligence that the Egyptians had disarmed [the hijackers]. They had Egyptian security aboard [Unit 777], so the expectation was that the Egyptians would not fire on the Americans. They would resist, but they would not go to the point of armed resistance and would surrender. . . . As for the Italians, there was not much concern because [the NSC staff] didn't think the Italians would really enter into the process. They thought the Italians would be very happy to see us take them off their hands and get them out of the way."[71]

After Teicher contacted Simhoni, the Israeli headed over to the White House Situation Room. Once there, Simhoni verified that the request for intelligence was official and then called the Israeli chief of intelligence, General Ehud Barak, to ask for information on the hijackers. Within an hour, Barak called back and said the hijackers were at the al Maza air base near Cairo. He also provided the tail number of the hijackers' plane, the runway they would depart from, the type of aircraft, the flight plan, and the time of day it would depart. They also learned that one additional passenger would be on board—Abul Abbas. This information was verified by American intelligence, and Simhoni returned to the Israeli embassy.[72] North then presented the detailed plan to Poindexter who approved it and kicked it up the chain of command.[73]

The president was unaware of the ongoing planning and showed it in Chicago during a question-and-answer session with reporters. When asked about the PLO's plans to try the hijackers, Reagan responded, "Well, I think that if [Arafat] believes that their organization has enough of a—sort of a kind of national court set up, like a nation that they can bring [the hijackers] to justice and—carry that out, all right; but just so they are brought to justice."

One of the reporters replied, "But you'd let the PLO punish them, then?" "What? Yes, I said if they were determined to do that," responded Reagan. Following the exchange, McFarlane "clarified" the president's remarks, indicating that the U.S. intended to pursue extradition so the hijackers could be punished in an American court of law.[74]

The president then headed to Deerfield, Illinois, for an appearance at the Sara Lee Bakery. Around noon, Poindexter called McFarlane on a secure data-link and told him, "Ollie thinks we can intercept these guys, and the Joint Chiefs believe it's feasible, but I'm having trouble with Cap. I want to know if you think Reagan will approve."[75]

McFarlane pulled the president aside and explained the intercept plan. Reagan's initial response was positive, but he wanted to know about the risks, potential gains and losses, possible reactions of other countries involved (including the impact on the Middle East peace process), and the "what ifs" in case the plan did not proceed as expected. McFarlane outlined the potential problems, including: (1) the Navy might intercept the wrong plane, (2) the Egyptian pilot could refuse to land, and (3) likely damage to diplomatic relations with Egypt, Italy, and the Arab states. Reagan wanted the intercept executed in accordance with precise rules of engagement, and provided "one or two elements of guidance on the concept and on the rules." He then approved the plan in principle, telling McFarlane, "Well, good God, they've murdered an American here, so let's get on with it."[76]

With that order, McFarlane called Poindexter and told him, "The President says, 'Go ahead with the planning and keep me advised.'"[77] He also instructed his aide to contact Shultz and Weinberger to have them register their views with Reagan as soon as possible. Then McFarlane left the president in Chicago and flew to New Jersey for a pre-arranged dinner with former president Richard Nixon, effectively leaving Poindexter in control at the NSC.[78]

Now that Reagan had tentatively approved the plan, Moreau requested that North draft a National Security Decision Directive for the president to sign authorizing the action. With Stark's help, North did so and faxed it to the president aboard Air Force One. The NSDD specified the rules of engagement that had been developed by Moreau: American planes were allowed to fire live ammunition in front of the plane, but not to shoot it down. Reagan wrote in his diary as he flew back to Washington that "Of course we will not attack the plane, just signal it to turn and crowd it a bit."[79]

On his way home from Ottawa, Weinberger phoned Reagan to express his objections. However, the two planes were unable to link their secure phone systems, so the two talked over an open channel, using the code names "Rawhide" and "Finley." In a conversation that was intercepted by a ham radio operator, Weinberger complained that the intercept would damage

American relations with Egypt and other moderate Arab states, as well as relations with Italy. He also thought the interception of the Egyptian airliner—a civilian plane—in international airspace would be a violation of international law. Further, diverting the plane might require firing shots across its bow. The president said he did not care what it took. When Weinberger persisted in his opposition, Reagan told him the plan was going ahead anyway, saying, "Cap, it is pretty cut and dried. This is a guilty party; we cannot let them go." When Weinberger attempted to call again to stop the operation, the NSC staff with Reagan would not let the Secretary of Defense get through.[80] At 4:37 pm, the President was notified that the hijackers' plane was leaving Cairo, whereupon Reagan signed the NSDD authorizing action and instructed Weinberger to phone Crowe and order the operation to proceed.[81]

When the administration learned that the plane was headed to Tunisia, North prepared a cable from Reagan to Tunisian President Habib Bourguiba requesting that the EgyptAir flight not be permitted to land. The NSC also prepared cables requesting that the Greek and Lebanese governments deny landing rights for the terrorists' plane. As soon as the hijackers' plane was airborne, these cables were transmitted.[82] When the plane's pilot requested permission to land at Tunis, the tower declined.[83] At Athens the scene was repeated, owing to pressure from the American State Department.

Shultz then cabled Veliotes and instructed him to tell Egyptian Defense Minister Abu Ghazala, "Let us take this problem off your hands." Ghazala apparently liked the idea. Veliotes' cable back to Shultz noted that the Egyptian was "thunderstruck."[84]

However, the question of where to force the plane to land was still not settled. The State Department was unable to get permission from the Italian government to land on Sicily because it could not reach Prime Minister Craxi. At the NSC, staffers were already considering other options. Egypt and Tunisia were ruled out because those governments would likely be overly sympathetic to the hijackers. Greece was not considered an option because the Papandreou government had friendly relations with the PLO and would be unlikely to let the Americans walk away with Abbas. The British base at Akrotiri, Cyprus was eliminated from the list because it was believed that the British would not give the necessary permission on such short notice. So attention turned to Israel. North phoned Simhoni at the Israeli embassy and asked if the plane could land at Tel Aviv. Simhoni put the request to Barak, but the Israeli intelligence chief wanted to know if this was an official request from the president. Simhoni passed this concern back to North asking, "Is this a presidential request, or an Oliver request?" Within a few minutes, North called back saying, "This is an official presidential request to land in Tel

Aviv." Simhoni made arrangements for the plane to land at Tel Aviv, or at a site in the Negev should it be necessary, and also arranged for Israeli warplanes to be in the air as a precaution. Despite the Israeli willingness to help, the State Department objected to using Israel. One official said that to do so would be "the biggest slap in the face to the Egyptians. What we have done is bad enough." Ultimately, it was decided that Italy was the best option.[85]

Even if the State Department had been able to reach Craxi right away, getting Italy's permission would still have been problematic. Since many Italian officials had friendly relations with the PLO and Egypt, there was a belief that if the U.S. asked permission to use Sigonella, someone in the Italian government would leak the operation to the PLO and Egypt, who might then alter the hijackers' escape plan. It was much more likely that the Italian government would acquiesce to the operation if it were presented with a fait accompli.[86]

After failing to land at Tunis and Athens, the EgyptAir plane attempted to contact Cairo for instructions, but was unable to get through. Moreau had anticipated this possibility and ordered U.S. forces to jam the plane's radio.[87] As a result, the pilots decided to head back over the Mediterranean to Egypt, at which point planes from the *Saratoga* intercepted the airliner and escorted it to Sigonella.

As the intercepted plane was on its way to Sicily, the administration continued its scramble to contact the Italian leadership. When the State Department still could not reach Craxi, North suggested that Michael Ledeen, an NSC consultant who happened to be old friends with the Italian prime minister, give it a try. Ledeen was able to track him down and proceeded to request permission to land the Egyptian airliner at Sigonella. After some banter, Craxi said he would "take care of it at once."[88] Permission was not crucial, though, since Admiral Crowe had ordered the *Saratoga*'s planes to put the hijackers down on Sicily with or without Italy's permission.[89]

At 6:30 pm EST, as the plane was being shepherded toward Sigonella, Shultz called Poindexter to make sure that there was a transport plane at Sigonella ready to fly the hijackers to the United States. Poindexter told Shultz, "Cap is against it. He's afraid of trouble with the Italians." Ten minutes later, Reagan, Shultz, and Weinberger held a conference call to discuss the fast-moving developments. Despite Craxi's assurances, the control tower at Sigonella had refused to let the plane land, and Italian warplanes were preparing to scramble to move the *Saratoga*'s F-14s away from the Egyptian plane. Weinberger argued that the operation should be called off, but Shultz encouraged the president to "just do it." Reagan agreed with the secretary of state and ordered the landing to proceed. The president also directed Weinberger to phone Italian defense minister Spadolini, and for Admiral Crowe to phone his Italian counterpart, to ask the Italians for landing permission. Attorney General Meese also contacted his counterpart, Italian interior minister Oscar Luigi Scalfaro, to ask for Italian cooperation. In the meantime, Reagan talked to Italian prime minister Craxi.[90] These multiple approaches were necessary because, as one member of the U.S. embassy staff in Rome later said, "the Italian government is not very centralized."[91]

North and several other members of the TIWG, including Noel Koch and Charles Allen, were on watch in the White House Situation Room as the intercept took shape. When fellow TIWG member Buck Revell arrived and saw what was in the works, he protested vigorously saying, "Damn it, Ollie! You can't force the plane down in Italian territory. They have jurisdiction. Their laws don't give them any discretion. They'll have to arrest the terrorists."

"Buck, don't worry. Carl Stiner will have those guys out before the Italians even know they were there," said North.

Revell was skeptical, saying, "The *Carabinieri* are practically an occupation force in Sicily. They'll be there when the wheels stop, and they won't back down. It's their country. It was their ship that was hijacked. They don't have any choice in this situation."[92]

Despite this, the intercept continued. Those in the Situation Room were relegated to the role of observers, though, as the Pentagon had cut communications between the NSC and forces in the Mediterranean to keep the NSC staff from meddling.[93]

When the hijackers' plane finally landed, it did so with Craxi's blessing. However, the Italian prime minister had not been told about the American planes carrying the JSOC forces, which landed moments later. Troops from Delta Force quickly surrounded the plane, only to find themselves surrounded by armed and angry Italian troops. Although the Italians did allow the hijackers' plane to land, they were not going to let the Americans just walk off with the plane's passengers. So now, if the United States wanted to take custody of the terrorists, it faced the prospect of conflict with the Egyptian commandos aboard the plane as well as with the Italians. General Stiner radioed Washington to ask permission to "shoot my way out," but was told an emphatic "no."[94] In Washington, Crowe briefly considered having his troops shoot out the plane's tires to "preempt the Italians from letting it go," but decided against it.[95]

Shultz was talking to Italian foreign minister Giulio Andreotti when Armacost informed the secretary about the stalemate at Sigonella. When Shultz told Andreotti that the U.S. was transferring the hijackers from one plane to another for transport to the United States, Andreotti replied, "I absolutely cannot give authorization to that. They should stand trial in Italy." The State Department's legal advisor, Abraham Sofaer, was in the office with Shultz and confirmed that the U.S. had no legal right to use the base for anything other than NATO activities. If the transfer was going to take place, the Italians would have to permit it. Shultz returned to Andreotti and pleaded, "An American has been murdered, and trial here is appropriate." The Italian still would not agree to let the American operation proceed; when the call ended, Shultz reported the situation to Reagan.[96]

The administration was also receiving feedback from the embassy in Cairo where Veliotes argued that, with the intercept completed, the Italians should now take custody of the hijackers. That way the United States could still claim that the terrorists had been brought to justice. He thought that with the hijackers all but captured, the administration's focus should turn to the state of U.S.–Italian and U.S.–Egyptian relations. Further, giving the hijackers to the Italians did not foreclose the option of extradition. If the Italians said no, the hijackers would still be prosecuted in Italy. As for Abbas, the Egyptians were saying he had come to Egypt as a guest and was responsible for ending the hijacking peacefully. As far as Cairo was concerned, Abbas was aboard the EgyptAir plane under Egyptian protection, and even pro-American elements in the Egyptian government were arguing that the United States should let Abbas go so that there would be something left with which to rebuild the U.S.–Egyptian relationship. To Veliotes, it was not worth damaging relations with two of America's closest allies just to get Abbas. Shortly after sending his input, someone at the State Department cut off the ambassador's information about the situation at Sigonella; when Veliotes figured out what had happened, he called Armacost and the cables began flowing to Cairo again.[97]

As the stalemate at Sigonella continued, Ledeen again called Craxi and told him that the American troops were not going to "do anything crazy, but that the President felt strongly about bringing the terrorists to justice." Craxi told Ledeen that it was out of his hands, explaining that the custody and prosecution of the hijackers was now a matter for the Italian courts to decide. When Reagan was told the Italians would not acquiesce, he ordered Stiner and his forces to stand down.[98]

Once the standoff ended, Ledeen contacted Craxi again with Ledeen translating for both men, Reagan said that the United States would be filing an extradition request for the hijackers immediately. Craxi wanted to know if the U.S. insisted on the arrest of all four hijackers, and Reagan, who had not been briefed in detail, said, "It might be acceptable if the two main terrorists were put in jail." Ledeen was aware that the U.S. had already demanded that all four be arrested pending extradition, and covered the president's mistake telling Craxi, "We want all four in prison." Shortly afterward, the Italians informed Mubarak that the hijackers aboard the plane were being arrested, and Abul Abbas was going to be taken into custody for questioning.[99]

However, Abbas refused to leave the plane, and the Italians were not prepared to go aboard what was technically sovereign Egyptian territory just to detain him. When the hijackers were leaving the plane, though, Abbas stood at the door watching, allowing JSOC snipers to acquire him "in the crosshairs." With this new opportunity, Stiner requested permission to fire, but was denied.[100] With nothing left to do, the JSOC forces prepared to depart, although Stiner remained behind to keep tabs on Abbas.[101]

## The Aftermath

There was jubilation at the White House over the successful intercept of the EgyptAir plane. An exuberant Reagan crowed at a news conference, "You can run but you can't hide." At the same time, the administration recognized that the U.S. had upset relations with two of its allies, so Reagan immediately set out to mend fences. At a press conference the president praised Italy, saying, "I want to point out the crucial role played by the Italian government in bringing this operation to a successful and peaceful conclusion. Throughout, Prime Minister Craxi has been courageous in his insistence that those apprehended shall be subject to full due process of law." As for Egypt, Reagan was not as forthcoming with his praise. In an official statement, the administration said, "The United States wants to emphasize the fundamental and durable interests that the United States and Egypt share, interests which transcend this difficult incident. . . . We will do all we can to ensure that the basic U.S.–Egyptian relationship—in which both our countries have taken so much pride for so long—remains unaffected."[102]

Despite this, relations with the U.S. remained severely damaged by the intercept, and a CIA assessment predicted "Egyptian relations with the United States and the PLO are likely to remain strained for some time."[103] On October 12, Mubarak accused the United States of "an act of piracy," and when the Syrian government returned Klinghoffer's body to the United States on October 16, the Egyptian president was reportedly enraged.[104] When Ambassador Veliotes issued a statement expressing "deep regret" over the incident on October 14 in an effort to ease tensions, many in the administration were angry, thinking that it was Mubarak who owed the U.S. an apology.[105] On October 15, Mubarak complained again that Egypt had not yet received a satisfactory apology for the incident. Additionally, the Egyptian president found himself under intense domestic pressure to take some punitive measure against the United States. Both moderate and radical Egyptian groups denounced the intercept, and protestors marched through Cairo demanding that Mubarak cancel upcoming joint Egyptian–American military exercises and deny America the use of Egyptian military facilities.

In Rome, passengers from the *Achille Lauro* identified the four hijackers in a police line-up, and the Italian government charged the four with premeditated murder, kidnapping, hijacking of a ship, and possession of arms and explosives. Hours after the hijackers were taken into custody, Meese called Mino Martinazzoli, the Italian minister of justice, and told him that the administration was preparing a provisional arrest warrant for the four and Abul Abbas. When Veliotes saw a draft of the cable intended to persuade the Italians to arrest and extradite Abbas, he immediately recognized that much of the background information had come directly from a Mossad report. He called Washington and argued that it should be rewritten, since its Israeli source would quickly be recognized. No change was made, and the cable was sent.[106] At 5:30 am on October 12, Rabb went to the home of Salvatore Zhara Buda, the assistant to Martinazzoli, and hand-delivered the U.S. extradition request.[107] Additionally, Revell informed Italian police, Italian domestic security services, and Interpol, that Federal District Court Judge Charles Richey had issued an arrest warrant for the hijackers and Abbas, charging them with piracy on the high seas, hostage taking and conspiracy.[108] Still, despite all the rhetoric, the White House was not overly upset about the situation. Chief of Staff Donald Regan noted during a staff meeting on October 11, "Our goal is to see that justice is done—where it is done is immaterial."[109]

Despite the administration's all-out push for extradition, the Italians were not prepared to hand Abbas and the hijackers over, even with a proper request. Instead, they decided to ignore the terms of the U.S.–Italian extradition treaty and allowed Abbas to go, facilitating his departure to Yugoslavia.[110] Craxi later claimed that "the request for the provisional arrest, though formally correct, did not, in the Justice Minister's opinion, satisfy the factual and substantive requirements laid down by Italian law. . . . This being so, there was no longer any legal basis . . . [for] detaining Abbas, since at the time he was on board an aircraft which enjoyed extraterritorial status."[111] As for the four hijackers, the Italians decided to put them on trial in an Italian court.

While Reagan was praising Italy for helping peacefully end the hijacking, a statement issued on October 13 deplored the Italian handling of Abul Abbas, saying, "The U.S. Government finds it incomprehensible that Italian authorities permitted Abul Abbas to leave Italy despite a U.S. Government request to the Italian Government for his arrest and detention. . . . The U.S. Government is astonished at this breach of any reasonable standard of due process and is deeply disappointed."

Before the *Achille Lauro* hijacking, Craxi and Spadolini were already personally at odds, and deep political divisions between Craxi's Socialist Party and Spadolini's Republicans over economic policy existed.[112] Because of the crisis, though, these preexisting cleavages within Craxi's coalition government erupted into open political warfare. Spadolini accused Craxi of releasing Abbas before a judge could review the extradition request and of failing to live up to Italy's international responsibilities. In protest, Spadolini withdrew his party from the coalition, and the Italian government collapsed on October 17, 1985.

In early 1986, the public prosecutor's Office in Genoa brought charges against three of the four hijackers, a number of other Palestinians, and Abul Abbas for the hijacking. In mid-1986, Abbas was tried in absentia, found guilty and sentenced to life in prison. The hijackers received jail sentences as well: Majed al Molqi received 30 years, Abdel Ibrahim received 24 years, and Hallah al Hassan, who cooperated with the prosecution, received 15 years. The fourth hijacker was a minor and prosecutors dropped the charges against him. Others involved in the hijacking received sentences ranging from time served to seven years. Abu Abbas remained at large until 2003 when he was captured by American forces in Baghdad following Operation Iraqi Freedom.

The capture of the *Achille Lauro* hijackers marked a turning point in American counter-terrorism policy. The consensus position (with the exception of Weinberger, who had little choice but to go along) favored using the military, first to launch the rescue mission, and later to intercept and capture the terrorists. However, this success seems to have satisfied the appetite of some in the administration for strong action, for when terrorists struck again just after Christmas 1985, the consensus was gone, and the debate started all over again.

*Chapter Six*

# The Rome and Vienna Airport Massacres

By the passage of time, everyone changes, through experience. In the 1970s we supported liberal movements without knowing which were terrorists and which were not. In the 1980s we began to differentiate between terrorists and those with legitimate political aspirations.

—Muammar al-Qaddafi, 1992[1]

## BACKGROUND

Libyan strongman Colonel Muammar al-Qaddafi was in the Reagan administration's crosshairs from day one. However, it was previous administrations' experiences with the Libyan leader that set the stage for confrontation in the 1980s. In 1969, Qaddafi overthrew the pro-Western King Idris in a military coup, and President Nixon subsequently blocked the sale of twelve C-130 cargo planes to the North African nation. When relations soured further and American forces vacated their base in Libya (Wheelus Air Force Base), Qaddafi declared "victory" over the Untied States. Then in 1973, contrary to international law and custom, Qaddafi claimed the entire Gulf of Sidra— including its international waters—as Libyan territorial waters, and vowed to defend them. During the Ford and Carter years, as Qaddafi tilted more and more toward Moscow, the United States extended its arms and technology embargo against Libya, and in 1979, the State Department took the dramatic step of placing Libya on its list of countries supporting terrorism. In response, Qaddafi allowed the U.S. embassy in Tripoli to be sacked and burned by a mob as Libyan officials stood by. Following this outrage, the United States significantly curtailed its diplomatic presence in Libya, moving its remaining

163

staff to the Belgian embassy. Following similar attacks against the French and Tunisian embassies in Tripoli, the United States withdrew the last of its diplomatic personnel from Libya. In a retaliatory move, Libya detained two Americans and expelled twenty-five others on espionage charges.[2]

Early in 1980, the CIA reported that Qaddafi had warned, "Libyan exiles . . . should return home, or they would be punished." True to his word, on October 14, 1980, Faisal Zagalai—a Colorado State University student and leader of the Libyan dissident community, was shot and seriously wounded in Fort Collins, Colorado. The following April, when a former Green Beret named Eugene Tafoya was arrested and charged with the attempted murder, police found an address book in his possession with the names and addresses of other Libyan exiles living in the United States.[3] Tafoya's arrest prompted the State Department to order the closing of the Libyan Peoples' Bureau (or LPB, Libya's version of an embassy) in Washington, D.C., and the expulsion of Libyan diplomats in May 1981.

So when Reagan and his foreign policy team came to Washington in January 1981, Libya was already a major concern. From the start, both the CIA and the State Department prepared to push hard for a new covert policy that would, in secretary of state-designate Alexander Haig's words, "bloody Qaddafi's nose." Even before the inauguration, Haig was working on a strategy to oust Qaddafi, convening a meeting with the deputy director of the State Department's Bureau of Intelligence and Research (INR), Herman Cohen, and Director of Current Intelligence Philip Stoddard, to determine what the United States could do to hurt the Libyan leader. Lillian Harris, INR's North African analyst later described the situation: "Qaddafi presented this marvelous target because you could fight the Soviets, you could fight terrorism, and you could fight evil Arabs." Qaddafi raised his profile even further when he ventured into Latin American politics, developing close ties with the Sandinistas in Nicaragua and aiding the Marxist government of Grenada in their effort to construct a runway long enough to accommodate Soviet military aircraft.[4]

Haig also conferred with State Department Counselor Robert McFarlane and asked what could be done to "put Qaddafi back in the box." McFarlane subsequently met with Egyptian president Anwar Sadat and the two discussed possible options against Qaddafi, including one in which Egypt would annex Libya. McFarlane and Haig were intrigued by this idea and asked the State Department's Bureau of Political and Military Affairs to investigate how it could be done militarily. Their report argued that it should be a purely Egyptian operation, but that unilateral action on the part of Cairo would be difficult since Egypt's military was primarily focused on its eastern front with Israel. The report also explored a simultaneous American–Egyptian operation, where the U.S. would airlift Egyptian paratroopers to Benghazi in conjunction with American naval bombardments and a Marine landing. However, when the plan was floated at the White House and the Pentagon, fierce opposition from the military caused the idea to be killed.[5]

William Casey, the newly confirmed Director of Central Intelligence, was also on Qaddafi's trail. On his third day as DCI, Casey received a Special National Intelligence Estimate (SNIE) entitled "Libya: Aims and Vulnerabilities." In a section called "Key Judgments," the analysis explained that, first, "Qaddafi's recent success in Chad [which he had recently invaded] ensures that his aggressive policies will pose a growing challenge to the U.S. and Western interests." Second, "The domestic and exile opposition to his regime is poorly organized and ineffective." In other words, active measures would be necessary if the U.S. intended to topple Qaddafi. Third, "Soviet objectives are served by Qaddafi's anti-Western policies. . . . The Soviets gain substantial hard currency earnings from massive arms sales to Libya," estimated to be worth one billion dollars a year. The report went on to say that, recently, Qaddafi had "employed political intrigue, diplomatic activism, terrorism, assassination, and now, in Chad, military occupation." Concerning the Gulf of Sidra, the estimate reported, "His military has standing orders to attack U.S. ships or aircraft penetrating this line [the so-called "line of death" at 32 degrees, 30 minutes in the Gulf of Sidra]. . . . Chances for an incident off Libya involving the U.S. are relatively high."[6]

As a result, Casey directed that more intelligence-collecting assets be directed against Libya, which led to a breakthrough when the Libyan diplomatic and intelligence codes were broken. Casey's challenge to obtain quality and timely intelligence was made easier, though, because Qaddafi often used unsecured phone lines, providing the United States with a fairly clear picture of his plans.[7]

To pressure Qaddafi into curtailing his troublesome activities, the administration adopted a series of active measures, including a plan to covertly aid Chad's former defense minister Hissen Habré's efforts to make the war there more costly for Qaddafi.[8] In addition, the administration began dispensing military assistance to other states that were resisting Libyan adventurism, including Tunisia, Morocco, Egypt, and Sudan. The United States also contributed twelve million dollars to maintain the international peacekeeping force in Chad, conducted joint military exercises with Egypt and Sudan, quietly notified Egypt that the United States would not block Egyptian action against Libya, and sent extensive military aid, including a Green Beret unit, to Liberia where Qaddafi was also meddling.[9]

In June 1981, the National Security Council (NSC) sought to increase pressure on Qaddafi, raising the possibility of renewing naval maneuvers inside the Gulf of Sidra—an operation that had been canceled by President Carter during the hostage negotiations with Iran. Secretary of Defense Caspar Weinberger favored the operation as a means of repudiating Qaddafi's claim to the area and maintaining freedom of navigation in international waters.[10] The Joint Chiefs of Staff (JCS), the Defense Intelligence Agency (DIA), and the U.S. European Command (EuCom) all supported the maneuvers, agreeing that the likelihood of a hostile reaction from Libya was low. With these reassurances, Reagan approved the operation, including a set of retaliatory measures the Navy would employ should the Libyans react militarily.[11]

When the freedom of navigation exercises commenced, Libya did not immediately respond. But on August 19, after American planes had patrolled the Gulf of Sidra for nearly twenty-four hours, two Libyan SU-22 fighter planes fired on two F-14s from the carrier *Nimitz* some sixty nautical miles from the Libyan coastline. The American pilots shot back, downing both Libyan planes. At the time, Qaddafi was visiting South Yemen, and when he was notified by phone of the defeat (a conversation the National Security Agency intercepted), he was livid and vowed to kill President Reagan.[12] Qaddafi repeated the threat several times over the next week, including once while visiting Lieutenant Colonel Mengitsu Haili Mariam, Ethiopia's Marxist leader, who was also attended by a CIA asset. Throughout September and October, the administration became increasingly concerned about intelligence that indicated Libyan assassination teams were on their way to the United States to kill the president and other top American officials, as well as reports that Qaddafi had enlisted a number of terrorist groups to attack American targets.[13]

Libya also stepped up its direct use of terrorist tactics, undertaking several operations in November. The first was thwarted when two loudspeakers filled with explosives were discovered in Nairobi, Kenya, as they were being loaded aboard a plane bound for the American Recreation Club in Khartoum. One intelligence report explained, "Bombs of this size could have completely destroyed the club and killed or maimed several hundred innocent people. . . . [The speakers] were prepared by Libyan intelligence officers assigned to the Libyan Peoples' Bureau. A Libyan intelligence officer personally assured that the bombs were [loaded] on a flight to Khartoum."[14] The second attack occurred in Paris, where U.S. charge d'affaires Christian Chapman was fired on but escaped unhurt. In addition, Libyan squads were reportedly sent to attack the U.S. embassies in Athens and Ankara, and Libyan operatives were seen surveilling American installations in Lebanon, Brazil, Turkey, and the Central African Republic.

At an NSPG meeting on November 30 to discuss the Libyan threat, Reagan asked his staff to develop plans for "a military response against Libya in the event of further Libyan attempts to assassinate American officials or attack U.S. facilities." As a result, Haig and Frank Carlucci (Weinberger's deputy) drafted a memo on "Counter-terrorism planning toward Libya." It said that the president "should immediately direct the Joint Chiefs of Staff to ready assets to carry out military action against Libya in self-defense, following a further Libyan provocation," and recommended five graduated responses: (1) attack terrorist training sites in Libya; (2) bomb Qaddafi's airfields; (3) attack Libyan naval facilities; (4) attack Libyan military equipment stockpiles; and (5) sabotage Libyan naval vessels in port, using the Navy SEALs.[15]

On December 6, Qaddafi appeared on ABC's *This Week With David Brinkley* and denied that he planned to assassinate Reagan, claiming that the U.S. had invented the story. The following day Reagan responded, "I wouldn't believe a word he says if I were you. . . . We have the evidence and he knows it." Within days, Reagan sent a message to Qaddafi through the Belgians, saying, "I have detailed and verified information about several Libyan-sponsored plans to assassinate U.S. government officials and attack U.S. facilities both in the U.S. and abroad. Any acts of violence directed by Libya or its agents against officials of the U.S., at home or abroad, will be regarded by the U.S. government as an armed attack upon the U.S. and will be met by every means necessary to defend this nation in accordance with Article 51 of the United Nations Charter."[16]

Dealing militarily with Libya, however, was problematic due to the 1,500 Americans living and working there. If the United States did react militarily to Libyan provocations, these American citizens could be in mortal danger. So on December 9, Deputy Secretary of State William Clark asked all Americans in Libya to depart immediately, with Reagan repeating the request the next day. Some left, but only temporarily.

Another problem the administration faced was what to do about the fairly substantial amount of American trade with Libya. The United States purchased fully one-third of Libya's oil, amounting to nearly ten percent of all U.S. imports.[17] On December 10, Reagan signed NSDD-16, setting up a task force to oversee implementation of the administration's new Libya policy, including limited economic sanctions that were imposed on March 10, 1982. Further, it declared that the U.S. would support other governments helping anti-Libyan forces in Chad's civil war.[18]

By late December both the CIA and the State Department concluded that the stories of Libyan hit squads or assassination teams in the United States were false. Nevertheless, the stories had made an impact. According to the INR's Philip Stoddard, "The top people suddenly felt Qaddafi was coming after them personally. They took umbrage at that."[19] By the end of 1981, Libya policy had become personal.

In 1982, Qaddafi continued to create problems for the administration, expanding his campaign against Libyan ex-patriots. In October, he announced that Libyan exiles working against the regime were "escaped agents of America" and faced assassination. As a further provocation, in December, Libya annexed the Aozou Strip in northern Chad—an area believed to be rich in uranium deposits.

Qaddafi was fairly quiet in 1983, but that did not slow the administration's efforts against him. In February, the U.S. launched Operation Early Call, a plan to lure Qaddafi into sending his air force to aid a fabricated pro-Libyan coup in Sudan. Once en route, the Libyan planes would be ambushed by Egyptian and American forces. However, the Libyans did not take the bait.[20]

In October, the State Department produced a report on Qaddafi's activities entitled, "The Libyan Problem." It reminded its readers about the seriousness of the challenge Qaddafi posed to Western interests, and pointed to a number of terrorist incidents in the late 1970s and early 1980s that he was responsible for. It also stated, "Qaddafi has established a series of camps in Libya for training foreign revolutionaries. . . . Several camps are devoted entirely to instructing terrorists in a range of explosives and arms for use in assassination and sabotage." The report went on to highlight the growing relationship between Qaddafi and the Soviet Union, bleakly concluding, "[Qaddafi's] ambitions and hatreds are so ingrained that there is little prospect for change." Additional intelligence showed that the KGB had trained Libyan intelligence officers at the Andropov Institute in Moscow, and regularly supplied Qaddafi with reports on American naval maneuvers in the Mediterranean.[21]

The year 1984 marked an increase in Qaddafi's subversive activities. In March, intelligence reports concluded that Libya was intervening in Sudan, and that Qaddafi had sent a TU-22 bomber to attack a CIA-backed exile radio station in Omdurman, Sudan, that had been broadcasting anti-Qaddafi propaganda. After the air attack in Sudan, the administration began to reevaluate its Libya policy.[22] Part of this new thinking was manifest in NSDD-138, signed by Reagan on April 3, 1984, which placed special emphasis on campaigns against states supporting terrorists and guerrillas, including the USSR, Iran, Syria, and Libya.[23] Additionally, the CIA appears to have provided intelligence to the Direction de la Sécurité Eterieure (the French intelligence service) in support of two operations meant to overthrow Qaddafi, one of which resulted in a failed coup attempt in May.[24]

In Washington, Casey recognized the growing problem and encouraged Secretary of State George Shultz to take the lead against Qaddafi. Shultz then assigned his deputy, Kenneth Dam, to conduct a review of U.S. policy toward Libya. By May, Dam had produced a provisional paper entitled "Countering Libyan Terrorism," in which he outlined ten options for the administration, ranging from "do nothing" to the extreme—"seek a regime change." Option eight proposed to "establish a pattern of directly reacting to Libyan terrorism by going after carefully selected Libyan targets . . . ," and option nine was to "Mount a program of covert action to preempt, disrupt and frustrate Libya's plans." On May 19, Dam convened a meeting at the State Department to review the proposals, which were subsequently toned down and consolidated into four, with the most extreme option—number four—proposing to "forcefully expand existing policy. . . . For example, re-examine the feasibility of other military or covert options."[25]

Meanwhile, the official Libyan news agency announced that the "masses have decided to form suicide commandos to chase traitors and stray dogs wherever they are and liquidate them physically." Shortly thereafter, in Philadelphia, police arrested two Libyans trying to buy handguns with silencers, while in Britain, Greece, and Italy, six Libyan exiles were killed by other assassination squads. In June, Qaddafi stepped up his rhetoric proclaiming, "We are capable of exporting terrorism to the heart of America."

Despite a willingness to confront Qaddafi, and the Libyan leader's continued penchant for troublemaking, the administration could not agree on a new Libya policy. On June 13, the CIA's Deputy Director for Intelligence, Robert Gates, received a request from Hugh Montgomery, head of INR: "In connection with the very sensitive policy review which he is now conducting, Ken Dam has asked for an interagency assessment of the threat which Libya poses to U.S. interests." Coincidentally, the CIA's national intelligence officer for the Near East, Graham Fuller, was already conducting such a review, trying to determine where Qaddafi was weak and in what ways U.S. policy might be effective against him. With input from the CIA, DIA, INR, and the National Security Agency, Fuller produced a 29-page interagency intelligence memo explaining that the current U.S. trade policy was not working and that Libya's oil production had not been hampered by American sanctions. In assessing Qaddafi's vulnerabilities, it argued that "no course of action short of stimulating Qaddafi's fall will bring any significant and enduring change in Libyan policies." The memo then advocated increased support for Libyan exiles opposed to Qaddafi, and "a broad program in cooperation with key countries [i.e., Egypt and Algeria] combining political, economic and paramilitary action." However, not everyone agreed with Fuller's analysis. Officials at the Pentagon were all in favor of increasing pressure on Qaddafi so long as military action was not required, while INR's analysts believed that the CIA had exaggerated Qaddafi's vulnerabilities and the opportunities to bring him down.[26]

On July 4, the CIA issued a threat assessment on Libya, stating that Qaddafi continued to act against U.S. interests, but that the only immediate concern was his involvement in Sudan. The assessment continued, "An act of Libyan terrorism in the US is possible, but we believe Libya would be hard-pressed to mount a successful operation. Libya almost certainly has a few agents among the approximately 1500 Libyan students in the U.S.," including "approximately 200 fanatic pro-Qaddafi students here."[27]

In the second half of 1984, a flurry of events caused tensions to mount. In July and August, the Libyan ferry *Ghat* laid mines in the Red Sea, damaging nineteen ships. As that episode ended, the administration discovered that Qaddafi had dispatched military advisors to Nicaragua.[28] Further, Libya was now allowing the Soviets to base naval vessels at Tobruk, and a Soviet-designed airfield opened at Jufra. In light of these developments, an NSC staff paper concluded that "Qaddafi's adventurism is accelerating and the constraints of his international behavior are fewer. NATO allies, despite Qaddafi's demonstrated capacity for mischief-making, compete with each other for profitable Libyan contracts while pronouncing the convenient rationale that it is better to collaborate with Qaddafi than to isolate him."[29] While the administration believed that something had to be done, it was unclear what, since the prospect of international cooperation seemed dim. In December, the State Department issued another warning for Americans to leave Libya, and the CIA issued a report outlining evidence that Libya was supplying weapons to terrorists throughout Europe and the Middle East.[30]

By late 1984, Donald Fortier, the NSC's director of politico-military affairs, joined the push for a major policy change toward Libya. Initially, he had the policy review group (the NSC's organ that planned covert operations) direct the CIA to draft a new presidential finding authorizing the Agency to supply "lethal aid" to Libyan opposition groups. In January 1985, he and Vincent Cannistraro, a CIA officer on temporary duty with the NSC staff, wrote a paper that concluded Qaddafi was still a significant threat to American interests worldwide. Fortier and Cannistraro believed the Libyan leader to be vulnerable to overt and covert operations, but that "active American participation in anti-Qaddafi activity by the Libyan opposition may result in the removal of the last restraints against Libyan-sponsored terrorism directed at American citizens and officials." Despite this fear, action against Libya was still advocated. Their first option was a less aggressive, or "broad," approach with three components: (1) press the remaining American citizens and businesses to leave the country, (2) reassure the Egyptians that the U.S. was still involved in anti-Qaddafi operations, and (3) have the Pentagon resume its naval exercises near Libya, "coupling these exercises with provocative ship movements into the Gulf of Sidra." Second was the "bold," or more aggressive option, containing two parts: (1) Maintain covert and overt actions aimed at removing Qaddafi from power and (2) encourage Egypt and Algeria "to seek a *casus belli* for military action against Tripoli and plan with these countries U.S. military support to their possible joint action."[31]

Vice President Bush, Shultz, Casey, and National Security Advisor Robert McFarlane wanted to significantly increase pressure on Qaddafi, and supported the "bold" option. However, Weinberger and the Joint Chiefs opposed any plan that required U.S. military action, claiming that the goals were not sufficiently clear and that the Soviet response to any such operation had not been thoroughly considered.[32]

Meanwhile, Reagan, Shultz, and Congress were insisting that Casey to pay more attention to the terrorism problem. In February, Gates sent Casey a summary of Iranian, Syrian, and Libyan support for terrorism and an assessment of each country's vulnerability to retaliation. According to Gates, the CIA did "targeting studies of Libyan and Iranian ports and military facilities, and examined similar targets in Syria. We analyzed the potential impact of various kinds of sanctions. We focused especially on Iran, the worst offender . . . [but] Iran proved to be 'too hard.' . . . Syria was not seriously considered as a target because such action would almost certainly bring a confrontation with the USSR. So the process of elimination brought CIA to Libya."[33]

In March, Casey issued a Special National Intelligence Estimate entitled "Libya's Qaddafi: The Challenge to the United States and Western Interests," in which he projected that Qaddafi would continue to cause trouble over the next eighteen months. He based this on intelligence reports showing that Libya was providing "money, weapons, a base of operations, travel assistance or training to some 30 insurgent, radical or terrorist groups." Casey concluded, "We believe Qaddafi would directly target U.S. personnel or installations if he (1) could get away with the attack without U.S. retaliation, or (2) believed the U.S. was engaging in a direct threat to his person or was actively trying to overthrow his regime." The SNIE included a map highlighting the countries in which Qaddafi was involved, including Guatemala, El Salvador, Colombia, Chile, the Dominican Republic, Spain, Turkey, Iraq, Lebanon, Pakistan, Bangladesh, Thailand, the Philippines, Niger, Chad, Sudan, Namibia, and eight other African countries.[34]

On April 30, Reagan signed NSDD-168, "U.S. Policy Toward Northwestern Africa." It assessed how "The evolving situation in North Africa poses opportunities and risks for American interests" and cited a number of concerns, among them "the potential for increased Soviet regional influence and the dangers of Libyan adventurism." The NSDD directed, "An NSC-chaired interagency group shall be established to review U.S. strategy toward Libya, and to prepare policy options to contain Qaddafi's subversive activities." It also ordered the Department of Defense to "review [the] Stairstep Exercise program and forward options and recommendations." Stairstep was the operational name for naval exercises in and around the Gulf of Sidra.[35]

NSDD-168 incorporated some of Cannistraro's suggestions and represented a major step forward in Fortier's push to revamp U.S. policy toward

Libya. The review of the Stairstep Exercise was a clear indication that a majority within the administration, despite Weinberger's and the Joint Chief's reservations, favored using the military to force Qaddafi to change his ways. At the same time, this showed that Reagan and his advisors were not concerned about Casey's belief that provoking Qaddafi would be dangerous.

However, Qaddafi did not need any encouragement to accelerate his campaign against the West. According to a national intelligence directive issued by the CIA in May, Qaddafi continued to be an active supporter of terrorism and had sponsored an attempt to truck-bomb the U.S. embassy in Cairo. In June, the Frankfurt airport was bombed, and again, Qaddafi was the prime suspect.[36] By mid-June, Libya was the central focus of the administration's retaliatory inclinations, and on June 15, Deputy National Security Advisor John Poindexter informed Fortier, "We will be working toward an NSPG on Libya."[37] Although the counter-terrorism focus shifted to Iran and Syria during the TWA hijacking, the NSC staff continued its campaign against Qaddafi. At a June 30 meeting, newly promoted Deputy National Security Advisor Fortier asked NSC staffer Oliver North to find out how many Russians were in Libya; if the United States was going to war against Qaddafi, it had to know how many Soviet military advisors were there and their locations.[38] An NSC staff research paper concluded that the Soviets would be cautious in regards to a military response, "even when Soviet personnel were killed or wounded and equipment destroyed."[39]

On July 8, Reagan gave a speech to the American Bar Association in which he claimed that the administration had evidence linking Libya and its agents to at least twenty-five terrorist incidents in 1984. He also revealed that Egypt had foiled an attempt to bomb the U.S. embassy in Cairo, and declared, "these terrorist states are now engaged in acts of war against the Government and people of the United States. And under international law, any state which is the victim of acts of war has the right to defend itself." He concluded by warning, "The American people are not—I repeat, not—going to tolerate intimidation, terror, and outright acts of war against this nation and its people."

On July 13, the NSPG met to discuss Libya policy. McFarlane explained that the economic sanctions in place against Libya were not effective, that diplomatic pressures were not working, and argued that stronger measures were necessary. Casey, Shultz, and Weinberger all agreed with the assessment, but could not agree on a course of action. Among the measures discussed was Operation Flower and its two components: Tulip and Rose. Operation Tulip was a covert CIA operation to overthrow Qaddafi using anti-Qaddafi exiles. Operation Rose was a proposed preemptive military strike against Libya in concert with Egypt to remove the Libyan dictator. According to the plan, Aziziyyah Barracks, Qaddafi's command and control center, would be targeted. However, this raised the question of assassination and the problems associated with it. Executive Order 12333 prohibited assassination, stating, "No person employed by or acting on behalf of the United States government shall engage in, or conspire to engage in, assassination." Still, Reagan said not to worry about this restriction, saying he would personally take the heat if Qaddafi were killed.[40]

As planning for Operation Rose continued, Casey assigned Gates to produce a study summarizing the pros and cons of preemptive action. However, instead of one study, Gates produced two. The first included updates of his vulnerability and targeting study on Libya, Syria, and Iran, while the second, entitled "Options Against Qadhafi," assessed the Libyan–Egyptian military balance, Egypt's likely needs and wants if asked to engage against the Libyan military, Libya's warning capabilities, and possible Libyan, Arab, and Soviet reactions.[41]

Despite the CIA's support, the real impetus behind Operation Rose was the NSC staff. McFarlane, Poindexter, and North all envisioned a combined U.S.–Egyptian operation against Libya, with the Egyptian army attacking across the desert and entering Libya from the east, while U.S. air and ground forces attacked Tripoli and other targets. When the Pentagon was tasked to draw up plans for an attack, Weinberger, his deputy, Richard Armitage, and the Joint Chiefs thought the whole idea was ludicrous and wanted no part of it. Still, the Pentagon did as it was asked but in a way that was sure to be rejected; planners designed an invasion that required at least three divisions be pulled from Europe. When Gates saw it, he thought the plan looked "a lot like the invasion of Normandy."[42]

As intended by its authors, the plan quickly developed opposition outside the Pentagon once its ramifications were understood. Gates wrote a memo to Casey opposing the invasion because the costs and risks included "a huge outcry globally against U.S. imperialism, a strong reaction in the Arab world against a U.S. invasion of an Arab country, potentially significant Soviet gains in the Middle East and elsewhere in the Third World, a probable short-term upsurge in terrorism against U.S. citizens and installations, and a potential setback in U.S.–Soviet relations." He concluded that Libyan terrorism had not yet reached the threshold for a major invasion of an Arab country, and urged more measured, proportional responses.[43] The regionalists at the State Department objected for similar reasons, and the American ambassador to Egypt, Nick Veliotes, believed that there was no way Egyptian president Mubarak would go for the idea. This, because American resolve and staying power in the region had already been found wanting in Lebanon, and Mubarak believed that the U.S. would retreat again when American blood was spilled, leaving Egypt to face Qaddafi's forces alone.

In preparation for an NSPG meeting on Operation Rose, under secretary of state Michael Armacost called Ambassador Veliotes and asked him to come to Washington to help prepare briefing papers for Shultz. Once in Washington, Veliotes and Shultz concluded that Mubarak would never agree to an invasion, and that under no circumstances should the administration try to push the Egyptian president on the matter.[44]

On July 22, the NSPG met to discuss the invasion proposal. The group was concerned about public and congressional opinion, as well as America's relations with "Fundamentalist Islam [and the] Gulf States" if the United States were to support or participate in an invasion of an Arab country.[45] In the end, not one of the principals supported the plan, effectively killing it. Nevertheless, quiet planning at the NSC staff continued, and on July 24, Poindexter wrote a note to McFarlane outlining their strategy:

> Bud,
>     This is an update of the elements of our action plan . . . that comes closer to what I think is required. Our approach to Egypt should be we are going to do it one way or the other and we would like them to help. In reality we really need them for the ground role.
>
>                                                                  —JP[46]

This continued enthusiasm for Operation Rose was predicated on the belief that Qaddafi's grip on power was slipping, that it would only require a small push from the U.S. and Egypt for an uprising to take place, and that Egypt could in fact be convinced to participate.[47] Consequently, Poindexter scheduled a visit to Cairo.

When Veliotes was informed of the Poindexter mission, he pleaded with the CIA to explain to the admiral that there was absolutely no prospect of an early overthrow of Qaddafi using Libyan exiles; the Libyan opposition was well-meaning but ineffective. Still, in September, while McFarlane focused on the upcoming Reagan–Gorbachev summit, Poindexter and Fortier visited Cairo to discuss the invasion proposal with Mubarak. When they arrived, Veliotes offered some advice to the NSC staffers on how to deal with Mubarak, explaining that the Egyptian president had a short attention span, especially if he did not like what he was hearing. Veliotes also told Poindexter that it was best to dispense with the formal briefing approach and cut straight to the heart of the matter.

As a preliminary to the Mubarak meeting, Poindexter first met with the Egyptian military and intelligence chiefs so that they could prepare Mubarak for the later meeting. After that, Poindexter, Fortier, and Veliotes sat down for their meeting with Mubarak and his national security adviser Osama al Baz.

Immediately, Poindexter began reading four pages of talking points, but Mubarak quickly grew impatient and interrupted, "It sounds like an invasion of Libya." Unmoved, Poindexter continued reading from his prepared notes, but before Poindexter could finish his presentation, Mubarak doused it with cold water, announcing, "When we decide to attack Libya it will be our decision and on our timetable."[48] Poindexter headed home empty handed.

In September, Qaddafi set off the administration's alarm bells when he gave a speech on the anniversary of his coup, declaring, "We have the right to fight America, and we have the right to export terrorism to them." In addition, Washington grew increasingly concerned that Qaddafi was trying to shoot down an American surveillance plane over the Mediterranean.[49] That same month, Abu Nidal met with Qaddafi, and according to claims made by the Libyan news agency, the two agreed on prices for a menu of potential terrorist attacks that Libya would pay to Abu Nidal if they were carried out.[50] The German magazine *Bild Am Sonntag* also reported that Qaddafi had agreed to give Abu Nidal an annual budget of 32 million dollars to attack American targets.[51] Subsequently, Abu Nidal bombed the British Airways office in Rome, injuring 15 bystanders, and threw grenades at Rome's Café de Paris, injuring 38 tourists, including some Americans.

In October, around the time of the *Achille Lauro* hijacking, Reagan signed a new intelligence finding authorizing the CIA to support Egyptian, Iraqi, and Algerian efforts to aid anti-Qaddafi groups in Libya. However, the operation was aborted after the chairman and vice-chairman of the Senate Intelligence Committee, Senators David Durenburger and Patrick Leahy, opposed the plan, threatened to shut it down, and leaked the story to the *Washington Post*.[52]

Meanwhile, the State Department was searching for new ways to undermine Qaddafi, and throughout the fall, its officials explored the option of severing all economic ties with Libya. Commerce Department figures showed that despite existing sanctions, Libya exported 190 million dollars worth of goods to the United States in 1983. In 1984 that figure had grown to 200 million, and the 1985 numbers were projected to be around 310 million dollars.[53]

In November, the Abu Nidal group hijacked an EgyptAir plane en route from Athens to Cairo. After a brief gunfight between the hijackers and an Egyptian air marshal on board, the cabin began to depressurize, and the plane was forced to land at Malta. Once on the ground, the hijackers demanded fuel, and when their demands were not met, they began executing passengers; two Americans and three Israelis were shot. When word reached Washington, the administration offered to send a team of special operations forces to help resolve the crisis, but Malta refused to allow the emergency support team or a special operations team into the country, in large part because of the Maltese government's pro-Libya sentiments. However, because the plane was an

Egyptian-flagged carrier, Malta allowed Egypt's "Thunderbolt" commando unit to enter the country and attempt to end the standoff. The team was American trained, but many of the original members had been promoted out, leaving an inexperienced team to conduct the operation. When they stormed the plane, the Egyptians used too many explosives; many passengers were killed in the initial blast, while others died in the ensuing crossfire between the hijackers and the commandos.

Before the Egyptians stormed the plane, though, U.S. intelligence detected evidence of Libyan complicity in the hijacking. While the plane was on the ground in Malta, the National Security Agency intercepted messages between Tripoli and the LPB in Malta that convinced the NSC staff that Libya was sending instructions to the hijackers and was sponsoring Abu Nidal's attacks.[54]

## THE CRISIS

On December 27, 1985, Abu Nidal terrorists launched simultaneous attacks in the passenger terminals at Leonardo da Vinci Airport in Rome and Schwechat International Airport in Vienna.[55] The terrorists later claimed that they had planned to hijack an El-Al plane and blow it up over Israel, but the nature of their assaults tells a different story. Upon entering the airports, the terrorists immediately threw hand grenades at a crowded area and then opened fire on the El-Al ticket counters. In Rome, Italian police and Israeli security forces killed three of the four attackers, wounding and capturing the fourth. In Vienna, the three terrorists fled in a stolen car, with the police in pursuit. After a mile-long chase, the police disabled the car and captured the terrorists. In all, the terrorists killed eighteen people, including five Americans: Don Maland, Elena Tomarello, John Buorocore, Frederick Gage, and eleven-year-old Natasha Simpson. In addition, over one hundred people were wounded, including fourteen Americans.

Reagan found out about the attacks when Donald Fortier briefed him and Donald Regan in the lower hallway of the White House residence, just before the president left Washington for a vacation in California. The president received further information aboard Air Force One on his way to the Annenberg Estate in Palm Springs, California. His initial response was one of stunned disbelief, and when he watched news coverage of the attacks, he was filled with "revulsion" and "anger," and immediately favored a strong U.S. response.[56]

In Jerusalem, the Israeli government was furious over the attacks at the El-Al counters and blamed the Palestinian Liberation Organization (PLO), warning that it would retaliate "in every place and at anytime it sees fit." Prime Minister Shimon Peres proclaimed, "Terror is blind, and anyone who attempts to justify any form of terror must know that he will also be hit by terror. The government of Israel will protect its citizens at home and abroad, and will fight in all ways against terrorists." Defense Minister Yitzhak Rabin told Israeli television that he did not rule out retaliation against terrorist targets "anywhere." Some Israeli officials tried to tie the attacks to Syria, with anonymous Israeli security sources saying that Abu Nidal probably carried out the attack at the behest of Syrian president Hâfez al Assad.[57] Meanwhile, foreign ministry spokesman Avi Pazner said that Israel would make no distinction between the Abu Nidal Organization and the PLO, adding to speculation that Israel would attack the PLO headquarters in Tunisia as it had after the September 1985 murder of three Israelis aboard a yacht near Cyprus.

Initially, the administration did not mind the Israeli rhetoric, and a Reagan spokesman said it would be "fine with us" if Israel takes military action against the sources of the attacks. As time passed, however, it became apparent that an Israeli strike would not be a positive development, as another major strike against the PLO would hamper continued administration efforts to pursue its Middle East peace agenda.

Additionally, some on the NSC staff were concerned that an Israeli operation would make it more difficult for the American military to do the same thing. One NSC staffer concluded, "there is a world of difference between, on the one hand, yet another Israeli lashing out half-way down the Mediterranean under the tolerant eye of an America unable to act on its own behalf. It is better for Israel, for our position in the Arab world, and for the domestic psychology of the American campaign against terrorism if we do this one OURSELVES." Consequently, the administration cautioned Israel to exercise restraint.[58]

On December 28, Fortier chaired a meeting of the CPPG to discuss the situation. The evidence implicated Abu Nidal, as the modus operandi of the attack bore a similarity to many of his previous attacks. In addition, shortly after the attacks, a man called a Spanish news service and claimed that the raids had been conducted by the Abu Nidal Organization; Muhammad Sarham, the lone surviving terrorist in Rome, also told Italian authorities that he was a member of that organization.[59]

However, behind Abu Nidal stood Muammar al-Qaddafi, whose news service JANA hailed the massacres as "daring" and "heroic operations." In a cable to the U.S. mission at NATO, Shultz commented, "There is one piece of very strong physical evidence tying Libya to [the attacks.]"[60] In fact, the evidence against Qaddafi quickly grew to include: Libyan-provided passports for the terrorists, intercepted communications (indicating that Libya was furnishing equipment and ammunition), the existence of terrorist training camps located throughout Libya, and the attackers' use of Eastern European-manufactured grenades that had been purchased by the Libyan Army.[61] Additionally, as the

FBI's Buck Revell explained, "At the time, Abu Nidal had most of his training operations in Libya. He himself was there most of the time, [and the] Libyan government was the principal source of his income. The perception was if Libya didn't order [the Rome and Vienna attacks] at least they were knowledgeable of and didn't take any action to in any way impede [them] and probably supported [the attacks]."[62] Police said that at least one of the four terrorists in the attack had a Moroccan passport from the same series used by the hijackers of the November EgyptAir hijacking in Malta.[63] According to a Tunisian security spokesman, three of the Tunisian passports used by the terrorists were among a group of documents confiscated by Libyan authorities during a recent expulsion of Tunisians.[64]

At the CPPG, the group next discussed non-military options that the U.S. could employ against Libya. NSC staffer Elaine Morton, on temporary assignment from the State Department, proposed strengthening the economic sanctions against Libya, arguing, "Both existing export trade to Libya and commerce done in Libya by U.S. oil companies can be eliminated by use of the International Emergency Economic Powers Act. . . . In addition, this Act can be used to make it a criminal offense for those U.S. citizens now in Libya to remain there in conscious subversion of the intent of our passport restriction." She concluded that economic sanctions were preferable to military retaliation because "the impact of economic sanctions is easier to control and unforeseen consequences less likely to arise."[65]

The group also considered military options, but came to no decision. However, Fortier argued that if the United States was going to react, it should avoid the limited, tit-for-tat approach that had characterized the Vietnam War. Instead, he advocated a "disproportionate response" to any Libyan provocation.[66] In the end, military *and* economic options were forwarded to the NSC.

By December 30, Shultz believed there was sufficient evidence to warrant military action against Libya. To him, the link between Abu Nidal and Qaddafi was clear, and retaliation was the best course of action to both punish those responsible and deter future attacks. A State Department White Paper prepared by Robert Oakley and David Long outlined the State Department's case against Libya. It asserted, "[Qaddafi] has provided safehaven, money, and arms to these groups—including the Popular Front for the Liberation of Palestine—General Command, the Fatah dissidents, and the notorious Abu Nidal group. . . . Libya's support has broadened to include logistic support for terrorist operations. . . . Since 1984, Libya began to provide increased support to the group, and Abu Nidal himself and many of the group's operations may have moved there within the last 12 months."[67]

Elsewhere in the government, support for this position was growing—most notably at the Pentagon. In a telegram from Chairman of the Jiont Chiefs of staff, William Crowe, to Shultz, Casey, and Weinberger, the admiral wrote, "Intelligence sources have linked the attacks to the Abu Nidal Organization with Libyan support. The [United States Government] has publicly stated that once positive [identification] of those responsible is made, appropriate retaliation will be taken."[68] Immediately after the attacks, Crowe met with his intelligence and operations officers, Rear Admiral Tom Brooks and Lieutenant General Richard Burpee, respectively, to study potential targets for retaliation. Crowe subsequently directed his assistant, Lieutenant General John Moellering, to present these sites—all Abu Nidal related—for consideration when the CPPG met again.[69]

Citing a number of reasons for opposing retaliation, Weinberger cautioned against military action. His first concern was American military casualties if the administration launched an attack. Libyan defenses were substantial, with 535 combat aircraft—including Mirage fighters, MiG-21s, 23s, and 25s; three brigades of surface-to-air missiles; 30 French Crotalé anti-aircraft systems; 72 Soviet surface-to-air missile batteries (SAM-2s and 3s); SAM-5 anti-aircraft missiles, as well as 1,500 Soviet advisors and technicians. Second, Weinberger maintained that military action would upset relations with U.S. allies in the region, especially those that currently welcomed American forces in their countries. Third, he also maintained that a strike would endanger the large number of American civilians that continued to live and work in Libya, since Qaddafi might retaliate by using them as pawns, creating a hostage scenario worse than the one Carter faced in Iran. Fourth, although most intelligence incriminated Abu Nidal, the secretary of defense believed that the evidence was not compelling enough, and that it would be wrong to strike without better information. After all, he argued, the United States did not want to hit the wrong people. There was also concern that such a strike would incite more terrorism against U.S. interests. Qaddafi added fuel to this fear when he declared during a January 2 news conference, "We [will] . . . pursue U.S. citizens in their country and street" if the U.S. retaliated for the Rome and Vienna massacres.[70]

Weinberger's opposition notwithstanding, by December 31, the NSC staff believed that the administration was moving toward the retaliatory option. NSC staffer Jock Covey sent an e-mail to Donald Fortier exclaiming that the administration now had a "smoking gun. Any concerns expressed yesterday afternoon about [a] weak linkage to Libya are withdrawn. I don't think we have EVER been so well positioned for forceful action, and it would be worthwhile emphasizing that point in the memo [to the president]."[71]

On December 31, Reagan wrote in his diary, "Of course, hanging over all of this was a cloud we tried to ignore completely—the matter of Qaddafi and his connection with the massacres at Rome and Vienna airports. We all feel we must do something, yet there are problems, including 1,000 Americans living and working in the mad clown's country."[72] Despite this concern, Reagan directed the Pentagon to begin compiling a list of potential targets in Libya, and to commence operational planning for an attack. On December 31, the JCS sent a cable to U.S. air bases in Britain and the carrier *Coral Sea* (then in the Mediterranean) saying, "The Secretary of Defense has approved alerting of forces and execution planning for Operation Prairie Fire," which was a strike plan against a preselected target package in Libya. The specific date for the attack had not yet been set, but was not expected to be before January 4, 1986.[73]

On January 1, a U.S. planning team at Britain's Lakenheath Royal Air Force Base began developing a strike plan against Libyan bases in Tripoli and Benghazi. Forces in the Mediterranean were beefed up, and the JCS forwarded a collection of potential military options to Reagan. The list covered a wide range of targets, from government facilities to anti-aircraft sites, and indicated that they could be attacked using FA-18 bombers based on the USS *Coral Sea*, Air Force F-111 bombers from the 48th Tactical Fighter Wing at Lakenheath, and B-52 bombers based in the United States. The B-52 option was an early favorite of planners because the Libyan military would not anticipate, or be able to defend against, that sort of attack. Using the *Coral Sea* would have alerted Libya that action was imminent since the carrier would have had to cut short a port call at Naples, Italy; the Soviets were monitoring the Sixth Fleet's movements and would have passed that intelligence on to the Libyans. However, when the carrier departed as scheduled—on January 2, carrier bombers and the F-111s became the leading option.[74]

On January 2, Ambassador William Eagleton delivered a message to the government of Syria urging "[Damascrus] could do much for its image as well as strike a blow against terrorism by getting rid of members of the Abu Nidal Organization now in the country." Selection of appropriate targets was a difficult task at best, and was made even more arduous by restrictions placed on the Pentagon's planners by Reagan and his advisors. A significant criterion used to compile the target list was that each site had to be away from civilian populations.[75] Accordingly, some military planners favored hitting anti-aircraft sites, including recently acquired Russian-built SAM-5s, that were stationed away from population centers. However, there were two drawbacks to attacking these emplacements. First, roughly 600 Soviet citizens worked at or near these sites; if any of them were injured or killed in a U.S. strike, the situation could quickly escalate into a superpower confrontation. Second, attacking anti-aircraft sites was inherently dangerous for warplanes, as these emplacements had the ability to shoot down the American planes. Sites that were linked to Libya's support for terrorism were even more problematic because of their proximity to civilians and the consequent risk of collateral damage.

On January 3, Reagan conferred with Shultz, Regan, and the new National Security Advisor, Admiral Poindexter, to review the military option. The president was leaning toward implementing economic sanctions only, primarily because a military operation would endanger the hundreds of Americans still living in Libya. Other arguments also played a part in his thinking—the likelihood of collateral damage, the chance that Soviet military advisors would be killed and that American planes would be shot down, and expected negative reactions in the Arab world.[76] Another factor that pushed Reagan in this direction was the media; many details of the military planning had leaked to the press, giving opponents of the plan another argument—Qaddafi knew what was coming and would be prepared for it.

Consequently, the president told the group, "Let's let the Austrians and the Italians bring these people to justice. It was their airports, it is in their jurisdiction." According to William Martin, the NSC staff's executive secretary, Reagan then instructed his staff to tell the Israelis to refrain from attacking Syrian positions in Lebanon's Bekaa Valley, including new missiles that Damascus had just placed there, explaining, "This is not a time to spread violence in the region."[77]

On January 6, the NSPG met in the White House Situation Room, with Reagan, Bush, Shultz, Weinberger, Casey, Crowe, Meese, Treasury Secretary James Baker, Regan, Poindexter, Fortier, Craig Fuller, James Miller (from OMB), and Major Carol Chandler (who "brought in charts") in attendance.[78]

Shultz argued again in favor of a military strike, and brought with him an opinion by Abraham Sofaer, the State Department's legal counsel, asserting that terrorism was "armed aggression and [the] military response [is] justifiable self-defense." Also advocating an attack were members of the NSC staff. North, Howard Teicher, and Navy captain James Stark prepared a briefing memo for the meeting arguing that the United States could attack Libya without putting American servicemen in harm's way if it used submarine-launched cruise missiles, or Tomahawks.[79]

Weinberger continued to oppose military action, again raising the specter of American citizens being held hostage by Qaddafi. The secretary of defense also argued that a single aircraft carrier was not enough to do the job properly, and at the time only the *Coral Sea* was in the Mediterranean. In Weinberger's opinion, three carriers were necessary, and the Joint Chiefs agreed with Weinberger, lending credence to this concern. The secretary of defense went on to argue that the evidence was not compelling enough to act militarily, and he questioned whether such a strike against Libya would really deter future attacks. Finally, he wanted all other options exhausted before resorting to force, and there were still some alternatives that had not been tried.

In the end, Reagan rejected the military option, and according to one report, when the meeting adjourned, Weinberger "left the Situation Room smiling."[80]

One administration official explained, "Unless Qaddafi does something completely outrageous, Weinberger and the Europeans won't want us to act the next time either."[81] Additionally, it appears that Reagan was not entirely convinced of Libya's culpability for the airport massacres.[82] While Abu Nidal was clearly responsible, and his ties to Libya clear, specific camps used by Abu Nidal in Libya were as yet unidentified. According to one White House aide, "We didn't know anybody to hit."[83]

These concerns notwithstanding, there was sufficient concern about Libya to do something. Qaddafi's well-documented support of various terrorist groups, and his adventurism throughout the Arab world, Sub-Saharan Africa, South Asia, Southeast Asia, and particularly in Latin American and the Caribbean, convinced the administration that it had to act. As one Reagan aide put it, to ignore Qaddafi's provocations would be "like reading *Mein Kampf* and saying he doesn't really mean it, and somebody has to put a stop to it."[84]

Despite shelving a retaliatory strike against Libya, a number of other military measures were approved in the hope that, as Reagan put it, Qaddafi would "go to sleep every night wondering what the United States might do."[85] The first was the renewal of naval maneuvers in the Gulf of Sidra to re-establish the freedom of navigation in recognized international waters. As a White House spokesman later explained, their purpose was to make "the legal point that beyond the internationally recognized 12-mile limit, the Gulf of Sidra belongs to none, and that all nations are free to move through international waters and air space."[86] To show that this move was a standard procedure for the United States, Shultz cited an instance in early March when the U.S. Navy had conducted a similar exercise in the Black Sea where waters had been "wrongfully claimed by the Soviets."[87] It was also hoped that by sending a large American presence into waters claimed by Qaddafi, the Libyan leader would do something stupid. The plan, according to Secretary of the Navy John Lehman, was to "challenge Qaddafi" by "reasserting our naval rights . . . even if it meant clobbering the Libyans to do so."[88] If Qaddafi responded with force, as he had in 1981, the U.S. would retaliate by bombing targets in Libya.

The naval maneuvers were designed to increase pressure on Qaddafi in stages. The first two exercises were to take place north of the Gulf, while the third, set to begin in mid-March, would involve three carrier battle groups and include forays into the international waters claimed by Libya. Although pre-existing plans already called for having two carrier groups in the Mediterranean, a third was added at the insistence of Weinberger and Crowe, who wanted to make sure there was enough American firepower in the region in case the shooting started.[89] The rules of engagement allowed the Navy to use "aggressive self-defense," which meant that American forces could destroy Libyan targets that had not fired but appeared hostile.[90] When a staffer asked the president if American planes could follow hostile aircraft into Libyan airspace, Reagan responded, "Right into their own damn hangars."[91] As Admiral Crowe later explained, "Requiring our units to wait until they were actually fired upon put American lives at great risk—our experience in Lebanon being the most recent example. I wanted them to be able to defend themselves as soon as a threat was apparent."[92] Reagan explained the decision in his diary the next morning: "After quite a session, I finally came down on the side of an executive order bringing Americans and American business home from Libya and canceling relations—trade, etc., with them. At the same time we beefed up the Sixth Fleet in the Mediterranean Sea. If Mr. Qaddafi decides not to push another terrorist act, okay, we've been successful with our implied threat. If on the other hand he takes this for weakness and does loose another one, we will have targets in mind and instantly respond with a [hell] of a punch."[93]

While planning for unilateral action moved forward, a bilateral approach also began to take shape when the NSPG approved a plan to contact the French about a joint effort to oust Qaddafi. To that end, Shultz dispatched Vernon Walters and Howard Teicher to Paris for discussions in March, resulting in an agreement from French president François Mitterrand to begin military planning with the United States—so long as the action taken against Qaddafi was *decisive*.[94]

Following the NSPG meeting, the CPPG met to plan the implementation of the NSPG's decisions. The sub-cabinet group reviewed plans to move another carrier group into the Mediterranean, a plan for follow-on action against Libya, and worked on a list of potential retaliation targets provided by the JCS. On this target list, two important sites were initially ruled out because of the danger to civilians: the Libyan Military Intelligence Service building and al-Marafiq (the Libyan External Intelligence Service building), which was located across the street from the French Embassy. However, the frogman base at Sidi Bilal was added to the list because it was specifically linked to terrorism and the port was home to the Libyans responsible for the 1984 mining of the Red Sea.[95]

The remainder of the CPPG's meeting was spent on the diplomatic strategy to ensure that the sanctions about to be imposed by the president's executive order would work. The group endorsed a proposal to send emissaries to Europe and Japan to seek their cooperation in enforcing the sanctions.[96]

At the NSC staff, Fortier headed up continued policy planning toward Libya, developing a strategy to modify Libya's behavior and, if unsuccessful, to pave the way for military action. The first step was what Fortier considered a "conditioning process"—expanding existing economic sanctions against Libya.[97] Despite previous sanctions, a number of U.S. corporations continued doing business in Libya, so Fortier directed Elaine Morton to prepare a proposal for severing all economic ties with Libya. Morton turned to the only law that had not been utilized up to that point in the economic crackdown on Libya—the

International Economic Emergency Powers Act (IEEPA). This act allowed the president to impose sanctions on a country when he deemed it a threat to the United States's national security.

Since Fortier did not have much faith that the sanctions would work, he had staffers Teicher, Stark, Cannistraro, North, and Morton design a strategy of "steadily increasing pressures" and "disproportionate responses" against Libya. In so doing, he hoped that Qaddafi would be persuaded to stop supporting terrorism if the associated costs were too high. One key to Fortier's strategy was a measure of sabre rattling in the form of the renewed freedom of navigation exercises in the Gulf of Sidra. Other components of the strategy included: (1) keeping Qaddafi and his misdeeds in the international spotlight through diplomacy and the press; (2) pressing the European allies (especially Belgium, France, and Italy) to discontinue arms sales to Libya or chance losing their own deals with the United States; (3) making it harder for Libya to sell its oil; (4) aiding Qaddafi's enemies—both dissident communities and belligerent neighboring countries; (5) pushing the Europeans to crack down on Libyan abuse of diplomatic privileges, such as transporting weapons in diplomatic pouches; and (6) preparing for military action. Fortier's strategy included every available option short of a military strike, ensuring that if Qaddafi continued to support terrorism in the future, a military response would be the administration's only option.[98]

On January 7, Reagan signed Executive Order 12543, imposing strict new economic sanctions on Libya. In a press conference announcing the sanctions, the president explained, "There is irrefutable evidence of [Qaddafi's] role in these attacks. . . . By providing material support to terrorist groups which attack U.S. citizens, Libya has engaged in armed aggression against the U.S. under established principles of international law, just as if it had used its own armed forces." Reagan went on to declare that Libya "constituted a threat" to national security, ordered American businesses to discontinue their activities in Libya and directed all American citizens to leave the country. Despite this, Reagan was not entirely sure that the sanctions would work, pledging that if the new measures "do not end Qaddafi's terrorism, I promise you that further steps will be taken."[99]

Despite his earlier uncertainties about Libyan culpability, on January 8, Reagan signed a new NSDD—number 205—which declared that Qaddafi's role in the airport massacres was "indisputable." NSDD-205 also determined that "the policies and actions in support of international terrorism by the Government of Libya constitute an unusual and extraordinary threat to the national security and foreign policy of the United States." The directive ordered the ban of all direct imports and exports with Libya, a ban on service contracts, a prohibition of travel to Libya, a clarification that Libya was not eligible for Most Favored Nation trade status, a prohibition of loans to Libya, and barred Libyan-flagged ships from entering U.S. ports. Later that day, the administration froze 240 million dollars' worth of Libyan assets in U.S. banks that Libya was trying to transfer elsewhere.[100]

Support from Europe, however, was shallow and short-lived. On January 11, British prime minister Margaret Thatcher warned the United States about retaliation, saying that such actions were "against international law." This made military planning more difficult, since contingency planning called for using American bombers based in Britain. So, to rally support for collective action against Libya, Reagan dispatched Deputy Secretary of State John Whitehead, Robert Oakley, and Robert Kimmitt to Europe to consult with the allies on terrorism. While visiting Great Britain, Turkey, West Germany, Italy, Greece, France, Belgium, the Netherlands, and Spain, where Whitehead asked the Europeans to reduce oil imports from Libya, stop selling Qaddafi weapons, discontinue granting credit to Libya, voice condemnation against Libyan support for Abu Nidal and other terrorist organizations, and to shut down the Libyan Peoples' Bureaus in each country. However, the mission failed to convince the Europeans to alter their behavior; they unanimously opposed any military action against Libya, and the British, French, Germans, and Italians expressed doubts about the wisdom and utility of sanctions, probably because Libya was a major importer of European Economic Community goods. Canada was the lone ally to fully support the American position, while Italy offered a small gesture by banning arms sales to Qaddafi and banning Italian companies from filling the void left by departing American companies.[101]

Meanwhile, planning for the naval exercises and Operation Prairie Fire continued. On January 8, the JSC requested detailed information on the strike plan from EuCom, and a few days later tasked EuCom "to be prepared to conduct strikes against the first four priority targets planned under Prairie Fire not later than 48 hours after receipt of an execute order." On January 21, EuCom sent the updated plans to the JCS.[102]

On January 13, the CPPG reviewed intelligence showing Qaddafi was probably about to conduct new terrorist actions against American targets in Western Europe or the Caribbean. The group also reviewed the diplomatic efforts against Libya, including the Whitehead/Oakley/Kimmitt mission to the allied governments, and was told that Canada was "most helpful." However, the Europeans continued to decry the lack of a "smoking gun," complained that the new sanctions would not work, and argued that the American course of action was inhibiting the Middle East peace process.[103]

On January 23, NSC staffer James Stark, General Burpee, Brigadier General Roland Lajoie (the defense attaché at the U.S. embassy in Paris), and

Admiral James Dorsey (the operations officer from EuCom), visited the Elysée Palace in Paris to discuss joint Franco-American operations against Libya. Meeting with President Mitterand's military *chef de cabinet*, General Jean Saulnier, they put two questions to the French government. First, would France join the United States in a freedom of navigation exercise in the Gulf of Sidra while simultaneously supporting Chad's southern offensive against Libya? Second, would the French grant overflight privileges to U.S. warplanes based in England should they be needed for an operation against Libya? While opposing the former, the French did give qualified approval for the latter, asking that Washington give a "reasonable" amount of time for the French to consider the request—at least 24 hours. Burpee told Saulnier that the U.S. could provide a "two- or three-day window."[104]

By January 29, trouble was brewing over enforcement of the sanctions. Shultz and the State Department were worried that enforcing them would strain relations with the Europeans, while the Treasury Department feared the sanctions' effect on withdrawing American companies. Consequently, three weeks after Reagan issued the executive order imposing sanctions, they had not yet been fully enacted. In an e-mail from Stark to Fortier and Poindexter, the NSC staffer complained, "[I]t seems to me that NSC, as the President's representatives, are going to have to force the issue . . . [the other Departments' concerns] are less important than the need for the U.S. to be seen as serious in enforcing the sanctions. If we declare sanctions and then, in the next breath, authorize U.S. firms to obviously circumvent those measures, we will go right back to the credibility problem which plagued our earlier half-measures."[105] By early March, sanctions were still a point of contention between the NSC staff, Treasury, and State; another e-mail lamented, "State charges that Treasury is giving too much favorable licence to the oil companies. . . . Treasury charges that State should tend to its own knitting . . . not a single demarche has been sent by State protesting European instances of backfill that are readily apparent from intelligence data."[106]

While the sanctions did not have the desired effect, other parts of Fortier's plan proved to be much more effective. Qaddafi did not sit quietly when American forces provoked him, and when Libya struck again—this time in Berlin, the administration was finally ready to respond.

# Chapter Seven

# The Bombing of the La Belle Disco

We have something planned that will make you very happy.

—Message to Qaddafi from his agents in Berlin,
April 4, 1986

## BACKGROUND

Following the massacres at the Rome and Vienna airports, despite seriously contemplating a military attack against targets in Libya, the Reagan administration rejected retaliation in favor of diplomatic and economic initiatives. From the outset, however, many in the administration did not believe that sanctions would successfully dissuade Qaddafi from continuing his support of terrorism. Part of the problem was how these measures were implemented; the Treasury Department told at least half of the American oil companies being forced out of Libya that the administration preferred that they transfer assets to their European subsidiaries rather than selling to foreign competitors. As NSC staffer Elaine Morton, the architect of the sanctions predicted in an e-mail to fellow staffer Robert Pearson, "If the goal of our sanctions was to cause dislocation in the Libyan oil economy, this certainly won't do the trick."[1]

Despite the less aggressive response by the administration, the U.S. remained wary of Libya's connection to terrorism and stepped up intelligence gathering against Qaddafi. Early in 1986, Reagan ordered the National Reconnaissance Office (NRO) to move a signals intelligence satellite from its orbit over Poland to one covering North Africa in order to monitor Libyan communications. In addition, National Security Agency eavesdropping stations in

Cyprus, England, and Italy intensified their monitoring of all communications emanating from Libya.[2] This increased surveillance paid quick dividends; in February the CIA reported that Libyan agents were watching thirty-five American installations abroad, studying them as potential targets for attack.

Meanwhile, military planning against Libya moved ahead on several fronts. First, contingency planning for unilateral strikes against targets in Libya continued. The Joint Chiefs of Staff (JCS) generated a list of thirty-six potential targets for Air Force bombers based in England to hit and 152 targets for planes from the Navy's carriers in the Mediterranean to attack. At Lakenheath Royal Air Force Base in Britain, F-111 bomber crews conducted Operation Ghost Rider—missions to Goose Bay, Canada and İnçirlik, Turkey to practice long-range bombing runs and work out the logistical problems associated with night-time refueling.[3]

Second, Assistant Secretary of Defense Richard Armitage chaired an interagency target selection committee. Here, though, the different opinions about what targets to hit were worked through. Committee members from the Pentagon wanted to bomb targets that were solely military in nature, not wanting to go after Qaddafi-related targets that could result in collateral damage. For this reason, the JCS opposed the inclusion of Aziziyyah Barracks—Qaddafi's residence and operational headquarters. In addition, targeting economic sites was harder to justify than military and terrorist targets, primarily because they did not match the administration's argument that the air strikes would be in self-defense.[4] Meanwhile, the NSC staff favored a broader target list, including oil facilities and other economic targets that, if destroyed, could cripple Qaddafi's regime. As Peter Rodman later explained, "The NSC staff view was the maximum. Do something really impressive, that has the shock effect, and we kept having to push the Pentagon to come up with more targets."[5] It was the NSC staff and CIA that advocated adding Aziziyyah Barracks, hoping to gain some "political benefit" from a military strike, such as a coup attempt by the Libyan military against Qaddafi.[6]

The tactics for the operation was another area of contention for the committee members. NSC staffers Oliver North and James Stark proposed using some of the newest weapons in the U.S. arsenal, including cruise missiles and Stealth fighter planes. They explained that if these weapons platforms were used, the Libyans could not defend against them, and fewer American servicemen would have to go into harm's way. However, Chairman of the Joint Chiefs of Staff Admiral William Crowe immediately vetoed the idea, arguing, "If we use these capabilities, our adversaries will know that we have them." By this he meant that if America's newest and most sophisticated weapons were used, there was a danger that they could fall into the hands of the Libyans, who would undoubtedly hand them over to Moscow.[7]

In addition to preparing for unilateral action, the administration continued its military planning in conjunction with Egypt (operations Flower and Rose), dispatching Lieutenant General Dale Vesser, the head of planning for the JCS, to Cairo for further discussions. Initially set for mid-January, the mission was delayed by several weeks when a newspaper article about the upcoming freedom of navigation exercises also mentioned that an unnamed envoy was being "sent to Egypt for further discussion about coordinating possible military options."[8] The original article included Vesser's name and some of the mission's specifics, but this information was deleted after National Security Advisor John Poindexter visited the *Washington Post* newsroom and told editor Ben Bradlee that if the story ran unchanged, it would foreclose Reagan's options for dealing with Qaddafi.[9]

Vesser eventually visited Egypt, bringing four options for consideration. Three proposals were defensive in nature, in case Libya attacked Egypt. However, the fourth option was a preemptive strike against Libya, which included Reagan's approval for the use of U.S. "combat support inside Libya."[10]

Additionally, the administration continued its efforts to keep Qaddafi's misdeeds in the public eye. In early 1986, CIA director William Casey invited the Washington chapter of the Harvard Law School Alumni Association to CIA headquarters where he discussed, among other things, Qaddafi's involvement in terrorism. He told the group, "As soon as Qaddafi took over, he started looking for a kindred spirit. He found it in the PLO. The PLO was Muslim, revolutionary, anti-imperialist, and fighting Israel. He opened his doors and treasury to the Palestinians. Libya runs twenty-five terrorist training camps. It's their second largest export, after oil."[11] However, it was not just the administration's public diplomacy campaign that kept the world's attention on Libya; Qaddafi managed to do this himself. In early January 1986, an arms cache, which British Prime Minister Margaret Thatcher described as among the largest ever found, was discovered at Sligo and Roscommon in the Republic of Ireland. The stash included rifles and ammunition supplied by Libya.[12]

In addition, Qaddafi's rhetoric continued to draw the administration's ire. On January 6, the Libyan leader declared, "A human being in America has no value." During another speech broadcast on Tripoli television, Qaddafi asserted, "The Arabs who are in Libya [will] be trained in the suicide missions. . . . [We] will allocate the trainers who will . . . train all members of the Arab People's congresses in the Arab territory on suicide operations. We will provide them with the required weapons to carry out such missions." Qaddafi concluded by declaring that the Mediterranean would become a "zone of all-out war" if the United States attacked Libya. In early February, he hosted a gathering of Muslim terror organizations that included Mustafa Murad, the operational commander of the Abu Nidal organization and head of its Syrian branch. During the course of the conference, the participants agreed "to escalate the armed struggle" and made plans for renewed attacks against Israeli and American interests.[13]

Despite the growing evidence against Qaddafi, members of the administration continued to disagree about how to respond to Libya's terrorist campaign, and a very public debate over counter-terrorism policy again erupted between Secretary of State George Shultz, and Secretary of Defense Caspar Weinberger. On January 15, Shultz spoke to a group at the National Defense University in Washington and argued that the United States should not wait for absolute proof that a group or government was responsible for an attack before carrying out military retaliation. Instead, he claimed that under international law, "A nation attacked by terrorists is permitted to use force to prevent or preempt future attacks, to seize terrorists or to rescue its citizens, when no other means is available." The next day Weinberger responded. He cautioned against attempting to solve the terrorist problem with military force, and in a thinly veiled attack on the secretary of state and his allies, criticized those who sought "instant gratification from some kind of bombing attack without being too worried about the details." Finally, he argued that reprisals "haven't eliminated terrorism or terrorist attacks on the people who made the immediate retaliation."

On March 6, Vice President George Bush added his voice to the debate. On the day his task force released its findings on American counter-terrorism policy, Bush tried to stake out the middle ground in the Shultz–Weinberger feud, lending qualified support to the retaliatory option. In a statement during the Task Force's news conference, the vice president announced, "We should reiterate the willingness of our Administration to retaliate swiftly when we feel we can punish those who were directly responsible."

Despite the lack of unanimity on how to respond to terrorism, however, the U.S. Navy's provocation of Libya went ahead as planned. Toward the end of January, a second carrier, the *Saratoga*, moved into the Mediterranean, and from January 26 to 30 joined the Sixth Fleet for maneuvers in the vicinity of Libya, code-named Operation Attain Document.[14] This phase included air and surface operations in the Libya Flight Identification Region—an area monitored closely by Libyan air controllers but not claimed by Qaddafi as Libyan territory. The operation's stated mission was to "Demonstrate U.S. resolve and capability against Libya . . . to keep Libyan armed forces uncertain as to U.S. intentions, and signal Libyan, European and Arab observers that the U.S. has the capability and the will to conduct military strikes if necessary."[15] The second phase, Operation Attain Document II, ran from February 12 through 15, and saw increased American action north of the Gulf of Sidra. Although American forces did not cross Qaddafi's "line of death" in either operation, both operations provided valuable intelligence about the capabilities and tendencies of the Libyan armed forces.[16]

On March 10, the CPPG convened to review the Libyan situation. In attendance were Assistant Secretary of State Michael Armacost, Assistant Secretary of Defense Richard Armitage, the CIA's deputy director for intelligence Robert Gates, Lieutenant General John Moellering from the JCS, and Donald Fortier, James Stark, and Howard Teicher from the NSC staff.[17] During the meeting, those present discussed whether the upcoming freedom of navigation exercises and contingency retaliatory strikes would strengthen or weaken Qaddafi's position, and reviewed the Operation Prairie Fire targets, re-evaluating whether or not they were the "right ones." No changes were recommended, but they did explore the possibility of "third echelon" responses in the event that Libya responded to American retaliation, including additional airstrikes against economic, political, and more military targets in Libya. Ultimately, the group concluded that an NSPG meeting was needed in the near future to approve plans for operations Attain Document III and Prairie Fire.[18]

Consequently, on March 14, the NSPG met at the White House to review U.S. policy toward Libya before the third phase of naval maneuvers began. Present were Reagan, Bush, Shultz, Weinberger, Casey, Crowe, Poindexter, Meese, Regan, and a number of NSC staffers, including Fortier, Teicher, and Rodney McDaniel.[19] Much of the meeting centered on a CIA report about Qaddafi's personality, but the discussion eventually turned when Reagan asked about the ramifications of the new naval exercise. He asked if the plan could lead to new trouble, and he wanted to know, "Could we end up with a less palatable situation than we have now?"[20] He was told that an aggressive Libyan response was highly probable. Shultz and the NSC staffers argued for a strong and immediate response should that happen, but Weinberger and Crowe were less enthusiastic about striking back and urged caution. Poindexter was able to find a compromise; the commander of the Sixth Fleet, Vice Admiral Frank Kelso, would have discretion to respond according to the "proportional response doctrine." If Qaddafi attacked U.S. forces massed near the Gulf of Sidra, the U.S. response would be proportional, counterattacking against the source of the attack only. If a Libyan attack resulted in a single U.S. casualty, and if Reagan approved, the Navy would set in motion the Prairie Fire contingency and bomb a list of predetermined sites in Libya.[21] Four of the targets were:

1. The military side of the Tripoli airport, location of the Libyan military's air transport planes (IL-76s) that were used for "subversive and terrorist activities."

2. The Benghazi Army Barracks East, which served as Qaddafi's alternative command post and the headquarters of his Jamahariyah guard in eastern Libya.
3. The Sidi Bilal training center for Libyan naval commandos, where the 1984 mining of the Red Sea was planned.
4. The Benina Airfield, which was the primary airbase for Libyan MIG-23 fighter interceptors.

If Qaddafi ordered particularly aggressive action, American warplanes would bomb oil-pumping facilities and other economic sites in addition to the designated military targets. This compromise apparently satisfied Reagan, who then ordered the three carrier battle groups (the *America* had just steamed into the Mediterranean) to commence with Operation Attain Document III, during which U.S. naval forces would operate inside Qaddafi's "line of death."[22]

The exercise began on Sunday, March 23, and although its start was supposed to be secret, the State Department's Bureau of Research and Intelligence mistakenly sent an unclassified alert to American diplomatic posts ahead of time. The NSC staff's James Stark observed, "This is exactly opposite of guidance from yesterday's . . . meeting. . . . Weinberger will hit the roof."[23] Fortunately, no damage was done and the exercise began as scheduled.

Within two hours, Qaddafi took the bait and two Libyan SAM-5 surface-to-air-missiles were fired at American F-14s from a battery at Sirte; both missed. News of the attack arrived at the White House around 9:00 am, but the Navy had not yet returned fire. An update arrived at 1:15 pm reporting that more SAMs had been fired and that the Navy still had not responded, whereupon Chief of Staff Regan contacted Poindexter to find out why the Navy had not returned fire. Poindexter explained that Weinberger had not yet confirmed the latest missile attacks.

Regan was concerned and told Poindexter, "The President [is] in a position of responsibility for potential loss of life in great numbers, and immediate steps should be taken."

Poindexter replied, "Cap . . . met with Admiral Kelso in London last week and [I am] uncertain about whether or not Cap . . . restricted the Admiral's retaliation ability."

"Regardless of what we [have] been told," responded Regan, "the next time the radar [comes] up [the Libyan missile emplacements] should be taken out."[24]

Poindexter then called Weinberger and asked him to commence operations against the Libyans. He also phoned Crowe to find out why the Navy had not attacked any of the Libyan patrol boats that had behaved aggressively toward the

American flotilla. Crowe counseled patience, but Poindexter replied, "You and Cap better come over here and talk to the President. He's pretty hot." On his way to the Oval Office, General Richard Burpee, the Joint Chiefs' operations officer, informed Crowe that three Libyan patrol boats had just been sunk.[25]

At 2:15 pm, Reagan met with Weinberger, Crowe, Bush, Poindexter, and Regan. Crowe briefed the president on the missile firings and said that Admiral Kelso had determined that it was best to wait until dark before commencing operations, and that the airstrike was currently underway. Reagan wanted and authorized immediate retaliation against the SAM sites and other related targets, but Crowe said that it would take twelve hours for the Navy to reconfigure the planes' weapons in order to conduct such an attack.

At 4:05 pm, Poindexter informed the president that American warplanes had successfully destroyed "one and probably two" SAM radar sites using HARM missiles. Reagan was also told that a Libyan patrol boat had been hit and was sinking, whereupon the president asked if provisions were being made to rescue the crew. Poindexter said he thought so. Reagan left the meeting glad that no Americans or civilians had been hurt in the day's engagements.[26]

## THE CRISIS

While the events in the Gulf of Sidra were conclusive militarily, they did not mark the end of the conflict between Qaddafi and the United States. Instead, just as Casey predicted, the encounter triggered a new Libyan terror offensive. On March 25, with the National Security Agency and the CIA monitoring, Qaddafi's intelligence service sent a three-line cable to at least eight Libyan Peoples' Bureaus (LPBs) in Europe (including East Berlin, Paris, Rome, and Madrid) instructing them to plan terrorist attacks against American military and civilian targets. Similar messages were sent to LPBs in a total of thirty countries, including Rwanda, Burundi, West Germany, Turkey, Yugoslavia, and Switzerland, instructing Libyan agents to "Cause maximum casualties to U.S. citizens and other Western people." This was the same type of instruction sent just before the April 1984 shooting that left a British policewoman dead and eleven anti-Qaddafi demonstrators wounded outside the LPB in London.[27] Additionally, over the next few days, American security monitored Libyan agents following U.S. diplomats, and one report indicated that the children of American diplomats were being cased by Libyan agents as they made their way home from school. As a result, the administration contacted representatives of each host government to seek their help in stopping the attacks. Most governments were responsive, but when the Soviet ambassador in Washington, Oleg M. Sokolov, was summoned to the State Department and told that Libyans from the East Berlin LPB planned to attack an American target in that city, he rejected the U.S. demarche. East Germany responded similarly.[28]

Publicly, Qaddafi railed, "It is a time for confrontation—for war. . . . If they want to expand the struggle, we will carry it all over the world." He then summoned all of the foreign ambassadors in Tripoli and informed them that a "state of war" existed between the United States and Libya, and that all American and NATO bases were considered legitimate targets.[29] On March 28, Qaddafi encouraged "all Arab people" to attack anything American, "be it an interest, goods, ship, plane or a person."

At the White House, Qaddafi's intentions were well known, and the NSC staff continued to plan for the administration's next round with Libya. An internal NSC e-mail stated, "We have collected [abundant evidence] over the past 3 months that [Qaddafi] is accelerating his plans for terrorist operations against American targets. . . . Libya's previous planning, together with the Gulf of Sidra beating he has taken, will certainly result in Libyan terrorism against Americans. . . . If the Libyans do turn to terrorism, we have several very well developed contingency plans. The only question is—will we use them?"[30] Peter Rodman wrote another e-mail to Fortier outlining the problems faced by the administration:

—We ought to make clear (if we haven't already) that we will hold Libya responsible for any such attacks on U.S. interests.

—Since such attacks are now predictable, do we have contingency plans for responding? Our ships will have left the area; how long will it take them to come back? (Or should we keep them there longer?) Are we prepared to retaliate against Libya if its responsibility for such acts is clear?

The dispersal of our ships in the next few days will not be the end of this. I hope we will be prepared.31

The administration's resolve, even if new terrorist attacks took place, remained in doubt.

On March 27, an interagency group consisting of Armacost, Arnold Raphel, Robert Oakley, and Nicholas Platt from the State Department, Ed Juchniewicz from the CIA, and Armitage and Moellering from the Pentagon, met to discuss Libya. Their concerns centered on the "cascading indicators of [an imminent] Libyan terrorist attack" and the departure of two of the three carrier battle groups from the Mediterranean. There was also some consternation expressed over the Pentagon's "unwillingness to forward any option other than four military targets already identified in Libya." The group decided: (1) that pending an NSPG decision, all three carriers should remain on station near the Libyan coast until their scheduled departures in case the president ordered airstrikes (the *Saratoga* was scheduled to leave on April 2 and the *Coral Sea* on April 10); (2) to meet again around April 7 to discuss options available when only one carrier remained, including the possible need to obtain permission to launch strikes using planes based in Britain; and (3) that the State Department should send cables to the British, French, and Italian governments "highlighting [the] extensive indicators of [the] Libyan terrorist threat, our resolve to respond, and giving [them a] heads up on [a] possible request to stage through them."[32]

As the administration inched closer to military action, the NSC staff's concern continued to grow about the Pentagon's unresponsiveness in providing additional targeting options. NSC staffer James Stark complained that "the [four] Prairie Fire targets are a limp-wrist response which [won't] even put a dent in Libya's military capability. If we have to go in and take casualties, which we surely will, then we ought to make it count for something."[33] Poindexter was at a loss over the Joint Chiefs' stance, complaining, "Why won't the JCS consider [bombing] the large military equipment depots in the desert? I am also concerned about [collateral] damage. . . . I think we have to be careful to go after [Qaddafi] and military equipment and facilities."[34]

On March 28, there were even more indications that an attack was imminent, with the NSC staff expecting something serious in Beirut. Stark warned, "If a terrorist attack is mounted, either in Lebanon or any of the other areas with hard evidence of Libyan involvement, we need to be ready to order implementation of PRAIRIE FIRE. As long as 3 [carrier battle groups] are in the Med[iterranean] this won't be a problem."[35] Also on March 28, France expelled two members of the LPB staff in Paris for involvement in a planned operation against the U.S. embassy there. In Istanbul, Turkish police arrested two Tunisians who claimed to have planned a terrorist operations against U.S. targets in Turkey on behalf of the Libyans. Additionally, on a tip from American intelligence, Turkish police followed a group of Libyans to the LPB in Ankara, observed the terrorists picked up weapons and proceeded to the American officers' club. Before the Libyans could attack, police arrested the group. In their possession were weapons with the same markings as those used by the terrorists who had attacked the Rome and Vienna airports and had hijacked an EgyptAir plane in November 1985.[36] Other attacks were foiled in Sudan and Italy. On April 2, a bomb exploded aboard TWA flight 840 en route from Rome to Athens. Although the plane managed to land, a large hole was blown in its side and four Americans, including a nine-month-old child, were sucked from the plane and fell 15,000 feet to their deaths. The Arab Revolutionary Cells, another name used by Abu Nidal, claimed responsibility. On April 3, French authorities expelled two Palestinians carrying Algerian and

Tunisian passports after they were observed picking up weapons at the LPB in Paris, apparently on their way to attack a line of visa applicants at the U.S. consulate.

On the evening of April 4, the National Security Agency and the General Communications Headquarters (Britain's signals intelligence agency) intercepted a message from the LPB in East Berlin to the Libyan Intelligence Service in Tripoli. The message proclaimed, "Tripoli will be happy when you see the headlines tomorrow," and predicted "a joyous event."[37] In the early hours of April 5, another message from the LPB in Berlin was intercepted. This one reported that an operation was "happening now" and would be untraceable to the Libyan mission.[38] Simultaneously, U.S. officials in Berlin knew that an attack was in the offing, and military police were dispatched to locations around the city frequented by American military personnel.[39] At 1:49 am Berlin time, a bomb exploded in the washroom of the La Belle Discotheque, instantly killing Army Sergeant Kenneth Ford and a young Turkish patron, while another American soldier, Sergeant James Goines was mortally wounded. In all, the explosion injured 230 people, including about fifty U.S. military personnel.

In addition to the intercepts, there was other intelligence that further incriminated the Libyans. Since their LPB was located in East Berlin, the Libyans had to cross the border into the western sector of the city to launch an attack. Richard Burt, the American ambassador to West Germany later explained, "[T]here was circumstantial evidence concerning their movements which coincided very well with other forms of special intelligence . . . it was very convincing."[40]

News of the bombing traveled quickly. Poindexter called the Situation Room from Santa Barbara, where he was with the vacationing Reagan. After conferring with the president, the National Security Advisor directed Fortier, North, Stark, and Teicher to prepare a memo for the next morning's national security briefing that summarized what was known about the attack and listed U.S. options "in the event of Libyan involvement."[41] In the afternoon, Poindexter briefed the president on the situation, explaining that one American soldier had been killed, and several hundred people were injured, including at least ten Americans.[42]

At the White House Situation Room, the national security team focused on transcripts of the intercepted messages, and it was immediately clear that Qaddafi had finally been caught red-handed. When this information was relayed to Reagan, it convinced him that Libya was responsible, and he directed the Pentagon to punish Qaddafi. Weinberger was on a trip to Thailand at the time, but when he spoke with Armitage, wanting to know if there was absolute evidence of Libyan responsibility, the assistant secretary said that the evidence was overwhelming. This convinced Weinberger, who from that time on supported a military strike.[43] Admiral Crowe also favored the retaliatory option; while Americans had been killed in the Rome and Vienna attacks, they had not been specifically targeted because of their nationality. By contrast, the La Belle disco bombing was meant to kill American servicemen.[44] Casey and Shultz also favored retaliation and were pleased when told by Poindexter, "The President will want to do something—Tuesday or Wednesday night [April 8 or 9]."[45] In addition to setting a military operation in motion, Reagan also directed that all necessary U.S. government resources, including explosives and forensic experts, be made available to aid the German bombing investigation.

Within hours of the attack, Shultz directed the U.S. mission in Berlin to present a demarche to the Soviets, the East Germans, and the West Germans, demanding the closure of the East Berlin and Bonn LPBs. The State Department believed it would be unnecessary to provide the East Germans with the incriminating intercepts because, "We assume, given normal DDR surveillance techniques, that DDR authorities have similar sorts of evidence of East Berlin LPB activities."[46] Later that day, the U.S. chargé d'affaires in Berlin, accompanied by the Mission's protocol officer, delivered the following demarche to Soviet Counselor Nikotin:

The United States Mission has incontrovertible information that the Libyan Peoples' Bureau located in the Soviet sector is responsible for this terrorist attack. The United States Mission notes that on March 27 it apprised the Counselor of the Soviet Embassy in a meeting at the Soviet Embassy of the threat of an imminent attack by members of the Libyan Peoples' Bureau in the Soviet sector against American installations and/or personnel in the western sector of Berlin. At that time, the United States Mission reminded the Soviet Embassy of its responsibility to ensure the safety and security of American personnel and installations from attacks planned and carried out by individuals resident in the Soviet sector. Nonetheless, as forewarned, on April 5 a savage terrorist attack took place. The United States Mission considers that the April 5 terrorist bomb attack is a direct result of the failure of Soviet authorities to take effective action on the information provided by the United States Mission on March 27.

The United States Mission protests in the strongest terms the disregard of the Soviet Embassy for its responsibilities. The United States Mission expects that the Soviet Embassy will take immediate steps to restore calm and security in and around Berlin. In particular, the United States Mission expects that the Soviet Embassy will take all necessary measures to eliminate the terrorist threat from Berlin by removing the terrorist outpost known as the Libyan Peoples' Bureau from the Soviet sector. The United States Mission reminds the Soviet

Embassy that continued failure by the Soviet Embassy to take action requisite
with its responsibilities to ensure safety and security in Berlin will create tensions in and around Berlin for which the Soviet Embassy alone will be fully
and directly responsible.

Nikotin "categorically rejected" the demarche, saying that the Soviet
Union was in no way liable because it could not be responsible where the
"sovereignty of and solidarity with" third countries was concerned. He continued, saying that the Soviets had "long ago" given up its "occupation rights"
in Berlin and that it was time to resolve the problem on the basis of the "actual situation." He then tried to shift blame to the Western allies, expressing
"concern" that the bombing showed how the U.S. mis-managed security in
West Berlin.[47]

In Washington, Ambassador Robert Oakley met with Soviet ambassador
Sokolov to register a similar protest. Like the demarche to the Soviet Mission
in Berlin, Oakley reiterated, "We know full well who perpetrated this action.
It was undertaken by the Libyan Peoples' Bureau in Berlin." When Sokolov
asked about the nature of the evidence, Oakley indicated that it was extensive.
In addition, the U.S. had identified specific individuals from the LPB (including some who had been expelled from Britain and West Germany for terrorism) who had crossed the inter-sector line around the time of the bombing.
Oakley also said that the U.S. had evidence showing the Libyans were planning at least ten more attacks in Europe. Sokolov concluded the meeting saying that this was all news to him, but that he would relay the message to his
government. When Sokolov left, Oakley immediately delivered the same demarche to the East German chargé d'affaires.[48]

While there was finally a consensus within the administration about retaliating, almost immediately, two areas of disagreement did arise. The first was over
target selection. Weinberger argued that only those directly responsible for the
bombing should be attacked. In addition, he only supported a single wave of
strikes rather than a broader campaign supported by others in the administration.[49] The NSC staff, Shultz, and Crowe argued that it was "next to impossible" to retaliate against those who were personally responsible for the attack.
As a sort of middle ground, Reagan's political advisors wanted to hit only targets that were directly related to terrorism, but not necessarily linked to the
Berlin bombing, thinking that these would be the easiest to justify to the American people. This, too, was problematic since attacking terrorist sites usually
meant bombing an empty training camp that would only cost the terrorists a few
thousand dollars to rebuild. Atop the Joint Chiefs' wish list was Libya's military infrastructure, because they believed this was the most significant danger
emanating from Libya.[50] The CIA wanted to include al-Marafiq (the headquar-

ters of the Libyan Intelligence Bureau) even though it was located in downtown Tripoli, surrounded by residential housing units and a number of foreign embassies, making it extremely difficult to hit.

As there was no consensus on target selection, each part of the bureaucracy put together its own list. At the Pentagon, Admiral Crowe instructed General Burpee to "find some military [and terrorist] targets in Libya and we are going to take them out." When Burpee wanted to know how many targets, Crowe said, "Take a look at all the military targets over there, but we'll select five or ten or something." Burpee and his staff worked through the night, but could not find any terrorist-related sites worth hitting. The lone candidate was a golf course at the old Wheelus Air Force Base where terrorists trained for combat in the sand traps. As Burpee later explained, "My thoughts were, if you're going to hit this guy, hit him where it hurts." That meant military targets, the best of which were already included in the Prairie Fire package.

Crowe also phoned General Richard Lawson in Stuttgart to ask for EuCom's list of targets. Lawson, General Bernard Rogers, and Admiral Kelso preferred bombing terrorist-related sites only, but since these enjoyed the protection of the Libyan military, they decided that Libyan military assets that endangered American forces during the operation should also be hit. Over the next thirty-six hours, they studied more than two dozen sites, but could not come up with a better selection than those already on the original Prairie Fire list. They also gave the forthcoming operation a new name: Operation El Dorado Canyon.[51]

At the CIA, Casey tasked Charles Allen to identify the Agency's preferred targets. Allen believed that the U.S. should go after the terrorist infrastructure in Libya, Qaddafi's command and control structure, and Qaddafi himself, and quickly put together a "top-ten" list. One specific target that Allen wanted was the Aziziyyah Barracks—the location of Qaddafi's command center. In addition, Allen wanted al-Marafiq (headquarters of Libyan intelligence), since this was the organization that had ordered the terrorist attacks back in March and had received the incriminating messages just before and after the disco bombing. However, Casey and Gates both observed that hitting al-Marafiq would be extremely difficult and would risk killing numerous civilians.

When the CIA and the Pentagon completed their target lists, they were forwarded to the CPPG targeting subcommittee. When Stark saw the two lists, he immediately recognized that they were not easily reconcilable. This was especially true of two CIA choices (Aziziyyah Barracks and al-Marafiq), which would be opposed by Weinberger and the Joint Chiefs because of probable collateral damage.[52] So Stark asked the CIA's Allen and Admiral Thomas Brooks (head of the Defense Intelligence Agency) to work together and produce a combined list. The two met at CIA headquarters in Langley and came up with a compromise set of targets that included the four Prairie Fire targets plus Aziziyyah Barracks. A list of secondary targets, should U.S. forces be unable to hit their primary targets, was also proposed.[53]

The administration's second area of contention was the method of attack. One option was to launch surgical military strikes. At the Pentagon, a group of special operations planners recommended such strikes, all of which were considered low risk and high gain with no chance of causing collateral damage. North and Poindexter also supported precision strikes, wanting the Navy to send a SEAL team into Tripoli to help guide "smart" bombs to their targets. However, the Pentagon's leadership balked at the idea of sending in ground troops.[54] Another proposal was to launch cruise missiles against al-Marafiq, but the Pentagon ruled this out as too imprecise.[55] EuCom sided with the Chiefs, but for different reasons. First, in the 1980s, Tomahawk cruise missiles were used primarily as a delivery platform for nuclear warheads, and were consequently not as accurate as today, primarily because dropping a nuclear weapon within ten or fifteen miles of an intended target was generally close enough to destroy it. Second, Tomahawks were new and there were not very many of them in the American arsenal; using them for this attack would have required removing the nuclear warheads and replacing them with conventional ones. Such a step would have been time-consuming and also would have reduced the number of missiles available should they be needed against the Soviet Union.[56]

At 9:30 am EST on April 7, the NSPG met in the Oval Office to discuss the American response to the La Belle bombing. Present were Reagan, Shultz, Meese, Casey, Crowe, Deputy Secretary of Defense William Taft (standing in for Weinberger), Poindexter, Fortier, and Regan. Casey opened with an intelligence brief, reminding the group that on March 25 Qaddafi had ordered Libyan diplomatic missions to attack Americans. He then presented evidence of Qaddafi's concerted terrorist campaign since the Gulf of Sidra incident and said that nine terrorist attacks had been tasked or were underway. Next he reviewed the April 5 intercepts and noted that even though the Libyans had been aware that the U.S. was "reading their mail" since 1982, they continued to use the same communications system anyway.[57]

The group moved quickly to a discussion on retaliation, with Poindexter reminding them, "We have talked about strikes against Libya if they retaliated against us for Sidra." The group did not need much persuasion at this point; they believed that Libya should now be punished and set a tentative date of April 12 for the strike. With this, Crowe and Taft spread out maps of Tripoli on the floor for the president to look at, and presented a proposed target list that included the Prairie Fire targets and a number of CIA priorities, including Aziziyyah Barracks, Tripoli radio, al-Marafiq, and the Peoples' Bureau communications center. Reagan insisted on a precision strike that avoided

civilian casualties, and directed that some targets be removed from the list because they were too close to populated areas. Crowe voiced the Joint Chiefs'
opposition to attacking Aziziyyah Barracks—based on the danger to nearby
civilians, but Reagan overrode this objection and Qaddafi's compound stayed
on the list.[58]

Shultz noted that there was a "growing consciousness of the Libyan threat in
the international community, but no readiness to join us in responding." He
thought that the U.S. had to justify its actions by going public with the evidence
against Qaddafi, arguing, "We must show our goods." He felt that under the circumstances, a large attack was called for, saying, "[We] can't show our information and just do something symbolic. [We] must do something massive."

Poindexter agreed with Shultz that the assault should be overwhelming and
said that the proposed target list should be broader. Recalling a plan approved
by the NSPG back in November 1985 that aimed to change the government
of Libya and get rid of Qaddafi, Poindexter suggested, "The best way [to pro-
ceed] is to convince the [Libyan] military [to overthrow Qaddafi]. Do installations, etcetera, and the place where Qaddafi is." Contemporaneous notes indicate that Poindexter's staff wanted to "hit directly at Qaddafi" and make
sponsoring terrorism "costly to Qaddafi."[59]

As for military preparations, Taft indicated that two carriers were available
for the attack. One was leaving port on Wednesday, and the other the following day. The attack envisioned by Shultz, though, entailed using more firepower than two aircraft carriers could provide, so the secretary of state suggested using American F-111 bombers based in Great Britain. There was no
disagreement, and the group decided to ask for permission to launch American F-111s from British bases and to request permission from Paris to allow
the bombers to overfly French territory en route to Libya.[60]

As the discussion about operational details wound down, the president
commented about public opinion, saying, "We must make our reasons public,
and justify [our] action." He asked Casey if the administration could release
the intercepts, and the DCI said yes. Shultz supported this decision, noting,
"We did this in the Korea 007 incident and were credible."

Reagan then reiterated, "We must do this . . . put out our info on what he
is doing." However, on targeting, the president insisted "[We] must not hit
civilian targets and hurt people. Use military targets—[that] hurts Qaddafi
more."

However, Attorney General Meese still wanted to go after economic targets.
He specifically wanted to hit oil-pumping stations, justifying them by drawing
a contrast between Libya and El Salvador. In El Salvador, he argued, the people could not affect change, but in Libya, Meese asserted, "If people are hurt
they will change the government."

Crowe countered that targeting economic sites would hurt the Europeans, who got much of their oil from Libya. Taft supported Crowe, saying, "[We] must have [the] enthusiastic support of [the] Europeans so they don't undercut us [like the] Italians did [after] the airport bombing. France is doing it today." Poindexter closed this stage of the discussion, observing that the "Europeans want to see us get rid of Qaddafi. Then they will cooperate."

The president asked how difficult it would be to go after the Libyan leader directly, since Qaddafi was known to switch residences frequently. Reagan also wanted to know, "How can we find him" without causing collateral damage?

With the discussion having returned to targeting, Casey tried to convince the group to focus on sites that would undermine Qaddafi, explaining, "Hitting military targets won't hurt Qaddafi. Hitting oil is not as good as it was. [We] must go after [the] leadership and targets that help the military get rid of him . . . Praetorian Guard and [the] security service around him, his palaces, and intelligence headquarters. [He] has two principal residences. Hit them and hurt his guard."

Crowe disagreed. He thought that military targets were important to Qaddafi, noting that the Libyan dictator did not want to lose more of his assets after the recent confrontation in the Gulf of Sidra. Crowe also cautioned, "If you make [an] attempt on Qaddafi and *miss*, he'll make a lot of it." As for Qaddafi-related sites, he explained, "[It] will be hard to hit those targets."

The president did not like the ramifications of Crowe's warning, since targets that were more difficult to hit also meant that American servicemen were more likely to die in the attempt. Reagan then explained, "I don't like writing letters to parents. Let's take a look at what else [we can do]."

Casey then presented photographs of Qaddafi's residences, and Poindexter suggested, "We have Stealth. Should we use them with [a] conventional raid . . . they can pinpoint a target."

Crowe immediately objected, saying, "[We] can't use Stealth and tip our hand [to the Soviets]." (At the time, their existence was not even acknowledged by the United States.) Taft supported Crowe, adding that Stealth bombers were "designed [to penetrate] thick defenses," not porous ones like in Libya.

After a few minutes of discussion, Shultz summed up what had been covered so far. "[We] must take action. [We] must use [the] information [we have] to tell everybody why we are taking [this action]. The question is what steps [to take]: military? economic? Qaddafi? The essence is to get rid of Qaddafi, [but] we cannot be sure of where to hit him. Economic [targets] are secondary, intelligence and military are the important ones. [We need to have] more focus on targets and give reasons" for hitting each.

Crowe raised one other concern, explaining, "[We] must look to the future to sustain the effort. [We may need to] keep two carriers in the Med and on station for long periods [of time]."

At this point, Chief of Staff Regan spoke up, noting that the group had not "thought [enough about] American public opinion. They would not approve of killing civilians. Military targets, intelligence facilities, and terrorist camps would be approved. [We] have to have the public with us. Economic targets might hurt European public relations. [Still, the attack] must be massive. Our media is setting the ground rules."

Meese, Casey, and Shultz all agreed, especially with Regan's last two points.

Crowe asked about talking to the Russians, and Shultz said that the State Department had given "Dobrynin both barrels on Libya this morning."

The president reiterated that he wanted to keep civilian casualties to a minimum, and that the U.S. had to use all of its information on Libya to justify the strike, "for example, their giving out weapons to mow down people standing in line outside our Embassy waiting for visas in Paris."

The secretary of state cautioned that the administration still needed to consult with the Europeans before striking, and Meese raised the issue of notifying Congress "under the War Powers Resolution." Poindexter said he was taking care of it, and the meeting adjourned.[61]

After the meeting, cables were dispatched to Egyptian president Hosni Mubarak, French prime minister Jacques Chirac, Dutch prime minister Ruud Lubbers, Italian prime minister Bettino Craxi, and British prime minister Margaret Thatcher, but it was the cable to Thatcher that was of prime importance. In it, Reagan requested the use of bases in Britain for the strike and the use of Cyprus as a landing site in case U.S. planes had to make an emergency landing. The president asked for a reply within twenty-four hours. Disregarding the deadline, Thatcher and her advisors sent a message back to Washington requesting more information:

1. How thoroughly had the Americans thought through the implications of an airstrike on Libya?
2. Why was it necessary for bases in Britain to be used?
3. Could American planes not fly from land bases in the United States or from American aircraft carriers in the Mediterranean?
4. How extensive would the raid be?
5. How many aircraft would be used?
6. What weapons would be employed?
7. What targets would be selected?
8. Could Reagan guarantee that only designated targets would be hit?
9. Was the Reagan Administration going to be able to present the raid as an act of self-defense?[62]

This last question was especially important because Thatcher had declared back in January that retaliatory strikes were against international law. However, she did not ask for more evidence against Libya; the British government had already seen the intercepts and had concluded that Qaddafi was guilty.

Meanwhile, Vice President Bush was conveniently on a previously scheduled trip to the Persian Gulf to familiarize himself with the region's issues and to meet those countries' leaders. In light of the terrorist attack and the impending American military action, he used these visits to explain the U.S. rationale for attacking Libya so as to "temper . . . the Arab response to what we did."[63]

On April 8, the CPPG met to coordinate planning for the attack. In attendance were North, Fortier, Gates, Taft, Raphel (from State), and General Moellering. They began by looking at non-military options against Libya, quickly dispensing with most; a diplomatic protest was deemed too weak, economic sanctions had already proven ineffective, and sabre rattling in the Gulf of Sidra had done nothing to deter Qaddafi. There was concern that the Europeans would decline the administration's request to close LPBs and expel Libyans suspected of being terrorists, so the group recommended that the Europeans be asked to defer their decisions on these matters until the administration could provide more evidence. It was also decided to forward information on Qaddafi's latest activities to Robert Oakley and Vernon Walters, who were on their way to Europe to consult with the Allies about the upcoming American action.[64]

The CPPG members unanimously agreed that military action was the administration's only option since diplomatic and economic measures had not worked, and because Qaddafi had all but declared war on the United States. The group recommended that the U.S. should request permission from Spain to use American bases there to launch refueling tankers for the operation and allow American planes to use these bases for emergency landings. However, two areas of disagreement continued to plague the planning: choice of targets and selection of weapons. Although the NSPG had tentatively selected five targets to attack, discussion about selection continued.

A small subcommittee of the CPPG that included NSC staffers North, Teicher, and Stark, and the CIA's Allen, worked to fashion a list of targets that all of the pertinent bureaucracies could agree to. They selected Tripoli International Airport, Sidi Bilal, Benina, Benghazi, Tarabulus naval base, Qaddafi's tents (which were not ready for "work-up" until the following Monday), Aziziyyah Barracks (referred to as "Qaddafi's Headquarters"), Qaddafi's compound at Surt, the radio transmitter in Tripoli, Jamahariyah military guard barracks in Tripoli, the Jamahariyah military barracks in Benghazi, and one other target that remains classified.[65] The only constraints were: (1) do not hit densely populated civilian areas and (2) only hit targets identified with Qaddafi's terrorist campaign.

On the intelligence front, despite stepped up efforts against Libya, the U.S. still had limited assets in the region. Therefore, Casey requested assistance from the Israelis, and the Mossad obliged, providing important information about the Aziziyyah compound. Not only was it Qaddafi's headquarters, but the compound also contained the primary residence of the Libyan leader and his family—a two-story house and a nearby tent. Mossad also tracked Qaddafi's movements and was able to pass the location of the Libyan leader to Washington virtually twenty-four hours a day.[66]

On the evening of April 8, Admiral Crowe met with Reagan to discuss a list of targets, including the Prairie Fire sites and a number of alternatives. The president reiterated his desire to hit the Aziziyyah Barracks, to which Crowe responded it would take more time to prepare for the attack since the Air Force had not planned to hit Qaddafi's headquarters. Tellingly, Aziziyyah Barracks was only priority number 37 on the JCS target list. The military's attitude toward Aziziyyah was a growing concern to the NSC staff, some of whom ordered the National Security Agency to monitor Sixth Fleet communications so that the White House would know if the Pentagon made any unauthorized changes to the target list.[67]

On April 9, the NSPG met in the Oval Office to continue discussing the airstrikes. Present were Reagan, Shultz, James Baker, Meese, Taft, Casey, Crowe, Poindexter, Fortier, and Regan. The president was ready for action, exclaiming, "The evidence is irrefutable. It is conclusive. We have to move to stop them from carrying out these terror operations." Poindexter said that the planning would take more time because of the need to brief Congress and Thatcher, "who is asking questions." He outlined the mission to consult with the Europeans and requested that Walters carry a letter from Reagan explaining the situation. The National Security Advisor explained that the Europeans were not convinced of Qaddafi's involvement—that the evidence given them so far was not good enough; they were concerned that the U.S. was going to act rashly. Finally, Poindexter argued that the administration had to release the intercepts to the media to justify the planned airstrikes.[68]

On the military front, Taft said that the Navy needed two carriers for the mission, and then Admiral Crowe launched into a discussion on the proposed targets. He explained, "A sustained effort means that the first attack has to be designed for public opinion. [There have to be] understandable and logical targets as Don [Regan] said, [and we must] cut down on collateral damage." He then proposed five targets: (1) the Tripoli airport, (2) Benghazi airport, (3) Benina terrorist camp, (4) Sidi Bilal, (5) the Libyan intelligence headquarters.

As the group discussed the list, Regan observed that there was not much worth hitting at Sidi Bilal, noting that it was a purely symbolic target. As for the Libyan intelligence headquarters, al-Marafiq, the group liked the idea of hitting it until they were informed that it was in the heart of downtown Tripoli, surrounded by residences. This set off alarm bells for the president, who was concerned about hitting nearby apartments, the French embassy, and a hospital only two blocks away. Consequently, he said, "Let's set it aside." In place of such a high-risk target, Reagan preferred going after Qaddafi's compound, his desert camp at Sebha, and the Tarabulus naval base, because these were home to the Libyan leader's Praetorian Guard, and because he regularly visited each. Crowe said that the military would need until Monday or Tuesday to prepare for the attack. With this, the president signed an NSDD authorizing the operation.

At 9:45 am the meeting recessed for a previously scheduled Republican congressional leadership meeting and reconvened at 10:45 am. As the group settled in again, Crowe said that the military barracks, the airports, and the terrorist camp—all of the proposed targets—could be hit in one night.

Reagan wanted to know what the Libyan military's reaction would be, saying, "We want [them] to overthrow the government." He also wanted to know if collateral damage could be minimized. He was told yes, except at Qaddafi's compound. Baker explained "Public opinion is needed here. If we do [cause] collateral damage we will have trouble." These questions were referred for study, and the meeting came to a close.[69]

Despite the administration's determination to act, neither the British nor the French had yet agreed to cooperate. So while the State Department sent a cable requesting permission to use the British bases, General Burpee telephoned his British counterpart, Lieutenant General Sandy Williams, to inform him about the administration's plans and ask permission to launch F-111s from Britain. Williams replied, "You know, we military . . . would really like to support [you], but politically it is really going to be difficult." The British Ministry of Defense subsequently sent a letter to Prime Minister Margaret Thatcher recommending against granting permission. When Burpee got a copy of that letter, he took it to Crowe, who showed it to Weinberger, who in turn met with Reagan and told the president, "We've got a little problem here, flying these airplanes off." Reagan decided that he needed to speak with Thatcher soon.[70]

At 4:00 am EST on April 10, British General Sammy Sanderson spoke with General Moellering and explained that he was about to brief Thatcher on the issue. Sanderson said that she was going to turn down the request unless she received answers to her previously posed questions. Ordinarily Moellering would have conferred with Crowe and Weinberger before giving out such information, but because of the time of day and the urgency of Sanderson's request, Moellering said, "I'll give you a four-day window. It is going to happen within the next four days, it is going to be a night raid, we will hit four military or terrorist targets, no civilian targets and . . . if we don't succeed we're going to go in the next [night] and do it again." When the conversation was over, Moellering notified Weinberger and Crowe of the call. Later that morning, Sanderson called back and said that permission had been tentatively granted.[71] However, Reagan and Thatcher still needed to talk in order to finalize the arrangement.

Later that day, Reagan and Thatcher spoke by phone, and the president answered each of her questions and allayed her concerns. He told her that the F-111s were needed "because by virtue of their special characteristics they would provide the safest means" of carrying out the attack "with the lowest possible risk of civilian casualties and casualties among United States service personnel." According to Thatcher, he also "assured me that the operation would be limited to clearly defined targets related to terrorism, and that the risk of collateral damage would be minimized." This satisfied Thatcher, but she encouraged the administration to publicly present the airstrike in terms of self-defense.[72] In addition to Reagan's argument, she may also have been swayed by a sense of indebtedness to Reagan for standing by Britain during the 1982 Falkland Islands War, by Libya's support for the Irish Republican Army, and by the murder of a British policewoman outside the London LPB two years earlier.

The CPPG targeting subcommittee finished the "final political and military review" in advance of the raid, recommending that the attack take place on April 15 at 2 am, Tripoli time. The timing was decided after intelligence indicated that the entire Libyan air defense system shut down after midnight and that a squadron of Syrian MIG-21s serving as a round-the-clock defense needed clearance from Tripoli before engaging in combat. According to North, American planners assumed that "it would take the Syrians hours before they could obtain clearance for an interception sortie." So it was that Weinberger issued the execute order on April 10, setting April 14/15 as "D-Day," indicating that the attack should take place after dark. That evening, General Rogers flew in from Europe and met with Crowe and Burpee. He was handed the strike orders, but was told that the total number of targets would ultimately depend on obtaining approval to fly the F-111s through French airspace.[73]

From overseas, pressure was building on the administration to slow its planning. Italian prime minister Craxi declared that Reagan needed to provide "clearer" evidence of Libyan complicity if he wanted the Europeans to support any sort of action against Qaddafi, while West German chancellor Helmut Kohl said that his country had evidence pointing to Libyan complicity but that he still opposed military retaliation. German resistance may have been on account of weak Syrian linkages to the attack; the brother of one La Belle suspect arrested for a separate terrorist incident had a direct link to Syrian intelligence. In addition, the investigation into the bombing showed that a Syrian organization—the Arab–German Friendship League—had smuggled the explosives into Berlin.[74]

Despite European reluctance, Vernon Walters departed for his mission to Europe on April 12. After a quick stop in London, he headed to Madrid to confer with Spanish prime minister Filipe González. Walters asked the Spanish for more than just moral support; the U.S. wanted permission for American F-111s to overfly Spain en route from bases in England. Although González did not give outright permission, he did suggest that the planes fly through Spanish airspace without authorization, and Spain would "pretend not to see them." The U.S. declined the Spanish offer. In Germany, Walters and Ambassador Burt briefed Foreign Minister Hans-Dietrich Genscher, who was noncommittal about supporting the American position. Then the Americans flew to Ludwigshafen to meet with Chancellor Helmut Kohl at his home. Kohl was much more supportive than his foreign minister and told his visitors that if the U.S. needed to use any facilities or bases in Germany, "you've got full access."[75]

Some in Congress were also voicing dissent over the administration's planning against Libya. During the previous week, Congressman Don Edwards wrote a letter to President Reagan claiming, "Secret planning for joint Egyptian–U.S. military action against Libya is the latest in a series of attempts to take unto yourself and your advisors the war-making power." He went on to say that this was not allowed by the Constitution, and that if the U.S. was to engage in a war against Libya, Congress should be the institution to make the decision. However, Edwards's letter had little effect on Reagan, except for the comment the president jotted in the margin: "I've never found [Edwards] a reliable authority on the U.S. Const[itution]."[76] In contrast, the congressional leadership from both parties was fairly supportive. For example, after being briefed by administration officials, Senator Richard Lugar, the Republican chairman of the Senate Foreign Relations Committee and Representative Matthew McHugh, a Democratic member of the House Select Committee on Intelligence, called for military retaliation against Libya.

On Sunday, April 13, Vernon Walters, accompanied by a "senior CIA analyst," met with French prime minister Jacques Chirac, and on April 14 with President Mitterrand about permission for American warplanes to overfly French territory. Both Frenchmen turned down the request, with Mitterrand declaring that the U.S. should not "do a pinprick" in its attack against Libya. Apparently the French did not think the operation was decisive (which was one of the conditions Mitterrand had mentioned back in January for joint Franco–American planning against Libya). He also felt it would not deter Qaddafi's adventurism in Africa, nor would it stop his support for terrorism.

People at the White House were so upset with Paris that a message was sent to the Elysée Palace asking, "What the hell do you guys want then?"[77]

By April 13, North wanted to delay the operation for a few days so that the National Security Agency and Israeli intelligence could gather more specific information about the proposed targets and more up-to-date information on Qaddafi's whereabouts. Casey also recommended postponing the operation. American and Israeli agents in Libya could be withdrawn. According to one Defense Department official, "Cap was furious at Casey" over the proposed delay and refused to change the date, saying that such a move would make the operation more dangerous for American pilots because it would allow the Libyans more time to prepare for the attack.[78]

Later that day, the NSC convened to review developments. The meeting opened with a briefing on the Walters mission to Europe. The State Department also reported that the European foreign ministers had requested an urgent meeting with the administration to discuss the rising U.S.–Libyan tensions. Admiral Crowe briefed the group on the military planning, noting that the British would allow the use of their bases, but that the French had refused to give overflight permission. This meant that if the British-based bombers were to participate in the attack, they would have to fly all the way around the European continent and through the Strait of Gibraltar on their way to and from Libya, adding thousands of miles to the mission. While it would be difficult, Crowe thought it could be done and supported the operation even without French cooperation. Reagan wanted to know how late he could recall the planes, to which Crowe explained that the attack could be aborted up to ten minutes before strike time. The operation was then confirmed for the night of "April 14, or on Tuesday morning, April 15, according to Libyan local time." A presidential address to the nation was also discussed, as was congressional notification. It was decided that Senators Dole, Byrd, Lugar, Goldwater, Speaker O'Neill, and Representatives Michel, Wright, Fascell, Broomfield, Aspin, and Dickinson would be informed just prior to the attack.[79]

During all of these deliberations, the question of intentionally targeting Qaddafi came up. Poindexter opposed killing the Libyan leader, thinking he would be "more dangerous dead than alive," becoming a hero and a martyr to radical Arabs. Instead, the National Security Advisor wanted to humiliate the Libyan dictator and show the Libyan people the price they were paying for his actions.[80]

However, North believed that the only way to end the Libyan threat was to get rid of Qaddafi, and at one CPPG meeting, pushed several plans. One was to "phone around" Tripoli to find Qaddafi just before the attack and then target that location. Another was to "have him take a call from somebody that he'll

have to take it from [like] the Pope. He would take the call. We'll hone in on it
and kill him." North also proposed using British hostage negotiator Terry Waite
to lure Qaddafi to talks at his Aziziyyah compound that evening, hoping that after a late meeting, Qaddafi would then spend the night there. Each of these
plans was discussed and rejected. While nobody in the administration would
have been upset if Qaddafi died during the attack, Executive Order 12333 ex-
pressly forbade assassination by American assets; intentionally targeting
Qaddafi was not an option. However, the targeting of his compound was allowed. Although that site had military value aside from Qaddafi, as Air Force
major general David Forgan later explained, "If we caught Qaddafi in bed, that
would be a bonus, but that was not the goal." Despite the CPPG's rejection of
the Qaddafi plans, North still drafted a contingency statement in case the
Libyan leader was caught in the bombing, calling his death "fortuitous." Aiding this effort, the Israelis managed to park a reconnaissance aircraft at Tripoli's
airport to collect last-minute intelligence, and continued to pass information to
the CIA on Qaddafi's whereabouts until forty minutes before the bombing
started. As the Israeli plane took off, it reported that Qaddafi was still working
in his tent at the Aziziyyah Barracks compound.[81]

Meanwhile, Walters's tour through Europe continued. On April 14, he met
with Italian prime minister Craxi, who tried to delay American action and urged
the U.S. to ask NATO to consider a joint action "against terrorism."[82] At the
same time, the European foreign ministers met in the Netherlands to discuss the
crisis. While they called on Libya to renounce its support for terrorism and
vowed to restrict the movement of Libyan diplomats, they again rejected economic sanctions and called on Reagan to show restraint. Although the Europeans had seen the evidence against Qaddafi and knew that he was guilty, they
did not believe that the United States would release the conclusive intercept
transcripts. Doing so would help swing public opinion in favor of an attack—
even among Europeans—but would compromise intelligence-gathering
sources and methods. So long as the administration did not go public with this
evidence, the Europeans believed that they were politically safe counseling restraint.[83] The Europeans had another reason for opposing action against Libya:
oil. Economic ties between Europe and Libya were extensive, and to openly
support the United States in its conflict with Libya would have created unwanted economic consequences.

At 4:00 pm EST on April 14, Reagan signed an executive order giving final
approval for a strike against "terror targets inside Libya."[84] Two hours later, the
president met with congressional leaders to consult about the airstrikes. Casey
presented evidence of Libya's central role in the Berlin bombing and Qaddafi's
ongoing terrorist campaign against the United States. Deputy Secretary of
State John Whitehead reviewed the diplomatic situation and presented evi-

dence of Libya's past support for terrorism, including the existence of terrorist training camps in Libya and canceled checks showing Libyan payments to terrorist groups. Reagan and Crowe outlined the military plan and told the legislators that their opposition could halt the operation. Even though the planes were already on the way to Libya, the president said he could still pick up the phone and recall them. He explained, "[The planes] will be refueled five times in the air before they arrive over Tripoli, so at the conclusion of this meeting, I could call off the operation. I am not presenting you with a *fait accompli*. We will decide in this meeting whether to proceed." Support for the plan split along partisan lines, but the opposition was not sufficiently strong to make Reagan call off the mission.[85]

At 7:00 pm, EST (2:00 am, April 15, Libya time), in retaliation for the bombing of the La Belle disco in Berlin *and* in order to deter and preempt Qaddafi's continuing terror campaign, U.S. naval and air forces struck designated targets in Tripoli and Benghazi. Two hours later, Reagan announced the airstrikes in a nationally televised address:

> The evidence is now conclusive that the terrorist bombing of the La Belle discotheque was planned and executed under the direct orders of the Libyan regime. . . . When our citizens are abused or attacked, anywhere in the world, on the direct orders of a hostile regime—we will respond, so long as I am in the Oval Office. . . . We believe that this preemptive action against his terrorist installations will not only diminish Colonel [Qaddafi's] capacity to export terror; it will provide him with incentives and reasons to alter his criminal behavior. . . . We Americans are slow to anger. We always seek peaceful avenues before resorting to the use of force. And we did. We tried quiet diplomacy, public condemnations, economic sanctions, and demonstrations of military force. None succeeded. Despite our repeated warnings, [Qaddafi] continued his reckless policy of intimidation, his relentless pursuit of terror. He counted on America to be passive. He counted wrong.

## Aftermath

One goal of the American operation was to show the Europeans that the U.S. would act alone if necessary, even in Europe's backyard. After Operation El Dorado Canyon, the Western allies were much more willing to cooperate with the U.S. in combating terrorism. Throughout Europe, Libyan diplomats and students suspected of planning or facilitating terrorist operations were deported. The British expelled twenty-one students and West Germany reduced the number of Libyan diplomats in Bonn from forty to fifteen. Also, new restrictions were placed on Libyan diplomats; deported diplomats were barred from serving in the same capacity in another Western European country. At the Tokyo Economic Summit on May 7, Reagan asked the leaders of the seven major industrialized countries to take a number of actions, including: (1) close the Libyan Peoples' Bureaus in allied countries; (2) boycott Libyan oil; (3) withdraw Western deposits from Libyan banks; (4) monitor or close down Libyan front organizations suspected of involvement in terrorism; (5) prohibit entry of Libyan [flagged] ships; (6) halt flights to and from Tripoli; (7) order citizens and companies out of Libya; (8) recall ambassadors from Libya; (8) ban sales of arms, spare parts, and sophisticated equipment to Libya; and (9) restrict cross-border travel of Libyans. The leaders assembled in Tokyo agreed to some of these requests, and issued a statement that singled out Libya, saying, "[We strongly] reaffirm our condemnation of international terrorism in all its forms, of its accomplices, and of those, including governments, who sponsor or support it."[86] In addition, at the May Trevi Meeting in The Hague, the European ministers of justice agreed to share intelligence on terrorist groups with each other and with the United States, and to crack down on the cross-border movements of suspected terrorists.[87]

In addition, the American attack also had a significant dampening effect on Libyan terrorism from an unexpected source. East German documents recovered after the reunification of Germany indicate that sometime after April 14, American officials approached Berlin with information about an upcoming Abu Nidal attack against a book fair in the West that was to be attended by a number of prominent Westerners. The East Germans put a halt to the operation, because, as one German memo on the matter stated, Berlin did not want to give the United States a reason "to pursue the policy of force against sovereign states and national liberation movements . . . it would be in our common interest if the friends would use the opportunities available to them to influence the Palestinian groupings known to them to prevent the carrying out of any terrorist actions in Europe."[88]

Lastly, the airstrikes had an effect on Libyan terrorism. After an initial spasm of retaliation, Qaddafi's terrorist activities abated—for a while. Prior to Operation El Dorado Canyon, Western intelligence had information that Qaddafi was attempting to purchase some of the American hostages held by Hezbollah in Lebanon. While they would not part with any of their captives, the Libyan leader was able to obtain an American held by another group. According to a CIA report, a Libyan intelligence officer bought Peter Kilburn and two British hostages and murdered them on April 17, 1986 in retaliation for the American airstrikes.[89] Several other attacks that had been set in motion before the U.S. air raid still occurred, including an assassination attempt against William Calkins, the communications officer at the American embassy in Khartoum, Sudan. After that, though, Libyan terrorism was relatively dormant until the bombing of Pan Am flight 103 over Scotland nearly a year and a half later.

## Chapter Eight

# Conclusion

Power wisely invested yields an enhanced reputation for effectiveness. Unsuccessful investments deplete both the stock of capital and the reputation.[1]

Ronald Reagan came to the presidency vowing "swift and effective retribution" against terrorists that attacked Americans. Contrary to this rhetoric, though, the administration rarely implemented any sort of action that could be construed as such. Out of the hundreds of terrorist attacks against American interests during the Reagan years, the administration responded to only a handful, while the overwhelming majority were either ignored or left for local law enforcement to manage. Of the few that the administration did react to, only two responses actually match Reagan's rhetoric and policy: (1) the intercept and capture of the *Achille Lauro* hijackers (and the planned assault on the cruise ship before the hijackers surrendered) and (2) the airstrikes against Libya in response to Qaddafi's terrorist campaign, including the bombing of the La Belle disco. Given such a wide disparity between policy and action, the question arises: Why was there such variation in response? The answer lies in the administration's makeup and power relationships.

*Reagan's management style.* In a way, a memo sent from Fred Iklé to Richard Allen on January 14, 1981, just days before Reagan was inaugurated is indicative of the president's approach to management. Iklé warned the soon-to-be National Security Advisor, "The President's prestige must be protected from becoming damaged by the hostage situation." He was, of course, talking about the Iranian hostage crisis that had destroyed Jimmy Carter's chances for reelection. Iklé continued, "Responsibility for all aspects of the hostage situation should be visibly delegated to an official at the sub-cabinet level or below . . . with only a supervisory role and strategic guidance reserved for the President."[2]

Reagan's management style has often been described as decentralized, hands-off, and a system in which he set the broad outlines of policy but gave little direction beyond that, in part because he was not interested in the details of policy. While this supposition is generally true, in the area of terrorism, Reagan seems to have been—at times—more involved than usual in formulating responses. However, even in the midst of many of these crises, he refused to settle conflicts between his advisors, and failed to give that authority to someone else, such as the National Security Advisor. When the administration's Lebanon policy began to flounder, Reagan was unwilling to interject himself into the feud between Shultz and Weinberger. Further, despite his desire to see the United States retaliate for the bombing of the Marine barracks, he was not engaged enough in the process to ensure that his wishes were carried out. Additionally, *if* it is true that Weinberger intentionally disobeyed a presidential order and canceled the airstrikes on his own, the secretary of defense undoubtedly would have taken comfort in the fact that Reagan rarely disciplined his subordinates and was even less likely to fire an old friend. Despite the enormity of the crisis during the hijacking of TWA Flight 847, there is little evidence of Reagan's involvement. Instead, he merely expressed that he wanted the situation ended peacefully and had McFarlane, Casey, and Shultz resolve it by giving the hijackers what they wanted. With the *Achille Lauro*, Reagan injected his desires into the process, pushing for the rescue attempt and supporting the subsequent mid-air intercept. With the massacres at the Rome and Vienna airports, he allowed the reservations of Weinberger and the Joint Chiefs to override his desire to punish Abu Nidal and Qaddafi, and was not able to push these advisors to action until the Libyans struck again, killing two American soldiers in Berlin. When the president's hands-off approach re-asserted itself, the decision-making process showed little resemblance to a truly deliberative process. In these cases, his lack of involvement allowed his advisors to unilaterally implement their own policy preferences. In response to terrorism during the Reagan years, there was very little compromise—only winners and losers.

*Beliefs.* Because the president allowed his advisors to act with little supervision, they had significant latitude in determining what policy options were implemented by the administration. Thus, the beliefs held by members of Reagan's national security team, beliefs that caused these men to take and hold certain positions, were critical to the process. Weinberger and most of the Joint Chiefs did not want to use the military for counter-terrorism operations because they believed that if American servicemen or innocent civilians were killed, the hard-earned goodwill of the American people in the post-Vietnam era would be lost. If that happened, Reagan's military buildup that was intended to counter the "true threat"—the Soviet Union—would be at risk. Additionally, since most counter-terrorist operations would have been conducted against Islamic extremists, it was feared that such actions would damage U.S. relations with the moderate Arabs. If this happened, Weinberger and the Joint Chiefs feared that America's access to Persian Gulf oil could be cut off, and in the event that Moscow made a military incursion into that region, the support of these governments could be lost.

On the other hand, another faction in the administration (including most of the NSC staff, Shultz, and Casey) saw terrorism as an extension of the Soviet campaign to undermine the West and that it should be responded to forcefully. In the Middle East, they believed that Israel was the region's only reliable ally and were not particularly concerned about the reaction of the moderate Arabs to American retaliatory acts. Still a third group (mostly State Department officials at the ambassadorial level), saw American interests as resting with the moderate Arabs and were unlikely to support military action against Muslims for fear of an "Islamic backlash" against Washington. They also tended to believe that terrorism was the result of localized issues, not the Cold War, and that the root causes should be addressed. American military action in response to terrorism only made solving these local problems more difficult.

In 1985, when Admiral Crowe replaced General Vessey as Chairman of the Joint Chiefs of Staff, a philosophical shift accompanied the change in command. While Vessey and Weinberger had virtually identical beliefs about the use of the military, Crowe had far fewer qualms about using force. The cases after Crowe became chairman (beginning with the *Achille Lauro*) show a marked shift toward the use of force in response to terrorism.

*Power.* Given Reagan's management style and the various beliefs of Reagan's advisors, what was it then that determined the administration's policy choices? The answer is power. Formal power is the authority that the individual participants in the process derive from their positions, while informal power is based on a participant's relationship with the president. As for formal power, Weinberger and the Joint Chiefs controlled the use of military force, Shultz controlled diplomatic channels, and Casey was in charge of intelligence-gathering tools. When Shultz wanted to launch an attack, he had to find a way to get Weinberger to support it, but if Weinberger was opposed and Reagan was unwilling to mediate their dispute, the secretary of defense could effectively kill any options calling for military strikes. On the other hand, Shultz had the formal power to prevent American diplomacy from being used to do things that Weinberger wanted, such as publicly pressuring Israel to release its Lebanese detainees during the TWA hijacking.

More important, though, is informal power, which is the key to understanding which advisor's preferences became reality. While formal power was a constant, informal power flowed from the confidence the president bestowed on his individual advisors. Like a pendulum swinging back and forth, the president's confidence in his advisors was in flux, so that whomever the "confidence pendulum" was closest to at a given moment had the most informal power. This fluctuation was based on previous experiences; if a particular advisor was successful in managing some crisis or had worked to see that the president's preferences were acted upon, the president was more likely to listen to that advisor the next time a similar crisis hit. Alternatively, if an advisor's advice or actions frustrated the president's desires, the president was less likely in subsequent cases to listen to that advisor or allow that advisor's preferences to be realized.

At the outset of the administration, Weinberger and the Joint Chiefs had an enormous informal power because Reagan deeply respected the military and had a long-standing friendship with Weinberger. Because of this, the Pentagon was able to, for the most part, use its forces as it saw fit. After the Marine barracks were bombed, Reagan wanted to retaliate and went so far as to order action, but Weinberger (according to one version) unilaterally canceled the mission. Weinberger had no fear of being disciplined because of his relationship with the president and had no fear of having his decision over-ridden because he and the Pentagon had Reagan's confidence. However, while the Pentagon continued to raise the same objections to retaliation after each terrorist incident, the attacks just kept coming. Reagan eventually began discounting their arguments and listening more to other advisors, including Shultz and the NSC staff. Because Shultz and McFarlane successfully negotiated an end to the TWA hijacking, when the *Achille Lauro* was hijacked, the president was much more willing to support their proposals. When the NSC staff devised the plan to intercept the hijackers' plane, Reagan approved it over Weinberger's objections, indicating that power had shifted to the NSC staff. It should be noted that it was during this period—late 1985 and early 1986—that Reagan overrode the concerns of Shultz and Weinberger and approved the NSC staff's plan to sell arms to Iran in exchange for their "help" releasing the American hostages in Beirut. It was mainly Reagan's respect for military advice, including Crowe's claim that forces were not ready to retaliate against Libya, that moved the president to implement economic sanctions instead of retaliating for the Rome and Vienna massacres. This again frustrated Reagan's desires, so when the La Belle disco was bombed, the hawks were in a position to drive policy because of their firm hold on informal power. Weinberger's demise was self-inflicted; his arguments began to sound like broken records to the president, and by the time of the disco attack, all of the secretary of defense's arguments were rendered moot because all of his conditions for using force had been met.

## OTHER OBSERVATIONS

In addition to highlighting the importance of power, beliefs, and the president's management style, this study was enlightening in two other areas: learning and domestic politics.

*Learning.* Learning on the job was an important part of the Reagan administration's counter-terrorism experience. When the president's advisors learned what worked to get their preferred policy option implemented, they acted accordingly. Weinberger and the Joint Chiefs were especially good at keeping the administration from implementing forceful action by playing to Reagan's aversion to collateral damage, and exploiting this concern repeatedly.

The National Security Council staffers and CIA director Casey were also adept at learning from past terrorism incidents. From the TWA hijacking, Casey and NSC staff (especially North, McFarlane, and Poindexter) discovered that it paid to bargain with, if not the hijackers directly, then forces allied with the terrorists. When Nabih Barri and Amal demanded the release of hundreds of Lebanese prisoners held by Israel, the NSC staff watched Shultz direct Charles Hill to open discussions with Benjamin Netanyahu on the matter, eventually leading to an agreement where the detainees would be freed after the American passengers were released. In other words, they learned that concessions work. There were a few other lessons from the TWA hijacking that would come into play later as well: (1) Iran could be helpful in resolving hostage crises; (2) secrecy was important; and (3) as long as there was no public quid pro quo, concessions could be plausibly denied.

From the *Achille Lauro* hijacking came two lessons. First, the NSC staff saw that it was much more effective at resolving terrorist crises than the bureaucracy. After all, it was the NSC staff—and not the bureaucracy—that had come up with the intercept plan, had found Craxi, and had come up with the intelligence revealing the location of the ship and then later the hijackers. If Stark had not come up with the intercept plan, and if Poindexter had not pushed it, the hijackers would likely have gotten away. If North and Teicher had never called their Israeli contacts, the administration would have been unable to find the ship at sea, and would not have been able to locate the hijackers after Mubarak lied about their location. If Ledeen had not had a personal relationship with Craxi, the administration never would have found the Italian prime minister to ask for landing rights at Sigonella. As North would later explain, "We could not have done *Achille Lauro* without a personal relationship between an NSC staff member and an Israeli intelligence official."[3] Thus, the NSC staff saw how effective it could be if it were to go operational.

Second, the NSC staff learned that it could bypass uncooperative members of the administration to accomplish its desired policy initiatives. The intercept plan was developed without Weinberger's input, and once his objections were registered with Reagan, the NSC staff ensured that the secretary of defense could not call the president again to try and scuttle the plan.

*Domestic politics.* An interesting and unexpected finding from this study is the irrelevance of both the Congress and public opinion in crisis decision making. Although there was congressional pressure toward the end of the Marine deployment in Lebanon, the legislative branch had no bearing on whether or not to retaliate. Responses during the other crises were the same; concern about Congress in the long run was occasionally mentioned but never really entered into the discussion as a decisive factor. This is perhaps most indicative in the La Belle disco case. Only after Reagan decided to launch a retaliatory attack against Libya and after the planes were in the air did he "consult" with the senior leaders of the House and Senate. Although he told the assembled group that he would turn the planes around if they did not approve of the mission, in reality, he had no intention of doing so, and was merely paying lip service to what the congressmen believed was their prerogative over the war power.

Likewise, public opinion was inconsequential, especially in the short term. When the president's national security team deliberated about how to respond to these terrorist attacks, there were occasional memos about public opinion, but their intent was only to highlight the danger that prolonged hostage crises would cause the public to compare Reagan's handling of terrorism to Carter's. Thus, the only effect of these polls and studies was to further encourage the administration to "do something" about each crisis. Reagan reflected this sentiment during the Beirut hostage crisis when he told his advisors that the public "would not forgive him" if he failed to do everything he could to bring the captive Americans home. Public opinion, though, was never a factor in the discussions about whether or not to use force in response to terrorist attacks.

It is likely, though, that the "no-deal deal" that ended the TWA hijacking was kept secret precisely because the administration expected a negative public reaction should it be revealed. Most documents from that crisis remain classified based on the argument that releasing them would damage national security. However, the governments and groups that could most exploit this information (Syria, Iran, Israel, Hezbollah, and Amal) already knew what happened and why. It was only the American public that was not told, leading to the conclusion that public opinion mattered in this case because full disclosure would have proven embarrassing and politically damaging.

## POLICY PRESCRIPTIONS

How, then, does all of this relate to the current war on terrorism? While many of the administration's officials are different and the terrorist groups have changed since the 1980s, enough parallels with today's campaign exist that lessons for the current conflict can still be learned.

As a point of departure, it is instructive to compare the 1980s with today, seeking to discover what about the two wars is the same and what has changed. For starters, many of the terrorist groups and state sponsors of terrorism are quite familiar. The State Department's 2003 report on terrorism cites Cuba, North Korea, Libya, Sudan, Syria, Iran, and Iraq as state sponsors of terrorism; all but Iraq and Sudan were members of that club in the mid-1980s. With the end of the Cold War, however, the context for the war against terrorism changed significantly. During the Reagan years, administration officials had to consider the possibility that launching a retaliatory strike against many of the state sponsors of terrorism risked escalating a crisis into a conflict with the Soviet Union. Strikes against Syria and Libya presented enormous risks because of their relationships with Moscow and because of the presence of Soviet advisors in each country. Should the United States attack, Soviet citizens could be killed and Moscow might feel sufficiently violated to respond. Meanwhile, the Cuban Missile Crisis and the Korean War were ever-present reminders of what could happen if the administration chose to challenge Cuba or North Korea. Attacking Iran risked pushing Tehran into the arms of the Soviets. Today, however, the Soviet sphere of influence is no longer a concern and Russia is viewed as a partner in the fight against international terrorism.

As for specific groups, many of the same organizations are still active, including FARC in Colombia, the Islamic separatist groups in the Philippines, and a number of groups in and around Israel, including Islamic Jihad, Hezbollah, and the Al-Aqsa Brigades (associated with Arafat's Fatah organization). However, there has been a significant decline in left-wing, communist terrorism, which can be attributed in large part to the end of the Cold War and the demise of the Soviet Union. The lack of support and encouragement from an ideological Moscow combined with effective police work meant that many of the (especially Western European) groups simply disappeared. The major terrorist groups of significance today appear to be motivated by religion and/or nationalistic self-determination, including Hamas, Abu Sayyaf in the Philippines, the Tamil Tigers in Sri Lanka, splinter groups from the Irish Republican Army, and the Basque separatist group ETA.

However, unlike the 1980s, when terrorist groups worked in relative isolation from one another, it is most significant that a new terrorist network arose during the 1990s. Osama bin Laden's Al-Qaeda became an umbrella organization for a number of radical Islamic groups, and has begun centralizing this loose affiliation by coordinating training and operations worldwide. In the 1980s, the organizations and individuals of greatest concern to the United States—Hezbollah, Abu Nidal, Abu Abbas, and various state apparatuses—did not have a truly global reach. Most of these groups could exert themselves throughout the Middle East, North Africa, and into Europe, but strikes against targets inside the United States were unlikely. Consequently, the American body politic deemed the fight against terrorism as less than urgent. However, in light of the events on September 11, 2001, the circumstances and stakes of terrorism have clearly changed. While some may have questioned the heightened importance accorded the war against terrorism during the Reagan years—declaring the effort less important than other issues, today terrorism is a top priority due to the clear and present danger posed by Al-Qaeda to America's national security.

*Proposal #1* The successful prosecution of the war on terrorism *should* remain a priority.

The costs of failing to engage and deter terrorist groups such as Al-Qaeda are far too high to ignore. Despite the magnitude of the attacks on the World Trade Center and the Pentagon, they were not worst-case scenarios. Terrorist groups have proven that they have the capability and willingness to conduct massive suicide missions on American soil, so it should not be surprising to see Al-Qaeda or other groups attempt even more savage attacks against the United States, including operations that use chemical, biological, or radiological weapons.

*Proposal #2* The military and intelligence agencies should be properly equipped to fight a war on terrorism. Consequently, they should have the resources necessary to develop new methods of warfare, including psychological and informational, that are effective against individuals and organizations that use the suicide attack as an operational tool.

The Reagan administration was—and the Bush administration is—committed to combating terrorism. It was a major component of American foreign policy during the 1980s, and in light of the attacks on September 11, is the paramount issue on the national security policy agenda today. This being said, why did the Reagan administration fail to prosecute its war consistently, and what lesson does the Reagan experience hold for the Bush team? During the 1980s, varying organizational views prevailed in different parts of the bureaucracy about how to handle the problem. Most obstructionist to the counter-terrorism effort was the Department of Defense, where decision-makers were more concerned about access to Persian Gulf oil and maintaining good relations with the moderate Arabs than with stopping terrorism. Consequently, the Pentagon regularly opposed launching attacks against Islamic extremists in the region for fear of upsetting the status quo. Further, the Pentagon's primary mission was (and is) to fight and win major wars; because of this, the military leadership discounted the importance of low-intensity conflict and special operations warfare. In the 1980s, decision-makers in the Department of Defense believed the primary threat to American national security were the Soviet ICBMs aimed at the continental

United States and the divisions of Russian tanks lining the Fulda Gap. As a result, the Pentagon's hierarchy believed that America's defense posture should be aimed at countering these threats instead of allocating time and money to special operations capabilities and missions—efforts that they thought diverted valuable resources away from the Pentagon's primary mission.

In the twenty-first century, however, the likelihood that the Pentagon will be called upon to fight a major global war in the next twenty years has diminished significantly relative to the Cold War era. Rather, as the last decade has shown, the United States will likely fight more regional or local wars that require precisely the types of capabilities needed for counter-terrorism operations. Somalia, Kosovo—even Grenada, Panama, and Iraq—all were operations that needed a potent unconventional warfare component in order to succeed. The war against the Taliban and Al-Qaeda in Afghanistan is no different, and the decision-makers in the Pentagon need to understand the new world they live in and plan accordingly. This is not to say that the dangers posed by China, North Korea, and other traditional military powers should be ignored; the United States will continue to need nuclear and conventional capabilities, such as a powerful blue-water navy, high-technology air force, and a well-trained and efficient army to deter such threats. But resources should not be allocated to these parts of the military to the exclusion of counter-terrorism units, since it is extremely likely that the latter will be used with increasing frequency.

In addition, the intelligence community needs to recognize the new enemy, task resources to meet this threat by increasing its analytical and language capabilities and by acquiring/placing more human intelligence assets (i.e., spies) within the radical communities that tend to produce terrorists.

*Proposal #3* The United States should pursue active diplomacy to resolve conflicts that give rise to terrorism against America.

While the upper echelons at the Pentagon need to recognize that America's interests are not significantly damaged by striking at terrorist groups responsible for attacking American targets (since America's ties with the moderate Arabs were not unduly strained by the war in Afghanistan), the State Department needs to appreciate the localized problems that create circumstances conducive to groups choosing terrorism. Case in point: the ongoing *intifada* and the seemingly intractable Israeli–Palestinian conflict that is more likely to hinder access to the region's oil (if the region's oil producers decide to curtail supplies because of U.S. support for Israel) and derail American relations with the region's moderate governments than harm American counter-terrorist operations. If this conflict were to be fairly and objectively resolved, much of the animosity toward the Untied States from the broader Arab population would radically diminish, as would anti-American terrorism. While terrorism will continue so long as there are rejectionists and absolutists in the world, the U.S. can go a long way toward reducing the threat by addressing the local causes and rationales for political violence.

*Proposal #4* When making appointments to an administration's national security team, a president and his advisors should take into account personal relations between prospective advisors. Where there is previously demonstrated stress in a relationship, one or both of the potential nominees should be removed from consideration.

One of the more detrimental components of the Reagan administration's war on terrorism was the personal dimension. Reagan chose advisors based on personal loyalty and ideological purity, but did not take into account whether or not these men and women could get along; nowhere was the problem more evident than in the Shultz–Weinberger relationship. It might be an overstatement to say that the two men hated each other, but they certainly were at each other's throats more often than not, so much so that one would oppose a policy position simply because the other supported it. Richard Armitage suggests that the problem was a clash of egos:

> They had both been cabinet officers, they were both formidable guys, both somewhat privileged. One had gone into the Marine Corps and the other had gone into the army during the war and they both fought well. There was an underlying competition.

And this competition was so personal that they refused to settle their differences. Armitage relayed a story indicative of the Shultz–Weinberger relationship:

> [Bashir] Gemayel had been assassinated, [and] Amin Gemayel had come to town . . . there was a reception at the embassy of Lebanon. I was there, just kind of standing in the corner and Shultz came over and said, "Rich, I just want to tell you how happy I am when we go to those NSC meetings and I see you sitting there because I know Cap will at least get good solid advice, whether he follows it, or not." I said, "Well, I'm not always on your side." He said, "No, I know it, but it will be reasoned." And I said, "Thank you very much, Mr. Secretary, that's a kind thing to say." Anyhow, I was standing alone and I was kind of emboldened by it and I said, "Mr. Secretary, to make a comment, why don't you just take a six pack of beer and grab Mr. Weinberger and go out in the middle of a lake and get things squared away between you two." He looked at me, he has the most piercing eyes, he looked right back and said, "He wouldn't come." Later, I told Secretary Weinberger that story, just as I told you and after I said that Shultz . . . said you wouldn't come, Weinberger said, "He's right."[4]

These conflicting personalities and bureaucracies add yet another dimension to the problem. When publicly aired in-fighting occurs, mixed signals are sent to America's adversaries, which only invites more violence.

*Proposal #5* There must be an enforcer in the administration. If the president is unwilling or unable to settle disputes between his foreign policy advisors, he *must* have a national security advisor (or the position's equivalent) with the stature and clearly designated power to settle disputes.

The previous chapters raise a significant set of questions about the governance of the national security apparatus: (1) Why was the Pentagon so unwilling to act in the battle against terrorism? (2) Why was it so effective in thwarting the will of the president? (3) How can a president overcome an intransigent bureaucracy?

The first question has been addressed already. In sum, the answer to this question is found in the individual beliefs of the president's advisors and their bureaucratic, parochial perspectives. The secretary of defense and the Joint Chiefs of Staff had very particular views about how and when the United States should use force—as outlined in the Weinberger Doctrine, while Shultz and the NSC staff viewed the problem and solution from an entirely differently point of view.

The second and third questions are interrelated, because they both pertain to a president's management of the process. As Harry Truman prepared to leave office, he noted that Eisenhower would encounter a lot of frustration with the bureaucracy: "He'll sit here and he'll say, 'Do this! Do that!' *And nothing will happen.* Poor Ike—it won't be a bit like the Army. He'll find it very frustrating."[5] In other words, it takes more than the president's will to make things happen. When the president's primary power—persuasion—is not enough, discipline and enforcement are required, especially when members of a particular bureaucratic organization do not agree with the course of action the president wants taken. Therefore, if a president is to see his wishes acted upon, he or an authorized deputy must hold an organization's feet to the fire, constantly monitoring performance to assure that the bureaucracy's actions match the president's orders.

*Proposal #6* Action *must* match rhetoric.

How can the United States maintain a consistent, even-keeled, and effective policy of responding to terrorism? This is perhaps the most vexing and overarching question, and the last four administrations have struggled to find the answer with little success. While Reagan's travails are explored in this book, Bush and Clinton did not fare much better. George Bush senior's administration downgraded the importance of terrorism so much that the president rarely dealt with the issue. Instead, the problem was largely ignored or left to the judicial process, as happened with the bombing of Pan Am Flight 103. Like Reagan, President Clinton relied on episodic responses to terrorist incidents that amounted to nothing more than a slap on the wrist. Clinton's order to attack targets in Afghanistan and Sudan following the bombing of the American embassies in Kenya and Tanzania had little effect, and there is even some question as to whether or not the pharmaceutical plant bombed in Sudan was in fact making chemical weapons for Al-Qaeda.

Rhetoric of the sort used by past administrations is counter-productive when not followed up by concrete action, for when inconsistencies are discovered, terrorists are emboldened. This is a cautionary note, as the current administration has already taken a step down this slippery slope and must correct its course before something truly tragic happens. In the Philippines, the Abu Sayyaf group has engaged in the kidnapping of foreign tourists and missionaries, including some Americans. According to press reports in April 2002, the Bush administration helped facilitate a private ransom payment to free two Americans, but the hostages in question were not released; one subsequently was freed and her husband died during a rescue attempt by the Philippine Army. Ransom payments and the granting of concessions send the wrong message to terrorists and invite more hostage taking—not only by Abu Sayyaf, but by other terrorist and criminal organizations as well. If the Bush administration does not renounce this action and reiterate its policy concerning concessions to terrorists, it is likely that more Americans will be taken in places where American counter-terrorism and counter-insurgency efforts are underway, such as Colombia, the Philippines, Iraq, and Pakistan.

Overheated rhetoric can also prove counter-productive. Toward the end of the TWA hijacking, when Reagan began calling the terrorists names and threatening massive retaliation even if the passengers were released, the hijackers backed away from the deal that would have freed the hostages. Likewise, the current administration needs to beware using inflated rhetoric in its war on terrorism. The "Axis of Evil" speech is a good example. Even if the label is appropriate, naming Iran as a member of the axis—at a time when Iran's help is necessary for the battle against Al-Qaeda and the rebuilding of Afghanistan—may make Tehran even less cooperative and become a self-fulfilling prophecy.

*Proposal #7* The war against terrorism must be a sustained campaign.

Wars are never won by launching a single attack. Despite the operational success of the bombing raid against military and terrorist targets in Libya, the lack of concerted military pressure against Qaddafi in the aftermath allowed him—at least in the short term—to resume his terrorist activities; eighteen months later his intelligence operatives destroyed Pan Am Flight 103 over Scotland, killing all 270 aboard. Clinton too was guilty of treating terrorism this way. Instead of effectively dealing with Al-Qaeda after the bombings of the embassies in Kenya and Tanzania, the issue returned to the back burner after the meager American response, allowing Osama bin Laden to continue his war against America with the subsequent bombing of the USS *Cole* in Yemen and the devastating attacks in New York and Washington on September 11, 2001.

If the past few administrations had truly seen terrorism as warfare instead of as a minor inconvenience, Libya and bin Laden would have been dealt with conclusively when they first attacked, rather than allowing them to regroup and carry out further operations. By turning a blind eye to the problem after some initial, superficial response, the American administrations only invited more problems later. A metaphor used to characterize the Clinton response to terrorism (and this applies equally to Reagan) is instructive here; a commentator described the response as "kicking a hornet's nest" once, and then walking away. However, once the nest is kicked, angry hornets will swarm after their attacker. So if one believes it is important enough to kick the nest in the first place, one must be prepared to stomp bugs until the job is done. Walking away after doing the initial deed only invites more danger. The lesson for the current administration: Finish the job. This does not mean that the United State should deal conclusively with every terrorist group in the world; some problems simply do not merit American military intervention. Further, this approach, if pursued, would be pure folly and would set up the United States for failure. In the cases where American interests are not threatened, such as in Northern Ireland or Sri Lanka (cases that could be termed civil wars), the United States should oppose the use of terrorism and support the search for a diplomatic solution only. However, where organizations and states demonstrate the intent and capability to target Americans—in the United States and abroad—the administration must be willing to wage a war intent on completely eradicating the danger, lest the remaining hornets strike again.

# Notes

## NOTES FOR CHAPTER ONE

1. See "Opinion Roundup," *Public Opinion* (December/January 1981), 27. The other factor that contributed to Carter's defeat was the economy. In the same September poll, only 15 percent of respondents said the president was doing an "excellent" or "good" job overall.

2. Roland Evans and Robert Novak, *The Reagan Revolution* (New York: E. Dutton, 1981), 195.

3. Theodore H. White, *America in Search of Itself: The Making of the President 1956–1980* (New York: Harper and Row, 1982), 21.

4. Laurence Barrett, *Gambling With History: Ronald Reagan in the White House* (Garden City, NY: Doubleday, 1983), 178.

5. Robert M. Gates, *From the Shadows* (New York: Simon and Schuster, 1996), 196.

6. R. W. Apple, "Reagan Confronts an Intractable Qaddafi," *New York Times*, April 13, 1986, section 4, 1.

7. George C. Wilson, "Pentagon Scrubbed a Second Iranian Rescue Plan as Too Dangerous," *Washington Post*, January 25, 1981, A19.

8. Lou Cannon, "Reagan Set to Warn Nations: 'Never Again' Seize Hostages," *Washington Post*, January 27, 1981, A9.

9. Reagan, October 24, 1983, Regional Broadcasters Luncheon. *Public Papers of the Presidents of the United States: Ronald Reagan, 1983, volume 2 (July 2–December 31, 1983)* (Washington, DC: United States Government Printing Office, 1985), 1500.

10. Reagan, October 27, 1983, Presidential Address to the Nation. *Public Papers of the Presidents of the United States: Ronald Reagan, 1983, volume 2 (July 2–December 31, 1983)* (Washington, DC: United States Government Printing Office, 1985), 1517.

11. "Draft speech on terrorism for delivery by Secretary Shultz at the Jonathan Institute Conference, June 24, 1984," 15, Donald Fortier Files, "Terrorism," [Shultz material] Box 90761, Ronald Reagan Presidential Library (henceforth RRL).

12. "Draft of Presidential Statement on the Release of Hostages," June 1985, Executive Secretary, NSC Records, System File, #8590727, RRL.

13. Robert McFarlane, briefing to the press, October 11, 1985.

14. Reagan, April 14, 1986, Address to the Nation. *Public Papers of the Presidents of the United States: Ronald Reagan, 1986, volume 1 (January 1–June 27, 1986)* (Washington, DC: United States Government Printing Office, 1988), 468.

15. Reagan, October 23, 1986, "A Time of Remembrance for Victims of Terrorism," Proclamation 5557. *Public Papers of the Presidents of the United States: Ronald Reagan, 1986, volume 2 (June 28–December 31, 1986)* (Washington, DC: United States Government Printing Office, 1989), 1416.

16. United States Department of State, *Patterns of Global Terrorism: 1988–1989* (Washington: U.S. Department of State, 1989), iii–iv.

17. Reagan, "Text of the Presidential Debate," *New York Times*, October 29, 1980, A27.

18. Reagan, February 7, 1984, Statement by the President on the Situation in Lebanon. *Public Papers of the Presidents of the United States: Ronald Reagan, 1984, volume 1 (January 20–June 29, 1984)* (Washington, DC: United States Government Printing Office, 1986), 185.

19. Reagan, October 23, 1986, "A Time of Remembrance . . ."

20. Robert Oakley, "International Terrorism: Current Trends and the U.S. Response," Circular #706 (Washington, DC: United States Department of State, Bureau of Public Affairs, Office of Communications, May 1985), 3.

21. Walter Pincus and Dan Morgan, "Agreement Has Something for Everybody—Including the Lawyers," *Washington Post*, January 21, 1981, A6.

22. For a different analysis of the administration's responses, see David Tucker, *Skirmishes At the Edge of Empire: The United States and International Terrorism* (Westport, CT: Prager Publishers, 1997), 72.

23. Operation Goldenrod, the capture of Fawaz Yunis—one of the terrorists who boarded TWA Flight 847 after Robert Stetham's murder—utilized the military and the FBI, but was after the fact and does not figure as an immediate military response. For a good account, see Duane Clarridge, *A Spy For All Seasons* (New York: Scribner, 1997), 349–359.

24. Even though the Clinton administration wrongly bombed a pharmaceutical plant in Sudan for a supposed connection to terrorist Osama bin Laden, it justified the attack by pointing to evidence (the flimsiness of that evidence notwithstanding).

25. The concept called *Nadelstichtaktik* ("tactics of the needle prick") provides a justification for responding even to small-scale incidents. Rather than viewing terrorist attacks as individual, isolated events, a government views them over time. When a pattern emerges, even though the magnitude of each attack is low, a state might be justified in responding. Individual pinpricks may not do much damage, but many such attacks could lead to irreparable damage. See Yehuda Blum, "The Legality of State Response to Acts of Terrorism," in Benjamin Netanyahu, ed., *Terrorism: How the West Can Win* (New York: Farrar, Straus, Giroux, 1986), 136.

26. For the most part, states do observe some basic set of international norms. Hedley Bull notes that this small, but universal set of rules and assumptions reflect the interests of states, and thus constitute a basic structure of international order—even when anarchy is the prevailing condition. See Hedley Bull, *Anarchical Society* (London: Macmillan, 1977).

27. Article 2(4) as revised in 1954, "Draft Code of Offenses Against the Peace and Security of Mankind," in *Yearbook of the International Law Commission, 1954, volume 1* (New York: United Nations, 1954), 150. For a different interpretation of "indirect aggression," see Brownlie, Ian, *International Law and the Use of Force by States* (Oxford: Carendon Press, 1963), 278–279, 369–378. One problem that has plagued the concept of "indirect aggression" is the international community's inability to define what constitutes this type of aggression, due to a dichotomy of views stemming from the East–West conflict and the North–South divide. For example, in a 1972 UN debate attempting to define terrorism, the representative from Madagascar declared that "Acts of terrorism inspired by base motives of personal gain were to be condemned. Acts of political terrorism, on the other hand, undertaken to vindicate hallowed rights recognized by the United Nations, were praiseworthy. It was, of course, regrettable that certain acts in the latter category affected innocent persons." Quoted in Abraham D. Sofaer, "Terrorism and the Law," *Foreign Affairs*, volume 64, number 5 (Summer 1986), 903–906. See also Isaak I. Dore, *International Law and the Superpowers: Normative Order in a Divided World* (New Brunswick, NJ: Rutgers University Press, 1984), 48–50.

28. "Draft Declaration on Rights and Duties of States," in *Yearbook of the International Law Commission, 1949* (New York: United Nations, 1949), 286–290. See also Sofaer (1986), 919.

29. See Hugo Grotius, *De Jure Belli ac Pacis*, Book 2, chapter 21 (1625); D. Costello, "International Terrorism and the Development of the Principle *Aut Dedere Aut Judicare*," *Journal of International Law and Economics*, volume 10 (1975). For examples from international law see the following: (1) for Britain's payment of damages to the United States for allowing the Confederate cruiser *Alabama* to escape from a British port during the Civil War, see Dean B. Mahin, *One War at a Time: The International Dimensions of the American Civil War* (Washington, DC: Brassey's, 1999), 158–160, 286–300; (2) for the Corfu Channel Case see *U.K. v. Albania, 1949 I.C.J. 4, 22* (Judgement on the Merits); Yves Daudet, "International Action Against State Terrorism," in Rosalyn Higgins and Maurice Flory, *Terrorism and International Law* (New York: Routledge, 1997), 207; (3) for the takeover of the U.S. embassy in Tehran, see *United States v Iran, 1980 I.C.J. 32–33, 36.*

30. Abraham D. Sofaer, "Terrorism, the Law, and the National Defense," *Military Law Review*, volume 126 (June 1989), 96. This idea is based on the ancient feudal concept of providing "protection" for one's people. The doctrine was developed by Lord Chief Justice Sir Edward Coke in the 1608 *Calvin's Case*, when he proclaimed "*protectio trahit subjectionem, et subjectio protectionem*" (protection draws with it subjection, and subjection protection). See 7 Coke's Reports 1, 5a (1608). The 1873 Supreme Court "Slaughter House Cases" recognized a constitutional obligation to protect American citizens abroad. Justice Miller said that the "right to demand protection of the Federal Government on the high seas, or abroad" is one of the privileges of U.S. citizenship as guaranteed by the 14th Amendment. For these and other cases, see Jean E. Smith, *The Constitution and American Foreign Policy* (St. Paul, MN: West Publishing Company, 1989), 277–309.

31. This is the basis of social contract theory. Locke states that men "unite for the mutual preservation of their lives, liberty and estates, which I call the general name—property. The great and chief end, therefore, of men uniting into commonwealths, and putting themselves under government, is the preservation of their property." See John Locke, *Second Treatise on Civil Government*, Chapter 9 (1690). Similarly, Rousseau states that "the only way in which [men] can preserve themselves is by uniting their separate power in a combination strong enough to overcome any resistance, uniting them so that their powers are directed by a single motive and act in concert." See Jean-Jacques Rousseau, *The Social Contract*, Book I, Chapter 6 (1762).

32. Michael Walzer, *Just and Unjust Wars: A Moral Argument with Historical Illustrations* (New York: Basic Books, Inc., Publishers, 1977), 42. See also Richard J. Regan, *Just War: Principles and Cases* (Washington, DC: Catholic University of America Press, 1996), 87.

33. Stephen D. Krasner, *Sovereignty: Organized Hypocrisy* (Princeton: Princeton University Press, 1999), 20.

34. I. W. Zartman, "Introduction: Posing the Problem of State Collapse," in I. W. Zartman, ed., *Collapsed States: The Disintegration and Restoration of Legitimate Authority* (Boulder: Lynne Rienner Publishers, 1995).

35. Sofaer (1989), 92.

36. Daniel Philpott, *Revolutions in Sovereignty: How Ideas Shaped Modern International Relations* (Princeton: Princeton University Press, 2001), 41. See also Francis Deng, "Changing Concepts of Displacement and Sovereignty," in Kevin M. Cahill, ed., *Preventive Diplomacy: Stopping Wars Before They Start* (New York: Routledge, 2000), 129; David Scheffer, "Toward a Modern Doctrine of Humanitarian Intervention," *University of Toledo Law Review*, volume 23, number 2 (1992), 262–263; William V. O'Brien, "Reprisals, Deterrence and Self-Defense in Counterterror Operations," *Virginia Journal of International Law*, volume 30, number 2 (Winter 1990), 421–478; Derek Bowett, "Reprisals Involving Recourse to Armed Force," *American Journal of International Law*, volume 66 (1972).

37. Brownlie, 292.

38. This would include most of the Western European allies, Canada, Algeria, Costa Rica, Kuwait, and possibly others.

39. These would include attacks in Greece, Malta, Pakistan, Lebanon, North Yemen, Jordan, Egypt, Sudan, Togo, Zimbabwe, Indonesia, the Philippines, México, El Salvador, Honduras, Guatemala, Colombia, Bolivia, Peru, and Chile, or attacks there or elsewhere sponsored by Iran, Libya, or Syria.

40. This does not mean that those who were pro-Israel were anti-Arab, or vice-versa. It simply means that each group saw American interests served best by pursuing closer ties to either Israel or the Arabs, and that the counter-policy was counter-productive.

41. There has been some debate over whether an attack against a military target such as the Marine barracks constitutes terrorism (see Frederic Hof's argument in "The Beirut Bombing of October 1983: An Act of Terrorism?" *Parameters*, volume 15, number 2 (Summer 1985), 69). Members of the Reagan administration unequivocally viewed this attack as terrorism, which makes this incident an appropriate case for this study. Additionally, the State Department's definition of terrorism supports this view: "The term 'terrorism' means premeditated, politically motivated violence perpetrated against noncombatant targets by subnational groups or clandestine agents, usually intended to influence an audience. . . . For the purpose of this definition, the term 'noncombatant' is interpreted to include, in addition to civilians, military personnel who at the time of the incident are unarmed and/or not on duty . . . [the definition] also consider[s] . . . attacks on military installations or on armed military personnel when a state of military hostilities does not exist at the site, such as bombings against US bases in Europe or elsewhere [to be terrorism]. . . . The US Government has employed this definition of terrorism for statistical and analytical purposes since 1983." See *Patterns of Global Terrorism, 1993* (Washington, DC: Department of State, Office of the Coordinator for Counterterrorism, 1994), iv.

# NOTES FOR CHAPTER TWO

1. John D. Steinbruner, *The Cybernetic Theory of Decision: New Dimensions of Political Analysis* (Princeton: Princeton University Press, 1974), 55.

2. Richard Betts, *Soldiers, Statesmen, and Cold War Crises* (Cambridge, MA: Harvard University Press, 1977), 11–12.

3. Richard Neustadt, *Presidential Power and the Modern Presidents: The Politics of Leadership from Roosevelt to Reagan* (New York: Macmillan, Inc., 1990), 29. See also Charles E. Lindblom, *The Intelligence of Democracy: Decision Making Through Mutual Adjustment* (New York: The Free Press, 1965), 21–22.

4. Morton H. Halperin, *Bureaucratic Politics and Foreign Policy* (Washington, DC: Brookings Institution, 1974), 107; Graham Allison and Philip Zelikow, *Essence of Decision: Explaining the Cuban Missile Crisis*, 2nd edition (New York: Addison Wesley Longman, 1996), 300.

5. Leslie Gelb, "Why Not the State Department?" *The Washington Quarterly* (Autumn 1980), 25–40.

6. 50 U.S.C. 401.

7. Raymond Tanter, *Who's At the Helm? Lessons of Lebanon* (Boulder, CO: Westview Press, 1990), 70; NSDD-3, in Simpson, 10, 29.

8. Doug Menarchik, "Organizing to Combat 21st Century Terrorism," Prepared for the Institute for National Security Studies, United States Air Force Academy, July 28, 1999, 18–19.

9. Marc Celmer, *Terrorism, U.S. Strategy, and Reagan Policies* (Westport, CT: Greenwood Press, 1987), 3.

10. Executive Order 12333 was modeled on EO 12036, signed by Jimmy Carter on January 24, 1978 and EO 11905, signed by Gerald Ford on February 18, 1976.

11. Quoted in Robert L. Pfaltzgraff and Jacquelyn K. Davis, eds., *National Security Decisions: The Participants Speak* (Lexington, MA: Lexington Books, 1990), 3.

12. Hendrick Smith, *The Power Game: How Washington Works* (New York: Random House, 1988), xxi, 46; Martin Hollis and Steve Smith, "Roles and Reasons in Foreign Policy Decision Making," *British Journal of Political Science*, volume 16, number 3 (July 1986), 282.

13. See Neustadt (1990), 152.

14. Kenneth E. Boulding, *The Image* (Ann Arbor, MI: University Press, 1956).

15. Halperin, 11–16. The strongest American shared image during the Cold War was that the Soviet Union was aggressive and expansionist and should be contained. For other, less prevalent views in the United States, see Ole Holsti and James N. Rosenau, "A Leadership Divided: The Foreign Policy Beliefs of American Leaders, 1976–1984," in Kegley and Wittkopf (1988), 31–37.

16. Harold Sprout and Margaret Sprout, *Man-Milieu Relationship Hypothesis in the Context of International Politics* (Princeton: Center of International Studies, 1956). See also Sprout and Sprout, "Environmental Factors in the Study of International Politics," *Journal of Conflict Resolution* volume 1 (December 1957), 318; Lloyd S. Etheredge, *A World of Men: The Private Sources of American Foreign Policy* (Cambridge, MA: MIT Press, 1978), xiii; Ole Holsti, "Foreign Policy Formation Viewed Cognitively," in Robert M. Axelrod, ed., *Structure of Decision: The Cognitive Maps of Political Elites* (Princeton: Princeton University Press, 1976), 34.

17. David Thompson, *The Listener*, volume 63 (London: May 5, 1960), 780.

18. John W. Kingdon, *Agendas, Alternatives, and Public Policies* (New York: Harper Collins, 1984), 99.

19. Betty Glad, "Black and White Thinking: Ronald Reagan's Approach to Foreign Policy," *Political Psychology*, volume 4, number 1 (1983), 33–76; John Lewis Gaddis, "The Rise, Fall, and Future of Détente," *Foreign Affairs*, volume 62 (Winter 1983–84), 372.

20. Tami R. Davis and Sean M. Lynn-Jones, "City Upon A Hill," *Foreign Policy*, volume 66 (Spring 1987), 21–23.

21. Ronald Reagan, "Communism, the Disease," May 1975, in Kiron K. Skinner, Annelise Anderson, and Martin Anderson, eds., *Reagan In His Own Hand: The Writings of Ronald Reagan That Reveal His Revolutionary Vision For America* (New York: The Free Press, 2001), 10. These latter depictions were identified by Robert L. Ivie, "Speaking 'Common Sense' About the Soviet Threat," *Western Journal of Speech Communication*, volume 48 (1984), 42.

22. Reagan, "Communism, the Disease," in Skinner, 12.

23. Reagan, "Russians," May 25, 1977, in Skinner, 34.

24. Reagan, "Two Worlds," August 7, 1978, in Skinner, 14.

25. Reagan, "Strategy I," May 4, 1977, in Skinner, 111.

26. Reagan, "'State of the Union' Speech," March 13, 1980, in Skinner, 479.

27. Fred Iklé, "Middle East Policy: Peace Through Security," Fred C. Iklé papers, Box 14, "Libya" folder, Hoover Institution, Stanford University; Samuel W. Lewis, "The United States and Israel: Constancy and Change," in William B. Quandt, ed., *The Middle East: Ten Years after Camp David* (Washington, DC: Brookings Institution, 1988), 217; William B. Quandt, *Peace Process: American Diplomacy and the Arab-Israeli Conflict Since 1967*, revised edition (Washington, DC: Brookings Institution Press, 2001), 246; Ronald Reagan, "Recognizing the Israeli Asset," *Washington Post*, August 15, 1979, A25.

28. Reagan, "Brezhnev," April 13, 1977, in Skinner, 213.

29. William B. Quandt, *Camp David: Peacemaking and Politics* (Washington, DC: Brookings Institution, 1986), 18; Lewis, in Quandt (1988), 227, 228; Brian Crozier, "Reagan and Israel," *National Review* (October 15, 1982), 1268.

30. Reagan, "Rostow II," October 10, 1978, in Skinner, et al., 93–94. See also "Strategy II," May 4, 1977, in Skinner, 111–112.

31. Reagan, "Peace," August 18, 1980, in Skinner, 480.

32. Reagan, "'State of the Union' Speech," in Skinner, 478.

33. Alexander M. Haig, Jr., *Caveat: Realism, Reagan, and Foreign Policy* (New York: Macmillan Publishing Company, 1984), 167.

34. Reagan, "'State of the Union' Speech," in Skinner, 478–479.

35. Reagan, "Palestine," March 27, 1979, in Skinner, 218; Crozier, 1268.

36. R. Emmett Tyrrell, Jr., "A World Without Russians," *The Alternative: An American Spectator*, volume 10, number 8 (May 1977). Quoted by Reagan in "Russians," May 25, 1977, in Skinner, 33.

37. Ronnie Dugger, *On Reagan: The Man and His Presidency* (New York: McGraw Hill, 1983), 340; See also Joseph E. Persico, *Casey: From the OSS to the CIA* (New York: Viking Penguin, 1990), 488.

38. Robert L. Pfaltzgraff and Jacquelyn K. Davis, eds., *National Security Decisions: The Participants Speak* (Lexington, MA: Lexington Books, 1990), 303.

39. Richard A. Melanson, *American Foreign Policy Since the Vietnam War: The Search for Consensus from Nixon to Clinton*, 3rd edition (New York: M. E. Sharpe, Inc., 2000), 130.

40. Reagan, "War," March 13, 1978, in Skinner, 102.

41. Ronald Reagan, *The Creative Society: Some Comments on Problems Facing America* (New York: Devin-Adair, 1968), 52.

42. Reagan, "Peace," April 1975, in Skinner, 8. See also Barrett (October 20, 1980), 20.

43. Interview with Lou Cannon, June 30, 2000, Summerland, California; interview with Peter Rodman, February 7, 2001, Washington, DC.

44. See "Korea," May 25, 1977 and "Korea," January 27, 1978, in Skinner, 66–69.

45. Reagan, "Chiefs of Staff," July 15, 1978, in Skinner, 71.

46. Reagan, "The Military," September 27, 1977, in Skinner, 70.

47. John Keraagac, *Between Promise and Policy: Ronald Reagan and Conservative Reformism* (Lanham, MD: Lexington Books, 2000), 82.

48. "CIA Facing Witch-Hunt—Reagan," *San Jose Mercury*, August 24, 1975. See also Reagan, "CIA Commission," August 1975, in Skinner, 121; and "Intelligence," June 15, 1977, in Skinner, 124–126.

49. "Show and Tell?" *Time*, March 31, 1975, 60. See also Richard Bergholz, "Reagan Calls for End of Agency Probes," *Los Angeles Times*, June 11, 1975.

50. "Reagan sees peril to agents of CIA," *Palo Alto Times*, March 4, 1975.

51. Richard E. Neustadt, *Presidential Power and the Modern Presidents: The Politics of Leadership From Roosevelt to Reagan* (New York: The Free Press, 1990), 18–23.

52. George P. Shultz, *Triumph and Turmoil: My Years as Secretary of State* (New York: Charles Scribners' Sons, 1993), 6.

53. "Statement of George P. Shultz of California to be Secretary of State," U.S. Congress, Senate, Committee on Foreign Relations, 97th Congress, 2nd session, 13–14 July, 1982.

54. Morton Kondracke, "Nowhere Man," *The New Republic*, May 16, 1983, 17.

55. Quandt (2001), 253; Smith (1988), 223; Ze'ev Schiff and Ehud Ya'ari (edited and translated by Ina Friedman), *Israel's Lebanon War* (New York: Simon and Schuster, 1984), 206; "Statement of George P. Shultz. . . ."

56. Smith (1988), 223. This was also the position of the Israeli opposition party—the Labor Party.

57. "Statement of George P. Shultz. . . ."

58. Herman Frederick Eilts, "The United States and Egypt," in Quandt (1988), 124; Barry Rubin, *Secrets of State: The State Department and the Struggle over U.S. Foreign Policy* (New York: Oxford University Press, 1985), 217.

59. George P. Shultz, "The United States and Israel: Partners for Peace and Freedom," *Current Policy* #690 (Washington, DC: United States Department of State, Bureau of Public Affairs, April 21, 1985); Smith (1988), 224; Lewis, in Quandt (1988), 243; Quandt (2001), 262.

60. "Soviets Using Terrorism, Shultz Asserts," *Washington Post*, June 25, 1984.

61. George Shultz, "Draft speech on terrorism for delivery by Secretary Shultz at the Jonathan Institute Conference, June 24, 1984," 8. Donald Fortier Files, "Terrorism," [Shultz material] Box 90761, RRL.

62. Neil C. Livingstone, *The Cult of Counterterrorism: The "Weird World" of Spooks, Counterterrorists, Adventurers, and the Not-Quite Professionals* (Lexington, MA: Lexington Books, 1990),

233; Michael B. Kraft, "Discussant," in Eric J. Schmertz, Natalie Datlof, and Alexej Ugrinsky, eds., *President Reagan and the World* (Westport, CT: Greenwood Press, 1997), 187.

63. Tanter (1990), 5–6; Winston Churchill, note to the First Sea Lord, October 15, 1942.

64. Gates, 278–279.

65. Glenn P. Hastedt, *American Foreign Policy: Past, Present, Future*, 2nd edition (Englewood Cliffs, NJ: Prentice Hall, 1991), 144–145.

66. Kevin V. Mulcahy, "Foreign Policy Making in the Carter and Reagan Administrations," in Karl F. Inderfurth and Loch K. Johnson, eds., *Decisions of the Highest Order: Perspectives on the National Security Council* (Pacific Grove, CA: Brooks Cole Publishing Co., 1988), 132; Smith, 581.

67. Interview with Bernard Kalb, February 15, 2001, Rockville, MD.

68. Leslie Gelb, "It's Mr. Reagan's Policy," *New York Times*, August 1, 1983; Kevin V. Mulcahy and Cecil V. Crabb, "Presidential Management of National Security: 1947–1987," in James P. Pfiffner, ed., *The Managerial Presidency* (Pacific Grove, CA: Brooks/Cole Publishing Co., 1991), 261.

69. Mulcahy, in Inderfurth and Johnson (1988), 132.

70. Smith (1988), 73.

71. "Nomination of Caspar Weinberger to be Secretary of Defense," Hearings before the Committee on Armed Services, United States Senate, 97th Congress, 1st session, January 6, 1981.

72. "Nomination of Caspar Weinberger. . . ."

73. Livingstone (1990), 233; Haig, 175; Samuel Segev, "The Reagan Plan: A Victim of Conflicting Approaches by the United States and Israel to the Syrian Presence in Lebanon," in Schmertz, et al. (1997), 50; Kondracke (May 16, 1983), 16; Schiff and Ya'ari, 64.

74. "Nomination of Caspar Weinberger. . . ."

75. Lewis, in Quandt (1988), 229.

76. Ibid., 241.

77. "Defense Chief Weinberger on Peace Prospects Now," *US News and World Report*, September 27, 1982, 26.

78. "Defense Chief Weinberger . . . ," 27.

79. Tanter, 109. For other examples, see I. M. Destler, "The Evolution of Reagan Foreign Policy," in Fred I. Greenstein, ed., *The Reagan Presidency: An Early Assessment* (Baltimore, MD: Johns Hopkins University Press, 1983), 124; Prados (1991), 468–469.

80. Weinberger's position changed over the course of the Reagan administration. What is presented here is his initial position.

81. Christopher C. Joyner, "In Search of an Anti-Terrorist Policy: Lessons from the Reagan Era," *Terrorism: An International Journal*, volume 11 (1988), 32.

82. "Weinberger Suggests Turning to the U.N. with Terrorist Woes," *New York Times*, June 26, 1984, A14.

83. Michael R. Gordon, "The Pentagon Under Weinberger May Be Biting Off More Than Even It Can Chew," *National Journal*, volume 16, number 5 (February 4, 1984), 204.

84. "Nomination of Caspar Weinberger. . . ."

85. Smith (1988), 201.

86. Karaagac (2000), 58; Livingstone (1990), 233.

87. Speech at the National Press Club, November 20, 1984. See also "Nomination of Caspar Weinberger. . . ."

88. Speech at the National Press Club, November 20, 1984. See also Tanter, 6.

89. Hastedt (1991), 148–149. See also James Roherty, "The Office of the Secretary of Defense," in John E. Endicott and Roy W. Stafford, eds., *American Defense Policy*, 4th edition (Baltimore, MD: Johns Hopkins University Press, 1977), 286–296.

90. Caspar Weinberger, *Fighting for Peace: Seven Critical Years in the Pentagon* (New York: Warner Books, 1990), 43; I. M. Destler, Leslie H. Gelb, and Anthony Lake, *Our Own Worst Enemy: The Unmaking of American Foreign Policy* (New York: Simon and Schuster, 1984), 227, 236; Samuel P. Huntington, "The Defense Policy, 1981–1982," in Fred I. Greenstein, ed., *The Reagan Presidency:*

*An Early Assessment* (Baltimore, MD: Johns Hopkins University Press, 1983), 91; "A Team Player for the Pentagon," *Time*, December 22, 1980, 10.

91. Amos A. Jordan, William T. Taylor, Jr., and Lawrence J. Korb, *American National Security: Policy and Process*, 3rd edition (Baltimore, MD: Johns Hopkins University Press, 1989), 172; Gordon (February 4, 1984), 204, 208.

92. Smith (1988), 581.

93. Ibid., 582.

94. Destler, Gelb, and Lake (1984), 227; Smith (1988), 208.

95. Bob Woodward, *Veil: The Secret Wars of the CIA, 1981–1987* (New York: Simon and Schuster, 1987), 37.

96. William Casey, "Building a National Consensus," Address to Denver Chief Executive Officers, Denver, CO, July 30, 1986, in Mark B. Liedl, ed., *Scouting the Future: The Public Speeches of William J. Casey* (Washington, DC: Regnery Gateway, 1989), 25.

97. Casey, "The Status of U.S. Intelligence," Address to the John Ashbrook Center for Public Affairs, Ashland College, Ashland, OH, October 27, 1986, in Liedl, 32.

98. Robert A. Manning, with Steven Emerson and Charles Fenyvesi, "Casey's CIA: New Clout, New Danger," *US News and World Report*, June 16, 1986, 30; Casey, "The Status of U.S. Intelligence," in Liedl, 35.

99. Casey, "Building a National Consensus," in Liedl, 26.

100. Woodward, 217; Tanter, 154.

101. Gates, 250.

102. Claire Sterling, *The Terror Network: The Secret War of International Terrorism* (New York: Holt, Rinehart and Winston, 1981), 10.

103. Livingstone (1990), 249–250.

104. Casey, "Fighting Terrorists: Identifications and Action," Address to the 14th Annual Conference of the Fletcher School of Law and Diplomacy's national security studies program, Tufts University, Cambridge, MA, April 17, 1985, in Liedl, 193.

105. Casey, "Responsible Journalism: Lives Are At Stake," Address to the American Jewish Committee, Washington, DC, May 15, 1986, in Liedl, 90.

106. "An Interview with William Casey," *Time*, October 28, 1985, 34.

107. Casey, "Analysis and Assessment," Address to the Commonwealth Club of California, San Francisco, CA, May 21, 1982, in Liedl, 51; See also Casey, "The First Line of Defense," Address to the Mid-America Club, Chicago, IL, April 14, 1984, in Liedl, 57; Casey, "Responsible Journalism," in Liedl, 91.

108. Casey, "Fighting Terrorism," in Liedl, 197–198.

109. Casey, "Analysis and Assessment," in Liedl, 51.

110. Tanter, 6.

111. Casey, "The Soviet Assault on Western Values," Address to the *Washington Times* Advisory Board and Editorial Board, Washington, DC, September 25, 1986, in Liedl, 158.

112. Casey, "Fighting Terrorism," in Liedl, 203.

113. Morton Kondracke, "Tinker, Tinker, Tinker, Spy," *The New Republic* (November 28, 1983), 17; see also Persico (1990), 60, 101, and 290.

114. Gates, 200–201; Woodward, 91.

115. John Prados, *Presidents' Secret Wars: C.I.A. and Pentagon Covert Operations since World War II* (New York: William Morrow, 1986), 360–67.

116. Manning, et al., 25–26; Ray S. Cline, *The CIA Under Reagan, Bush and Casey* (Washington, DC: Acropolis Books, 1981), 277.

117. Kondracke (November 28, 1983), 13.

118. Smith, (1988), 73.

119. Robert C. McFarlane, "The Political Potential of Parity," *U.S. Naval Institute Proceedings*, February 1979, 35.

120. Robert Timberg, *The Nightingale's Song* (New York: Touchstone, 1995), 218–220.

121. Timberg, 294.

122. Robert C. McFarlane with Zofia Smardz, *Special Trust* (New York: Cadell and Davies, 1994), 18; McFarlane (1979), 34.

123. Robert C. McFarlane, "Foreword," in Neil C. Livingstone and Terrell E. Arnold, eds., *Fighting Back: Winning the War Against Terrorism* (Lexington, MA: Lexington Books, 1985), ix–x.

124. Leslie H. Gelb, "Taking Charge: The Rising Power of National Security Advisor Robert McFarlane," *New York Times Magazine*, May 26, 1985, 25.

125. Gelb (May 26, 1985), 25.

126. Timberg, 125.

127. Ibid., 58.

128. Gelb (May 26, 1985), 21.

129. Ibid., 24; Robert S. Dudney, "How NSC Director Exercises Power," *US News and World Report* (October 31, 1983), 29.

130. "The Crisis Manager at Reagan's Elbow," *US News and World Report* (July 8, 1985), 13; Alexander George and Juliette L. George, *Presidential Personality and Performance* (Boulder, CO: Westview Press, 1998), 229; Prados (1986), 481–496; Gelb (May 26, 1985), 25.

131. Leslie H. Gelb, "Where Anonymous Power Accrues," *New York Times*, June 4, 1985, A22.

132. "The Crisis Manager . . . ," 13.

133. Gelb (May 26, 1985), 31.

134. The morning briefings were given by the National Security Advisor, and included the president, vice president, the White House chief of staff, and other aides. The president's Daily Brief is a CIA publication, augmented by documents and memos from the NSC staff, the State Department, and the Pentagon. See Gerlad Felix Warburg, *Conflict and Consensus: The Struggle Between Congress and the President over Foreign Policymaking* (New York: Harper and Row Publishers, 1989), 75–76; John Prados, *Keeper of the Keys: A History of the National Security Council from Truman to Bush* (New York: William Morrow, 1991), 494–495.

135. Timberg, 374.

136. James M. Hildreth, "A Quiet Voice, with Authority," *US News and World Report*, June 16, 1986, 33.

137. Timberg, 164.

138. Hildreth, 33.

139. Keith Schneider, "Poindexter at the Security Council: A Quick Rise and a Troubled Reign," *New York Times*, January 12, 1987, A6.

140. Timberg, 48.

141. Ibid., 171. See especially Poindexter's time as commanding officer of the USS *England*.

142. Ibid., 243.

143. George and George (1998), 230; Karl F. Inderfurth and Loch K. Johnson, "Transformation," in Inderfurth and Johnson, 102.

144. "Summary of Recommendations from the Special Review Board Interview with Richard Allen," President's Special Review Board (Tower Board): Records, Case Studies, Wise Men Master Book, AOD 1193 Unclass [3 of 14], Box 93224, RRL.

145. Schneider (January 12, 1987).

146. Ibid.

147. Timberg, 379–380.

148. Dick Kirsschten, "White House Notebook," *National Journal*, volume 19, number 32, 2043.

149. Betts, 160, 170.

150. Samuel P. Huntington, *The Soldier and the State: The Theory and Politics of Civil-Military Relations* (Cambridge, MA: Harvard University Press, 1957), 79.

151. Pfaltzgraff and Davis (1990), 20.

152. John W. Vessey, Jr., "To Provide for the Common Defense," in Hoxie, ed., 24–31; "Nomination of John W. Vessey, Jr., to be Chairman of the Joint Chiefs of Staff," Hearings before the Committee on Armed Services, United States Senate, 97th Congress, 2nd session, May 11, 1982.

153. William Crowe, "The Persian Gulf: Central or Peripheral to United States Strategy?" *U.S. Naval Institute Proceedings* (May 1978), 205.

154. Tanter, 210.

155. Brian M. Jenkins, "The American Response to State-Sponsored Terrorism," in Steven L. Spiegel, Mark A. Heller, and Jacob Goldberg, eds., *The Soviet-American Competition in the Middle East* (Lexington, MA: Lexington Books, 1988), 184–185.

156. Glenn P. Hastedt, with R. Gordon Hoxie, "The Intelligence Community and American Foreign Policy: The Reagan and Carter Administrations," in Hoxie, ed., 70. See also *US News and World Report* (June 25, 1984), 28.

157. Shawn R. McCarthy, *The Function of Intelligence in Crisis Management* (Brookfield, VT: Ashgate Publishing Co., 1998), 91.

158. "Nomination of William J. Crowe, Jr., to be Chairman, Joint Chiefs of Staff," Hearings before the Committee on Armed Services, United States Senate, 99th Congress, 1st session, July 30, 1985.

159. Jennet Conant, with John Barry, "An Officer and Intellectual," *Newsweek* (July 22, 1985), 29.

160. Betts, 11–12.

161. Margaret Hermann, "The Role of Leaders in the Making of American Foreign Policy," in Kegley and Wittkopf (1988), 297.

162. Ann Reilly Dowd, "What Managers Can Learn from Manager Reagan," *Fortune*, September 15, 1986, 36.

163. James W. Ceaser, "The Theory of Governance of the Reagan Administration," in Lester M. Salamon and Michael S. Lund, eds., *The Reagan Presidency and the Governing of America* (Washington, DC: The Urban Institute Press, 1985), 63.

164. See David Stockman, *The Triumph of Politics: The Inside Story of the Reagan Revolution* (New York: Avon Books, 1986), 100–108; Larry Speakes with Robert Pack, *Speaking Out: The Reagan Presidency from Inside the White House* (New York: Scribner, 1988), 135–136; Donald Regan, *For the Record: From Wall Street to Washington* (New York: Harcourt, Brace Jovanovich, 1988), 142, 188; Martin Anderson, *Revolution* (New York: Harcourt Brace Jovanovich, 1988), 283–286, 291–292.

165. George and George, 224; Lou Cannon, *President Reagan: Role of a Lifetime* (New York: Simon and Schuster, 1991), 55; Bert Rockman, "The Style and Organization of the Reagan Presidency," in Charles O. Jones, *The Reagan Legacy: Promise and Performance* (Chatham, NJ: Chatham House Publishers, Inc., 1988), 8.

166. Cannon, chapter 10.

167. Fred I. Greenstein, "Ronald Reagan—Another Hidden Hand Ike?" *Political Science and Politics*, volume 33, number 1 (March 1990), 10; George and George (1998), 224; Stephen L. Robertson, "Executive Office of the President: White House Office," in *Cabinets and Counselors: "The President and the Executive Branch* (Washington, DC: Congressional Quarterly, 1989), 10.

168. Gary G. Hamilton and Nicole Woolsey Biggart, *Governor Reagan, Governor Brown: A Sociology of Executive Power* (New York: Columbia University Press, 1984), 193.

169. Dowd, 35.

170. Memo from Richard Allen to Ray Tanter, December 9, 1981, in Kemp files, Libya Crisis 1981 [1/2], Box 90219, RRL.

171. "Summary of Recommendations from the Special Review Board, Interview with Richard Allen," President's Special Review Board (Tower Board): Recommendations, Case Studies, Wise Men Master Book, AOD 1193 Unclass [3 of 4], Box 93224, RRL. See also Hamilton and Biggart, 11, 186.

172. Regan, 142–144.

173. Melanson (2000), 145; Dowd, 34.

174. Hamilton and Biggart, 196.

175. Roger Hilsman, *The Politics of Policy Making in Defense and Foreign Affairs: Conceptual Models and Bureaucratic Politics*, 2nd edition (Englewood Cliffs, NJ: Prentice Hall, 1990), 104.

176. Hamilton and Biggart, 35.

177. Ibid., 198.

178. George J. Church, "How Reagan Decides," *Time*, volume 120, number 24 (December 13, 1982), 16.

179. Barrett (1980), 22.

180. "Conclusions of Probe," *Washington Post*, May 24, 1984; see also Prados (1991), 454.

181. Timberg, 359–361. See also Woodward, 183; Hamilton and Biggart, 46, 195.

182. Alexander George, "The President and the Management of Foreign Policy: Styles and Models," in Kegley and Wittkopf (1988), 122–123; Smith, 572; Cannon, 176, 210; George and George, 225.

183. Stewart Powell, with Joseph P. Shapiro, O. Kelly, Dennis Mullin, and Robert S. Dudney, "White House's Key Players When the Chips are Down," *US News and World Report* (July 1, 1983), 23.

184. David Ignatius, "Foreign-Policy Rows Make McFarlane's Job Unusually Tough One," *Wall Street Journal*, August 10, 1984, 10.

# NOTES FOR CHAPTER THREE

1. Ze'ev Schiff and Ehud Ya'ari (edited and translated by Ina Friedman), *Israel's Lebanon War* (New York: Simon and Schuster, 1984), 98; see also chapters 1–6 for an excellent recounting of Sharon and Begin's war planning. U.S. intelligence knew as early as September 1981 that Syria was pushing Abu Nidal to conduct operations that would undermine Arafat and the PLO. Apparently, Assad feared Arafat would "open a dialogue with the US and moderate Arabs on the Palestinian question, without reference to Syria. They are determined to bring the PLO under Syrian control, because they view their leverage over the Palestinians as the principal bargaining chip in any future negotiations for the return of the Golan Heights." "Syria-PLO" CIA assessment, "PLO 1981 (3 of 3)" folder, RRL.

2. David Martin and John Walcott, *Best Laid Plans* (New York: Harper & Row, 1988), 92.

3. Ibid., 92.

4. Michael Deaver and Michael Herskowitz, *Behind the Scenes* (New York: William Morrow, 1987), 165–166.

5. David Kennedy and Richard Haass, "The Reagan Administration and Lebanon," *Pew Program in Case Teaching in International Affairs*, Case #340 (Pittsburgh, PA: Pew Charitable Trusts, 1988), 4.

6. Robert M. Gates, *From the Shadows* (New York: Simon & Schuster, 1996), 283.

7. Robert L. Pfaltzgraff and Jacquelyn K. Davis, eds., *National Security Decisions: The Participants Speak* (Lexington, MA: Lexington Books, 1990), 302–303.

8. Phone interview with James D. Watkins, January 22, 2002, Washington, DC.

9. Kennedy and Haass, 4.

10. Roy Gutman, "Battle Over Lebanon," *Foreign Service Journal*, June 1984, 30.

11. Gutman, 30; Kennedy and Haass, 4.

12. Eric Hammel, *The Root: The Marines in Beirut, August 1982–February 1984* (New York, NY: Harcourt Brace Jovanovich Publishers, 1985), 15–16; Kennedy and Haass, 3.

13. Kennedy and Haass, 4–5.

14. John Prados, *Keepers of the Keys: A History of the National Security Council from Truman to Bush* (New York: William Morrow and Co., 1991), 471; Kennedy and Haass, 12; Martin and Walcott, 97.

15. Kennedy and Haass, 12.

16. Robert Murray, "Lebanon—1982–1983," 2. Presidential Special Review Board (Tower Board): Recs, Case Studies, Wise Men, Scowcroft, AOD 1193, Unclass [2 of 6], Box 93225, RRL.

17. "Troubles in Lebanon (A)," Draft study (Kennedy School of Government, Harvard University), 4.

18. Martin and Walcott, 95; "Troubles in Lebanon (A)," 4.

19. Interview with Richard Armitage, February 16, 2001, Arlington, VA.

20. Gutman, 31.

21. Gutman, 31; Robert C. McFarlane and Zofia Smardz, *Special Trust* (New York: Cadell & Davies, 1994), 211; Caspar W. Weinberger, *Fighting for Peace: Seven Critical Years in the Pentagon* (New York: Warner Books, 1990), 151.

22. Benis M. Frank, *U.S. Marines in Lebanon, 1982–1984* (Washington, DC: History and Museums Division, Headquarters, United States Marine Corps, 1987), 17, 22, 50.

23. Hammel, 38, 52.

24. Phone interview with Samuel Lewis, January 23, 2001, Manassas, VA.

25. Interview with Robert Gallucci, September 25, 2001, Washington, DC.

26. David Long, *The Anatomy of Terrorism* (New York: Free Press, 1990), 101.

27. Martin and Walcott, 83.

28. This is not the same organization as the Palestinian Islamic Jihad, which is active in the Gaza Strip.

29. Long, 102.

30. CIA Report GI M 84-10165, September 24, 1984.

31. According to Robert Gates, Ames "was the only senior intelligence officer on Middle East affairs I thought really had the confidence of George Shultz . . . [Ames] had a reputation within the government of being probably the best person in the government on the PLO, on the Middle Eastern things generally . . ." Interview with Robert Gates, February 23, 2001, College Station, TX. Ted Gup, *Book of Honor: Covert Lives and Classified Deaths* (New York: Doubleday, 2000), 262; Robin Wright, *In the Name of God: The Khomeini Decade* (New York: Simon and Schuster, 1989), 117; Robert Dillon, "Caught in the Crossfire," *Duke Alumni Magazine*, summer 1986, 4–7; interview with Robert Dillon, September 25, 2001, Arlington, VA.

32. Interview with Robert Gates.

33. Bob Woodward, *Veil: The Secret Wars of the CIA, 1981–1987* (New York: Pocket Books, 1987), 271–272; Martin and Walcott, 105.

34. Shawn R. McCarthy, *The Function of Intelligence in Crisis Management* (Brookfield, VT: Ashgate Publishing Co., 1998), 112.

35. Woodward, 273; Martin and Walcott, 105.

36. Martin and Walcott, 106. On April 30, 1983, Rifaat al Assad's chef de cabinet, Captain Joseph Szansil, met with the deputy chief of mission from the American embassy in Damascus. Speaking for Assad, Szansil said that Rifaat "strongly denounces" the bombing and noted that Rifaat wanted to cooperate with the US government's investigation in any way possible. Szansil said that Rifaat had already begun an investigation and would let the Americans know if and when he came up with any leads. Cable #301139Z APR 83, from American Embassy Damascus to Secretary of State, Document #1983DAMASC03264, State Department Archives.

37. Woodward, 320; Martin and Walcott, 105.

38. Martin and Walcott, 105.

39. Ronald Reagan, *An American Life* (New York: Simon and Schuster, 1990), 443; Edmund Morris, *Dutch: A Memoir of Ronald Reagan* (New York: Random House, 1999), 480.

40. Martin and Walcott, 106.

41. Jeffrey T. Richelson, "Truth Conquers All Chains: The U.S. Army Intelligence Support Activity, 1981–1989," *International Journal of Intelligence and Counterintelligence*, volume 12, number 2 (Summer 1999), 168–200.

42. Ben Bradlee, Jr., *Guts and Glory: The Rise and Fall of Oliver North* (New York: Donald I. Fine, Inc., 1988, 150. For a fairly extensive history of the ISA, see www.specwarnet.com/americas/isa.htm; Caryle Murphy and Charles R. Babcock, "Army's Covert Role Scrutinized," *Washington Post*, November 29, 1985, A8.

43. Interviews with Bill Cowan, Arlington, Virginia, on February 7, 2001 and December 5, 2001.

44. Richard Armitage believes the report never got past the European Command headquarters. Interview with Richard Armitage.

45. Memorandum of Conversation between President Reagan and President Gemeyel, April 18, 1983, Executive Secretariat, NSC: Records: Country File, Lebanon, volume VIII, 1/1/83–9/30/83 [8390505], box 91354, RRL.

46. Angus Deming, with Holger Jensen, James Pringle, and Joyce Barnathan, "Blood and Terror in Beirut," *Newsweek*, May 2, 1983, 22.

47. George P. Shultz, *Turmoil and Triumph: My Years as Secretary of State* (New York: Charles Scribner's Sons, 1993), 221.

48. Schiff and Ya'ari, 293–294. See also William B. Quandt, *Camp David: Peacemaking and Politics* (Washington, DC: The Brookings Institution, 1986), 25.

49. Gutman, 32. For Shultz's account of the May 17 Agreement negotiations, see Shultz, chapter 14.

50. Richard B. Parker, *The Politics of Miscalculation in the Middle East* (Bloomington, IN: Indiana University Press, 1993), 186–187, 209.

51. Kennedy and Haass, 15.

52. Robert Timberg, *The Nightingale's Song* (New York: Simon and Schuster, 1995), 321.

53. Raymond Tanter, *Who's At the Helm? Lessons of Lebanon* (Boulder, CO: Westview Press, 1990), 233; Timberg, 322–324.

54. NSDD-103, in Christopher Simpson, ed., *National Security Directives of the Reagan and Bush Administrations: The Declassified History of U.S. Political and Military Policy, 1981–1991* (Boulder, CO: Westview Press, 1995), 324.

55. Reagan, 446.

56. Hendrick Smith, *The Power Game: How Washington Works* (New York: Random House, 1988), 444, 583–584.

57. Martin and Walcott, 120; McFarlane and Smardz, 250–251.

58. Addendum to NSDD-103, in Simpson, 326.

59. Smith, 444.

60. Frank, 18.

61. Pfaltzgraff and Davis, 308.

62. Interview with P. X. Kelley, October 2, 2001, Washington, DC.

63. Interview with Nick Veliotes, September 24, 2001, McLean, VA; Interview with Robert Gallucci.

64. McFarlane and Smardz, 253; Timberg, 334.

65. Talking points for Robert C. McFarlane, NSPG meeting, 10/18/83, Executive Secretariat, NSC: Country File, Lebanon Chronology (1), Box 91354, RRL.

66. Lou Cannon, *President Reagan: The Role of a Lifetime*, revised edition (New York: Public Affairs, 2000), 384; Hammel, 279.

67. John Prados, *Keepers of the Keys* (New York, New York: William Morrow & Co., Inc., 1991), 475; text of Reagan speech, *New York Times*, March 24, 1983; McFarlane and Smardz, 257.

68. Gregory F. Treverton, with Douglas Horner and James Dickinson, "Deciding to Use Force in Grenada," Case Study #C96-88-795.0 (Kennedy School of Government, Harvard University, 1986); Prados (1991), 478.

69. Frank, 3.

70. Cable 2305002, CTF 62 (Commodore France) to CTF 61, in Frank, 94.

71. Timberg, 337; McFarlane and Smardz, 262–263.

72. Timberg, 337.

73. Juan Williams, "Reagan's Days Off Erupt in Crisis," *Washington Post*, October 24, 1983, A14; President's Daily Schedule [10/22/83–10/28/83], Presidential Daily Diary, Box 11, Office of the President, RRL.

74. Oliver L. North with William Novak, *Under Fire: An American Story* (New York: Harper Collins Publishers, 1991), 196. See also John F. Lehman, Jr., *Command of the Seas* (New York: Charles Scribner's Sons, 1988), 326.

75. Martin and Walcott, 132–133, 137.

76. NSPG, 10/23/83, list of participants, Executive Secretariat, NSC: Country File, Lebanon Chronology (1), box 91354, RRL; *Weekly Compilation of Presidential Documents*, volume 19, number 43, 1504; Cannon, 392.

77. Talking Points for the DDCI, 23 October 1983, Executive Secretariat, NSC: Records: Country File, Lebanon Bombing/Airport, Oct. 23, 1983, Box 91353, RRL.

78. NSPG, 10/23/83, agenda, Executive Secretariat, NSC: Country File, Lebanon Chronology (1), box 91354, RRL; McFarlane and Smardz, 267.

79. Interview with Robert Gates.

80. Lehman, 326.

81. Martin and Walcott, 137–138.

82. Interview with Richard Armitage.

83. Martin and Walcott, 138.

84. Interview with P. X. Kelley.

85. Interview with Howard Teicher, February 15, 2001, Washington, DC.

86. Mark Perry, *Four Stars: The Inside Story of the Forty-Year Battle Between the Joint Chiefs of Staff and America's Civilian Leaders* (Boston, MA: Houghton Mifflin, 1989), 316.

87. Pfaltzgraff and Davis, 309; Timberg, 337.

88. Pfaltzgraff and Davis, 309; Timberg, 337.

89. Howard Teicher, *Twin Pillars to Desert Storm: America's Flawed Vision in the Middle East from Nixon to Bush* (New York: William Morrow and Company, Inc., 1993), 264; Timberg, 337; Frontline interview for "Target America" with Robert McFarlane, www.pbs.org/wgbh/pages/frontline/shows/target/ interviews/mcfarlane.html.

90. The details from the passage ordering "efforts to identify and punish those responsible" are still classified. Simpson, 244–245, 341–342; Oliver "Buck" Revell, *A G-Man's Journal* (New York: Simon and Schuster, 1998), 291; Perry, 313.

91. Draft Presidential Remarks, Regional Broadcasters Luncheon, October 24, 1983, Philip Dur files, box 90595, RRL.

92. Cable #261143Z OCT 83, from American Embassy Cairo to Secretary of State, Document #1983CAIRO31620, State Department Archives.

93. Memorandum from Charles Hill to Robert McFarlane, National Security Affairs, Office of the Assistant to the President for: Records: Chronological File, file #8391352, RRL.

94. Cable #241539Z OCT 83, from American Embassy Amman to Secretary of State, Document #1983AMMAN09222, State Department Archives.

95. Cable #252135Z OCT 83, from American Embassy Amman to Secretary of State, Document #1983AMMAN09286, State Department Archives.

96. Talking Points for call to President Mitterrand, Executive Secretariat, NSC: Records: Country File, Lebanon Bombing/Airport, Oct. 23, 1983, Box 91353, RRL; President's Daily Schedule, October 24, 1983 [10/22/83–10/28/83], Presidential Daily Diary, Box 11, Office of the President, RRL.

97. Cable 241517Z OCT 83, Executive Secretariat, NSC: Records: Country File, Lebanon Bombing/Airport, Oct. 23, 1983, Box 91353, RRL.

98. *Weekly Compilation of Presidential Documents*, volume 19, number 43, 1504.

99. Eleanor Randolph, "O'Neill Scuttles House Push for Quick Lebanon Pullout," *Los Angeles Times*, October 27, 1983.

100. Memo from Brennan McKinley (for Charles Hill) to Robert McFarlane, October 26, 1983, Executive Secretary, NSC: System File, file #8391277, RRL.

101. Interview with Bill Cowan; Interview with Noel Koch, January 23, 2001, Potomac, MD.

102. Outline of points on Lebanon, Executive Secretariat, NSC: Records: Country File, Lebanon Bombing/Airport, Oct. 23, 1983, Box 91353, RRL.

103. Talking points, 10/25/83, Executive Secretariat, NSC: Records: Country File, Lebanon Bombing/Airport, October 23, 1983, Box 91353, RRL.

104. Cable #271957Z OCT 83, from Secretary of State to Reagan, Document 1983SECTO12012, State Department Archives.

105. NSDD-111, Executive Secretariat, NSC: Records: Nsdds, NSDD 111 (1) [Next Steps Toward Progress in Lebanon and the Middle East], Box 91291, RRL; Simpson, 246.

106. John Goshko, "State Department Official Says U.S. Sees Iranian Hand in Assault on Marines," *Washington Post*, October 31, 1983, A17.

107. Cable #311021Z OCT 83, from American Embassy Damascus to Secretary of State, Document #1983DAMASC08516, State Department Archives.

108. Cable #031826Z NOV 83, from American Embassy Damascus to Secretary of State, Document #1983STATE314116, State Department Archives.

109. Foreign Intelligence and National Security Policy Developments, October–December 1983, FPB 1-84, Central Intelligence Agency document, 18. Crisis Management Center, NSC: Records, Foreign Intelligence and National Security Policy Developments, October–December 1983 (1), Box 91129, RRL. Also, interview with P. X. Kelley.

110. A report in *Newsweek* says the second intercept was made on September 24, 1983—almost one month before the bombing of the Marine barracks. "New Evidence Ties Iran to Terrorism," *Newsweek,* November 15, 1999, 4; McFarlane and Smardz, 270. Radio Monte Carlo reported that Musawi had "praised" the attacks, calling them "a legitimate reply to the presence of the Multinational Force in Lebanon." See "Special Memorandum/Beirut Bombings: Middle East and Soviet Reactions," Foreign Broadcast Information Service bulletin, FB 83-10044/Middle East-9, October 28, 1983, 2; Woodward, Harwood, and Williams; Pfaltzgraff and Davis, 308–309; Joseph E. Persico, *Casey: From the OSS to the CIA* (New York, New York: Viking Penguin, 1990), 369; Memorandum from General P. X. Kelley to Reagan, November 2, 1983, 2. Executive Secretariat, NSC: Records: NSDDs, NSDD-111 (3), Box 91291, RRL; Interview with P. X. Kelley; McFarlane and Smardz, 270. In the years since the bombing, the evidence against Hezbollah mounted. In February 1998, Lebanon's high court announced its intention to try Hezbollah leader Tufayli for the bombing of the Marine barracks. See "Plans to Prosecute Shaykh for Marine Barracks Bombing," *Terrorism Review* (Langley, VA: Director of Central Intelligence, Counterterrorist Center, February 1998), 26; "Planning to Prosecute Shaykh for Bombing," *National Intelligence Daily*, February 13, 1998 (Langley, VA: Director of Central Intelligence), 4; Woodward, Harwood, and Williams, A14. Forensic evidence was very slow in coming. The FBI examined an axle from the truck, and three years later they concluded that the truck had come from Iran, and the explosives were from Bulgaria. See interview with P. X. Kelley; Wright, 122; Jeffrey D. Simon, *The Terrorist Trap: America's Experience with Terrorism* (Bloomington, IN: Indiana Press University, 1994), 175; Martin and Walcott, Teicher, 264; 133–134; Woodward, 320–321; Cable #281243Z OCT 83, from American Embassy London to Secretary of State, Document #1983LONDON23223, State Department Archives. Musawi was interviewed by *The Times* reporter Robert Fisk; Cable #262007Z OCT 83, from American Embassy Paris to Secretary of State, Document #1983PARIS40118, State Department Archives.

111. Memo from Philip Dur to Donald Fortier, and "The Destabilization of Syria" paper, Donald Fortier files, Lebanon (2/5), box 90753, RRL.

112. Interview with Richard Armitage.

113. Timberg, 338.

114. Michael Getler, "Weinberger Discounts Attack on U.S. Planes," *Washington Post*, November 11, 1983, A21.

115. Michael Dobbs, "France Confident it Knows Identity of Beirut Bombers," *Washington Post*, November 12, 1983, A1, A12.

116. George C. Wilson, *Super Carrier* (New York: Macmillan Publishing Company, 1986), 116–118; Teicher, 265; Martin and Walcott, 135–136.

117. Martin and Walcott, 135.

118. Wilson, 116–123.

119. President's Daily Schedule, November 14, 1983 [11/4/83–11/14/83], Presidential Daily Diary, Box 11, Office of the President, RRL.

120. Teicher, 265; Martin and Walcott, 138; Pfaltzgraff and Davis, 309; Timberg, 338; "A U.S. Reprisal Raid: On Hold," *Newsweek*, December 12, 1983, 33. Following the Syrian defeat by Israel, and without sustained American pressure on the Syrians to withdraw from Lebanon, the Soviet Union resupplied the decimated Syrian armed forces, this time with two billion dollars worth of top-of-the-line materials, and sent Soviet advisors and crews to man new SAM anti-aircraft batteries.

121. Timberg, 338.

122. Pfaltzgraff and Davis, 309.

123. Timberg, 340.

124. Lehman, 326. This was confirmed in an off-the record interview with a high-ranking administration official.

125. Interview with Howard Teicher; McFarlane and Smardz, 270; Martin and Walcott, 138.

126. Martin and Walcott, 139.

127. Pfaltzgraff and Davis, 309.

128. Smith, 583. For a slightly different version, but essentially the same conversation, see McFarlane and Smardz, 270–271.

129. McFarlane and Smardz, 271.

130. Smith, 583.

131. For a full account of the French and Israeli attacks, see Mark Whitaker, with James Pringle, Milan Kubic, and Jane Whitmore, "Lebanon: An Eye for an Eye," *Newsweek*, November 28, 1983, 55–58.

132. Reagan, 463–464.

133. Ronald Reagan, *Weekly Compilation of Presidential Documents*, volume 19, number 51, 1715.

134. Milton Coleman, "Identity of Attackers Eludes U.S. Probers," *Washington Post*, November 7, 1983, A6.

135. Smith, 583, 748 (footnote 10)

136. Martin and Walcott, 139; Smith, 748 (footnote 10).

137. Weinberger, 161–162; Timberg, 339.

138. Interview with William Cowan; William V. Cowan, "Intelligence, Rescue, Retaliation, and Decision Making," in Barry Rubin, ed., *Terrorism and Politics* (New York: St. Martin's Press, 1991), 2. However, there is some indication that a group of Marines did conduct a reconnaissance mission in the Shouf Mountains shortly after the bombing, scouting Druze and Syrian artillery positions. See article by Robert Fisk, *The Times*, November 10, 1983, 1.

139. Cowan, 2–3; Martin and Walcott, 133–134.

140. Interview with William Cowan.

141. Cowan, 3–4; interview with William Cowan.

142. List of participants, NSPG, December 1, 1983, Executive Secretariat, NSC: Country file, Lebanon chronology (2), box 91354, RRL.

143. Draft NSDD, Executive Secretariat, NSC: Records: NSDDs, NSDD 117 [Lebanon], Box 91292, RRL.

144. Lehman, 327, 329.

145. See Angus Deming, with James Pringle, Ray Wilkinson, John Walcott, Kim Willenson, and Milan Kubic, "A U.S. Clash with Syria," *Newsweek*, December 12, 1983, 34–35.

146. Douglas Watson and Robin Knight do a nice job laying out these options in their article. "Lebanon: High Risk in Staying On—Or Getting Out," *US News and World Report*, November 7, 1983, 26–29.

147. Joseph Fromm with Don Reeder, James M. Hildreth, Robert A. Kittle, and Jeffrey L. Sheler, "Agonizing Decisions," *US News and World Report*, November 7, 1983, 24.

148. On October 30, a *Washington Post*/ABC News Poll showed that the president had significant support for his Lebanon policy. Question 1: Do you approve of Reagan's handling of the situation in Lebanon? Before Reagan's October 27 speech, 41 percent of respondents approved. On October 30, that was up to 52 percent. Question 2: What should Reagan do with the Marines in Lebanon? Send more—17 percent. Leave about the same—41 percent. Remove the Marines—37 percent. See "Washington Post/ABC News Poll," *Washington Post*, October 30, 1983, A18.

149. Cannon, 394–395.

150. David Ignatius, "Foreign-Policy Rows Make McFarlane's Job Unusually Tough One," *Wall Street Journal*, August 10, 1984, 10.

151. Cannon, 397.

152. Weinberger, 167.

153. Handwritten note from Richard Armitage to Bob Kimmitt and Robert McFarlane, December 24, 1983, Donald Fortier files, Lebanon (4/5), Box 90753, RRL.

154. Memorandum from John Poindexter to Fred Iklé, et. al, December 20, 1983, Donald Fortier files, Lebanon (2/5), Box 90753, RRL; Weinberger, 167–168.

155. Martin and Walcott, 147.

156. Dear Colleague letter from Representatives Thomas Downey, Charles Bennett, and Leon Panetta, December 14, 1983. Donald Fortier files, Lebanon (5/5), box 90753, RRL.

157. Press release by Representative Dante Fascell, December 14, 1983. Donald Fortier files, Lebanon (5/5), box 90753, RRL.

158. "Adequacy of U.S. Marine Corps Security in Beirut, Summary of Findings and Conclusions," Report of the Investigations Subcommittee of the Committee on Armed Services, House of Representatives, 98th Congress, 1st session, December 19, 1983, 3.

159. "Adequacy of U.S. Marine Corps Security in Beirut," 69.

160. Eytan Gilboa, "Effects of Televised Presidential Addresses on Public Opinion: President Reagan and Terrorism in the Middle East," *Presidential Studies Quarterly*, volume 20, number 1, 47.

161. Interview with P. X. Kelley.

162. Report of the DOD Commission on Beirut International Airport Terrorist Act, October 23, 1983 (Long Commission), December 20, 1983, 121.

163. Long Commission, 68, 117.

164. Cannon, 397.

165. Leslie H. Gelb, "Taking Charge: The Rising Power of National Security Advisor Robert McFarlane," *New York Times Magazine*, May 26, 1985, 25.

166. List of participants, NSPG meeting, January 3, 1984. Executive Secretariat, NSC: Country file, Lebanon chronology (2), box 91354, RRL.

167. Agenda, NSPG meeting, January 3, 1984. Executive Secretariat, NSC: Country file, Lebanon chronology (2), box 91354, RRL.

168. Memorandum from Geoffrey Kemp to McFarlane and Talking Points, January 3, 1984. Executive Secretariat, NSC: Country file, Lebanon chronology (2), box 91354, RRL.

169. Interview with Peter Rodman, February 7, 2001, Washington, DC.

170. Cable 190242Z JAN 84, State Department archives.

171. William B. Quandt, "Reagan's Lebanon Policy: Trial and Error," *The Middle East Journal*, volume 38, number 2 (Spring 1984), 249.

172. Cannon, 398.

173. NSDD-123, in Simpson, 359–360, 380–382.

174. Gilboa, 47.

175. Pfaltzgraff and Davis, 310; Cannon, 399–400.

176. Martin and Walcott, 150.

177. Reagan handwritten notes, with typewritten version and cover memo (memo dated April 9, 1984), CO 086, RRL.

178. Bradlee, 190; Martin and Walcott, 156.

179. Martin and Walcott, 156.

180. Bradlee, 189.

181. Neil C. Livingstone, *The Cult of Counterterrorism: The 'Weird World' of Spooks, Counterterrorists, Adventurers, and the Not-Quite Professionals* (Lexington, MA: Lexington Books, 1990), 233–234.

182. "Secret Policy on Terrorism Given Airing," *Washington Post*, April 18, 1984, A1; Livingstone (1990), 234; Simpson, 366, 405–411.

183. George Shultz, "Realism, Strength, Negotiations: Key Foreign Policy Statements of the Reagan Administration," (Washington, DC: United States Department of State, Bureau of Public Affairs, May 1984), 8.

184. Draft speech on terrorism for delivery by Secretary Shultz at the Jonathan Institute Conference, June 24, 1984, Donald Fortier files [Terrorism] [Shultz material], box 90761, RRL.

185. See Mark Whitaker, with James Pringle, Nicholas Horrock, Eleanor Clift, Nikke Finke Greenberg, and Howard Fineman, "More Madness in Bloody Beirut," *Newsweek*, October 1, 1984, 18–21.

186. Philip Taubman, "U.S. Agencies Link a Moslem Group to Beirut Blast," *New York Times*, October 5, 1984, A1, A7; Woodward, 433; Martin and Walcott, 159; McCarthy, 177.

187. Oliver North Notebooks, September 20, 1984, volume 5, National Archives.

188. Martin and Walcott, 158–159.

189. James Berry Motley, "Target America: The Undeclared War," in Livingstone and Arnold, 74–75; Martin and Walcott, 159.

190. "Washington Whispers," *US News and World Report*, November 26, 1984, 23.

191. George Shultz, "Terrorism and the Modern World," Current Policy, number 629 (Washington, DC: United States Department of State, Bureau of Public Affairs, October 25, 1984).

192. Bernard Gwertzman, "Bush Challenges Shultz's Position on Terror Policy," *New York Times*, October 27, 1984, 1, 6; Don Oberdorfer and Juan Williams, "Officials Split on Shultz's Antiterrorism Speech," *Washington Post*, October 27, 1984, A1, A8.

193. Interview with P. X. Kelley; interview with Peter Rodman.

194. See Richard Halloran, "U.S. Will Not Drift Into Latin War, Weinberger Says," *New York Times*, November 29, 1984, A1, A4.

195. Memo from Oliver North to John Poindexter, December 6, 1984. Oliver North files, Terrorism: Kuwaiti hijacking, 12/3/84: Cable Traffic [2 of 5], Box 101, RRL.

196. Simpson, 370–371; Russell Watson, with Nicholas Horrock and Abdul Hajjaj, "Fighting Terror with Terror," *Newsweek*, May 27, 1985, 32–33. In a *Frontline* interview with Bob Woodward, the *Washington Post* journalist claims that the bombing was an "off the books" operation set up by Casey and the Saudi ambassador to Washington, Prince Bandar. See *Frontline* interview for "Target America," www.pbs.org/wgbh/pages/frontline/shows/target/interviews/woodward.html.

197. Martin and Walcott, 157.

198. Robert M. Sayre, "International Terrorism: A Long Twilight Struggle," Department of State Bulletin #84 (October 84), 48–50.

# NOTES FOR CHAPTER FOUR

1. The safety of the people shall be the highest law.

2. "The Beirut Hostages: Background to the Crisis," (Washington, D.C.: Foreign Affairs and National Defense Division, Congressional Research Service, The Library of Congress, June 21, 1985), 3.

3. All times are local. Athens, Beirut, and Damascus are seven hours ahead of Washington, while Algiers is five hours ahead.

4. David Martin and John Walcott, *Best Laid Plans* (New York: Harper and Row, 1988), 167.

5. The *Washington Post* published an article on May 12, 1985 exposing a linkage between the CIA and the Lebanese hit team that conducted the bombing.

6. Martin and Walcott, 169.

7. Ibid., 162.

8. Cable #140949Z, White House Situation Room, June 14, 1985, Oliver North files, Cables— Incoming (14–15 June) TWA #847 [1 of 4], Box 89, RRL.

9. Martin and Walcott, 169.

10. "Summary of Events: The Hijacking of TWA 847," Office of the Press Secretary, White House, June 30, 1985, 1; Joan Mower, "U.S. Leaders Maintain 24-Hour Vigil During Hijacking," *Associated Press*, June 17, 1985.

11. Interview with Noel Koch, January 23, 2001, Potomac, MD; Mark Whitaker and Harry Anderson, with Rod Nordland, Michael A. Lerner, John Walcott, and Kim Willenson, "An Odyssey of Terror," *Newsweek*, June 24, 1985, 27; Oliver North, *Taking the Stand*, 296; Martin and Walcott, 179; Constantine C. Menges, *Inside the National Security Council: The True Story of the Making and Unmaking of Reagan's Foreign Policy* (New York: Simon and Schuster, 1989), 221; Oliver North Notebooks, volume 13 [145-181-545105-23], June 14, 1985 (AMX000781), National Archives.

12. Interview with David Long.

13. A cable from the U.S. embassy in Paris indicated that there was some concern that the plane might be forced to land in Libya. Cable #141312A, National Security Council Secretariat, June 14, 1985, Oliver North files, Cables—Incoming (14–15 June), TWA #847 [1 of 4], Box 89, RRL.

14. Interview with Nathaniel Howell, June 6, 2000, Charlottesville, VA; interview with Michael Newlin, January 23, 2001, Rockville, Maryland; Martin and Walcott, 170.

15. Interview with Nathaniel Howell.

16. Cable #141716Z, Department of State, June 14, 1985, as released by the CIA.

17. Interview with Nathaniel Howell; interview with Michael Newlin.

18. Interview with David Long; Martin and Walcott, 173, 176.

19. Cable #150356Z, Department of State, June 15, 1985, as released by the CIA; Joseph E. Persico, *Casey: From the OSS to the CIA* (New York: Viking Penguin, 1990), 441.

20. Interview with Michael Newlin.

21. Martin and Walcott, 179. Reagan wrote an "urgent" letter to President Bendjedid on June 15. The most likely reason for the letter was to request either that Delta Force be allowed into the country or that the Algerians act on their own. Declassification of the letter was denied on May 23, 2000 (at the RRL).

22. Interview with Nathaniel Howell.

23. Martin and Walcott, 178, 179. Early military planning also included using Army Rangers to secure the Beirut Airport, and after the hostages were off-loaded, using Air Force special operations aircraft to drop counter-terrorism forces at locations where intelligence believed the hostages were being held. William V. Cowan, "Intelligence, Rescue, Retaliation, and Decision Making," in Barry Rubin, ed., *Terrorism and Politics* (New York: St. Martin's Press, 1991), 12.

24. Shawn R. McCarthy, *The Function of Intelligence in Crisis Management* (Brookfield, CT: Ashgate Publishing Co., 1998), 220–221.

25. Martin and Walcott, 179.

26. Interview with David Long.

27. Martin and Walcott, 180.

28. Donald Regan, handwritten notes, June 15, 1985, "White House: Notes, daily meetings, May–June, 1985," folder 2, box 190, Donald T. Regan Collection, Library of Congress.

29. Memorandum from George Shultz to Ronald Reagan, June 15, 1985, Executive Secretariat file, NSC, Records, System File, #8590671, RRL.

30. Memorandum No. 2 from George Shultz to Ronald Reagan, June 15, 1985, Executive Secretariat file, NSC, Records, System File, #8590671, RRL.

31. Oliver North Notebooks, volume 13, National Security Archives.

32. Neil Livingston claims that the U.S. also had "other military assets waiting in Israel for the word to move." *The Cult of Counterterrorism: The Weird World of Spooks, Counterterrorists, Adventurers, and the Not-Quite Professionals* (Lexington, MA: Lexington Books, 1990), 240.

33. Amy Wilentz, "Managing the Crisis," *Time*, June 15, 1985, 24.

34. "Summary of Events," 2.

35. David Ottaway, "Early Swap of Hostages Said Foiled," *Washington Post*, June 20, 1985, A1; "Report U.S. Asked Red Cross to Broker Hostage Deal," *UPI*, June 20, 1985.

36. Russell Watson, with Rod Nordland, Milan J. Kubic, John Walcott, Margaret Garrard Warner, and Kim Willenson, "We Eat, We Sleep, We Pray," *Newsweek*, July 1, 1985, 21.

37. Cable #151219Z, Department of State, June 15, 1985, as released by the CIA.

38. Cable #152015Z, Department of State, June 15, 1985, as released by the CIA.

39. Cable #251215Z, Department of State, June 25, 1985, as released by the CIA.

40. Interview with Michael Newlin.

41. Interview with Nathaniel Howell; interview with Robert Oakley, April 8, 2000; Martin and Walcott, 182.

42. George Shultz, *Turmoil and Triumph: My Years as Secretary of State* (New York: Charles Scribner's Sons, 1993), 655; interview with Caspar Weinberger, March 29, 2000 (phone); interview with Charles Hill, January 19, 2001, New Haven, CT.

43. Interview with Michael Newlin.

44. Regan, handwritten notes, June 15, 1985, "White House: Notes, daily meetings, May–June, 1985," folder 2, box 190, Donald T. Regan Collection, Library of Congress.

45. Interview with Robert Oakley.

46. Both NBC and ABC News reported the departure of Delta Force from Ft. Bragg.

47. Interview with David Long; interview with Michael Newlin.

48. Interview with Parker Borg, October 4, 2001, Manassas, VA; Martin and Walcott, 183.

49. Interview with Michael Newlin.

50. Regan, handwritten notes, conference call, June 16, 1985, "White House: Notes, daily meetings, May–June, 1985," folder 2, box 190, Donald T. Regan Collection, Library of Congress.

51. Watkins, et al., July 1, 1985, 22.

52. Barri was initially asked by Ambassador Bartholomew to help on June 14. Oliver North Notebooks, volume 13 [145-181-545105-23], June 14, 1985 (AMX000781), National Archives.

53. Regan, handwritten notes, conference calls, June 16, 1985, "White House: Notes, daily meetings, May–June, 1985," folder 2, box 190, Donald T. Regan Collection, Library of Congress.

54. Robert A. Snyder, "Negotiating With Terrorists: TWA Flight 847" (Washington, DC: The Institute for the Study of Diplomacy, School of Foreign Service, Georgetown University, 1994), 6.

55. President's Daily Schedule, June 16, 1985 [6/14/85–6/17/85], Presidential Daily Diary, Box 17, Office of the President, RRL.

56. Lou Cannon, *President Reagan, Role of a Lifetime* (New York: Simon and Schuster, 1991), 606; Martin and Walcott, 185.

57. Wilentz, 24.

58. Oliver North said that McFarlane actually visited Beirut during the hijacking to meet with Barri, but came back empty-handed. Interview with Oliver North, January 30, 2001, Washington, DC. Wilentz, 24; Martin and Walcott, 186–87.

59. Shultz, 656; interview with Parker Borg.

60. Howard Teicher, *Twin Pillars of Desert Storm: America's Flawed Vision in the Middle East from Nixon to Bush* (New York: William Morrow and Company, 1993), 332; interview with Charles Hill; Shultz, 664; Martin and Walcott, 192.

61. Shultz, 656; Martin and Walcott, 186; Cannon, 607.

62. Memorandum from Nicholas Platt to Robert McFarlane, June 17, 1985, Executive Secretariat file, NSC, Records, System File, #8504868, RRL.

63. Ronald Reagan, *An American Life* (New York: Simon and Schuster, 1990), 494.

64. Christopher Dobson and Ronald Payne, *Never-Ending War: Terrorism in the 80's* (New York: Facts on File, 1987), 43; Shultz, 655; Martin and Walcott, 185.

65. "An FBI Report on the Hijacking of TWA Flight 847, June 14, 1985," United States Department of Justice, September 1985, volume 5; from North, Oliver: Files, Box 53, RRL.

66. Shultz, 656; Martin and Walcott, 186; Cannon, 607.

67. Regan, handwritten notes, NSPG—June 16, 1985, "White House: Notes, daily meetings, May–June, 1985," folder 2, box 190, Donald T. Regan Collection, Library of Congress.

68. Memorandum from Elizabeth Penniman to David Chew, June 18, 1985, file PR014-08, RRL.

69. Christopher Dickey, "Multiple Pressures Build on Amal in Beirut," *Washington Post*, June 25, 1985.

70. The Syrian government was given 24-hour advance notice about the start of maneuvers.

71. Regan handwritten notes from June 17, 1985 daily operations meeting, "White House: Notes, daily meetings, May–June, 1985," folder 2, box 190, Donald T. Regan collection, Library of Congress.

72. Cannon, 606.

73. Regan, handwritten note, June 17, 1985, "White House: Notes, daily meetings, May–June, 1985," folder 2, box 190, Donald T. Regan Collection, Library of Congress.

74. Shultz, 656; Martin and Walcott, 186–87.

75. Cable #180030Z JUN 85, from US Mission U.N. New York to Shultz, June 18, 1985, Document # 1985USUNN01360, State Department Archives.

76. Whitaker and Anderson, et al., June 24, 1985, 19.

77. David Martin, *CBS Evening News*, June 17, 1985. The CIA was forced to withdraw its agents from Beirut following the Buckley kidnapping on the assumption that the CIA station chief had been forced to divulge their identities. See McCarthy, 170.

78. Interview with Robert Oakley; interview with Parker Borg.

79. North/Teicher Comment on Situation as of 0900 EST, June 17, 1985, "White House: Notes, daily meetings, May–June, 1985," folder 2, box 190, Donald T. Regan Collection, Library of Congress.

80. Shultz, 658.

81. Regan, handwritten notes from June 18, 1985 daily operations meeting, "White House: Notes, daily meetings, May–June, 1985," folder 2, box 190, Donald T. Regan collection, Library of Congress.

82. Regan, handwritten note, June 18, 1985, "White House: Notes, daily meetings, May–June, 1985," folder 2, box 190, Donald T. Regan Collection, Library of Congress.

83. Barry Sussman, *Washington Post*, June 19, 1985, A25.

84. NEA Press Guidance, "Hijacking: Algerian Proposal," June 19, 1985, Bush Vice Presidential Records; National Security Affairs; TWA 847 hijacking; [OA/ID 19851] [2 of 7]; GBPL; interview with Nathaniel Howell.

85. Cable #211025Z, Department of State, as released by the CIA.

86. Oliver North Notebooks, volume 13 [145-171-545104-23], June 19, 1985 (AMX000805), National Archives.

87. "Islamic Terror in U.S.?" *Washington Times*, June 20, 1985, A1.

88. Memo, Rodney McDaniel to Robert McFarlane, June 19, 1985. File SRB 378–TWA 847 (6), box 93207, President's Special Review Board (Tower Board): Recommendations, RRL.

89. Interview with Parker Borg.

90. "Talking Points for Meeting with Mother of James (Jeffrey) Hoskins Hijacked Hostage Held in Beirut," from Executive Secretariat file, NSC, Records, System File, #8504909, RRL.

91. Reagan wanted to retaliate for the Zona Rosa attack in El Salvador with an attack on a rebel training base inside Nicaragua. However, he decided against it after Weinberger argued that civilians would be killed in the strike. Interview with Lou Cannon, June 30, 2000, Summerland, CA.

92. *Nightline*, June 19, 1985.

93. Reagan, 495.

94. *ABC World News Tonight*, June 20, 1985.

95. President's Daily Schedule, June 20, 1985 [6/18/85–6/22/85], Presidential Daily Diary, Box 18, Office of the President, RRL.

96. Regan, handwritten notes, NSPG—June 20, 1985, "White House: Notes, daily meetings, May–June, 1985," folder 2, box 190, Donald T. Regan Collection, Library of Congress; Reagan, 495.

97. Regan, handwritten notes, NSPG—June 20, 1985, "White House: Notes, daily meetings, May–June, 1985," folder 2, box 190, Donald T. Regan Collection, Library of Congress; Shultz, 659.

98. Oliver L. North, with William Novak, *Under Fire: An American Story* (New York: Harper Collins Publishers, 1991), 196–197; Oliver North Notebooks, volume 13 [145-171-545104-23], June 20, 1985 (AMX000810), National Archives. This eventually became NSDD-179.

99. Memo, Bob Cynkar to Edwin Meese, June 19, 1985, White House Office file, June 1985, box 43, Edwin Meese Collection, Hoover Institution.

100. NSDD-180, July 19, 1985. Bush Vice Presidential Records, National Security Affairs; Combatting Terrorism Task Force [1 of 7] [OA/ID 19849], GBL.

101. Interview with Charles Hill; Shultz, 657, 659; handwritten note, author unknown, on "Office of the Vice President" letterhead, Bush Vice Presidential Records; National Security Affairs; TWA hijacking/ II; [OA/ID 19850] GBL; Shawn McCarthy confirmed this in an interview with Israeli official Ariel Merari. McCarthy, 220; Martin and Walcott, 198.

102. Interview with Howard Teicher, February 15, 2001, Washington, DC.

103. Shultz, 659–660.

104. President's Daily Schedule, June 20, 1985 [6/18/85–6/22/85], Presidential Daily Diary, Box 18, Office of the President, RRL; Oliver North Notebooks, volume 13 [145-171-545104-23], June 17, 1985 (AMX000799), National Archives.

105. Bernard Gwertzman, "U.S. Aides Say Hostage Release Would Free 766 Held in Israel," *New York Times*, June 21, 1985, A1; Shultz, 660.

106. Memo, Donald Fortier, Jock Covey, and Oliver North to Robert McFarlane, June 20, 1985. President's Special Review Board (Tower Board): Records, TWA (8), AOD 1193, box 93207, RRL.

107. Cable 210635Z, Department of State, June 21, 1985, as released by the CIA.

108. Reagan, 495.

109. Shultz, 661; Martin and Walcott, 195; Cable #220528Z JUN 85, from Shultz to numerous stations, June 22, 1985, Document #1985STATE192175, State Department Archives.

110. Shultz, 662.

111. Martin and Walcott, 195.

112. Memorandum from Pat Buchanan to Donald Regan, June 22, 1985, PR015, file #325960, RRL.

113. Cable #220414Z JUN 85, from Shultz to American embassy Damascus, June 22, 1985, Document #1985STATE192161, State Department Archives.

114. Cable #220153Z JUN 85, from Shultz to American embassy Lisbon, June 22, 1985, Document #1985STATE191986, State Department Archives.

115. Martin and Walcott, 194.

116. *This Week with David Brinkley*, June 23, 1985.

117. "Next Steps After the Hijacking," CIA Analysis, July 9, 1985. Office of Vice President George Bush, National Security Affairs, Terrorism—II: Terrorism Article [3 of 3] [OA/ID #19839], GBL; Martin and Walcott, 196; Robin Wright, *In the Name of God: The Khomeini Decade* (New York: Simon and Schuster, 1989), 131.

118. Vice President Bush was not at the meeting, as he had just departed on a trip to visit with the European allies. President's Daily Schedule, June 24, 1985 [6/23/85–6/27/85], Presidential Daily Diary, Box 18, Office of the President, RRL.

119. Reagan, 496.

120. Withdrawal sheet, item #1, Memo to Reagan RE: Telephone call to President Assad of Syria, June 24, 1985. Bush Vice Presidential Records, National Security Affairs, TWA 847 hijacking [OA/ID 19851] [7], GBL.

121. Regan, handwritten notes, NSPG—June 24, 1985, "White House: Notes, daily meetings, May–June, 1985," folder 2, box 190, Donald T. Regan Collection, Library of Congress.

122. Memorandum from Oliver North and Christopher Lehman to Robert McFarlane, June 25, 1985, Executive Secretariat, NSC, Records, System File, #8505073, RRL.

123. Interview with Oliver North, January 30, 2001, Washington, DC.

124. President's Daily Schedule, June 25, 1985 [6/23/85–6/27/85], Presidential Daily Diary, Box 18, Office of the President, RRL.

125. Regan, handwritten notes from daily operations meeting, June 25, 1985, "White House: Notes, Daily meetings, May–June, 1985," folder 2, box 190, Donald T. Regan Collection, Library of Congress; "Summary of Events," 5; Martin and Walcott, 195.

126. Interview with Robert Oakley.

127. Martin and Walcott, 195; Shultz, 663.

128. Robert Oakley later asked Robert Gates what the Soviet reaction would be if the United States were to launch such an attack. Gates replied that it would likely increase Soviet influence and arms in the region, and increase anti-American sentiment in the Arab world. Interview with Robert Oakley.

129. Shultz, 663.

130. Regan, handwritten notes, NSPG—June 25, 1985, "White House: Notes, daily meetings, May–June, 1985," folder 2, box 190, Donald T. Regan Collection, Library of Congress.

131. Martin and Walcott, 195.

132. Regan, handwritten notes, NSPG—June 25, 1985, "White House: Notes, daily meetings, May–June, 1985," folder 2, box 190, Donald T. Regan Collection, Library of Congress.

133. Martin and Walcott, 198.

134. Shultz, 664.

135. Regan, handwritten notes from meeting with Reagan, June 26, 1985, "White House: Notes, daily meetings, May–June, 1985," folder 2, box 190, Donald T. Regan Collection, Library of Congress; President's Daily Schedule, June 26, 1985 [6/23/85–6/27/85], Presidential Daily Diary, Box 18, Office of the President, RRL.

136. Reagan, 496.

137. Regan, handwritten notes, NSPG—June 26, 1985, "White House: Notes, daily meetings, May–June, 1985," folder 2, box 190, Donald T. Regan Collection, Library of Congress.

138. Jim Hoagland, "Barri Offers to Shift American Hostages to Western Embassy," *Washington Post*, June 27, 1985, A1.

139. *Frontline* interview with Robert Oakley, http://www.pbs.org/wgbh/pages/frontline/shows/target/interviews/oakley.html.

140. Bradley H. Patterson, Jr., *The Ring of Power: The White House Staff and its Expanding Role in Government* (New York, Basic Books, 1988), 168.

141. Interview with Howard Teicher.

142. "France Won't Accept Barri's Terms," UPI, June 28, 1985.

143. Memorandum from Nicholas Platt to Robert McFarlane, June 27, 1985, Executive Secretariat file, NSC, Records, System File, #8570726, RRL.

144. Jonathan Randal, "Syria Tries to Boost Mideast Role with Offers of Help in Hostage Crisis," *Washington Post*, June 28, 1985, A32; *CBS Evening News*, June 27, 1985. Assad came to this position after a meeting with United Nations special envoy Jean-Claude Aime, who convinced the Syrian president to take the hostages if the U.S. provided assurances that Israel would release the detainees. McCarthy, 220.

145. Shultz, 665.

146. Interview with Caspar Weinberger, March 29, 2000; interview with Robert Oakley; interview with David Long.

147. Cable #291133Z JUN 85, Ambassador Rentschler to Shultz, June 29, 1985, Document #1985VALLET01356, State Department Archives.

148. NSC memo, Poindexter to McFarlane, June 28, 1985, from Executive Secretariat files, NSC, Records, System File, #8590727, RRL.

149. Cable #291046Z JUN 85, Shultz to Ambassador Bartholomew, June 29, 1985, Document #1985STATE200232, State Department Archives.

150. Shultz, 667.

151. Martin and Walcott, 199–201.

152. David Halevy and Neil C. Livingston, "The Ollie We Knew," *The Washingtonian* (July 1987), 144; Livingstone (1990), 241.

153. Shultz, 666.

154. Interview with Robert Oakley.

155. Martin and Walcott, 199; Michael Ledeen relates an additional aspect of the Iranian story. He claims that while Syria said it could produce the hostages held by Amal, it could not guarantee those held by Hezbollah. So the United States turned to Israel who suggested using Iranian arms dealer

Manucher Ghorbanifar as an intermediary with Tehran. Ledeen implies that it was Ghorbanifar's efforts that succeeded in freeing the four hostages still held by Hezbollah. Michael A. Ledeen, *Perilous State-craft: An Insider's Account of the Iran-Contra Affair* (New York: Charles Scribener's Sons, 1988), 114.

156. David Ignatius and Jane Mayer, "Radicals Free 39 Hostages in Accord Preserving U.S. Anti-Terrorist Stance," *Wall Street Journal*, July 1, 1985, A3.

157. "Hostages Fly to Freedom," Reuters, July 2, 1985; Edward Walsh, "Israel Announces Prisoner Release," *Washington Post*, July 2, 1985, A12. The rest of the detainees were repatriated to Lebanon by September 10, 1985.

158. Cannon, 607; Donald T. Regan, *For the Record: From Wall Street to Washington* (New York: Harcourt Brace Jovanovich, Publishers, 1988), 17; Whitaker, et al., July 15, 1985, 18; Dave Doubrava, "U.S. Has Identified Hijackers—Shultz," *Washington Times*, July 2, 1985, A1. Also present for the call to Assad were NSC staffer Jock Covey and State Department interpreter Zaki Aslan. President's Daily Schedule, July 1, 1985 [6/28/85–7/4/85], Presidential Daily Diary, Box 18, Office of the President, RRL.

159. Presidential Determination #85-14, July 1, 1985, from file CA 302948, RRL.

160. Mark Whitaker, with Kim Willenson and John Walcott, "Reagan's Options," *Newsweek,* July 8, 1985, 22; Martin and Walcott, 202.

161. Reagan, 497.

162. E-mail from Wilma Hall to Robert McFarlane and others, June 27, 1985, Executive Secretariat files, NSC, Records, System File, #8590724, RRL.

163. *ABC's World News Tonight*, July 1, 1985.

164. David Ignatius, "A Clear Plan to Handle Terrorism Still Eludes Divided Reagan Camp," *Wall Street Journal*, July 6, 1985, A1.

165. Ronald Reagan, "Remarks at the Annual Convention of the American Bar Association," July 8, 1985. *Public Papers of the Presidents of the United States: Ronald Reagan; 1985, Book II—June 29–December 31, 1985* (Washington, DC: United States Government Printing Office, 1988), 894–900. In the first draft, he mentioned the governments the U.S. believed were sponsoring or supporting terrorism, including Cuba, Nicaragua, Vietnam, North Korea, Libya, and Syria. As a signal of favor to Damascus for their help in resolving the hijacking, McFarlane had the reference to Syria removed from the speech. See Menges, 222.

166. Talking points (for Vice President Bush) for meeting with selected ambassadors, October 31, 1985, and NSDD-179, Bush Vice Presidential Records, National Security Affairs, Terrorism file [5 of 9] [OA/ID 19849], GBL.

167. Memo, from Admiral Holloway to George Bush, November 7, 1985, Bush Vice Presidential Records, National Security Affairs, Terrorism file [5 of 9] [OA/ID 19849], GBL; interview with Noel Koch.

168. "Public Report of the Vice President's Task Force on Combatting Terrorism" (Washington, DC: United States Government Printing Office, February 1986), 22.

169. David Kennedy, "The Extradition of Mohammed Hamadei" (Cambridge, MA: Case Program #C15-88-835.0—Kennedy School of Government, Harvard University, 1988), 15–18.

170. Interview with Duane Clarridge, March 21, 2001, Escondido, CA; interview with Oliver "Buck" Revell, February 22, 2001, Carrollton, TX; Duane R. Clarridge, with Digby Diehl, *A Spy For All Seasons: My Life in the CIA* (New York, NY: Scribner, 1997), 349–359; Oliver Revell, *A G-Man's Journal* (New York, NY: Simon and Schuster, 1998), 313–326.

# NOTES FOR CHAPTER FIVE

1. On October 13, 1985, a PLF spokesman claimed responsibility for the hijacking of the *Achille Lauro*, but claimed the ship was not the intended target, and denied that any passengers had been

killed. Cable #130509Z, from Michael Armacost, October 13, 1985, White House Situation Room, CMC: NSC: Records Achille Lauro [10 of 23], box 91131, RRL.

2. "Ship Hijack," from Bush Presidential Records, NSC, Robin Frank Files, OLN—New AL: Press 28 JAN 89 [OA/ID CF00943] in "AL: Press, Oliver L. North, NSC Staff"; Christopher Dobson and Ronald Payne, *The Never-Ending War: Terrorism in the 80's* (New York: Facts on File, 1987), 216.

3. David Martin and John Walcott, *Best Laid Plans* (New York: Harper and Row), 236.

4. Interview with Nick Veliotes, June 13, 2000; "Terrorism Review" (Washington: Directorate of Intelligence, CIA, October 21, 1985), 11; Antonio Cassese, *Terrorism, Politics and Law: The* Achille Lauro *Affair* (Princeton, NJ: Princeton University Press, 1989), 24; John Walcott, with Rod Nordland, Theodore Stanger, Milan J. Kubic, Andrew Nagorski, John Barry, and Susan Agrest, "Getting Even," *Newsweek*, October 21, 1985, 25.

5. Interview with Charles Allen, February 14, 2001, Langley, VA; Oliver L. North with William Novak, *Under Fire: An American Story* (NY: Harper Collins, 1991), 200; Deborah Hart Strober and Gerald S. Strober, *Reagan: The Man and His Presidency, The Oral History of an Era* (New York: Houghton Mifflin, 1998), 374.

6. North and Novak, 200.

7. Oliver "Buck" Revell and Dwight Williams, *A G-Man's Journal* (New York: Simon and Schuster, 1998), 268–269.

8. Interview with Noel Koch, January 23, 2001, Potomac, MD.

9. John Prados, *Keepers of the Keys: A History of the National Security Council from Truman to Bush* (New York: William Morrow and Company, 1991), 20.

10. Interview with David Long, April 8, 2000; Duane Clarridge, *A Spy For All Seasons: My Life in the CIA* (New York: Scribner, 1997), 307; North and Novak, 201.

11. E-mail from Howard Teicher to John Poindexter, October 8, 1985, 16:32:22, National Security Archives; Cable #081425Z, October 8, 1985, George Shultz to Reginald Bartholomew, State Department Archives; Bolger, 364.

12. Vlad Jenkins, "The *Achille Lauro* Hijacking (A)" (Cambridge, MA: Kennedy School of Government), 3.

13. Interview with David Long and Robert Oakley, (2000); Michael Ledeen, *Perilous Statecraft: An Insider's Account of the Iran-Contra Affair* (New York: Charles Scribner's Sons, 1988), 175; Clarridge, 307. At the same time, the Italians deployed a force of paratroopers from the "Colonel Moschin" battalion and a naval raiding party from the "Teseo Tesei" group to Akrotiri. One source claims that they had prepared to assault the ship, and anticipated at least twenty deaths—a number that included some of the hostages. See Cassese, 27.

14. E-mail, Jock Covey to Situation Room, October 7, 1985, 18:52:26. National Security Archives.

15. One interviewee in a position to know said that an American submarine in fact trailed the *Achille Lauro* throughout the crisis. Ben Bradlee, *Guts and Glory: The Rise and Fall of Oliver North*, (New York: Donald I. Fine, Inc., 1988), 291–292; Neil C. Livingstone, *The Cult of Counterterrorism: The Weird World of Spooks, Counterterrorists, Adventurers, and the Not-Quite Professionals* (Lexington, MA: Lexington Books, 1990), 252.

16. Jenkins (A), 5.

17. E-mail from Stark to Poindexter, 10/8/84, 18:44, Tom Blanton, ed., *White House E-mail* (New York: The New Press, 1995), 102.

18. Shultz, *Turmoil and Triumph: My Years As Secretary of State* (New York: Charles Scribner's Sons, 1993), 669–670.

19. Cable #081107Z, October 8, 1985, American Embassy Damascus to Secretary of State, State Department Archives; Shultz, 679.

20. "Terrorism Review" (Washington: Directorate of Intelligence, CIA, October 21, 1985), 12.

21. Interview with Robert Oakley and David Long, (2000); Cable #081120Z, October 8, 1985, State Department Archives; Shultz, 669; Cable #081605Z, October 8, 1985, American Embassy Athens to Secretary of State, State Department Archives.

22. Interview with Charles Hill, January 18, 2001, New Haven, CT; interview with Parker Borg, October 4, 2001, Manassas, VA; Oliver L. North, *Taking the Stand: The Testimony of Lieutenant Colonel Oliver L. North* (New York: Pocket Books, 1987), 299; Jenkins (A), 5; Shultz, 670; Clarridge, 307; North and Novak, 202.

23. Cable #081356Z, October 8, 1985, George Shultz to Eagleton, State Department Archives.

24. Presidential Daily Brief, CIA Spot Commentary, October 8, 1985, Crisis Management Center, NSC: Records, Achille Lauro [1 of 23], Box 91131, RRL.

25. Shultz, 670.

26. Israeli intelligence was monitoring these ship-to-shore communications. Prados (1991), 21; Martin and Walcott, 239.

27. Cable #081404Z, October 8, 1985, American Embassy Damascus to Secretary of State, State Department Archives; interview with Parker Borg.

28. Cable #081330Z, October 8, 1985, American Consul Egypt to Secretary of State, State Department Archives; Martin and Walcott, 241.

29. Shultz, 671.

30. Jenkins (A), 9; Cassese, 30.

31. List of participants, NSPG meeting, October 8, 1985, President's Special Review Board (Tower board), Recommendations, SRB 0350 Achille Lauro Prelim File (3), Box 93211, RRL; President's Daily Schedule, October 8, 1985 [10/8/85–10/12/85], Presidential Daily Diary, Box 19, Office of the President, RRL.

32. CIA assessment, MORI DocID: 40146, October 9, 1985, CIA Archives; CIA assessment, MORI DocID: 40147, October 10, 1985, CIA Archives.

33. Martin and Walcott, 240, 241; Shultz, 671.

34. Jenkins (A), 7. The Genoa Court later ruled that the hijackers' claim—that they intended to attack Israelis in Ashdod—was a "smokescreen," and that the only operation planned by Abul Abbas was the hijacking of the ship. The Court said, "To land at Ashdod . . . would not have been possible. . . . The checks carried out by the Israeli agents before passengers are allowed to land at the port are so thorough and efficient that not only would the four never have got[ten] off the ship, but they would never have got[ten] as far as the gangplank . . . according to the witnesses, the [Israeli] officials could certainly not have missed the fact that Fataier, who looks typically Middle Eastern and speaks only Arabic, could not pass for a Norwegian called Stale Wan, as his passport declared . . . the operation would have been of a 'suicide' type, but it is also true that such operations require that, before dying, as many of the enemy as possible are killed and maximum damage is wrought. In our case, as we have seen, neither of these requirements could have been fulfilled, not only because the arms and munitions were totally inadequate, but, above all, because of the extremely stringent security measures adopted by the Israelis." Cassese, 109–112.

35. Interview with Robert Oakley (2000); interview with Morton Abramowitz, January 24, 2001, Washington, DC; interview with David Long and Robert Oakley, February 13, 2001, Washington, DC. Subsequently, the Syrian government identified that the hijackers belonged to the PLF faction controlled by Abbas and passed the information on to the administration. Jenkins (A), 8.

36. Jenkins (A), 8–9.

37. Jenkins (A), 6; North and Novak, 201.

38. Ronald Reagan, *An American Life* (New York: Simon and Schuster, 1990), 508.

39. Interview with Charles Allen; William J. Crowe, Jr., with David Chanoff, *The Line of Fire: From Washington to the Gulf, the Politics and Battles of the New Military* (New York: Simon and Schuster, 1993), 119; Daniel P. Bolger, *Americans At War: 1975–1986, An Era of Violent Peace* (Novato, CA: Presidio Press, 1988), 364; Prados (1991), 20; Jenkins (A), 3, 9.

40. Interview with Parker Borg.

41. A CIA map entitled "Track of the *Achille Lauro*" shows the ship heading first to Larnaca before returning to Egyptian waters, and a CIA review of the crisis indicated that after the ship left Tartus, it was denied entry to ports in Cyprus and Lebanon before finally making for Egypt. "Terrorism Review" (Washington: Directorate of Intelligence, CIA, October 21, 1985), 11.

42. Ledeen, 176; Livingstone (1990), 254. In an interview on March 29, 2000, Weinberger denied this assertion.

43. Martin and Walcott, 241; "Testimony of Joint Hearings before House Select Committee to Investigate Covert Arms Transactions with Iran and Senate Select Committee, 1987," Oliver North, 100–107, Part I, 223.

44. North and Novak, 204.

45. CIA assessment, MORI DocID: 40146, October 9, 1985.

46. North and Novak, 204; Strober and Strober, 375.

47. Martin and Walcott, 241.

48. Spot commentary, October 9, 1985, Central Intelligence Agency.

49. Flashboard #FB548047, Bush Presidential Records, NSC, Robin Frank Files, OLN—New AL: Flashboards 28 JAN 89 [OA/ID CF00943], in folder "AL: Flashboards, Oliver L. North, NSC Staff," GBL.

50. Interview with Nick Veliotes (2000). The CIA thought the Italians would be "relieved" that the hijacking was over. However, a CIA analysis predicted that "the decision to grant free passage to the hijackers will anger some elements of the governing coalition. Spadolini and his Republicans are likely to be particularly unhappy, and during the parliamentary debate over the government's handling of the incident, Craxi may find that his coalition's cohesion has been seriously shaken." CIA assessment, MORI DocID: 40147, October 10, 1985, CIA Archives.

51. Interview with Nick Veliotes (2000).

52. Bradlee, 292.

53. Shultz, 671; Jenkins (A), 13.

54. Interview with Nick Veliotes (2000); Martin and Walcott, 243; Clarridge, 307; Shultz, 672.

55. Shultz, 672.

56. E-mail from Jock Covey to Poindexter, October 9, 1985, 15:44:21, in Blanton, 103.

57. "Press Guidance," October 9, 1985, Bush Presidential Records; NSC; Robin Frank Files; OLN—New AL: Press, 28 Jan. 89 [OA/ID CF00943] in "AL: Press, OL North, NSC Staff, GBL; E-mail from Covey to Poindexter, October 9, 1985, 15:44:21, in Blanton, 103.

58. CIA assessment, MORI DocID: 40146, October 9, 1985, CIA Archives.

59. Interview with Nick Veliotes (2000).

60. North and Novak, 205.

61. Bradlee, 293; Jenkins (A), 18; Livingstone (1990), 253; David Halevy and Neil C. Livingstone, "The Ollie We Knew," *The Washingtonian* (July 1987), 145.

62. Robert McFarlane and Zofia Smardz, *Special Trust* (New York: Cadell & Davies, 1994), 103; Howard Teicher and Gayle Radley Teicher, *Twin Pillars of Desert Storm: America's Flawed Vision in the Middle East from Nixon to Bush* (New York: William Morrow, 1993), 338; Strober and Strober, 376; North (1987), 299; Bradlee, 293; Martin and Walcott, 244. One of the intelligence sources was quickly compromised. After a briefing for members of Congress, Senator Leahy went to a morning news show and disclosed, "Through sources in President Mubarak's office, we have learned. . . ." Most in the administration were incensed at the leak, but none more so that Casey, who later "blew up" at the senator. See Joseph E. Persico, *Casey: From the OSS to the CIA* (New York: Viking Penguin, 1990), 532.

63. E-mail from Jock Covey to Poindexter, October 10, 1985, 12:04:27, in Blanton, 104. The e-mail describes the Armacost—Egyptian ambassador encounter, saying the assistant secretary was "working him over forcefully."

64. A similar plan was developed at the State Department by Morton Abramowitz, the head of INR, who suggested it to Shultz during a meeting. This undoubtedly helped smooth the administration's overall decision on the intercept, since it already had support at State. Interview with Morton Abramowitz; interview with Richard Clarke, February 13, 2001, Washington, DC.

65. Reagan (1990), 375; Strober and Strober, 376; Martin and Walcott, 245; Robert Timberg, *The Nightingale's Song* (New York: Simon and Schuster, 1995), 347; Teicher, 337.

66. North and Novak, 207; Bradlee, 294; Halevy and Livingstone, 145–146.

67. Strober and Strober, 376, 379; Crowe, 121.

68. John F. Lehman, Jr., *Command of the Seas* (NY: Charles Scribner's Sons, 1988), 365; interview with James Dorsey, September 26, 2001, Solomons, MD.

69. Interview with William Crowe, January 29, 2001, Washington, DC; interview with Richard Armitage, February 16, 2001, Arlington, VA; Crowe, 123.

70. Jenkins (A), 19.

71. Interview with Noel Koch; Jenkins (A), 22.

72. Interview with Oliver North, January 30, 2001, Washington, DC; Bob Woodward, *Veil: The Secret Wars of the CIA, 1981–1987* (New York: Simon and Schuster, 1987), 477; Jenkins (A), 18; map of Cairo "for Ollie North" from Bush Presidential Records, NSC, Robin Frank Files, OLN-New AL: Flashboards 28 JAN 89 [OA/ID CF00943] in folder "AL: Flashboards, Oliver L. North, NSC staff." Strober and Strober, 376–377; Martin and Walcott, 248.

73. Bradlee, 295.

74. Sam Donaldson, *Hold On, Mr. President!* (New York: Random House, 1987), 99–100; Prados, 23.

75. Strober and Strober, 376; Martin and Walcott, 246; Bradlee, 295.

76. Timberg, 348; McFarlane press briefing, October 11, 1985; Martin and Walcott, 247.

77. Strober and Strober, 376.

78. Timberg, 348.

79. Reagan (1990), 508; interview with William Crowe; Strober and Strober, 379; North and Novak, 208; Martin and Walcott, 248.

80. Jill Smolowe, David Halevy, and Bruce van Voorst, "Piecing Together the Drama," *Time*, October 28, 1985, 31; Jenkins (A), 20; Walcott, with Nordland, et al., 24; McFarlane, 314; Martin and Walcott, 249, 379; Teicher, 339; Strober and Strober, 376, 379. In an interview with Weinberger, the secretary said he did not oppose the plan. Instead, he claims he was raising concerns that he thought had not been fully thought through.

81. The NSDD, which is still classified, was unnumbered. The rules of engagement allowed the intercepting planes to shoot across the bow of the EgyptAir plane, but did not authorize the use of lethal force. Interview with Richard Armitage; Christopher Simpson, ed., *National Security Directives of the Reagan and Bush Administrations: The Declassified History of U.S. Political and Military Policy* (Boulder, CO: Westview Press, 1995), 459; Martin and Walcott, 249, 379; Jenkins (A), 21; Crowe, 122.

82. Shultz, 673; Cable #112033Z, October 11, 1985, Department of State; Bradlee, 295; Martin and Walcott, 249; North and Novak, 207.

83. Neil Livingstone claims that the pilot of the EgyptAir plane did not actually talk to the Tunis control tower, but in fact, to a masquerading Israeli intelligence agent. See Livingstone (1990), 259.

84. Shultz, 673.

85. Ledeen, 177; Strober and Strober, 377–378; Jenkins (A), 18; Bradlee, 295; Livingstone (1990), 257.

86. Ledeen, 177; Bradlee, 295; "Remarks of the President in Q&A Session With Press," October 11, 1985.

87. North and Novak, 209; Livingstone (1990), 259.

88. Ledeen, 179; Strober and Strober, 378; Memorandum, Tyrus Cobb to John Poindexter, October 11, 1985, NSC, Robin Frank Files, Oliver L. North—New Terrorism: Achille Lauro 28 JAN 89, [1 of 2], [OA/ID CF00943], GBL.

89. Martin and Walcott, 251–252.

90. Interview with Edwin Meese, February 8, 2001, Washington, DC; Edwin Meese III, *With Reagan: The Inside Story* (Washington, DC: Regnery Gateway, 1992), 210; Shultz, 674.

91. Vlad Jenkins, "The *Achille Lauro* Hijacking (B)" (Cambridge, MA: Kennedy School of Government), 1.

92. Revell, 270–271.

93. Interview with Duane Clarridge, March 21, 2001, Escondido, CA; Strober and Strober, 379.

94. Interview with Richard Armitage.

95. Interview with William Crowe; Crowe, 125.

96. Shultz, 674.

97. Interview with Nick Veliotes (2000).

98. Martin and Walcott, 253; Bolger, 385.

99. Ledeen, 181; Martin and Walcott, 253.

100. Off-the-record interview.

101. Jenkins (B), 9. On Friday, October 11, when the EgyptAir plane departed for Rome with Abbas aboard, Crowe ordered Stiner to follow. The two were worried that the plane might not actually be headed to Rome and that the Italians were going to let Abbas go despite the pending U.S. request to hold him for extradition. Stiner took off from Sigonella without Italian permission, and followed the plane to Ciampino Airport near Rome, where he made an unauthorized landing.

102. "Statement by the Principal Deputy Press Secretary," October 10, 1985.

103. "Terrorism Review" (Washington: Directorate of Intelligence, CIA, October 21, 1985), 2. Egypt was not the only Arab nation to encounter turmoil. In Tunisia the CIA reported that "Bourguiba . . . will be obliged by internal political considerations to seek a lower U.S. profile in Tunis." *Near East and South Asia Review* (Washington: Directorate of Intelligence, CIA, October 25, 1985), 8.

104. Woodward, 477; Situation Report No. 17, Department of State Operations Center, Achille Lauro Working Group, October 16, 1985, NSC, Robin Frank Files, Oliver L. North—New Achille Lauro: Situation Reports, 28 JAN 89, [OA/ID CF00943], GBL.

105. Interview with Nick Veliotes (2000); "Threat To Withdraw U.S. Facilities," *Kuwait KUNA* (in Arabic), October 16, 1985, FBIS, V, October 16, 1985.

106. Interview with Nick Veliotes (2000).

107. Cassese, 41.

108. "Warrant for Arrest against Abu el-Abas, aka Mohammad Zaydan, aka Mohammad Abas," "Terrorism" file, Attorney General Subject Files, box 108, Edwin Meese collection, Hoover Institution.

109. Handwritten notes by Donald Regan, daily operations meeting, October 11, 1985, folder #6, White House: notes, daily meeting, October 1985, box 190, Donald Regan Collection, Library of Congress.

110. Situation Report No. 12, Department of State Operations Center, Achille Lauro Working Group, October 13, 1985, NSC, Robin Frank Files, Oliver L. North—New Achille Lauro: Situation Reports, 28 JAN 89 [OA/ID CF00943]; Clarridge, 16.

111. Cable #130021A OCT 85, Max Rabb to George Shultz, Oliver North Files, Achille Lauro: Incoming Cables, 10/13/85 (1 of 2), Box 89, RRL; Martin and Walcott, 255.

112. CIA Analysis, October 19, 1985, MORI DocID: 40151, CIA Archives.

# NOTES FOR CHAPTER SIX

1. Geoff Simons, *Libya: The Struggle for Survival*, second edition (New York: St. Martin's Press, 1996), 263.

2. For a brief history, see Edward Schumacher, "The United States and Libya," *Foreign Affairs*, volume 65, number 2 (Winter 1986/87), 329–348.

3. Christopher Dobson and Ronald Payne, *The Never-Ending War* (New York: Facts on File, 1987), 56; David C. Martin and John Walcott, *Best Laid Plans: The Inside Story of America's War Against Terrorism* (New York: Harper & Row, Publishers, 1988), 74.

4. Memo, Richard Allen to Ronald Reagan, July 24, 1981, Libya 1981 [3/4], Box 90219, Geoff Kemp Files, RRL; Oliver L. North, with William Novak, *Under Fire: An American Story* (New York: Harper Collins Publishers, 1991), 221; Martin and Walcott, 73.

5. Interview with Richard Clarke, February 13, 2001, Washington, DC.

6. Bob Woodward, *Veil: The Secret Wars of the CIA, 1981–1987* (New York: Simon & Schuster, Inc., 1987), 87–89.

7. Ibid., 176.

8. Interview with Charles Duelfer, February 14, 2001, Washington, DC.

9. Donald Rothchild and John Ravenhill, "Global Perspectives on Africa Becomes Ascendant," in Kenneth Oye, Robert Lieber, and Donald Rothchild, eds., *Eagle Defiant* (Boston: Little, Brown and Company, 1983).

10. Caspar Weinberger, *Fighting for Peace* (New York: Warner Books, 1990), 176–77; Robert M. Gates, *From the Shadows* (New York: Simon and Schuster, 1996), 253.

11. Martin and Walcott, 68.

12. Edwin Meese III, *With Reagan: The Inside Story* (Washington, DC: Regnery Gateway, 1992), 202; Martin and Walcott, 73.

13. Philip Taubman, "U.S. Officials Say F.B.I. Is Hunting Terrorists Seeking to Kill President," *New York Times*, December 4, 1981, A1; Gates, 253; Woodward, 178; Meese, 202.

14. Woodward, 372.

15. Woodward, 198–199; Martin and Walcott, 80–81.

16. Woodward, 199–200.

17. Libya 1981 [4 of 4], box 90219, Geoffrey Kemp files, RRL.

18. Martin and Walcott, 82; Edward R. Prachman, Alan Shank, and Richard M. Pious, *Presidents and Foreign Policy: Countdown to Ten Controversial Decisions* (Albany, NY: SUNY Series on the Presidency—Contemporary Issues, 1997), 250; Christopher Simpson, ed., *National Security Directives of the Reagan and Bush Administrations: The Declassified History of U.S. Political and Military Policy, 1981–1991* (Boulder, CO: Westview Press, 1995), 17–18.

19. Martin and Walcott, 80.

20. Martin and Walcott, 260–261.

21. "The Libyan Problem," Special Report No. 111, October 1983 (Washington, DC: United States Department of State, Bureau of Public Affairs, 1983); Christopher Andrew, *For the President's Eyes Only: Secret Intelligence and the American Presidency from Washington to Bush* (New York: Harper Collins Publishers, 1995), 464.

22. Memo, Richard Beal to Robert McFarlane, March 16, 1984, Buckley Kidnapping and Omdurman Bombing, 3/16/84, Crisis Management Center, National Security Council, Records, Box 91130, RRL; Howard Teicher and Gayle Radley Teicher, *Twin Pillars to Desert Storm: America's Flawed Vision in the Middle East from Nixon to Bush* (New York: William Morrow and Co., 1993), 307.

23. For more on NSDD-138, see Chapter 3.

24. Seymour M. Hersh, "Target Qaddafi," *New York Times Magazine*, February 22, 1987, 48.

25. Woodward, 414.

26. Martin and Walcott, 262; Teicher, 308; Woodward, 415–418.

27. Woodward, 418.

28. Oliver North Notebooks, volume 11, March 8, 1985, National Security Archive.

29. Martin and Walcott, 261.

30. Directorate of Intelligence, "Libya: Supplying Terrorist Weapons," December 3, 1984, Libya (3), James Stark Files, Box 91095, RRL.

31. Interview with Vincent Cannistraro, February 8, 2001, McLean, VA; Martin and Walcott, 263–264; Teicher, 340.

32. Teicher, 340–341.

33. Gates, 351; interview with Robert Gates, February 23, 2001, College Station, TX.

34. Woodward, 470–471.

35. NSDD-168, in Simpson, 448–449, 528–529; Woodward, 471.

36. "Libya Under Qadhafi: A Pattern of Aggression," Special Report No. 138, January 1986 (Washington: Bureau of Public Affairs, United States Department of State), 2; Woodward, 472.

37. Memo, Poindexter to Fortier, June 15, 1985, Libya strike follow-up (1 of 3), Box CPC-1; FBI098, Craig P. Coy files, RRL; Gates, 352.

38. Oliver North Notebooks, volume 13, June 30, 1985 [AMX000826], National Archives.

39. Memo, James Stark to Donald Fortier, July 20, 1985, and attachment, Libya, July 1985 (1 of 3), Donald Fortier files, Box 90753, RRL.

40. Interview with Richard Armitage, February 16, 2001, Arlington, VA; Brian L. Davis, *Qaddafi, Terrorism, and the Origins of the U.S. Attack on Libya* (New York: Praeger Publishers, 1990), 70–71; Woodward, 472–475; Hersh, 48.

41. Oliver North Notebooks, volume 14, July 16, 1985 [AMX001234], National Archives; Martin and Walcott, 265; Gates, 352.

42. Interview with Robert Gates; Gates, 352; interview with Robert Oakley, April 8, 2000, Washington, DC; Woodward, 482–483; Robert Timberg, *The Nightingale's Song* (New York: Simon and Schuster, Inc., 1995), 375.

43. Gates, 352–353.

44. Interview with Nick Veliotes, June 13, 2000, McLean, VA.

45. Handwritten notes, July 22, 1985, White House—Notes, daily meetings, July 1985, Box 190, folder 2, Donald T. Regan Collection, Library of Congress.

46. Handwritten note, Poindexter to McFarlane, July 24, 1985, SRB378 TWA 847 (12), President's Special Review Board (Tower), Records, Box 93207, RRL.

47. "Libya: Qadhafi's Prospects for Survival," August 5, 1985, Directorate of Intelligence, CIA, Libya (3), Box 91095, James Stark Files, RRL.

48. Interview with Nick Veliotes (2000); Gates, 352; Woodward, 476–481; interview with Robert Oakley (2000); Teicher, 341; John Prados, *Keeper of the Keys: A History of the National Security Council from Truman to Bush* (New York: William Morrow, 1991), 504.

49. E-mail, Vincent Cannistraro to Ron Sable, October 18, 1985, National Security Archive.

50. Interview with Oliver North, January 30, 2001, Washington, DC; Davis, 80.

51. FBIS, North Africa, December 30, 1985, Q1; FBIS, North Africa, December 31, 1985, Q1.

52. Martin and Walcott, 265–266; Hersh, 48.

53. General Accounting Office, "Libya Trade Sanctions (draft)," Libya Background [1986–1988] (2 of 4), box 91843, William J. Burns files, RRL.

54. Interview with Robert Oakley (2000); Martin and Walcott, 267.

55. On January 2, Belgian police announced the arrest of two Arabs suspected of planning an attack at the Brussels airport similar to those at Rome and Vienna. The Madrid airport also heightened security after reports it was being targeted.

56. Note, December 27, 1985, White House: Notes, Daily meetings, December 1985, Box 191, folder 1, Donald Regan Collection, Library of Congress; President's Daily Schedule, December 27, 1985 [12/18/85–12/31/85], Presidential Daily Diary, Box 19, Office of the President, RRL; interview with William Martin, October 1, 2001, Washington, DC; Bernard Weinbraub, "Response to Terrorism: How President Decided," *New York Times*, January 12, 1986, A1, A12.

57. National Intelligence Daily, December 28, 1985, CIA Archives. The Syrian link, however, is weak. In an October 1985 interview with *Der Spiegel*, Abu Nidal openly declared that he was a loyal disciple of the Syrian Baath Party and believed firmly in the doctrine of a "greater Syria." But according to Robert Oakley and David Long, the Abu Nidal Organization, while accepting assistance from the Syrians during this period, was primarily a mercenary group that worked for whomever would pay. Reports that some of the surviving terrorists from Rome and Vienna were trained in the Bekaa Valley by Syrian intelligence probably hold true. However, all of the available evidence points to Libyan sponsorship of this operation, and his statement about Qaddafi in the same *Der Spiegel* article paints an equally strong relationship with Libya: "We have a deep and strong friendship. . . . He is a big help for us."

58. E-mail from Jock Covey to Donald Fortier, December 31, 1985, National Security Archive.

59. National Intelligence Daily, December 28, 1985, CIA Archives; FBIS, North Africa, December 31, 1985, Q1.

60. Telegram, Shultz to U.S. Mission at NATO, December 1985, 8, National Security Archive.

61. Interview with William Crowe, January 29, 2001, Washington, DC; interview with Vincent Cannistraro; interview with Duane Clarridge, March 21, 2001, Escondido, CA; interview with Oliver North; Teicher, 341; Daniel P. Bolger, *Americans At War: 1975–1986, An Era of Violent Peace* (Novato, CA: Presidio Press, 1988), 386. The lot numbers on the grenades were identical to those used in the Egypt Air hijacking to Malta. In addition, markings on the ammunition matched caches of weapons seized from the Libyan military in Chad in April 1987.

62. Interview with Oliver "Buck" Revell, February 22, 2001, Carrollton, TX.

63. Loren Jenkins, "Gunmen Use Grenades, Rifles," *Washington Post*, December 28, 1985.

64. "Libya Under Qadhafi . . . ," 4; Abraham Sofaer, "International Law and the Use of Force," *The National Interest*, number 13 (Fall 1988), 57.

65. Position paper, December 28, 1985, 12-28-85 (1st Post [Terrorist Attacks in] Rome, Vienna), CPPG on Libya, Elaine Morton files, Box 91758, RRL.

66. Timberg, 376.

67. "Libya Under Qadhafi . . . "; Cable #110628Z February 1986, State Department, National Security Archive; "State Support for International Terrorism, 1985," Directorate of Intelligence, 3, CIA Archives.

68. Telegram, CJSC to Secretary of State, Director of Central Intelligence, and the Secretary of Defense, December 29, 1985, National Security Archive.

69. Interview with Richard Burpee, February 26, 2001, Oklahoma City, OK; Davis, 81; William J. Crowe, Jr., with David Chanoff, *The Line of Fire: From Washington to the Gulf, the Politics and Battles of the New Military* (New York: Simon and Schuster, 1993), 132–133.

70. Phone interview with Caspar Weinberger, March 29, 2000, Washington, DC; David Blundy and Andrew Lycett, *Qaddafi and the Libyan Revolution* (London: Weidenfeld and Nicolson, 1987), 3; Prachman, et al., 263; Teicher, 342, 351.

71. E-mail from Jock Covey to Donald Fortier, December 31, 1985, National Security Archive.

72. Ronald Reagan, *An American Life* (New York: Simon and Schuster, 1990), 513–514.

73. Cable #312234Z December 1985, Department of Defense, JCS Message Center, National Security Archive; Teicher, 341–342; Weinberger, 188.

74. Martin and Walcott, 258–259.

75. George C. Wilson, "Reagan Denounces Warning By Qaddafi on Retaliation," *Washington Post*, January 3, 1986.

76. Davis, 82.

77. Interview with William Martin.

78. Appointment schedule, NSPG 125, 1-6-86 CPPG Libya (following morning NSPG), Elaine Morton files, Box 91758, RRL; Edwin Meese Schedule, January 6, 1986, Schedules, January 1986, Department of Justice Office File, Box 45, Edwin Meese Collection, Hoover Institution; President's Daily Schedule, January 6, 1986 [1/1/86–1/11/86], Presidential Daily Diary, Box 19, Office of the President, RRL.

79. Prados (1991), 503; Ben Bradlee, Jr., *Guts and Glory: The Rise and Fall of Oliver North* (New York: Donald I. Fine, Inc., 1988), 349.

80. Woodward, 498.

81. Bernard Gwertzman, "Why Reagan Shuns Force," *New York Times*, January 8, 1986.

82. Bradlee, 349; Martin and Walcott, 274.

83. Harry Anderson, with John Walcott, Thomas M. DeFrank, Margaret Garrard Warner, Kim Willenson, and Rich Tomas, "Get Tough: The Reagan Plan," *Newsweek*, January 20, 1986, 16–17.

84. See William Casey, "Collapse of the Marxist Model: America's New Calling," Address to the Union League Club, New York City, January 9, 1985, in Mark B. Liedl, ed., *Scouting the Future: The Public Speeches of William J. Casey* (Washington, DC: Regnery Gateway, 1989), 176; Anderson, 16–17.

85. Davis, 83.

86. Bernard Weinraub, "U.S., Citing Libyan Fire, Reports Attacking a Missile Site and Setting 2 Ships Ablaze in Disputed Area," *New York Times*, March 25, 1986.

87. Phone interview with George Shultz, July 24, 2001, Palo Alto, CA.

88. John F. Lehman, Jr., *Command of the Seas* (New York: Charles Scribner's Sons, 1988), 367; Robert Oakley, "International Terrorism," *Foreign Affairs*, volume 65, number 3 (February 1987), 616.

89. The joke around the Pentagon was that the level of the Mediterranean was rising because there were so many American ships there. Interview with William Crowe; interview with Richard Burpee.

90. Teicher, 343.

91. Interview with Edwin Meese, February 8, 2001, Washington, DC.

92. Crowe, 130.

93. Reagan, 515.

94. Teicher, 344–345; e-mail from Howard Teicher to John Poindexter, February 27, 1986, National Security Archive; interview with Peter Rodman, February 7, 2001, Washington, DC.

95. Lehman, 367; Charles G. Cogan, "The Response of the Strong to the Weak: The American Raid on Libya," *Intelligence and National Security*, volume 6, number 3, 614; Fred Iklé Appointment Calendar, January 6, 1986, Box 18, Fred Iklé Collection, Hoover Institution; Andrew, 483; Oliver North Notebooks, volume 17, January 6, 1985 [AMX000855], National Archives.

96. Oliver North Notebooks, volume 17, January 6, 1985 [AMX000854], National Archives.

97. Teicher, 343.

98. Anderson, et al., 16–17; Teicher, 343.

99. In addition to the IEEPA, the National Emergencies Act, Section 1114 of the Federal Aviation Act of 1958 as amended, and section 301 of title 3 of the United States Code were used to terminate American economic activity with Libya.

100. NSDD-205, in Simpson, 631, 654–655; e-mail from John Poindexter to Paul Thompson, January 8, 1986, National Security Archive.

101. Interview with John Whitehead, January 17, 2001, New York, NY; interview with Robert Oakley (2000); Martin and Walcott, 276; Frederick Zilian, Jr., "The U.S. Raid on Libya—and NATO," *Orbis*, volume 30, number 3 (Fall 1986), 503; Jo Thomas, "Britain Rules Out Joining Sanctions," *New York Times*, January 17, 1986; *The Times* (London), January 8, 1986, 5; Davis, 87.

102. Cable #082139Z, JCS to USCINCEUR, January 8, 1986, National Security Archive; Cable #121428Z January 1986, Department of Defense, JCS Message Center, National Security Archive; Cable #312234Z, USCINCEUR to JCS, January 21, 1986, National Security Archive.

103. Oliver North Notebooks, volume 14, January 13, 1986, National Security Archive.

104. Interview with Richard Burpee; Martin and Walcott, 292; Cogan, 608–609.

105. E-mail, James Stark to Donald Fortier, January 29, 1986, National Security Archive.

106. E-mail, Elaine Morton to Donald Fortier, March 7, 1986, National Security Archive.

# NOTES FOR CHAPTER SEVEN

1. E-mail, Elaine Morton to Donald Fortier, January 13, 1986, in Tom Blanton, ed., *White House E-mail* (New York: The New Press, 1995), supplementary floppy disk.

2. Edward R. Prachman, Alan Shank, and Richard M. Pious, *Presidents and Foreign Policy: Countdown to Ten Controversial Decisions* (Albany, NY: SUNY Series on the Presidency—Contemporary Issues, 1997), 256.

3. Robert E. Stumpf, "Air War with Libya," *Proceedings, US Naval Institute* (August 1986), 42; David Martin and John Walcott, *Best Laid Plans: The Inside Story of America's War Against Terrorism* (New York: Harper and Row, 1988), 274.

4. Martin and Walcott, 272; Charles G. Cogan, "The Response of the Strong to the Weak: The American Raid on Libya," *Intelligence and National Security*, volume 6, number 3 (1991), 614; Tim Zimmerman, "Coercive Diplomacy and Libya," in Alexander L. George and William E. Simons, eds.,

*The Limits of Coercive Diplomacy* (Boulder, CO: Westview Press, 1994), 213, 220–221; interview with Peter Rodman, February 7, 2001, Washington, DC.

5. Interview with Peter Rodman.

6. Interview with Howard Teicher, February 15, 2001, Washington, DC.

7. Interview with William Crowe, January 29, 2001, Washington, DC; interview with Richard Clarke, February 15, 2001, Washington, DC; interview with John Moellering, February 12, 2001, Annapolis, MD; interview with Howard Teicher; Robert Timberg, *The Nightingale's Song* (New York: Simon and Schuster, 1995), 378; Martin and Walcott, 273.

8. Bob Woodward and George Wilson, "U.S. Navy Plans to Begin Operations North of Libya," *Washington Post*, January 24, 1986, A-1, A-26.

9. Interview with Bob Woodward, February 15, 2001, Washington, DC; Bob Woodward, *Veil: The Secret Wars of the CIA, 1981–1987* (New York: Pocket Books, 1987), 502.

10. Woodward, 503.

11. Joseph E. Persico, *Casey: From the OSS to the CIA* (New York: Viking Penguin, 1990), 497.

12. Christopher Dobson and Ronald Payne, *The Never-Ending War: Terrorism in the 80's* (New York: Facts on File, 1987), 64.

13. Dobson and Payne, 72–74. On February 4, Israeli jets intercepted an airliner believed to be carrying participants from the conference on their way back to Damascus, and forced it to land in Israel. However, the Israelis picked the wrong plane, as no terrorist leaders were found aboard.

14. Interview with Richard Burpee, February 26, 2001, Oklahoma City, OK; Brian L. Davis, *Qaddafi, Terrorism, and the Origins of the U.S. Attack on Libya* (New York: Praeger Press, 1990), 89; Daniel P. Bolger, *Americans at War: 1975–1986, An Era of Violent Peace* (Novato, CA: Presidio Press), 389.

15. Cable #172220Z January 1986, Department of Defense, JCS Message Center, National Security Archive.

16. Interview with Richard Burpee; Cable #081881Z February 1986, Department of Defense, JCS Message Center, National Security Archive; Bolger, 392.

17. List of participants, March 10, 1986, 3-10-86 CPPG Libya, Box 91758, Elaine Morton files, RRL.

18. Memo, from James Stark and Howard Teicher to Donald Fortier, March 7, 1986, Libya Policy (2), Box 91747, James Stark files, RRL; Memo, James Stark to John Poindexter, March 10, 1986, Libya policy (2), Box 91747, James Stark files, RRL.

19. Schedule Proposal for NSPG meeting (129), March 10, 1986, "NSPG, Libya," box 91834, William J. Burns collection, RRL; Edwin Meese Schedule, March 14, 1986, Schedules, March 1986, Department of Justice Office File, Box 45, Edwin Meese Collection, Hoover Institution.

20. Richard Stengel, with David Beckwith and Bruce van Voost, "Sailing Into Harm's Way," *Time*, April 7, 1986, 18; Davis, 103.

21. Memo, Admiral Crowe to Caspar Weinberger, February 27, 1986, National Security Archive; Cable #280015Z February 1986, Department of Defense, JCS Message Center, National Security Archive.

22. Woodward, 508; John Prados, *Keepers of the Keys: A History of the National Security Council from Truman to Bush* (New York: William Morrow, 1991), 503–504; Seymour M. Hersh, "Target Qaddafi," *New York Times Magazine*, February 22, 1987, 71; Caspar Weinberger, *Fighting for Peace: Seven Critical Years in the Pentagon* (New York: Warner Books, 1990), 182–183.

23. E-mail, James Stark to John Poindexter, March 21, 1986, National Security Archive.

24. Contemporaneous account by Donald Regan, White House—Subject File—Libya, 1986, Donald Regan Collection, Library of Congress.

25. Interview with Richard Burpee; William J. Crowe, Jr., with David Chanoff, *The Line of Fire: From Washington to the Gulf, the Politics and Battles of the New Military* (New York: Simon and Schuster, 1993), 131.

26. Contemporaneous account by Donald Regan, White House—Subject File—Libya, 1986, Donald Regan Collection, Library of Congress; e-mail, Rod McDaniel to Ron Sable, March 24, 1986, National Security Archive; interview with Richard Burpee.

27. Gwertzman (April 16, 1986); Martin and Walcott, 284; Woodward, 513; David Halevy and Neil C. Livingstone, "The Ollie We Knew," *The Washingtonian*, July 1987, 148; Gerald Boyd, "Reagan Based Mission Approval on Reports of Danger to Envoys," *New York Times*, March 26, 1986; Oliver L. North and William Novak, *Under Fire: An American Story* (New York: Harper Collins, 1991), 215.

28. Robert Oakley, "International Terrorism," *Foreign Affairs*, volume 65, number 3 (February 1987), 617; David Blundy and Andrew Lycett, *Qaddafi and the Libyan Revolution* (London: Weidenfeld and Nicolson, 1987), 4–5; Questions and Answers for the Press Spokesman, April 14, 1986, Libya strike follow-up (1 of 3), Box CPC-1; FBI098, Craig P. Coy Files, RRL.

29. Shultz, 682; Robert M. Gates, *From the Shadows* (New York: Simon and Schuster, 1996), 353.

30. E-mail, from James Stark to Donald Fortier, March 25, 1986, in Blanton, supplemental disk.

31. E-mail note from Peter Rodman to Donald Fortier, March 25, 1986, in Blanton, supplemental disk.

32. E-mail, from James Stark to Robert Pearson, Oliver North and Rod McDaniel, March 27, 1986, in Blanton, supplemental disk.

33. E-mail note from James Stark to Robert Pearson, Oliver North and Rod McDaniel, March 27, 1986, in Blanton, supplemental disk.

34. E-mail, from John Poindexter to Robert Pearson, March 28, 1986, in Blanton, supplemental disk.

35. E-mail, from James Stark to Rod McDaniel, March 28, 1986, in Blanton, supplemental disk.

36. Oakley, 617; MORI DocID: 637388, CIA Archives.

37. Interview with Noel Koch, January 23, 2001, Potomac, MD; Christopher Andrew, *For the President's Eyes Only: Secret Intelligence and the American Presidency from Washington to Bush* (New York: Harper Collins Publishers, 1995), 483; Woodward, 513; Martin and Walcott, 285.

38. Interview with Morton Abramowitz, January 24, 2001, Washington, DC; interview with Richard Burt, February 6, 2001, Washington, DC; interview with Mark Lowenthal, January 31, 2001, Fairfax, VA; interview with Duane Clarridge, March 21, 2001, Escondido, CA; Woodward, 513; Martin and Walcott, 286.

39. Cable #050333Z APR 86, from U.S. Mission Berlin to Secretary of State, Document #1986US-BERL01013, State Department Archives.

40. Interview with Richard Burt.

41. Howard Teicher and Gayle Radley Teicher, *Twin Pillars to Desert Storm: America's Flawed Vision in the Middle East from Nixon to Bush* (New York: William Morrow and Company, 1993), 347. Reagan's Daily Schedule does not say that Poindexter was with the president in Santa Barbara, but does indicate that NSC staffer Donald Fortier was traveling with the presidential party. It is likely that Fortier called the Situation Room and then briefed the president. President's Daily Schedule, Air Force One Manifest, March 27, 1986 and April 6, 1986 [3/25/86–4/6/86], Presidential Daily Diary, Box 20, Office of the President, RRL.

42. Handwritten notes, Donald Regan, April 5, 1986, White House—Notes, Daily meetings, April 1986, Box 191, folder 5, Donald T. Regan Collection, Library of Congress.

43. Interview with Caspar Weinberger, March 29, 2000, Washington, DC; Edwin Meese III, *With Reagan: The Inside Story* (Washington, DC: Regnery Gateway, 1992), 203; Teicher, 347; Weinberger, 188; Martin and Walcott, 298; Gwertzman (April 16, 1986).

44. Interview with William Crowe.

45. Shultz, 683.

46. Cable #050725Z APR 86, from Secretary of State to US Mission Berlin, State Department Archives; Cable #051214Z APR 86, US Mission Berlin to Secretary of State, Document # 1986US-BERL01015, State Department Archives.

47. Cable #052014Z APR 86, from US Mission Berlin to Secretary of State, State Department Archives. American ambassador to Bonn, Richard Burt, delivered a similar demarche to the East German ambassador. Cable #052213Z APR 86, from Secretary of State to American Embassy Bonn, State Department Archives.

48. Cable #052344Z APR 86, from Secretary of State to US Mission Berlin, Document #1986STATE106398, State Department Archives; Cable #062055Z APR 86, from Secretary of State to US Mission Berlin, Document #1986STATE106418, State Department Archives.

49. Hendrick Smith, *The Power Game: How Washington Works* (New York: Random House, 1988), 582.

50. Interview with William Crowe; Crowe, 133.

51. Interview with Richard Burpee; Bolger, 405, 409–410; Cable #011417Z April 1986, Department of Defense, JCS Message Center, National Security Archive; Martin and Walcott, 286. According the Charles Allen, Admiral Thomas Brooks, the head of the Defense Intelligence Agency, also had a major hand in the target selection. Interview with Charles Allen, February 14, 2001, Langley, VA.

52. Teicher, 348.

53. Interview with Charles Allen.

54. William V. Cowan, "Intelligence, Rescue, Retaliation, and Decision Making," Barry Rubin, ed., *Terrorism and Politics* (New York: St. Martin's Press, 1991), 19.

55. Clarridge, 337–338; Ben Bradlee, Jr., *Guts and Glory: The Rise and Fall of Oliver North* (New York: Donald I. Fine, Inc., 1988), 353–354. Whether or not al-Marafiq was an intended target during Operation El Dorado Canyon remains open to debate. Numerous memoirs, including Clarridge's, claim that al-Marafiq was not on the final target list specifically because Reagan feared there would be too much collateral damage. This was backed up in numerous interviews, including: Richard Armitage, February 16, 1986, Arlington, VA; Richard Burpee; and William Crowe. Nonetheless, other interviewees have said that the Libyan Intelligence Headquarters was indeed the intended target of bombs that went off course, damaging the nearby French, Swiss, and Romanian embassies and the Bin Ashur residential area. These include: Caspar Weinberger; Robert Oakley, April 8, 2000, Washington, DC; James Dorsey, September 26, 2001, Solomons, MD; Vincent Cannistraro, February 8, 2001, McLean, VA; and Christopher Ross, February 6, 2001, Washington, DC.

56. Interview with James Dorsey.

57. President's Daily Schedule, April 7, 1986 [4/7/86–4/13/86], Presidential Daily Diary, Box 20, Office of the President, RRL; Donald Regan, handwritten notes, NSPG April 7, 1986, Regan Collection, Library of Congress; Ronald Reagan, *An American Life* (New York: Simon and Schuster, 1990), 518; Gates, 353.

58. Meese, 205; interview with Colonel Charles Brower, Reagan's military aide, 9/18/93, in Andrew, 483; Deborah Hart Strober and Gerald S. Strober, *Reagan: The Man and His Presidency, the Oral History of an Era* (New York: Houghton Mifflin, 1998), 382; Cogan, 614–615.

59. Oliver North Notebooks, volume 18, April 7, 1986 [AMX001058], National Archives.

60. Regan, handwritten notes, NSPG April 7, 1986. Despite Shultz's reservations, it was possible for the three aircraft carriers then in or near the Mediterranean to conduct the operation alone. Secretary of the Navy John Lehman later asserted that the Joint Chiefs' insistence that the operation be "for maximum effect" meant involving the Air Force as well. Admiral Crowe defended the move, saying that since there would only be a single round of attacks, the Navy's tools were "too limited in the weight of ordinance it could deliver." Instead, he wanted to use Air Force F-111's because their "superb fire control ideally suited them for a low-level one-pass night attack against heavy flak" (Crowe, 137). Consequently, Crowe directed the Sixth Fleet's commander, Admiral Kelso, to design a joint operation; Kelso quickly warmed to the idea, believing that if he only was going to get one shot at Qaddafi, it should be "the heaviest he could mount" (Lehman, 372). Therefore, the targets in Tripoli were assigned to the Air Force and the Navy was left to attack the targets in Benghazi. See James A. Winnefeld and Dana J. Johnson, *Joint Air Operations: Pursuit of Unity In Command and Control, 1942–91* (Annapolis, MD: Naval Institute Press, 1993), 84; Shultz, 683.

61. Regan, handwritten notes, NSPG April 7, 1986; interview with William Crowe; Teicher, 348.

62. Withdrawal sheet, #13–18, "Libya—El Dorado Canyon [6 of 10]," James Stark Collection, RRL; Geoffrey Smith, *Reagan and Thatcher* New York: W. W. Norton and Co., 1991), 189–192; Strober and Strober, 383.

63. Interview with Doug Menarchik, February 20, 2001, College Station, TX; Strober and Strober, 381.

64. Teicher, 347; Hersh, 20; Prados (1991), 506; Appointment Schedule, April 8, 1986, Fred Iklé Collection, Box 18, Hoover Institution; Duane R. Clarridge, *A Spy for all Seasons: My Life in the CIA* (New York: Scribner, 1997), 337; Neil Livingstone, *The Cult of Counterterrorism: The Weird World of Spooks, Counterterrorists, Adventurers, and the Not-Quite Professionals* (Lexington, MA: Lexington Books, 1990), 263–264.

65. Oliver North Notebooks, volume 18, April 8, 1986 [AMX001063–64], National Archives; John F. Lehman, Jr., *Command of the Seas* (New York: Charles Scribner's Sons, 1988), 371–372.

66. Persico, 498.

67. Martin and Walcott, 287–288.

68. President's Daily Schedule, April 9, 1986 [4/7/86–4/13/86], Presidential Daily Diary, Box 20, Office of the President, RRL; Halevy and Livingstone, 148; Livingstone (1991), 266.

69. Donald Regan, handwritten notes, NSPG April 9, 1986, Regan Collection, Library of Congress; Reagan, 518; Shultz, 684; Davis, 119.

70. Interview with Richard Burpee.

71. Interview with John Moellering.

72. R. W. Apple, Jr., "U.S. Plays Down Idea of NATO Split," *New York Times*, April 16, 1986, A14; Dobson and Payne, 79; Strober and Strober, 383.

73. Oliver North Notebooks, volume 18, April 9, 1986 [AMX001066], National Archives; Halevy and Livingstone, 149; Cable #100200Z April 1986, Department of Defense, National Security Archive; Martin and Walcott, 292.

74. Prados (1991), 506; Bolger, 404.

75. Interview with Robin Raphel, January 25, 2001, Washington, DC; interview with Richard Burt; interview with Richard Burpee; interview with Richard Clarke; interview with William Crowe; Crowe, 137; Cogan, 610; Davis, 127–128; Frederick Zilian, Jr., "The U.S. Raid on Libya—and NATO," *Orbis*, volume 30, number 3 (Fall 1986), 517.

76. Mail log, April 1–15, 1986, RRL.

77. Davis, 126. See also: Gerald Boyd, "U.S. Stepping Up Rebuke to Allies on World Terror," *New York Times*, April 17, 1986; Bernard Weinraub, "U.S. Says Allies Asked for More in Libya Attack," *New York Times*, April 22, 1986. These articles seem to indicate that it was the U.S. defense attaché who met with the French to request overflight on April 12; Teicher, 349; Richard Bernstein, "French Say They Favored Stronger Attack on Libya," *New York Times*, April 23, 1986; Martin and Walcott, 293.

78. Persico, 498; Halevy and Livingstone, 149; Russell Watson, with John Barry and John Walcott, "Reagan's Raiders," *Newsweek*, April 28, 1986.

79. NSC Agenda, 4/12/86, Stark files, RRL; Halevy and Livingstone, 149.

80. Timberg, 377.

81. Interview with Robert Oakley (2000); interview with David Long, April 8, 2000, Washington, DC; interview with Richard Armitage; Martin and Walcott, 296–297; George Wilson, "Colonel 'was the target,'" *The Guardian* (London), April 19, 1986. Waite and Qaddafi had met together in the past to discuss a variety of issues. See Gavin Hewitt, *Terry Waite and Ollie North: The Untold Story of the Kidnapping and the Release* (Boston, MA: Little, Brown and Company, 1991), 10–12; Persico, 498–499.

82. E. J. Dionne, "Italy Urged Consultations," *New York Times*, April 24, 1986; James M. Markham, "Libya Raids: Behind Allies' Reaction," *New York Times*, April 25, 1986.

83. Interview with Robert Oakley (2000); interview with David Long (2000).

84. Halevy and Livingstone, 150.

85. When Admiral Crowe was later asked whether Reagan would have canceled the mission if congressional opposition had been strong enough, he responded, "Hell no. He had no intention of recalling them." interview with John Whitehead, January 17, 2001, New York, NY; interview with William Crowe; NSC Talking Points for Congressional Leadership [Top Secret—Flower], Teicher files: El Dorado Canyon [1 of 4], box 91671, RRL; Strober and Strober, 381–382.

86. Interview with Parker Borg, October 4, 2001, Manassas, VA; Action against Terrorism list, May 1986, Next Steps (2/2), Box 91747, James Stark Collection, RRL.

87. Interview with Robert Oakley and David Long, February 13, 2001, Washington, DC.

88. *Die Welt*, April 16, 1991; FBIS, June 27, 1991, 29.

89. Davis, 110; interview with Neil Livingstone, January 29, 2001, Washington, DC; Martin and Walcott, 314; North, 43;

# NOTES FOR CHAPTER EIGHT

1. Graham Allison and Philip Zelikow, *Essence of Decision: Explaining the Cuban Missile Crisis*, second edition (New York: Addison Wesley Longman, Inc., 1999), 300.

2. Memo, Fred Iklé to Richard Allen, January 14, 1981, "Iran" folder, Box 14, Fred C. Iklé Collection, Hoover Institution Archives.

3. Oliver L. North, *Taking the Stand: The Testimony of Lieutenant Colonel Oliver L. North* (New York: Pocket Books, 1987), 508.

4. Interview with Richard Armitage, February 16, 2001, Arlington, VA.

5. Richard E. Neustadt, *Presidential Power and the Modern Presidents: The Politics of Leadership from Roosevelt to Reagan* (New York: Free Press, 1990), 10.

# Bibliography

## BOOKS

Allison, Graham, and Philip Zelikow. *Essence of Decision: Explaining the Cuban Missile Crisis*, 2nd edition. New York: Addison Wesley Longman, 1996.

Anderson, Martin. *Revolution*. New York: Harcourt Brace Jovanovich, 1988.

Andrew, Christopher. *For the President's Eyes Only: Secret Intelligence and the American Presidency from Washington to Bush*. New York: Harper Collins Publishers, 1995.

Barrett, Laurence. *Gambling With History: Ronald Reagan in the White House*. Garden City, NY: Doubleday, 1983.

Betts, Richard. *Soldiers, Statesmen, and Cold War Crises*. Cambridge, MA: Harvard University Press, 1977.

Bill, James A. *The Eagle and the Lion: The Tragedy of American-Iranian Relations*. New Haven, CT: Yale University Press, 1988.

Blanton, Tom. *White House E-Mail*. New York: The New Press, 1995.

Blundy, David, and Andrew Lycett. *Qaddafi and the Libyan Revolution*. London: Weidenfeld and Nicolson, 1987.

Bolger, Daniel P. *Americans at War: 1975–1986, An Era of Violent Peace*. Novato, CA: Presidio Press, 1988.

Bradlee, Ben, Jr. *Guts and Glory: The Rise and Fall of Oliver North*. New York: Donald I. Fine, Inc., 1988.

Brownlie, Ian. *International Law and the Use of Force by States*. Oxford: Carendon Press, 1963.

Brzezinski, Zbigniew. *Power and Principle*. New York: Farrar, Straus, Giroux, 1983.

Bull, Hedley. *Anarchical Society*. London: Macmillan, 1977.

*Cabinets and Counselors: The President and the Executive Branch*. Washington, DC: Congressional Quarterly, 1989.

Cahill, Kevin M., ed. *Preventive Diplomacy: Stopping Wars Before They Start*. New York: Routledge, 2000.

Cannon, Lou. *President Reagan: The Role of a Lifetime*. New York: Simon and Schuster, 1991.

———. *President Reagan: The Role of a Lifetime*, revised edition. New York: PublicAffairs, 2000.

Carter, Jimmy. *Keeping Faith: Memoirs of a President*. New York: Bantam Books, 1982.

Cassese, Antonio. *Terrorism, Politics and Law: The* Achille Lauro *Affair*. Princeton, NJ: Princeton University Press, 1989.

Celmer, Marc A. *Terrorism, U.S. Strategy, and Reagan Policies*. Westport, CT: Greenwood Press, 1987.

Clarridge, Duane R. *A Spy for all Seasons: My Life in the CIA*. New York: Scribner, 1997.

Cline, Ray S. *The CIA Under Reagan, Bush and Casey*. Washington, DC: Acropolis Books, 1981.

Crowe, William J., Jr., with David Chanoff. *The Line of Fire: From Washington to the Gulf, the Politics and Battles of the New Military*. New York: Simon and Schuster, 1993.

Davis, Brian L. *Qaddafi, Terrorism, and the Origins of the U.S. Attack on Libya*. New York: Praeger Publishers, 1990.

Deaver, Michael, and Michael Herskowitz. *Behind the Scenes*. New York: William Morrow, 1987.

Destler, I. M., Leslie H. Gelb, and Anthony Lake. *Our Own Worst Enemy: The Unmaking of American Foreign Policy*. New York: Simon and Schuster, 1984.

Dobson, Christopher, and Ronald Payne. *The Never-Ending War: Terrorism in the 80's*. New York: Facts on File, 1987.

Donaldson, Sam. *Hold On, Mr. President!* New York: Random House, 1987.

Dore, Isaak I. *International Law and the Superpowers: Normative Order in a Divided World*. New Brunswick, NJ: Rutgers University Press, 1984.

Dugger, Ronnie. *On Reagan: The Man and His Presidency*. New York: McGraw Hill, 1983.

Endicott, John E., and Roy W. Stafford, eds. *American Defense Policy*, 4th edition. Baltimore, MD: Johns Hopkins University Press, 1977.

Etheredge, Lloyd S. *A World of Men: The Private Sources of American Foreign Policy*. Cambridge, MA: MIT Press, 1978.

Evans, Roland, and Robert Novak. *The Reagan Revolution*. New York: E.P. Dutton, 1981.

Frank, Benis M. *U.S. Marines in Lebanon, 1982–1984*. Washington, DC: History and Museums Division, Headquarters, United States Marine Corps, 1987.

Gates, Robert M. *From the Shadows*. New York: Simon and Schuster, 1996.

George, Alexander. *Presidential Decisionmaking in Foreign Policy: The Effective Use of Information and Advice*. Boulder, CO: Westview Press, 1978.

———, and William E. Simons, eds. *The Limits of Coercive Diplomacy*. Boulder, CO: Westview Press, 1994.

———, and Juliette L. George. *Presidential Personality and Performance*. Boulder, CO: Westview Press, 1998.

Greenstein, Fred I., ed. *The Reagan Presidency: An Early Assessment*. Baltimore, MD: Johns Hopkins University Press, 1983.

Gup, Ted. *Book of Honor: Covert Lives and Classified Deaths*. New York: Doubleday, 2000.

Haig, Alexander M., Jr. *Caveat: Realism, Reagan, and Foreign Policy*. New York: Macmillan Publishing Company, 1984.

Halperin, Morton H. *Bureaucratic Politics and Foreign Policy*. Washington, DC: Brookings Institution, 1974.

Hamilton, Gary G., and Nicole Woolsey Biggart. *Governor Reagan, Governor Brown: A Sociology of Executive Power*. New York: Columbia University Press, 1984.

Hammel, Eric. *The Root: The Marines in Beirut, August 1982–February 1984*. New York: Harcourt Brace Jovanovich Publishers, 1985.

Hastedt, Glenn P. *American Foreign Policy: Past, Present, Future*, 2nd edition. Englewood Cliffs, NJ: Prentice Hall, 1991.

Hewitt, Gavin. *Terry Waite and Ollie North: The Untold Story of the Kidnapping and the Release*. Boston, MA: Little, Brown and Company, 1991.

Higgins, Rosalyn, and Maurice Flory, *Terrorism and International Law*. New York: Routledge, 1997.

Hilsman, Roger. *The Politics of Policy Making in Defense and Foreign Affairs: Conceptual Models and Bureaucratic Politics*, 2nd edition. Englewood Cliffs, NJ: Prentice Hall, 1990.

Hoxie, R. Gordon, ed. *The Presidency and National Security Policy*. New York: Center for the Study of the Presidency, 1984.

Huntington, Samuel P. *The Soldier and the State: The Theory and Politics of Civil-Military Relations*. Cambridge, MA: Harvard University Press, 1957.

Inderfurth, Karl F., and Loch K. Johnson, eds. *Decisions of the Highest Order: Perspectives on the National Security Council*. Pacific Grove, CA: Brooks/Cole Publishing Co., 1988.

Jervis, Robert. *Perception and Misperception in International Politics*. Princeton, NJ: Princeton University Press, 1976.

Jones, Charles O. *The Reagan Legacy: Promise and Performance*. Chatham, NJ: Chatham House Publishers, Inc., 1988.

Jordan, Amos A., William T. Taylor, Jr., and Lawrence J. Korb. *American National Security Policy and Process*, 3rd edition. Baltimore, MD: Johns Hopkins University Press, 1989.

Kegley, Charles W., Jr., and Eugene R. Wittkopf, eds. *The Domestic Sources of American Foreign Policy: Insights and Evidence*. New York: St. Martin's Press, 1988.

Keraagac, John. *Between Promise and Policy: Ronald Reagan and Conservative Reformism*. Lanham, MD: Lexington Books, 2000.

Ledeen, Michael A. *Perilous Statecraft: An Insider's Account of the Iran-Contra Affair*. New York: Charles Scribner's Sons, 1988.

Lehman, John F., Jr. *Command of the Seas*. New York: Charles Scribner's Sons, 1988.

Liedl, Mark B., ed. *Scouting the Future: The Public Speeches of William J. Casey*. Washington, DC: Regnery Gateway, 1989.

Lindblom, Charles E. *The Intelligence of Democracy: Decision Making Through Mutual Adjustment*. New York: Free Press, 1965.

Livingstone, Neil C, ed. *Beyond the Iran-contra Crisis: The Shape of U.S. Anti-Terrorism Policy in the Post-Reagan Era*. Lexington, MA: Lexington Books, 1988.

———. *The Cult of Counterterrorism: The "Weird World" of Spooks, Counterterrorists, Adventurers, and the Not-Quite Professionals*. Lexington, MA: Lexington Books, 1990.

———, and Terrell E. Arnold, eds. *Fighting Back: Winning the War Against Terrorism*. Lexington, MA: Lexington Books, 1985.

Long, David. *The Anatomy of Terrorism*. New York: Free Press, 1990.

Martin, David C., and John Walcott. *Best Laid Plans: The Inside Story of America's War Against Terrorism*. New York: Harper and Row, 1988.

McCarthy, Shawn R. *The Function of Intelligence in Crisis Management*. Brookfield, VT: Ashgate Publishing Co., 1998.

McFarlane, Robert C., and Zofia Smardz. *Special Trust*. New York: Cadell and Davies, 1994.

Meese, Edwin III. *With Reagan: The Inside Story*. Washington, DC: Regnery Gateway, 1992.

Melanson, Richard A. *American Foreign Policy Since the Vietnam War: The Search for Consensus from Nixon to Clinton*, 3rd edition. New York: M. E. Sharpe, Inc., 2000.

Menges, Constantine C. *Inside the National Security Council: The True Story of the Making and Unmaking of Reagan's Foreign Policy*. New York: Simon and Schuster, 1989.

Morris, Edmund. *Dutch: A Memoir of Ronald Reagan*. New York: Random House, 1999.

Netanyahu, Benjamin, ed. *Terrorism: How the West Can Win*. New York: Farrar, Straus, Giroux, 1986.

Neustadt, Richard. *Presidential Power and the Modern Presidents: The Politics of Leadership from Roosevelt to Reagan*. New York: Macmillan, 1990.

North, Oliver L. *Taking the Stand: The Testimony of Lieutenant Colonel Oliver L. North*. New York: Pocket Books, 1987.

———, and William Novak. *Under Fire: An American Story*. New York: Harper Collins, 1991.

Oye, Kenneth, Robert Lieber, and Donald Rothchild, eds. *Eagle Defiant*. Boston, MA: Brown and Company, 1983.

Parker, Richard B. *The Politics of Miscalculation in the Middle East*. Bloomington, IN: Indiana University Press, 1993.

Patterson, Bradley H., Jr. *The Ring of Power: The White House Staff and its Expanding Role in Government*. New York: Basic Books, 1988.

Perry, Mark. *Four Stars: The Inside Story of the Forty-Year Battle Between the Join Chiefs of Staff and America's Civilian Leaders*. Boston, MA: Houghton Mifflin, 1989.

Persico, Joseph E. *Casey: From the OSS to the CIA.* New York: Viking Penguin, 1990.

Pfiffner, James P., ed. *The Managerial Presidency.* Pacific Grove, CA: Brooks/Cole Publishing Co., 1991.

Pfaltzgraff, Robert L. and Jacquelyn K. Davis, eds. *National Security Decisions: The Participants Speak.* Lexington, MA: Lexington Books, 1990.

Philpott, Daniel. *Revolutions in Sovereignty: How Ideas Shaped Modern International Relations.* Princeton, NJ: Princeton University Press, 2001.

Prachman, Edward R., Alan Shank, and Richard M. Pious. *Presidents and Foreign Policy: Countdown to Ten Controversial Decisions.* Albany, NY: SUNY Series on the Presidency—Contemporary Issues, 1997.

Prados, John. *Presidents' Secret Wars: C.I.A. and Pentagon Covert Operations since World War II.* New York: William Morrow, 1986.

——. *Keepers of the Keys: A History of the National Security Council from Truman to Bush.* New York: William Morrow, 1991.

Quandt, William B. *Camp David: Peacemaking and Politics.* Washington, DC: Brookings Institution, 1986.

——. *The Middle East: Ten Years after Camp David.* Washington, DC: Brookings Institution, 1988.

——. *Peace Process: American Diplomacy and the Arab-Israeli Conflict since 1967,* revised edition. Washington, DC: Brookings Institution, 2001.

Reagan, Ronald. *The Creative Society: Some Comments on Problems Facing America.* New York: Devin-Adair, 1968.

——. *An American Life.* New York: Simon and Schuster, 1990.

Regan, Donald. *For the Record: From Wall Street to Washington.* New York: Harcourt, Brace and Jovanovich, 1988.

Regan, Richard J. *Just War: Principles and Cases.* Washington, DC: Catholic University of America Press, 1996.

Revell, Oliver "Buck," and Dwight Williams. *A G-Man's Journal.* New York: Simon and Schuster, 1998.

Rubin, Barry. *Secrets of State: The State Department and the Struggle over U.S. Foreign Policy.* New York: Oxford University Press, 1985.

——, ed. *Terrorism and Politics.* New York: St. Martin's Press, 1991.

Salamon, Lester M., and Michael S. Lund, eds. *The Reagan Presidency and the Governing of America.* Washington, DC: The Urban Institute Press, 1985.

Schmertz, Eric J., Natalie Datlof, and Alexej Ugrinsky, eds. *President Reagan and the World.* Westport, CT: Greenwood Press, 1997.

Schiff, Ze'ev, and Ehud Ya'ari (edited and translated by Ina Friedman). *Israel's Lebanon War.* New York: Simon and Schuster, 1984.

Shultz, George P. *Triumph and Turmoil: My Years as Secretary of State.* New York: Charles Scribners' Sons, 1993.

Simon, Jeffrey D. *The Terrorist Trap: America's Experience with Terrorism.* Bloomington, IN: Indiana University Press, 1994.

Simons, Geoff. *Libya: The Struggle for Survival,* 2nd edition. New York: St. Martin's Press, 1996.

Simpson, Christopher, ed., *National Security Directives of the Reagan and Bush Administrations: The Declassified History of U.S. Political and Military Policy, 1981–1991.* Boulder, CO: Westview Press, 1995.

Skinner, Kiron K., Annelise Anderson, and Martin Anderson, eds. *In His Own Hand: The Writings of Ronald Reagan That Reveal His Revolutionary Vision For America.* New York: The Free Press, 2001.

Smith, Geoffrey. *Reagan and Thatcher.* New York: W. W. Norton and Company, 1991.

Smith, Hendrick. *The Power Game: How Washington Works.* New York: Random House, 1988.

Smith, Jean E. *The Constitution and American Foreign Policy.* St. Paul, MN: West Publishing Company, 1989.

Speakes, Larry, with Robert Pack. *Speaking Out: The Reagan Presidency from Inside the White House*. New York: Scribner, 1988.

Spiegel, Steven L., Mark A. Heller, and Jacob Goldberg, eds. *The Soviet-American Competition in the Middle East*. Lexington, MA: Lexington Books, 1988.

Sterling, Claire. *The Terror Network: The Secret War of International Terrorism*. New York: Holt, Rinehart and Winston, 1981.

Stockman, David. *The Triumph of Politics: The Inside Story of the Reagan Revolution*. New York: Avon Books, 1986.

Strober, Deborah Hart, and Gerald S. Strober. *Reagan: The Man and His Presidency, The Oral History of an Era*. New York: Houghton Mifflin, 1998.

Tanter, Raymond. *Who's At the Helm? Lessons of Lebanon*. Boulder, CO: Westview Press, 1990.

Teicher, Howard, and Gayle Radley Teicher. *Twin Pillars to Desert Storm: America's Flawed Vision in the Middle East from Nixon to Bush*. New York: William Morrow and Company, Inc., 1993.

Timberg, Robert. *The Nightingale's Song*. New York: Simon and Schuster, Inc., 1995.

Tower, John, Edmund Muskie, and Brent Scowcroft. *The Tower Commission Report*. New York: Random House, 1987.

Tucker, David. *Skirmishes at the Edge of Empire: The United States and International Terrorism*. Westport, CT: Prager Publishers, 1997.

United Nations, *Yearbook of the International Law Commission, 1949*. New York: United Nations, 1949.

———, *Yearbook of the International Law Commission, 1954, volume 1*. New York: United Nations, 1954.

Walzer, Michael. *Just and Unjust Wars: A Moral Argument with Historical Illustrations*. New York: Basic Books, 1977.

Warburg, Gerlad Felix. *Conflict and Consensus: The Struggle Between Congress and the President over Foreign Policymaking*. New York: Harper and Row Publishers, 1989.

Weinberger, Caspar. *Fighting for Peace: Seven Critical Years in the Pentagon*. New York, Warner Books, 1990.

White, Theodore H. *America in Search of Itself: The Making of the President 1956–1980*. New York: Harper & Row, 1982.

Wilson, George C. *Super Carrier*. New York: Macmillan Publishing Company, 1983.

Winnefeld, James A., and Dana J. Johnson. *Joint Air Operations: Pursuit of Unity In Command and Control, 1942–91*. Annapolis, MD: Naval Institute Press, 1993.

Woodward, Bob. *Veil: The Secret Wars of the CIA, 1981–1987*. New York: Pocket Books, 1987.

Wright, Robin. *In the Name of God: The Khomeini Decade*. New York: Simon and Schuster, 1989.

# ARTICLES AND PAPERS

"An Interview with William Casey." *Time*, October 28, 1985.

Anderson, Harry, with John Walcott, Thomas M. DeFrank, Margaret Garrard Warner, Kim Wiltenson, and Rich Tomas. "Get Tough: The Reagan Plan." *Newsweek*, January 20, 1986.

"A Team Player for the Pentagon." *Time*, December 22, 1980.

Barrett, Laurence. "Meet the Real Ronald Reagan." *Time*, October 20, 1980.

Bowett, Derek. "Reprisals Involving Recourse to Armed Force." *American Journal of International Law*, volume 66 (1972).

Church, George J. "How Reagan Decides." *Time*, December 13, 1982.

"CIA Facing Witch-Hunt—Reagan." *San Jose Mercury*, August 24, 1975.

Cogan, Charles G. "The Response of the Strong to the Weak: The American Raid on Libya." *Intelligence and National Security*, volume 6, number 3 (1991).

Conant, Jennet, with John Barry. "An Officer and Intellectual." *Newsweek*, July 22, 1985.

Costello, David. "International Terrorism and the Development of the Principle *Aut Dedere Aut Judicare*." *Journal of International Law and Economics*, volume 10 (1975).

"The Crisis Manager at Reagan's Elbow." *US News and World Report*, July 8, 1985.

Crowe, William. "The Persian Gulf: Central or Peripheral to United States Strategy?" *U.S. Naval Institute Proceedings*, May 1978.

Crozier, Brian. "Reagan and Israel." *National Review*, October 15, 1982.

Davis, Tami R., and Sean M. Lynn-Jones. "City Upon A Hill." *Foreign Policy*, volume 66 (Spring 1987).

"Defense Chief Weinberger on Peace Prospects Now." *US News and World Report*, September 27, 1982.

Deming, Angus, with Holger Jensen, James Pringle, and Joyce Barnathan. "Blood and Terror in Beirut." *Newsweek*, May 2, 1983.

———, with James Pringle, Ray Wilkinson, John Walcott, Kim Willenson, and Milan Kubic. "A U.S. Clash with Syria." *Newsweek*, December 12, 1983.

Dillon, Robert. "Caught in the Crossfire." *Duke Alumni Magazine*, Summer 1986.

Doubrava, Dave. "U.S. Has Identified Hijackers—Shultz." *Washington Times*, July 2, 1985, A1.

Dowd, Ann Reilly. "What Managers Can Learn from Manager Reagan." *Fortune*, September 15, 1986.

Dudney, Robert S. "How NSC Director Exercises Power." *US News and World Report*, October 31, 1983.

Fromm, Joseph, with Don Reeder, James M. Hildreth, Robert A. Kittle, and Jeffrey L. Sheler. "Agonizing Decisions." *US News and World Report*, November 7, 1983.

Gaddis, John Lewis. "The Rise, Fall, and Future of Détente." *Foreign Affairs*, volume 62 (Winter 1983–1984).

Gelb, Leslie. "Why Not the State Department?" *The Washington Quarterly*, Autumn 1980.

———. "Taking Charge: The Rising Power of National Security Advisor Robert McFarlane." *New York Times Magazine*, May 26, 1985.

Glad, Betty. "Black and White Thinking: Ronald Reagan's Approach to Foreign Policy." *Political Psychology*, volume 4, number 1 (1983).

Gordon, Michael R. "The Pentagon Under Weinberger May Be Biting Off More Than Even It Can Chew." *National Journal*, volume 16, number 5 (February 4, 1984).

Greenstein, Fred I. "Ronald Reagan—Another Hidden Hand Ike?" *Political Science and Politics*, volume 33, number 1 (March 1990).

Gromoll, Robert H. "The May 17 Accord: Studies of Diplomacy and Negotiations on Troop Withdrawals from Lebanon." Pittsburgh, PA: Graduate School of Public and International Affairs, University of Pittsburgh, 1987.

Gutman, Roy. "Battle Over Lebanon." *Foreign Service Journal*, June 1984.

Halevy, David, and Neil C. Livingstone. "The Ollie We Knew." *The Washingtonian*, July 1987.

Hersh, Seymour M. "Target Qaddafi." *New York Times Magazine*, February 22, 1987.

Hildreth, James M. "A Quiet Voice, with Authority." *US News and World Report*, June 16, 1986.

Hollis, Martin, and Steve Smith. "Roles and Reasons in Foreign Policy Decision Making." *British Journal of Political Science*, volume 16, part 3 (July 1986).

"Islamic Terror in U.S.?" *Washington Times*, June 20, 1985.

Jenkins, Vlad. "The *Achille Lauro* Hijacking." Cambridge, MA: Kennedy School of Government.

Joyner, Christopher C. "In Search of an Anti-Terrorist Policy: Lessons from the Reagan Era." *Terrorism: An International Journal*, volume 11 (1988).

Kennedy, David, and Richard Haass. "The Reagan Administration and Lebanon." *Pew Program in Case Teaching and Writing in International Affairs*, Case number 340. Pittsburgh, PA: Pew Charitable Trusts, 1988.

———. "The Extradition of Mohammed Hamadei." Case Program #C15-88-835.0. Berkeley, MA: Kennedy School of Government, Harvard University, 1988.

Kirsschten, Dick. "White House Notebook." *National Journal*, volume 19, number 32.

Kondracke, Morton. "Nowhere Man." *The New Republic*, May 16, 1983.

————. "Tinker, Tinker, Tinker, Spy." *The New Republic*, November 28, 1983.

Manning, Robert A., with Steven Emerson and Charles Fenyvesi. "Casey's CIA: New Clout, New Danger." *US News and World Report*, June 16, 1986.

McFarlane, Robert C. "The Political Potential of Parity." *U.S. Naval Institute Proceedings*, February 1979.

Menarchik, Doug. "Organizing to Combat 21st Century Terrorism." Paper prepared for the Institute for National Security Studies, United States Air Force Academy, July 28, 1999.

"New Evidence Ties Iran to Terrorism." *Newsweek*, November 15, 1999.

*New York Times*, December 4, 1981–January 12, 1987.

Oakley, Robert. "International Terrorism," *Foreign Affairs*, volume 65, number 3 (February 1987).

O'Brien, William V. "Reprisals, Deterrence and Self-Defense in Counterterror Operations." *Virginia Journal of International Law*, volume 30, number 2 (Winter 1990).

"Opinion Roundup." *Public Opinion* (December/January 1981).

Powell, Stewart, with Joseph P. Shapiro, O. Kelly, Dennis Mullin, and Robert S. Dudney. "White House's Key Players When the Chips are Down." *US News and World Report*, July 1, 1983.

Quandt, William B. "Reagan's Lebanon Policy: Trial and Error." *The Middle East Journal*, volume 38, number 2 (spring 1984).

Randolph, Eleanor. "O'Neill Scuttles House Push for Quick Lebanon Pullout." *Los Angeles Times*, October 27, 1983.

"Reagan sees peril to agents of CIA." *Palo Alto Times*, March 4, 1975.

Richelson, Jeffrey T. "Truth Conquers All Chains: The U.S. Army Intelligence Support Activity, 1981–1989." *International Journal of Intelligence and Counterintelligence*, volume 12, number 2 (Summer 1999).

Rubin, Barry, and Laura Blum. "The May 1983 Agreement Over Lebanon." *Pew Program in Case Teaching and Writing in International Affairs*, Case #312. Pittsburgh, PA: Pew Charitable Trusts, 1988.

Scheffer, David. "Toward a Modern Doctrine of Humanitarian Intervention." *University of Toledo Law Review*, volume 23, number 2 (1992).

Schumacher, Edward. "The United States and Libya." *Foreign Affairs*, volume 65, number 2 (Winter 1986/87).

"Show and Tell." *Time*, March 31, 1985.

Smolowe, Jill, David Halevy, and Bruce van Voorst. "Piecing Together the Drama." *Time*. October 28, 1985.

Snyder, Robert A. "Negotiating with Terrorists: TWA Flight 847." Washington, DC: The Institute for the Study of Diplomacy, School of Foreign Service, Georgetown University, 1994.

Sofaer, Abraham D. "Terrorism and the Law." *Foreign Affairs,* volume 64, number 5 (Summer 1986).

————. "International Law and the Use of Force." *The National Interest*, volume 13 (Fall 1988).

————, "Terrorism, the Law, and the National Defense." *Military Law Review*, volume 126 (June 1989).

Sprout, Harold, and Margaret Sprout, "Environmental Factors in the Study of International Politics." *Journal of Conflict Resolution*, volume 1 (December 1957).

Stengel, Richard, with David Beckwith and Bruce van Voost. "Sailing Into Harm's Way." *Time*, April 7, 1986.

Stumpf, Robert E. "Air War with Libya," *Proceedings, US Naval Institution* (August 1986).

Thompson, David. *The Listener*, volume 63 (London, May 5, 1960).

Treverton, Gregory F., with Douglas Horner and James Dickinson, "Deciding to Use Force in Grenada," Case Study number C96-88-795.0. Kennedy School of Government, Harvard University, 1986.

"Troubles in Lebanon." Draft case study, Kennedy School of Government, Harvard University.

Tyrrell, R. Emmett, Jr. "A World Without Russians." *The Alternative: An American Spectator*, volume 10, number 8 (May 1977).

"U.S. Reprisal Raid: On Hold." *Newsweek*, December 12, 1983.

Walcott, John, with Rod Nordland, Theodore Stanger, Milan J. Kubic, Andrew Nagorski, John Barry, and Susan Agrest. "Getting Even." *Newsweek*, October 21, 1985.

*Wall Street Journal*, January 3, 1984–July 1, 1985.

*Washington Post*, August 15, 1979–January 24, 1986.

"Washington Whispers." *US News and World Report*, November 26, 1984.

Watson, Douglas, and Robin Knight. "Lebanon: High Risk in Staying On—or Getting Out." *US News and World Report*, November 7, 1983.

Watson, Russell, with Nicholas Horrock and Abdul Hajjaj. "Fighting Terror with Terror." *Newsweek*, May 27, 1985.

———, with Rod Nordland, Milan J. Kubic, John Walcott, Margaret Garrard Warner, and Kim Willenson. "We Eat, We Sleep, We Pray." *Newsweek*, July 1, 1985.

———, with John Barry and John Walcott. "Reagan's Raiders." *Newsweek*, April 28, 1986.

Whitaker, Mark, with James Pringle, Milan Kubic, and Jane Whitmore. "Lebanon: An Eye for an Eye." *Newsweek*, November 28, 1983.

———, and Harry Anderson, with Rod Nordland, Michael A. Lerner, John Walcott, and Kim Willenson. "An Odyssey of Terror." *Newsweek*, June 24, 1985.

———, with Kim Willenson and John Walcott. "Reagan's Options." *Newsweek*, July 8, 1985.

———, with John Walcott, Margaret Garrard Warner, and Kim Willenson. "Diplomacy by Carrot and Stick." *Newsweek*, July 15, 1985.

Wilentz, Amy. "Managing the Crisis." *Time*, June 15, 1985.

Wilson, George C. "Colonel 'was the target.'" *The Guardian* (London), April 19, 1986.

Zilian, Frederick, Jr. "The U.S. Raid on Libya—and NATO." *Orbis*, volume 30, number 3 (Fall 1986).

# GOVERNMENT PUBLICATIONS

"Adequacy of U.S. Marine Corps Security in Beirut, Summary of Findings and Conclusions." Report of the Investigations Subcommittee of the Committee on Armed Services, United States Congress, House, 98th Congress, 1st session, December 19, 1983.

"The Beirut Hostages: Background to the Crisis." Washington, DC: Foreign Affairs and National Defense Division, Congressional Research Service, The Library of Congress, June 21, 1985.

"Libya Under Qadhafi: A Pattern of Aggression." *Special Report #138*. Washington, DC: United States Department of State, Bureau of Public Affairs, 1986.

"The Libyan Problem." *Special Report #111*. Washington, DC: United States Department of State, Bureau of Public Affairs, 1983.

"Nomination of Caspar Weinberger to be Secretary of Defense." Hearings before the Committee on Armed Services, United States Senate, 97th Congress, 1st session, January 6, 1981.

"Nomination of John W. Vessey, Jr., to be Chairman of the Joint Chiefs of Staff." Hearings before the Committee on Armed Services, United States Senate, 97th Congress, 2nd session, May 11, 1982.

"Nomination of William J. Crowe, Jr., to be Chairman, Joint Chiefs of Staff." Hearings before the Committee on Armed Services, United States Senate, 99th Congress, 1st session, July 30, 1985.

Oakley, Robert. "International Terrorism: Current Trends and the U.S. Response." *Circular #706*. Washington, DC: United States Department of State, Bureau of Public Affairs, Office of Communications, May 1985.

Perry, William. *Report of the Secretary of Defense to the President and Congress.* Washington, DC: United States Government Printing Office, 1996.

"Public Report of the Vice President's Task Force on Combatting Terrorism." Washington, DC: United States Government Printing Office, February 1986.

Reagan, Ronald. *Public Papers of the Presidents of the United States: Ronald Reagan.* Washington, DC: United States Government Printing Office.

———. *Weekly Compilation of Presidential Documents.*

"Report of the DOD Commission on Beirut International Airport Terrorist Act, October 23, 1983 (Long Commission)," December 20, 1983.

Sayre, Robert M. "International Terrorism: A Long Twilight Struggle," Department of State Bulletin #84. Washington, DC: Department of State, Bureau of Public Affairs, October 1984.

Shultz, George P. "Statement of George P. Shultz of California to be Secretary of State." U.S. Congress, Senate, Committee on Foreign Relations, 97th Congress, 2nd session, 13–14 July, 1982.

———. "Realism, Strength, Negotiations: Key Foreign Policy Statements of the Reagan Administration." Washington, DC: United States Department of State, Bureau of Public Affairs, May 1984.

———. "The United States and Israel: Partners for Peace and Freedom." *Current Policy*, number 690. Washington, DC: United States Department of State, Bureau of Public Affairs, April 21, 1985.

———. *Report of the Secretary of State's Advisory Panel on Overseas Security.* Washington, DC: United States Department of State, June 1985.

———. "Terrorism and the Modern World." Current Policy, number 629. Washington, DC: United States Department of State, Bureau of Public Affairs, October 25, 1984.

United States Department of State. *Patterns of Global Terrorism: 1988–1989.* Washington, DC: United States Department of State, 1989.

## ARCHIVAL RESOURCES

Central Intelligence Agency
George Bush Presidential Library, Texas A&M University, College Station, Texas
Hoover Institution, Stanford University, Palo Alto, California
Library of Congress, Washington, DC
National Archives, College Park, MD
National Security Archive, George Washington University, Washington, DC
Ronald Reagan Presidential Library, Simi Valley, California
United States Department of State

## INTERVIEWS

Abramowitz, Morton. January 24, 2001, Washington, DC.
Allen, Charles. February 14, 2001, Langley, VA.
Armitage, Richard. February 16, 2001, Arlington, VA.
Borg, Parker. October 4, 2001, Manassas, VA.
Burpee, Richard. February 26, 2001, Oklahoma City, OK.
Burt, Richard. February 6, 2001, Washington, DC.
Cannistraro, Vincent. February 8, 2001, McLean, VA.
Cannon, Lou. June 30, 2000, Summerland, CA.
Clarke, Richard. February 13, 2001, Washington, DC.
Clarridge, Duane. March 21, 2001, Escondido, CA.
Cowan, William V. February 7, 2001, Arlington, VA.
———. December 5, 2001, Arlington, VA (phone).
Crowe, William. January 29, 2001, Washington, DC.
Dillon, Robert. September 25, 2001, Arlington, VA.

Dorsey, James. September 26, 2001, Solomons, MD.
Duelfer, Charles. February 14, 2001, Washington, DC.
Gallucci, Robert. September 25, 2001, Washington, DC.
Gates, Robert. February 23, 2001, College Station, TX.
Hill, Charles. January 19, 2001, New Haven, CT.
Howell, Nathaniel. June 6, 2000, Charlottesville, VA.
Kalb, Bernard. February 15, 2001, Rockville, MD.
Kelley, P. X. October 2, 2001, Washington, DC.
Kemp, Geoffrey. February 7, 2001, Washington, DC.
Koch, Noel. January 23, 2001, Potomac, MD.
Lewis, Samuel. January 23, 2001, Manassas, VA (phone).
Livingstone, Neil. January 29, 2001, Washington, DC.
Long, David. April 8, 2000, Washington, DC.
——. February 13, 2001, Washington, DC.
Lowenthal, Mark. January 31, 2001, Fairfax, VA.
Martin, William. October 1, 2001, Washington, DC.
Meese, Edwin. February 8, 2001, Washington, DC.
Menarchik, Doug. February 20, 2001, College Station, TX.
Miller, James C., III. January 31, 2001, Washington, DC.
Moellering, John. February 12, 2001, Annapolis, MD.
Motley, Langhorne. January 30, 2001, Washington, DC.
Murphy, Richard. February 8, 2001, Washington, DC.
Newlin, Michael. January 23, 2001, Rockville, MD.
North, Oliver. January 30, 2001, Washington, DC.
Oakley, Robert. April 8, 2000, Washington, DC.
——. February 13, 2001, Washington, DC.
Odom, William. October 4, 2001, Washington, DC.
Raphel, Robin. January 25, 2001, Washington, DC.
Revell, Oliver "Buck." February 22, 2001, Carrollton, TX.
Rodman, Peter. February 7, 2001, Washington, DC.
Sable, Ron. January 25, 2001, Roslyn, VA.
Shultz, George, July 24, 2001, Palo Alto, CA (phone).
Teicher, Howard. February 15, 2001, Washington, DC.
Veliotes, Nick. June 13, 2000, McLean, VA.
——. September 24, 2001, McLean, VA.
Walcott, John. February 15, 2001, Washington, DC.
Walsh, Lawrence. February 26, 2001, Nichols Hills, OK.
Watkins, James D. January 22, 2002, Washington, DC (phone).
Weinberger, Caspar. March 29, 2000, Washington, DC (phone).
Whitehead, John. January 17, 2001, New York, NY.
Woodward, Bob. February 15, 2001, Washington, DC.

# WEB SITES

www.pbs.org/wgbh/pages/frontline/shows/target/interviews/mcfarlane.html
www.pbs.org/wgbh/pages/frontline/shows/target/interviews/oakley.html
www.pbs.org/wgbh/pages/frontline/shows/target/interviews/woodward.html
www.specwarnet.com/americas/isa.htm

# Index

# About the Author

**David C. Wills** received his Ph.D. from the University of Virginia and is currently living in Santa Barbara, California.